Becoming Ecological

BECOMING ECOLOGICAL
An Expedition Into Community Psychology

James G. Kelly

OXFORD
UNIVERSITY PRESS
2006

OXFORD
UNIVERSITY PRESS

Oxford University Press, Inc., publishes works that further
Oxford University's objective of excellence
in research, scholarship, and education.

Oxford New York
Auckland   Cape Town   Dar es Salaam   Hong Kong   Karachi
Kuala Lumpur   Madrid   Melbourne   Mexico City   Nairobi
New Delhi   Shanghai   Taipei   Toronto

With offices in
Argentina   Austria   Brazil   Chile   Czech Republic   France   Greece
Guatemala   Hungary   Italy   Japan   Poland   Portugal   Singapore
South Korea   Switzerland   Thailand   Turkey   Ukraine   Vietnam

Copyright © 2006 by Oxford University Press

Published by Oxford University Press, Inc.
198 Madison Avenue, New York, New York 10016

www.oup.com

Oxford is a registered trademark of Oxford University Press

Library of Congress Cataloging-in-Publication Data
Kelly, James G.
Becoming ecological : an expedition into community psychology / by James G. Kelly.
p. cm.
Includes bibliographical references and index.
ISBN-13 978-0-19-517379-6
ISBN 0-19-517379-1
1. Community psychology.   I. Title.
RA790.55.K455 2005
362.2'2—dc22   2005004297

9 8 7 6 5 4 3 2 1
Printed in the United States of America
on acid-free paper

For
Seeley
and Tolstoy
(our Russian Blue)

Foreword

REBECCA CAMPBELL
JULIAN RAPPAPORT

The volume you hold in your hand is a much-anticipated collection. Here, in a single place, are some 40 years of major papers (along with considerable additional material and personal reflections) by James G. Kelly, one of the founders and perhaps the foremost theoretician of community psychology. We, along with just about anyone who teaches or practices community psychology, have often introduced Kelly's work as either required reading for students or recommended reading for colleagues. We have often wished that he would put it all together in book form. Now that it is here, all in one place, it is a bit easier to see why to "get it" (that is, to grasp what community psychology is about) one has to read Kelly.

In these 40 years of papers, we can see the history of community psychology unfold. History is everything to Kelly—one cannot possibly know where to go next, what to do next without an understanding, a feel, for what came before. The history of community psychology, as created by Kelly and throughout this volume, told by Kelly, is one grounded in the history of many other disciplines. For Kelly, history is also personal. Events and ideas are shaped by whom you have lunch with, whose office is next door, and who happened to be in the same space at the same time. This volume tells these stories, too: who and what influenced Kelly, who then influenced the entire field of community psychology. This volume reminds us to look around and see our own history in the works— where we were when we read these papers first (and then again and again), with whom we discussed them, and how we applied them to our own work. These encounters weave the history of tomorrow.

Perhaps the overarching impact of reading Kelly is that attentive readers will acquire a powerful way of looking at the world. The shorthand term for this worldview is *ecological*, and Kelly is the one who made this term come alive well before it became widely accepted. He has taken it very seriously, more than once explicating the ecological principles of interdependence, succession, adaptation, and cycling of resources. Once this viewpoint is adopted, nothing seems to be the same; it becomes impossible to ignore what one now sees. Kelly's world (the social ecology) is complex, multilayered, and filled with interesting people, organizations, communities, venues, values, and ideas that point us toward process and interconnections. It is no coincidence that he taught us to look for radiating effects in our interventions and research projects.

It can be difficult to communicate this ecological worldview to students in their introduction to community psychology. Human behavior in real-world settings is messy enough, but then Kelly demands that we examine that behavior in the context of interconnected dynamic cycles that change over time. It is a wonderful teaching moment when you sense that your students have started thinking ecologically. They start a sentence, but then stop themselves with, "well, wait, no, that is related to that, which would probably cause that . . . hang on, this is bigger than I thought." Every time those of us who teach community psychology bear witness to that intellectual transformation, we, too, are transformed again by Kelly's work. Every trip through these writings brings something new. As a teacher, this process will be easier now: Hand students this volume, and let Kelly do what he does best—take us on an intellectual journey that challenges and inspires.

Often his theoretical writings on ecology and communities garner the most attention, but this volume reintroduces us to Kelly the methodologist. As with his theoretical writings, methodology is embedded in context and history. Kelly taught us "Tain't what you do, it's the way that you do it." Kelly's methods reflect a radical way of thinking about the methods of our scholarship. Method defined by experimental field designs, questionnaires, and data files is too narrow, and community psychology methods must be broader, richer, and undoubtedly more complicated. If context matters, then race, ethnicity, gender, social class, age, disability, sexual orientation, and other markers of our individual and collective identities will shape how we conduct our research. For Kelly, these are resources for scholarship as they shape how we interact with the community. His own projects articulate a methodology of collaboration. Through his research, Kelly showed us how we can create partnerships with our community collaborators and how such work can stimulate new methodological approaches. The trees from Kelly's Developing Communities Project are both method and metaphor, fitting that both his theory and his methods return to the natural world.

In this volume one will not find specific methodological techniques so much as viewpoints. These viewpoints are simultaneously straightforward and philosophically sophisticated. They provide a theoretical skeleton on which to hang the empirical, if sometimes amorphous body of work that makes up community psychology. Partly from reading the previously published papers and partly from reading Kelly's current reflections on them, we are provided with a window into his mind. But Jim Kelly is more than an intellectual. He is also a practitioner of his craft, and his concern with practice is reflected here in his interest in locating hidden community and human resources, training, mentoring and nourishing students and colleagues, and fostering the continued development of our knowledge base in a wide variety of forms.

In addition to telling us what he was thinking about at the time that he wrote each of the chapters included here, Kelly gives us a narration of his own autobiography. For anyone who (like us) sees him as a hero, there will be considerable delight in his willingness to share his own life story. Kelly believes in interdependence as more than an abstraction. He understands interdependence as a concrete reality, and here the reader is treated to an example of that reality in the author's narration of his own life experiences. And that is not all this volume provides. In the last section Kelly brings us up to date on his current thinking on ecological topics as they are played out in theory, research, action, and training. Throughout this remarkable collection of essays, Kelly maintains an intellectually generous spirit. He continuously credits specific people and circumstances with stimulating his own thinking. It is ultimately Kelly's generosity toward ideas, methods, people, and practice that one comes away from this volume understanding. That generosity has made Jim Kelly a beloved figure in community psychology, but it is his ideas that have sustained the field for more than four decades.

Kelly is the kind of scholar/social scientist who is rare today. He is old fashioned in his breadth of interests and expertise and in the broad scope of his ideas; but he is postmodern in his ability (to steal his own phrase) to cross boundaries between fields, social statuses, and methodologies. Read this volume to become educated in a way that will make you more curious, more appreciative of social environments, more open to research methods that are liberating, and more responsive to others, including students and ordinary citizens.

Preface

This volume presents 13 selections of published work covering the period of 1968 to the present. To offer a more personal context for the published articles, I have prepared an autobiographical statement of factors that set the direction for my work.

The Autobiography

The book begins with an autobiographical statement that relates features of my life that I believe are salient to understand the topics I chose to think about and study. In addition, I hope that the comments expressed in the autobiography are not a sanitized reporting but reveal some of the complexities of my personal and professional development. My story is not linear but is marked by searches, trial runs, uncertainties, anxieties, accidental events, and coincidences that have provided the grounding for a life and a point of view.

The personal story is organized by seven concepts that are chosen to help make more explicit the connections between the personal and the professional. I must tell you that these concepts were formed as a result of my editor at Oxford University Press, Jennifer Rappaport, asking me to remold a much longer series of detailed recollections to condense my story. She advocated making explicit the connections between the personal and professional. So the opening autobiographical statement is not a conventional chronological recitation. The seven topics are my solution to prepare a more exacting statement. I hope that this solution works for the reader as it now does for me.

The Articles

The 13 articles that appear next were chosen based on the advice of 10 colleagues who believed that these particular publications were both representative of my work and catalytic for the field of community psychology. Before each of the selected articles there are Reflections, where I set the scene and suggest personal and professional events and issues that were present when these articles or chapters were being prepared. The reader will notice, too, that several of the early articles use "man" or the masculine pronoun "he" when the intended meaning is "humanity." They were written before the norms for gender-neutral language were established, and their original language has been preserved. They are presented chronologically to illustrate the very process of the work, crisscrossing from theory to research, practice, and education as these pieces were in fact developed. Because my work has explored the role of some of the contextual factors that impact behavior, I wanted to organize this book to emphasize that these contextual connections are real and influential. Personal and professional expeditions can be connected—interdependent, if you will.

There is not much emphasis in the available published literature in community psychology, on personal reports, or on the connections between the personal and the professional. So I wanted to be explicit and lay out some groundwork for such an endeavor. These connections can be known, and it may be useful to the next generation of community psychologists for me to say publicly what they are.

The Essays

These four essays prepared especially for this book are my effort to reflect on current topics that are apt for the field of community psychology. I am suggesting that the issues of today in community psychology can be examined in terms of concepts that have had a long evolutionary process. In this way, the new essays demonstrate continuities between the autobiographical remarks, the re-published articles, and contemporary work of others.

Summing Up

The final section is my effort to step back and reflect on my total body of work. The emphasis is on the vital significance of interdependence, a major concept for thinking ecologically. In this section, I offer seven facets of interdependence that can suggest future work, which in turn can potentially connect research, practice, and theory.

This book is not just a report of my personal journey into this profession; rather, it is an effort to describe early experiences that may seem in retrospect to have contributed to my later professional interests. The intended experience for the reader is to note possible themes that have provided continuity for the integration of my life and my work.

Throughout the book, I have noted many of the people and places that were essential in helping me think and develop the ideas presented herein. These people and circumstances are key contributors to this volume.

Acknowledgments

This book was begun and completed with the investment of many people. I am indebted to friends and colleagues who encouraged me to tell my story. Without their support, I may have plowed ahead but with much less joy and élan.

Completing this book has reaffirmed friendships that were always there. This has been a capstone celebration of those deep ties that in some cases cover a period of 70 years.

My grateful appreciation to:

Tracey Revenson, who suggested the idea for the book, nurtured its very early beginnings, and read the autobiographical segment.

Dan Romer, who has encouraged me with his steadfast support.

Becki Campbell, Len Jason, Robin Miller, Julian Rappaport, Dick Reppucci, Tracey Revenson, Lonnie Snowden, Steve Stelzner, Rhona Weinstein, and Marc Zimmerman, who offered their suggestions about which of my publications should be included in the selection of articles and chapters. I took their advice with very few changes.

The following people, who read every part of the book, on some occasions several times. They paused from their busy schedules to read drafts and shared their impressions and critiques: David Altman, B. Eileen Altman, Dan Cervone, Janet Chang, Paul Dolinko, Carol Schneider, Lonnie Snowden, Myrna Shure, Steve Stelzner, and Marc Zimmerman. Each of them encouraged me to move on and move ahead.

Meg Bond, Bart Hirsch, Keith Humphreys, Chris Keys, Don Klein, Cindy Kingry-Westergaard, Cecile Lardon, Lynne Mock, Ricardo Munoz, Dan Romer, Dick Reppucci, William M. Runyan, Beth Shinn, Anna Song, and Rhona Weinstein, who read the autobiography and were enthusiastic about my efforts to tell this story.

Colleagues Keith Humphreys, Len Jason, Murray Levine, Ken Maton, Phil Newman, Beth Shinn, and Anna Song, who read one or more of the contemporary essays and offered their perspectives and reviews with candor and good spirit.

The following commented on those parts of the autobiography where they shared experiences with me as friend, fellow student, teacher, or colleague.

Bob Helton, who read the sections dating back to West Oakley Elementary School in Cincinnati, Ohio, and Lew Keck, who supplemented Bob's recollections and commentary during the high school years.

Ira Iscoe, who recalled with me my graduate school years at the University of Texas and 50 years beyond.

Jack and Fran Glidewell, who have known me over 40 years. Jack commented on my recollections in chapter 4.

Bob Newbrough and Bob Shellow, who read those parts focusing on the years when we were all at the Mental Health Study Center of NIMH.

Betty Lindemann, who first knew me during the two incubating years at the Human Relations Service of Wellesley and who has offered advice and encouragement for over 40 years, including the presentation reported in chapter 9.

Norm Sundberg, who reflected on my story and knew me during most of my tenure at the University of Oregon.

Mort Silverman, who reviewed my report of the presentation in chapter 8.

The following who worked with me at the University of Michigan: David Todd and Dan Edwards read and commented on my recall of events in chapter 2, as did Joe Dimento for chapter 5. Dave Todd did so as well for chapter 7.

Those who read and commented on specific sections or pieces: Steve Goldston, Thom Moore, Monty Hunter, and Susan Ryerson Espino.

Those who worked directly with me at the University of Illinois at Chicago in documenting community leadership: L. Sean Azelton, Cecile Lardon, Lynne Mock, and Darius Tandon, who commented on chapter 12.

Wade Pickren of the American Psychological Association (APA), who read the autobiography; Tamra Washington of APA, who provided historical material; and Linda Bailey of the Cincinnati Historical Society, who checked my memory of important details about Cincinnati, Ohio, circa 1935–1953.

To all of the above, I express my appreciation for their friendship and their willingness to check my memory with theirs.

Jennifer Rappaport, my supportive and diligent editor at Oxford University Press, who made me feel that I was able to take on this opportunity and succeed.

Anne Zanzucchi, who helped in the final phases with formatting and editing, offered good advice on style and phrasing, and did so with gentleness and attentiveness to my desire to compose a good book. She supported my aspirations.

To all of you, my appreciation and deepest recognition of your care and love.

Credits

The articles appearing in chapters 1 through 13 of this book have been reprinted with permission.

"Toward an ecological conception of preventive interventions" originally appeared in J. W. Carter Jr. (Ed.), 1968, *Research contributions from psychology to community mental health,* New York, Behavioral Publications.

"Adolescent boys in high school: A psychological study of coping and adaptation" originally appeared as "Exploratory behavior, socialization, and the high school environment," in J. G. Kelly (Ed.), 1979, *Adolescent boys in high school: A psychological study of coping and adaptation,* Hillsdale, NJ, Lawrence Erlbaum Associates.

"Antidotes for arrogance" originally appeared as "Antidotes for arrogance: Training for community psychology," in *American Psychologist, 25*(6), 1970.

"The quest for valid preventive interventions" originally appeared in G. Rosenblum (Ed.), 1971, *Issues in community psychology and preventive mental health,* New York, Behavioral Publications.

"Community as Teacher" originally appeared in Don M. Flournoy & Associates (Ed.), 1972, *The New Teachers,* San Francisco, Josey-Bass.

"Qualities for the community psychologist" originally appeared in *American Psychologist, 26*(10), 1971.

"Tain't what you do, it's the way that you do it" originally appeared in *American Journal of Community Psychology, 7*(3), 1979.

"Seven criteria when conducting community-based prevention research: A research agenda and commentary" originally appeared in J. A. Steinberg & M. M. Silverman (Eds.), 1987, *Preventing mental disorders: A research perspective,* Rockville, MD, National Institute of Mental Health.

"Generating social settings for a public's health" originally appeared in D. G. Satin (Ed.), 1994, *Insights and innovations in community mental health: Ten Erich Lindemann memorial lectures,* Northvale, NJ, Jason Aronson.

"A contextualist epistemology for ecological research," originally appeared in P. Tolan, C. Keys, F. Chertok, & L. Jason (Eds.), 1990, *Researching community psychology: Issues of theory and methods,* Washington, DC, American Psychological Association.

"Wellness as an ecological enterprise," originally appeared in D. Cicchetti, J. Rappaport, I. Sandler, & R. P. Weissberg (Eds.), 2000, *The promotion of wellness in children and adolescents,* Washington, DC, Child Welfare League of America.

"Contexts and community leadership: Inquiry as an ecological expedition," originally appeared in *American Psychologist, 54*(11), 1999.

"The spirit of community psychology," originally appeared in *American Journal of Community Psychology, 30*(1), 2002.

Contents

Becoming Ecological

Being Autobiographical

Roots and the Varied Soils for Ecological Inquiry

> We are more honest as scholars when we acknowledge the myriad ways in which our personal lives and emotions are intertwined with who, what and how we study.
>
> —Blee (2003, p. 22)

This will not be a finished statement. Gertrude Stein's view was that telling an autobiography is not reporting facts but discovering new insights. Following this cue, my recollections will focus on the roots, supportive places, and people that contributed to multifaceted discoveries. I hope that these discoveries will express some plausible interconnections of times and settings that in retrospect illuminate how I may have become an ecological thinker and contributor to the field of community psychology.

I will present the discoveries under seven headings, which illustrate topics for further discussion. These seven topics in sequence are social class, the power of place, the diversity of roles, the sources of social support, coping with noxious events, the benefit of ideas from other places, and the role of coincidence. I am reasonably confident that these topics are salient because they are based not solely on my own appraisal of my career. They also include the reviews of others who have observed me in a professional or personal context. Their recollections were either congruent with my memory or they reported that it seemed to be an accurate depiction of what took place.

Each of these seven topics will be presented as points of orientation. They are offered in the spirit of guesses as to events and themes that were possibly decisive in how I chose to work on the topics for research, theory, and community practice as well as my philosophy about how the field of community psychology could be constructed.

The Seven Topics Linking Biography to Career Interests

In what way has my early life experiences contributed to my much later interests in the field of community psychology? How direct are those influences? Some would consider it problematic to attempt to reconstruct the past *and* connect the past with my later work. This task is incomplete and vulnerable to misremembering or condensing subtleties. This is particularly so in thinking back to the people, events, and places that created feelings and meanings for me when it all took place over 60 or 70 years ago.

What I will express are those critical or essential memories that I do recall. Others no doubt were forgotten, repressed, and considered unintentionally insignificant. As I mentioned, this is intended to be neither a true story nor a revisionist report, but as close to a veridical view that in good conscience I can recall.

External factors, like places, determined my professional interests. There is no question that several major societal events affected my professional opportunities and choices. They also influenced public opinion and my own points of view. Although I was not directly affected by the Depression, it created a worldview of frugality. World War II made everyone very patriotic and public duty was praised. During the 1960s, when my career was just beginning, there were substantial, interlinked social movements for civil rights, feminism, free speech, and Vietnam War protests. These movements and events made me more self-conscious of how outside social forces can either constrain or liberate ideas or positions, though I may not have been explicitly aware of it except during these massive pleas for social justice. In addition, there were the public assassinations of John F. Kennedy, Martin Luther King Jr., Robert Kennedy, and Malcolm X. All of these social forces liberated me from conforming to positions that were elitist or participating in work that was subjecting others to remain in subservient conditions. These external events also made me more aware of the power of the concept of community or its absence. Certainly, the 1960s provided a positive background that supported community research and practice.

Each and all of these various events both impacted and challenged my own growth. They each were environmental intrusions. I either adapted to them or they motivated me to right a wrong. They gave me pause to assess my moral courage to either address, escape from, deny, or increase my desire to work with my emerging ideas. I had variable responses depending on my situation at the time. My responses were not always uniform, explicit, or well articulated. I was often simply immersed in them.

Now for the seven concepts.

The Role of Social Class

The feelings I had about class no doubt contributed to my appreciation and understanding of context. Early on during trips to downtown Cincinnati, life in my neighborhood in West Oakley, or visits to the adjacent neighborhood to the south, Hyde Park, I was aware that there were household products superior to what my parents owned, such as a large radio console or modern waffle iron. Most important, I became aware that other people might be better off. In Hyde Park, for example, there was a definite air of comfort, self-satisfaction, and style that my parents and I did not have. We did not radiate self-confidence. It was clear that we were not part of mainstream society or affluent. My parents and I were more subdued, compliant, hesitant in gait, and modestly dressed.

Going from West Oakley to Hyde Park intensified my feelings of discrimination, which ultimately made me feel less worthy. Throughout my life these feelings have been carried with me, not always with my full awareness, leading me to become interested in variables, situations, and events that were beyond my control. As an adult, I read a statement attributed to Karl Marx that expresses an unspoken notion I had at the time: "While people may make their own history, they do not do so in circumstances of their own choosing." This quote illustrates how I felt at the time as I recall thinking, "Can you be poor and be happy?" These experiences, no doubt, intensified my interest in social justice and research that offers a potential benefit to others. I had a sense that I was not all bad. I was enmeshed in a social drama defined by key actors who often had more social power than I did.

These vague musings were validated when I rushed for a high school fraternity. I was asked, "Who are you?" When I said "Jim Kelly," the two guys who had asked me the question looked at each other. I knew I made a social gaffe and, as a consequence, would not be recruited. Later, I realized that they wanted to know who my parents were and my social standing. Could they have thought because of the last name Kelly that I was an Irish Catholic? There certainly was a pervasive prejudice against Catholics at that time. This was an event that made it clear that I was a "have-not" in the vocabulary of the times. As I became more informed about my fellow high school students, it was also apparent that they had educational opportunities that I lacked for economic reasons. They went to summer camp, traveled to Europe, and had more contact with the world beyond West Oakley. Personally, I felt that being less advantaged meant humiliation, anger, frustration, and a nagging sense of inevitable hopelessness.

It affected my self-esteem, posture, and possibly health habits. There could have been a spiraling downturn. I was not sure what would happen to me.

Could I change my circumstances? Where would I find the help I needed to make a better life for myself? In retrospect, I lived with unstated worries. I kept on doing what I thought was best. Without realizing it or having the words for it, I was more invested in friends who helped me go beyond my heritage. Many years later when I discovered Samuel Beckett and his work, I revered a phrase in his novel *The Unnamable:* "Where I am, I don't know, I'll never know, in the silence you don't know, you must go on, I can't go on, I'll go on."

My family's white Protestant heritage and racist beliefs also made me aware of how feelings and attitudes could impact innocent targets. In my neighborhood, Protestants did not talk much with Catholics. Italians were suspect. No Jewish or African Americans lived close enough to demean. Not only did I experience the suspicion of being an outsider in Hyde Park, I also witnessed how prejudice limited the options of its victims. I saw how the accident of where you lived might limit or expand your opportunities. Without having any words for it, I felt the power of social norms as shared beliefs that could determine your future. I developed a keen sensitivity of how opportunities, influenced by social norms, could be restricted by the history of the place and its inhabitants. Where you grew up would probably impact your future.

This was the yet unknown grounding for my later convictions that preventive interventions must include an assessment of the surroundings as well as the individual. Not giving full attention to multiple contexts was not only incomplete but also invalid. I was not pleased with the current implicit premises for viewing individuals outside of context. I wanted a view that included the development of persons in natural settings and physical environments. I needed a framework to articulate these intuitions, which I found in biological ecology. The concept of interdependence had immediate salience.

The field of community psychology needed to have a systematic framework to conduct research on how individuals and social environments were connected and related. This realization shaped how I viewed theoretical issues (chapter 1), suggested that preventive interventions recognize context and not just persons (chapter 2), and advocated for research to include measures of settings as well as persons (chapter 3). A corollary of this idea was that the training of community psychologists could be designed to foster learning about social environmental effects on individuals. Most important, through their cumulative understanding and this pedagogical design, community psychologists could realize how they may improve the quality of schools, neighborhoods, or surrounding community (chapter 5).

Premises about the value of limited heritage drove the ecological perspective that evolved. Natural resources in a social setting became a guidepost when supervising doctoral psychology students and psychiatry residents in consultation methods at the University of Michigan. Until that time, the theorists of consultation primarily focused on the school principal and classroom teacher as the preferred consultee. It was often an eye opener for the students when we focused on the roles of the school secretary, custodian, and crossing guard as potential resources for children and faculty despite their allegedly low social status. My earlier sensitivities about the limiting influence of class and social status informed these and other new perspectives.

The Power of Place

Early on, I realized that the bounded quality of my neighborhood in Cincinnati defined how I thought about myself. Somehow the way that the streets were organized, like the bungalow houses arranged in predictable patterns or the location of key grocery stores and schools, defined me in surprising ways. My identity was bounded by terrain as well as experience. My surroundings implied that nobody was home, for I did not see people, only edifices. My world was not open—it was closed. It was up to me to bring meaning to myself. The larger social environment offered little apparent help for a good while.

My first real place of optimism and comfort was Crosley Field, a small stadium near downtown where the Cincinnati Reds played home games. On a Sunday afternoon during 1938, I went to my first major league game with my father to see his favorite player, Stan Hack, the third basemen for the Chicago Cubs. I was overwhelmed by not only the size and the grandeur of the stadium but also by the celebration, excitement, and emotion. Before then, I never saw much public display of emotion in West Oakley. Most memorable was how strangers at Crosley Field talked with each other. The audience was mostly men, and it was refreshing to see men emote and communicate. This was terrific; men did not need to be always trapped in work or provider roles.

I lived in the city until 1953, and Crosley Field became an important place for me to be expressive and to have a momentary sense of community and ritual. Early on, I saw how places could become special and influence one's perspective if not behavior. Crosley Field, as a world beyond my limited scope, gave me my first sense of community. These visits to Crosley Field and interest in baseball became so defining that until I graduated from high school I wanted to be a baseball announcer. My hero was Red Barber. It's odd that many strangers over the years have asked me if I was an announcer. Little did they know how affirming it was to hear this friendly and innocent question.

A little later, I became aware of differences between the front yard and the backyard. Front yards were for display with flowers, shrubs, and cut grass, whereas backyards were more private. If you were in a friend's backyard, you knew that you were special. You had been accepted. Backyards were like the intimate sides of a family, revealing what was important to the resident, which could be as simple as an expanse of grass with a floral border like iris or a small toolshed to store bicycles or supplies for outdoor eating in the summer. When the residents were in their backyard, they were more so themselves because it was their private sanctuary.

Following that realization, I noticed how department stores in downtown Cincinnati influenced identity. Only a 30-minute streetcar ride away from West Oakley, they were symbols of solidity and class. They were revered magnets for aspirations, because it wasn't necessary to be a paying customer. You felt good strolling through the stores, especially the first floor where unaffordable items could be inspected. Handsome tall men known as floor walkers with their boutonnieres and carefully placed folded handkerchiefs in their left suit coat pocket walked around. Their formal appearance made you feel important. They were friendly and not condescending despite their attire. They were regal and far beyond my reality of what men looked like in West Oakley. On Saturdays, my mother and grandmother and I would make regular pilgrimages to these department stores: Shillitoes, Pogues, Mabley & Carew, Alms & Doepke, and McAlpins.

Each of these stores had a unique culture. Pogues was high class, where you could walk leisurely and feel important. Alms & Doepke was farther away and had sawdust on the floor, which made it seem like a warehouse. Mabley & Carew had less snob appeal because it had a friendly and approachable environment. McAlpins and Shillitoes were like Oakley, unpretentious and not putting on airs. Each of these places was inviting and conveyed their uniqueness. I changed as I entered each store. I was dignified in Pogues and playful in Shillitoes.

All of these places—the neighborhood, Crosley Field, the yards, and the department stores—had an impact because I saw how people, including myself, would behave according to where they were. It was not until much later that I had the pleasure of knowing that psychologists shared my interest in the role of place. Roger Barker's research on social settings in Oskaloosa, Kansas, and Harold Raush's work on the behavior of aggressive and normal boys inspired me. This notion of place fit in with an ecological perspective. Similarly, while Bill Fairweather with his community lodge for mental patients and Rudolph Moos in his analysis of various treatment settings had begun to address these issues, they had not yet found a way to interrelate the person and the setting.

Eventually, as a researcher, I wanted to understand if and how the social settings in high schools impacted the behavior of students. The high school study that is reported in chapter 2 is a direct result of these early experiences with place. This study was designed to test out a notion: Did boys with exploratory behavior in one high school have a different adaptive history than boys with a similar behavior in a different high school? In psychology, I had experienced the traditional emphasis on individual differences as largely defined by qualities of people with little regard for context. I wanted to know more about contexts, particularly their meanings and effects.

I became convinced that psychologists had to become more aware of environmental factors. Equally important, no preventive program could be designed without specific elaboration on the particular ways in which place and the person could benefit from a community or prevention program. The intervention would not endure without the researcher knowing how to assist the community to become their own resource.

My emphasis on the ecology of place grew out of these very early personal experiences with the power and variety of places. Even though there is a commonsense truism about ecological concepts, only a small amount of attention is given to the ecology of people and places. I wanted to give empirical and theoretical meaning for ecological thinking in research and practice in the new field of community psychology.

Diversity of Experiences and Roles

It is common knowledge that being in places and situations requires performing roles and expressing a range of behaviors. Adopting different roles, like son, employee, baseball player, student, parent, or caretaker, allows us to become aware of how events, circumstances, and expectations influence our identities.

The social sciences have tended to emphasize either qualities of people *or* environments. Less emphasis is placed on the interdependence of the two. Certainly, the number of different jobs I had as a boy and bosses with different patterns of authority made me acutely aware that I was expected to rise to the specific occasion.

One of my first jobs was delivering telephone books in a wheelbarrow. It was clumsy and difficult to manage when piled with phone books. I quickly developed respect for those who labored with this vehicle. Whenever I saw a person with one, I gave a greeting. I also learned that I did not want to do this as an adult. This may have been a defining moment. I respected laborers but realized that I wanted something more for myself.

Other jobs required more direct contact with people. One such job was being a drugstore clerk during World War II with cigarette rationing and thus fewer name brands. I was instructed by the drugstore owners to sell only Lucky Strike, Camels, and Chesterfields to preferred customers. Others were sold Wings and Tareytons. I had been an employee for about a month when a stranger appeared and asked for a name brand. I had never seen him before, and the owners were not there, so I refused. The customer complained, and I was fired. Apparently, he was a major customer. I became acutely aware that I was solely dependent on the goodwill of my employer. The environment had spoken. I experienced for the first time the apparent whim of arbitrary authority.

Later on in high school, I became familiar with a different dimension of diversity—ethnic and religious status. At the time, Protestants did not date Jews.

I liked several Jewish girls, and we dated. I received looks and stares from the non-Jewish boys. No one said a word, but the message was clear: "What are you doing?" Despite their prejudice, I had wonderful experiences. I was welcomed into the homes of the girls. I was treated as a special person, more special than in my own home. The same energy and warmth was expressed with my male Jewish friends. These experiences gave me the first clear impression that life could be approached differently. It was exhilarating and validating. My role and status as a white Protestant was augmented by new experiences with those from a different heritage.

In college, I came to truly understand the power of occupational roles and their impact on my behavior. One of my most painful realizations of occupational behavior came from being an aide in a male psychiatric ward and then an attendant in a juvenile detention home. Sociologists and organizational psychologists have studied the requirements for behavior in work environments. I became aware of the meaning of these role expectations in a powerful way. I learned that a psychiatric aide was beholden to the nurse. Because I worked at night, I was there to protect the nurse from any possible aggression from male patients. I was expected to adopt the medical role of being caring and in control, consequently acquiring some self-importance despite my lower status.

When I left that role and became a night attendant at a juvenile detention center, I had a comeuppance. When with these delinquent boys, I was not expected to be regal but open, playful, approachable—almost a surrogate older brother. I was not aware of how much of the psychiatric aide role I had absorbed. The boys confronted me, and I needed to shape up. I was shocked, realizing that I had become potentially aloof. I must have eventually adapted better to my new circumstances because later I was spared from a threat of violence. The boys had procured a crowbar and were planning to break out. They decided not to do it during my shift. I might have been seriously hurt.

Such experiences made me sensitive at an intuitive level that my behavior stemmed from something more than a coherent sense of self. The surrounding world affected me whether or not I was aware of it. Roles made a difference, like places. These diverse experiences and roles developed for me an unstated notion that *I really was* different in different environments. Most important, environments affected the roles I played for better or worse.

This notion of the diversity of settings carried with me. I believe that such experiences affected my thinking and outlook. One feature of the ecological premise is that an environment can affect people differently, perhaps not all in the same way. There is an endless array of reports on how a disaster will affect individuals differently. I developed, without knowing it, the premise that any intervention had to take into account the particular place as well as express itself according to the community. This idea, I discovered later, was counter to the dominant paradigm in psychology, where the emphasis was on creating a method that could generalize and could be replicated. There has been little recognition of how interventions and treatments *should* vary with the circumstances. I found myself challenged to explicate these ideas accumulated from my lived experience that had yet to gain currency in psychology.

Because the word *community* comes before the word *psychology*, a logical and philosophical expectation follows that communities will be considered as varied, especially the way interrelationships between people and communities are defined. An ecological perspective precludes any inadvertent ethnocentrism. An ecological perspective provides an alternative way to view the development of people and the emergence of social settings without being unconsciously influenced by a colonialist or elitist mindset. Community psychology provided me with a foundation for expressing some ideas that were intuitively salient and a catalyst for systematic inquiry. Each and every one of my publications has been influenced by my search for rationales to illustrate or extend my intuitions. Earlier intuitions have become concepts and principles culled and illustrated by the work displayed in this book.

The Power of Social Support

It is axiomatic that the well-being of the giver is enhanced when caring about another. Not only did I benefit from the love of parents, a grandmother, and other relatives, but I also became aware that personal and organizational resources were essential for my well-being and self-esteem, especially because I lacked many key resources and wanted to move beyond my past. Moving from one sector of society to another is in many ways similar to adapting to a whole new culture. A new language, expectations, and rules must be acquired to learn this new world. The availability and care of others are essential and often define a positive social environment. This is another feature of the ecological perspective that I will discuss in the following chapters. When a place, setting, or social environment has resources to share, then opportunities exist to contribute not only to morale but also to the belief that others can achieve their aims. Many of the collective efforts to improve a community are designed to provide personal and organizational resources for the participants to achieve these ends.

My first meaningful need for community resources was when I moved from elementary school to the college preparatory high school, Walnut Hills High School. Although my family wanted me to be educated, they were not highly educated themselves. Consequently, I had little experience with important ideas. On beginning seventh grade, I immediately heard the name *Shakespeare*. Several students were kind when I asked, "Who is Shakespeare?" Rather than laughing or jeering at my ignorance, they oriented me.

In the eighth grade I had the good fortune to meet Lew Keck, who was interested in jazz. He was more knowledgeable than I and was willing to share his extensive record collection with me. Eventually, we began to attend jazz concerts together at a time when swing was dominant and bop was emerging. During these high school years, we heard the historic concerts of Nat Cole, Duke Ellington, Dizzy Gillespie, Woody Herman, Billie Holiday, Django Reinhardt, Sarah Vaughn, and on and on. This was a time, according to my mother's view and others, that jazz was close to sin. Additionally, few whites would attend black concerts, especially at black venues. Through this friendship with Lew, my experiences became more diverse as I felt the rewards of other powerful settings like the concert and jazz session. Lew and I still discuss jazz on a weekly basis by phone.

Whether it was high school teachers, college professors, or mentors, I have benefited from their care and investment in me. They are legion, but it is worth mentioning a few. Cecil Max Freeburne (Bowling Green State University); Wayne Holtzman, Ira Iscoe, and Lou Moran (University of Texas); Louisa Howe, Don Klein, Betty Lindemann, and Erich Lindemann (Harvard Medical School); Joe Bobbitt, Jerry W. Carter, and Len Duhl (NIMH); Harold Pepinsky and George Thompson (Ohio State); and Dan Katz, Bill McKeachie, and Harold Raush (University of Michigan). Outside my academic setting were those who responded to my intellectual interests: Seymour Sarason, Jack Glidewell, and Phil Mann. I mention these contributors to my well-being because they helped me adapt and grow, if not survive, in different settings. Bowling Green State University (1953–1954) and the University of Texas (1954–1958) were different in visions, cultural norms, and adaptive requirements as were Harvard, NIMH, Ohio State, and Michigan in their times. Demands and opportunities for growth were unique to each institution, requiring varied skills. The people mentioned are key resources because they supported me during the formative years of my professional career. That is not to discount the legions thereafter that did the same. Their care and investment nurtured my understanding of a variety of settings as well as their related demands and norms. Some of those listed are no longer with us, but they all have contributed to my ability to think ecologically.

I began to appreciate the nuances, foibles, and hidden supports as the mentioned persons taught me the power of social resources available to me in these quite different places. This was all cumulative learning about how casual acquaintances can become social resources by providing kindness, guidance, and validation. These individuals believed in me, showed me the ropes or helped me cope with possible roadblocks, *and* assuaged my anxieties. Implicitly, I considered the notion of nutrients as essential for life such that support and resources were analogs to these essential life-giving processes. It is no surprise that one of the concepts that underlies the ecology thesis is that settings can provide individual and organizational resources that support personal development. I became interested in such questions as: Do social environments vary in how they define and allocate resources? How does the availability of resources facilitate supportive relationships? I also thought that to really get at the question of how resources are defined and allocated, one has to become familiar with the more subtle aspects of a setting and community. To do this, you have to be trusted by the community so as to elucidate the more basic and overlooked features of life that are the grounding for identifying resources. Then it might be possible to illustrate how social support is defined, expressed, and maintained.

This was not a conventional idea in psychology, where the emphasis was on the *methods* of technology, not the recipient of the technology—the community itself. Over time, I gained more experience with research and theory construction, leading me to the topic of process. I believed that the success of a program depended on not only the content of the method or preventive intervention but also how these activities were done. Above all, how the relationship between the professional and the client was worked out was critical. I wanted to know how the program was absorbed in the community. Would the program evolve to enable the participants to really control this new program? These ideas were elaborated in several books cited in the four new essays in this collection. The first statement of this interest is presented in chapter 7 in an address being presented with an award from the Society for Community Research and Action in 1978 and elaborated in chapter 9 in the Lindemann Lecture.

This idea led me to the conviction that celebrations and rituals would be an essential part of any community-based intervention or research. By celebrations I do not mean looking for an excuse to have a party. What I mean is that time needs to be taken to acknowledge and validate the work just begun or completed. There need to be occasions where key participants acknowledge one another and their achievements. From what I have seen, celebrations are powerful rituals for further achievements built on the traditions of the community. For some psychologists, the idea of including celebrations within the context of professional work perhaps lacks the dignity expected in a professional role. As many become immersed in conducting community research, the utility of the concept no longer seems hokey but essential for long-term maintenance and evolution of a program. These rituals acknowledge shared activities and meanings, providing a basis for integrating past activities and beliefs with new activities and beliefs based on these common experiences. These ideas were stimulated by my own personal experiences, where social support led to a new sense of self, supported my resolve to carry on no matter what the challenge, and created pride in understanding some fundamental features of being a community psychologist.

Reducing the Impact of Noxious Events and Places

For me, this topic is essential. It directly addresses how we can prevail rather than just endure as William Faulkner phrased it in his 1950 Nobel Prize acceptance speech. All of us somehow learn to make do when crises occur. I tried to view noxious experiences as opportunities as well as dangers, an epigram first articulated by the sixth-century sage Lao Tzu. This idea gained currency when community and prevention ideas were emerging in the late 1940s and early 1950s.

During childhood, I unknowingly experienced noxious places and events. These occasions spoke "to my condition." They also influenced my later professional commitment to an ecological perspective as a resource for understanding crises. A few examples from my past became the grist for my desire to define a systematic view of calamities. My father died suddenly from a heart attack at the age of 45 when I was a sophomore in high school. This was the most disorienting experience I have ever had. Suddenly, a benefactor was gone. In retrospect, my grieving mother was clinically depressed. I felt that I was more alone than ever. As best I can recall, I mobilized my incipient support systems without knowing quite what I was doing. My friends, like Lew Keck and Bob Helton from high school, responded. Most important, their parents responded as well. I began to see that others supported, often with combined spoken and unspoken encouragement, my efforts to attend school and carry on. For instance, Lew's mother was particularly caring when my father died and very encouraging about my desire to attend college. Lew's friendship and his mother's interest in my well-being made it possible to seek out the resources that would enable me to achieve my goals. The collective meaning of these acts I gathered, whether it was verbalized or not, was that they were there for me. Boys and girls came through. So did teachers, as well as my employer and staff of the deli where I worked.

True to the isolated quality of life in West Oakley, I do not recall much local support except from the family physician, Dr. F. R. Stansbury, who stayed in my corner until his death, which occurred shortly after the completion of my doctorate in 1958. These experiences of mobilizing and activating necessary resources later convinced me that the success of a community-based prevention program depended on utilizing local resources. During a visit to Cincinnati shortly after receiving my doctorate, I visited Dr. Stansbury's widow. She told me that he wanted me to have his library of homeopathic medical books. I was flabbergasted—what would I do with 50 medical books? I declined her offer, which was a mistake. In retrospect, I should have accepted the gift. I regret that I did not honor him and his commitment to me.

When I read Ella Baker, a civil rights leader, her words resonated with my convictions: "My basic sense of it has always been to get people to understand that in the long run they themselves are the only protection they have against violence or injustice. People have to be made to understand that they cannot look for salvation anywhere but to themselves." I took this to mean that it was not just the individual but the individual's support systems as well as personal and social resources that were the potential sources of prevailing against injustice. This was reflected in my desire to document the development of citizen leaders, which I discuss further in chapter 12.

Once again, I understood the value of resources being organized on my behalf in response to a noxious event while at Bowling Green State University working on my master's degree. I asked a Professor Brenda Combs (not her real name) to write a letter for me for admission to a doctoral program in clinical psychology. I had received A's in her classes, and to my awareness I never had any problems with her. Early in the process, six other students working on their master's degrees predicted that I would be the first to be accepted to doctoral programs. Contrary to their predictions, they were all accepted while many schools turned me down.

I was getting distraught. Faculty sought me out, and I sought them out. One hypothesis was that Combs might have written a negative letter. A faculty member, not in clinical, found out that Combs had said, "Kelly is rigid, authoritarian and unteachable" among other comments. Some faculty did not agree. Professor Cecil M. Freeburne phoned some schools where my application was still pending, and I assume put in a good word for me. I was accepted at the University of Texas and the University of Colorado.

I was really distraught. This time resources were mobilized not by me but by people in critical positions, like faculty. Without their intervention, I would not have begun graduate school in fall 1954, perhaps not at all. Professor Robert Guion, a longtime member of the department of psychology at Bowling Green, was just beginning his academic career back then. He heard about my situation. Years later, when I would see him at meetings of the American Psychological Association, he would proudly introduce me to colleagues as "the most unteachable student Bowling Green ever had." Then he would roar. I was vindicated and validated. Resources mobilized made a difference in my coping with a bad situation.

An important quality of the ecological perspective is that resources, however latent, must be identified. Community-based research and practice have an ethical obligation to do this. This is a basic premise of the theoretical statement published in *The Handbook of Community Psychology* (2000) edited by Julian Rappaport and Ed Seidman. The challenge is to learn enough about the community to help identify and then mobilize resources while carrying out the particular program.

In this sense, the ecological perspective is a meta-concept serving as a conceptual anchor for community-based activities and also as a reservoir against succumbing to noxious events. This idea is applied to a discussion of mental health consultation and conducting community-based research, which is presented in two books: *The Ecology of Prevention* (1987) and *A Guide to Conducting Prevention Research in the Community: First Steps* (1988). These ideas are summarized in chapter 10. Activating resources is potentially a diagnostic index of the community's competence to become self-sufficient, empowered, and able to withstand imposed noxious events. At its core, the ecological perspective is a way of thinking about the life of the community and recognizing its capacity to sustain resources for itself. People are not passive but are energized by the knowledge of how to create and maintain resources for themselves. They have the adaptive capacity to transform bad events into potentially viable opportunities for their own living system. Resources are established within the system and connected to other resources outside the system. Linkage is encouraged. Insularity is discouraged. Interdependencies are valued.

Research could be accomplished more easily with the host community's increased direct support. More possibilities exist for the intervention being adapted and sustained. The ecological perspective affirms that "good" work is done, especially when there is an organic connection with the host community and the community owns the work. The belief is that the professional serves as a resource for the community to mobilize local resources for the next unknown event, an idea compatible with Ella Baker's thinking. My life experiences instilled this idea in me. These influences have been multifaceted, showing me that other people share this view that systems, contexts, and cultures are credible. They have been intellectual resources, relieving me of anxieties about being heretical and thereby devalued.

The Power of Ideas From Other Places

There is no question that I was fortunate to have been selected to be a postdoctoral fellow at Massachusetts General Hospital in 1958, eventually earning a degree in public health from the Harvard School of Public Health in 1960. As a new Ph.D. in psychology in 1958, I was trained to conduct research in a positivistic framework. My focus as a clinician was on the difficulties of individuals either from an assessor or therapist perspective. I was looking for another way to see the clinical enterprise without the constraints and confines of a pathology emphasis. Those two years opened my eyes to the excitement of concepts like prevention, consultation, and social systems. I learned about community health programs and the role of culture in the delivery of community-based services. I was developing alternative anchors for my incipient interests.

From this fellowship experience, I learned an additional professional role to the one I gained in clinical psychology. These ideas supported and validated my search for alternative professional roles. New methods of epidemiology and case history studies on the evolution of community health programs were striking. These public health ideas have been central to my later thinking. The ideas of Dan Katz and Bob Kahn in organizational psychology at the University of Michigan have influenced my thinking, as have the writings of Clifford Geertz in anthropology and Ludwig Wittgenstein in philosophy. Geertz has inspired me to keep at the task of paying attention to the particulars of place. Wittgenstein has validated my desire to escape the limitations and narrow perspectives of positivistic science.

Ecological thinking is an interdisciplinary enterprise. Without the connection to ideas beyond one's discipline, the scope and implication of one's work could be limited. The sociological studies of places like Crestwood Heights, Middletown, Midtown, and Yankee City convinced me of the need to understand community dynamics. The community perspective defines the purpose and methods of inquiry, not the needs of the researcher. This premise was stimulated by the writings and performances of others outside of psychology. Although I am very connected to psychological research, I have often been stimulated by the ideas of those who I find as kin in other fields. This has been important to the extent that my work is atypical within psychology. The idea of kin became an essential source of intellectual lifeblood for my work. That is one reason that the University of Michigan was such a good resource when I was developing the theory, research and practice. During the time that I was there (1966–1972), I benefited from a long tradition of crossing boundaries at the university. I sought out those persons in other fields, such as Roy Rappaport in anthropology and Richard Meier in urban and regional planning. None of us could have anticipated how formative those few conversations would be.

Ella Baker is a personal hero because she stood for the dignity of the individual, arguing that the ultimate obligation for community work is to ennoble and inspire people to action. I have been also inspired by the art of Romare Bearden. His collages of African American culture have been very important to me. As he said: "There are roads out of secret places within us along which we all must move as we go to touch others."

The arts have been a constant source of inspiration. Novelists have inspired, enlightened, or challenged me, notably Jane Austen, Herman Hesse, Thomas Mann, W. Somerset Maugham, and George Orwell, who reminded me of the significance of the complexities of personality and how history defines character. Poems by W. H. Auden, e.e. cummings, Stephen Spender, and William Stafford have enlightened me and made me laugh. Serge Koussevitsky, the conductor of the Boston Symphony Orchestra before and during World War II, told an audience: "Of all the arts, music is a powerful medium against evil and destruction. It has the power to heal, to comfort and to inspire." It has been that for me, too. Both classical music and jazz especially have been a constant source of solace. Fifteen years ago my wife, Seeley Chandler, introduced me to opera. This is another musical exploration. I admit that I most enjoy the more modern, contemporary operas. Going to the opera is like visiting Crosley Field. They are both powerful communal places.

Theater, dance, and museums have had a similar impact. But no doubt, for me, movies, especially films created outside the United States, have helped me both gain new insights as well as reduce feelings of alienation. *Rules of the Game, The Band of Outsiders, The Conformist,* and *8½* are examples that were enlightening and especially moving for me. American films have also been powerful influences. Examples are *Trouble in Paradise, Chinatown, The Third Man,* and

Singing in the Rain. The film directors who have communicated deep insights to me over the years are John Cassavetes, Mike Leigh, Yasujiro Ozu, and Andrey Tarkovsky. I continue to seek films by new (to me) directors, like Robert Bresson and Chris Marker. Novelist Walker Percy and movie critic Jonathan Rosenbaum have written about the power of movies, which has confirmed my opinions as viewer. These films and directors have been important because they have inspired me to think beyond convention, moving me to consider artistic efforts as equally credible as scientific ones. They have given me energy and continue to do so.

All of these different sources have encouraged me to adopt multiple methods, such as those in the high school research presented in chapter 2 and community leadership in chapter 12. The ideas have inspired me to chart my own direction and to create methods that fit the community, such as the leadership tree presented in chapter 12 as a plausible way to create methods that are unique to a community. This is almost a heretical idea in psychology: to design a method unique to a community without concern for the generalizability of the method but instead validate the method for that particular time and place. The primary goal is the development of the community, not just the visibility of the method across time and place.

I have not just talked about open systems, I have benefited from being part of several. When I first arrived in Chicago, community organizers and community psychologists rarely communicated with one another. There was some temerity, possibly impatience on the part of the psychologists and suspicions by the organizer that the community psychologist was just another researcher to exploit the community for professional gain. Redefining these tensions during this decade of work further convinced me that the integrity of the field of community psychology depends on being a genuine partner in community development. An organic fit between the tenets of community organizing and an ecological perspective was confirmed during my documentation of the development of African American community leaders presented in chapter 12. This is another example of not only the value of outside ideas but also the synergistic effects of collaboration. In chapter 12 with the presentation of the 10 years of work with African American leaders, the connections between community organizing and community research were enlivened by being closely connected to the host organization, the Developing Communities Project.

The Power of Coincidence

Beyond the usual topics of professional interest, one topic is systemic but for the most part outside of the interests of academic researchers. It is too common or perhaps beyond the bounds of the serious scientist. This is the role of accidents, those apparently unplanned, unsought, and maybe even inexplicable events that do in fact make a difference. Some filmmakers, like Eric Rohmer, feature coincidence as a major theme. John Hartford, a folk singer, wrote a song about this subject in "I Would Not Be Here." Except for the interests of Carl Jung and of esteemed social scientists Robert Merton and Albert Bandurra, the concept of coincidence is not featured as an explanatory subject.

My work has been directly determined by the incidental juxtaposition of people, time, and circumstances. I will mention a few. In the seventh grade, the fact that Lew Keck and I were climbing the stairs at Walnut Hills High School at the same time was indeed coincidental. We were two total strangers. The small talk walking up the stairs made it possible for me to ask about what he did over the weekend. He reported that he had gone to a jazz event. Neither of us can recall now which one. On the basis of that casual meeting grew our friendship over jazz and our mutual support of each other. Because we lived in different parts of the city, hailed from different social classes, and attended different academic classes, chances are we might have never met. If we were to meet, it was more likely to have occurred later on in our high school careers, depriving me of at least some good times with such a knowledgeable and good friend. As I mentioned, 61 years later we are still talking about jazz.

Another significant coincidence occurred in 1956 when Professor Wayne Holtzman at the University of Texas was moving his office from Mezes Hall to the University Tower, where he was to become an official of the Hogg Foundation for Mental Health. I had taken courses and done research with him. I asked him if I could help him move some boxes. As I helped, he asked me how my graduate career was going. When I no doubt mumbled that I could not decide between social psychology and clinical psychology, he told me that there was a new field about to emerge for which he thought I would be a natural. When I asked what it was, he said, "community mental health." He was unsure what the new field was but promised to recommend me as a research fellow if the Austin Community Guidance Center received an NIMH grant. The grant was received. The project, directed by Carl Hereford, was a stimulating idea—to assess the effects of training parents to serve as group discussion leaders for other parents in an effort to improve parental attitudes toward childrearing.

I was involved in creating and conducting measures of children's behavior in the classroom and going to schools to collect the data. I watched Frank Cheavens train parents. This was heady and novel. I said to myself that this was it! I liked the work so much that I wanted to do my internship on this project. Professor Phil Worchel, director of the Clinical Program, wanted me to go to the Houston VA Hospital. I balked. If I agreed to go to the VA, the department would find a postdoctoral fellowship in community mental health for me. I had read about the work of Erich Lindemann at Harvard and was impressed. When Worchel said that there was a postdoctoral fellowship at Harvard with Lindemann, I agreed immediately to go to the Houston VA for the year's predoctoral internship in clinical psychology.

The two years at Harvard defined my career. I felt so fortunate to find my niche even though the field was so new. It all came about as a result of being at the right place at the right time when I asked to help Holtzman move his office. Because there were few informal occasions with faculty at that time, his advice might never have been given in more formal conversations, especially because I no longer had classes with him.

In 1960, when I was a student at the Harvard School of Public Health, I received notice that my ROTC seven-year delay for a call to active duty had expired. I was to fulfill my military obligation as a forward observer in the antiaircraft artillery. I was frantic. I could not receive a transfer to the medical service corps. One of my Harvard classmates, Mel Reid, told me that Jerry Carter from NIMH was visiting the school and I should meet with him. Carter suggested that if I could get a release from the army, I could fulfill my military obligation with the U.S. Public Health Service. I became even more frantic when the army denied my request. I phoned my Congressman, Jackson Betts, covering the Tiffin, Ohio region, which was my permanent residence. The following day I was released from the army and assigned to the NIMH Mental Health Study Center, rising from second lieutenant to lieutenant colonel in four years. This assignment further consolidated my career. National community mental health legislation was being passed by Congress while I was at NIMH, which gave further grounding for our field. The happenstance of Jerry Carter's visit during my crisis saved my career, and he remained a terrific mentor until his death in the mid-1980s.

In 1964, when I began my academic career at Ohio State University, I met a second-year graduate student, Ed Trickett, who had an unusual talent of being incisive with a wonderful sense of humor. I chaired his master's thesis and doctoral dissertation and am pleased that we have been coauthors and colleagues for 40 years. The timeliness of his being there when I arrived made my work most stimulating, especially because I was beginning to articulate ecological concepts. He was an enthusiastic observer of what I was trying to do. Soon he became a coauthor and joined in contributing in major ways to the articulation of ecological ideas together and in his own way.

This was repeated in 1966 when I joined the University of Michigan. This time another doctoral student, Dave Todd, was there in his second year. We worked together on several projects, one of which was a coauthored chapter with Ed Trickett describing how you could view the high school environment as a social system. He did his doctoral dissertation on the high school project presented in chapter 2. Not only have we remained colleagues, our friendship has been equally lasting. The informal aspects of university life are that as a professor you have the opportunity to meet gifted students. I have been blessed throughout my career. Ed and Dave were my first students, making them most memorable.

The last example I will mention occurred some years later. In the mid-1970s while I was dean of the School of Community Service and Public Affairs at the

University of Oregon, I was invited to prepare an *Annual Review* chapter on social and community interventions. I considered the invitation an honor. Because of the substantial amount of work involved, I asked the university administration for a short leave. My request was denied because deans at that time at the University of Oregon were not encouraged to do scholarly work. Still, I wanted to do the review. I had worked with a doctoral student in psychology, Ricardo Munoz, who was interested in prevention. I also knew there was a new assistant professor, Lonnie Snowden, in clinical psychology. I asked them to join me in doing this work. We were a very good team, productive and collegial. We finished the chapter. Then I had the idea of asking 10 of the people whom we discussed as doing exemplary research to summarize their work. We divided up and interviewed them to focus on the processes of doing their work. This way of communicating research was not done at the time. We published the book in 1979, and it was well received. I really appreciated this experience and recall it with much pride. The significance of these coincidences may be that they created opportunities for knowing, connecting, and creating resources. The topic of coincidence is an opportunity for other future ecological expeditions.

Putting These Comments in Perspective

These seven concepts and their examples were intended to make connections between my biography and later work, which is presented in the following pages. I think it is important to delineate links between our studies, ourselves as did the 22 social scientists in *Our Studies, Ourselves* (Glassner & Hertz, 2003) who made these connections explicit. Our personal histories and professional choices are connected, though they are infrequently noted. When noted, they are often expressed as anecdotal remarks at award ceremonies. There is merit, I believe, in attempting to make these connections explicit so that future generation of scholars and practitioners reveal and articulate how past experiences influenced their decision to seek out their career. Coincidences influence personal and professional paths, as do the other six concepts mentioned here. A personal ecology is as valid as a social one. The following chapters include 13 examples of my work over the years, reflecting both the evolution of the work and how each new learning experience contributed to the next idea about teaching, research, and practice. All of these projects are interdependent, helping continue what became an ecological expedition.

PART I

A SELECTION OF THIRTEEN ARTICLES
WITH REFLECTIONS

1

Toward an Ecological Conception of Preventive Interventions

Reflections

An introductory statement of the ecological thesis was first presented at the American Psychological Association meetings in 1965 and published in American Psychologist *in 1966 as "Ecological Constraints on Mental Health Services." However, the following 1968 article is the first major statement of the ecological thesis, which developed in the following way. Jerry W. Carter Jr. of the National Institutes of Mental Health (NIMH) organized a symposium for the 75th annual meeting of the APA in New York in 1967 on "Research Contributions to Community Mental Health." Emory Cowen, Nicholas Hobbs, Robert Kahn, J. M. Hunt, and Melvin Zax were the presenters. I had suggested that Bob Kahn represent an organizational perspective at the session. For two other symposia, I presented papers. Carter read these papers and must have thought well of them, as he invited me to be a contributor to the publication related to his symposium. I integrated the two papers and they became "Toward an Ecological Conception of Preventive Interventions." Jack Glidewell was asked to be a discussant for the printed volume. I was honored to be included with such a distinguished group.*

As I reread this publication, I remind myself that the motivation for the presentation of ecological concepts was to propose ideas for preventive interventions. At that time, the primary reference point was to categorize people by diseases when considering prevention work. I wanted to develop a point of view that would free the community psychologist from such a heritage by suggesting concepts for seeing people as contributors to living systems. In this way, the community psychologist could consider varieties of healthy or positive behavior as expressed in real-world settings. The concept of interdependence was the major axiom. I found that the search for independent and dependent variables was not salient for living systems. Living systems do not stand still for the observer.

My belief was that a vital notion of a preventive intervention would derive from a working knowledge of real students and faculty in a community context, like contrasting high schools. At those APA meetings, I offered the idea that individuals would have different adaptive histories in different high school environments. These ideas were a combination of my readings in ecology while in Columbus, Ohio, and some preliminary work at two local high schools. The chapter included a brief statement of the orienting ideas and guesses as to possible examples of results in four high schools in Michigan. The chapter presented the orienting structure for designing the high school study later published in Adolescent Boys in High School (1979). The final chapter of this 1979 book is chapter 2 of this volume.

The work described in this paper on natural environments is designed as an aid in conceptualizing preventive interventions. Primary interest is in such questions as: (1) What types of psychological treatments are relevant for social settings? (2) What are the effects of such treatments upon the behavior of participants in social settings? (3) What change in organizational functions will emerge as a result of interventions?

From the writer's experience in developing preventive services in different parts of the country, the effects of geographical and cultural diversity in limiting or accelerating the development of community services have been clearly observed. The attempt in this paper is to contribute a conception of preventive interventions by a study of natural environments.

More specifically, an emerging ecological thesis will be presented by illustrating the kinds of integrative tasks involved in this research program. As an introduction for this thesis, four principles from field biology will be presented to provide the context for the discussion of the research program and its implications for preventive services.

Ecological Analogies

Elsewhere the writer has presented a case for the ecological analogy, both for studying social environments and for changing them (Kelly, 1966a, 1966b, 1967). The premise for this analogy is relevant for studying the expression of effectiveness in varied environments, e.g., this axiom states that functions of individuals and organizations are interdependent.

The translation of this particular ecological analogy affirms that as the structure and functions of social units vary, modes of dealing with disruptive events also shift, with a corresponding variation in the behavior of individuals who perform adaptive and maladaptive roles in the specific society. Interrelationships between the functions of social units and the participation of individual members then become a primary focus for designing programs of interventions where the intervention rearranges the interrelationships or couplings between individual behavior and social functions as much as it alters the behavior of one social unit or the expressive behavior of any one member of the society. The work of the writer includes such specific variables as: (a) individual preferences for dealing with environments (coping styles); (b) the development of role requirements for social settings (adaptive role functions); (c) the type and range of units for social interaction that are characteristic of specific environments (social settings); and (d) the structural properties of the environment, such as rate of population exchange. The development of a conception for these four types of variables can then lead to the design of interventions based upon knowledge for topics like: (1) What styles of coping behavior are correlated with effective performance in varied environments? (2) How are adaptive roles distributed in different environments? (3) How do changes in the structures of social environments effect changes in social functions? The primary integrative and conceptual task is to specify how these four types of variables are interrelated.

Before discussing the interrelationships for these variables in more detail, a few comments are in order about ecological analogies. Ecology, with its concern with the relationship of organisms or groups of organisms with their environment, historically has been a multidisciplinary enterprise. Smith (1966) cites Macfadyen (1957), who has made the following observations about the scope of ecology:

> The ecologist is something of a chartered libertine. He roams at will over the legitimate preserves of the plant and animal biologist, the taxonomist, the physiologist, the behaviorist, the meteorologist, the geologist, the physicist, the chemist, and even the sociologist; he poaches from all these and from other established and respected disciplines. It is indeed a major problem for the ecologist, in his interest, to set bounds to his divagations. (Smith, 1966, p. 5)

In spite of the breadth of the field and the number of relevant disciplines involved, there are some principles that have an empirical basis in field biology and that offer a point of departure for the study of social environments.

Principle 1: Functions Within a Social Unit Are Interdependent (The Ecosystem Principle)

One of the primary analytic terms in field biology is the concept of the ecosystem, the interdependence of living and nonliving elements. This term uniquely defines the emergence of ecology as an identifiable point of view. A brief summary of the principle can be stated like this:

> a naturally occurring assemblage of plants and animals that live in the same environment, are mutually sustaining and interdependent, and are constantly fixing, utilizing and dissipating energy. The interacting populations are characterized by constant death and replacement and usually by immigration and emigration of individuals. The populations are always fluctuating with seasonal and environmental changes. The community depends upon and is influenced by the habitat, the specific set of conditions that surround the organisms, such as sunlight, soil, mineral elements, moisture, temperature, and topography. The biotic (living) and the abiotic (nonliving) interact, thus creating an ecological system or *ecosystem*. (Smith, 1966, pp. 12–13)

This principle of interdependence or reciprocity between structures and functions is one of the axioms for the ecologist (see Watt, 1967, as a very recent example). One implication of the knowledge generated from ecosystem studies of the natural habitat is the awareness that organisms depend not only upon food sources but also directly or indirectly upon one another for their well-being and existence.

The translation of this axiom for a study of social environments presents difficulties since psychologists do not often view the coupling of structure and function as the focus for theory construction. More often we select one aspect of social structure, i.e., social class, and study its effects upon individuals who vary along certain dimensions, such as response to psychotherapy. We also will select individuals, such as persons who vary in their attitudes (dogmatism) and identify how they function in an organization (resist change). Both of these prototypic methods do not, however, usually include hypotheses or inferences that focus on a conception of cause and effect as one of interdependence between social class and response to therapy or dogmatism and organizational participation.

Roger Barker's work and that of his students and colleagues is a distinguished and notable exception in psychology not only for the methodological contributions in defining the social setting, but for their efforts to identify the effects of such variables as size and physical distance upon the behavior of participants (Barker, 1960, 1964, 1965). However, as Sommer's (1967) recent review indicates, much of this type of work and other research on the ecology of group behavior is taxonomic or descriptive and is not concerned with explicating the social processes that mediate between such variables as size or density of a setting and the behavior of individual group members.

The translation of the ecological analogy for designing preventive services requires a definition of the functions of a society in conjunction with a view of those persons who are unique in performing or not performing adaptive functions. The creation of hypotheses for such interdependence should be derived from a motivational theory that is ecological. For the present work I am asking: What social functions are generated for high school students attending a school with a high rate of exchange? How do students attending a school with high preferences for exploration fulfill or take part in such functions? and, What are the effects of such interrelationships for the performance of adaptive and maladaptive behavior of the organization and its members?

Principle II: The Cycling of Resources

This principle as it applies to field biology is a corollary of the first principle and is a direct derivation from the laws of thermodynamics. The first law of thermodynamics is often translated to mean that energy is transferred, neither created nor destroyed, while the second law of thermodynamics states that the transformation of energy assumes a form that cannot be passed on any further. In biology this principle is expressed by methods for defining how energy is transferred from one organism to another and how a large part of that energy is degraded as heat with the remainder stored as living tissue. An example of the cycling of resources in animal ecology is the food chain. Marsh vegetation is eaten by the grasshopper, the grasshopper is consumed by the shrew, the shrew by the marsh hawk or the owl, with the effect that no organism lives wholly on another but resources are shared. From this principle, measurement of the production of energy in different plant or animal communities has been attempted in order to specify how net and gross production varies among plant communities and to determine the efficiency of production of communities—the useful output of energy in relation to input.

The translation of this principle of energy transfer to the measurement of social environments is undeveloped. Except for contemporary organizational psychologists such as Katz and Kahn (1966) and a few of the studies cited by Pugh's (1966) recent review, an equivalent concept is not developed. For the development of interventions, assessment of the procedures for utilizing resources is essential in order to clarify how skills are distributed in an organization and how an organization shares competence.

Viewing social environments in this light does make it possible to view the developmental history of an organization in terms of its management of resources. Katz and Kahn (1966, p. 161), for instance, present as one approach for defining organizational efficiency the ratio of energic output to energic input. They attempt to conceive how much input to an organization emerges as product and how much is absorbed by the system.

One implication of this principle for my own work is a study of the effects of population exchange of high school students upon the development and absorption of informal leaders. My guess is that high exchange environments make more efficient use of resources than low exchange environments. One of the predicted adaptive responses an organization can make to a high rate of population exchange is an unplanned-for increase in utilizing rare resources.

Principle III: The Environment Affects Styles of Adaptation

This principle derives from Von Lubig's law of minimum and Shelford's later modification of the law of tolerance (Smith, 1966, p. 60). The modern derivation of these laws states that the availability of nutrient substances affects the presence of an organism. The empirical research on this law has demonstrated that an organism that exhibits a wide range of tolerance for all environmental influences will be widely distributed in multiple and contrasting settings (Ardrey, 1966; Smith, 1966). Current research in field biology concerned with this principle is focusing upon a reexamination of evolutionary theory, and is leading to restatements of natural selection (Simpson, 1967; Williams, 1966).

Levins, in discussing the context for the construction of model building on biology, concludes that work on the joint evolution of habitat selection and niche breadth, on the role of productivity of biotic environments and on food-getting procedures, all converge in supporting the theorem that environmental uncertainty (randomness) leads to increased niche breadth while unchanging environments lead to specialization of members (Levins, 1966, pp. 426–427). Such work as Levins's and that of Lewontin (1938), who has defined adaptive behavior as the relative diversity of environments in which a unit of evolution can survive and reproduce, provides a provocative set of questions for specifying the form of adaptations for varied social environments.

Principle IV: The Succession Principle: The Evolution of Natural Communities

The principle of succession is characterized by progressive changes in species structure, in organic structure, and in energy flow. In field biology, the principle assumes that there is a gradual and continuous replacement of one kind of plant and animal by another, until the community itself is replaced by another that is more complex. This principle focuses on those factors that contribute toward progressive change in species structure and the changes in the flow of energy distribution and community production. This process in biology assumes that as organisms exploit the environment, their own activities make a habitat unfavorable for their own survival. But in doing so, they create an environment for a different group of organisms, with an equilibrium or steady state with the environment that is more or less achieved for a limited period of time. As natural environments receive greater and greater modification, the succession process is altered, affecting the composition and even the functions of communities. This later phenomenon is the subject for much of the theory, research, and contemporary work in conservation. As Smith summarizes:

> To provide food for himself, man has cleared away natural vegetation and replaced it with simple, highly artificial communities of cultivated species, adapted to grow on disturbed sites. This has brought about an explosion of insect pests and accelerated erosion of unprotected soil. Nowhere is land change more complete than in industrial and urban areas, a climax type of human succession. Natural communities are completely destroyed and replaced by the concrete, asphalt, and steel of cities, highways, and dams. And the process is accompanied by air and water pollution from industrial and human wastes. Most communities exist only through man's continued, deliberate interference, usually motivated by economic interests. In these "economic climaxes," the animals and plants present either are desired by man or are adaptable to existing conditions. (Smith, 1966, p. 155)

This principle of succession is particularly relevant for studying social environments, for the principle defines a time perspective for the organization, and alerts the investigator to assess and define the systemic change already present in the organization prior to any proposed intervention. It is also an aid in drawing implications for the relevance of the adaptive effects of specific coping processes. To the extent that a high exchange environment is approaching constancy or a low exchange environment is unsettling, changes will be expected in how persons who vary in their coping preferences assume adaptive or maladaptive roles. For example, persons with high preferences for exploration will be able to assume more adaptive roles as the environment becomes less constant and more fluid.

Summary of a Research Example: A Study of Adaptive Behavior in Varied High School Environments

These four principles have provided the context for the development of a conception of the coupling process between individuals and organizations and provides a dynamic understanding of the role of individuals in large organizations, and the relative levels of ineffectiveness and effectiveness that are specific for particular environments.

The major work is a study of teenagers' preferences for coping with their high school environment. The specific coping style selected for study is exploratory behavior. Exploration is defined as preferences for trying out alternative behaviors and sampling diverse social situations in the high schools. A 30-item paper and pencil questionnaire and the description of preliminary work carried out in two high schools in Columbus, Ohio, has been described previously (Kelly, 1966a, 1967).

The current research is planned as a longitudinal study of four cohorts of male high school students, who vary in their preferences for exploratory behavior, and who are attending high school environments that contrast in the number of students who enter and leave during a school year. Two high schools of equal size have been selected from a suburban area of Detroit. One of these high schools has an exchange rate of students that is 22%, while the other school has an exchange rate that is only 6 per cent. Two other high schools of equal size and of equal demographic characteristics have been selected in the inner city of Detroit. One of these inner city schools has an exchange rate of 50% of its students, while the second school has an exchange rate of 15%.

Population exchange has been selected as the main independent variable for defining the social environments of these two schools, because of the premise that rate of population turnover has predictable effects not only upon the social functions in these two environments but also upon the coping preference of the students. For example, one hypothesis states that students who have high preferences for exploration will have a high probability of emerging as adaptive members in a fluid environment but will develop maladaptive roles in a constant environment. Male high school students who are low explorers will have a contrasting adaptive history and are predicted to emerge as effective members in a constant society, but are more likely to assume maladaptive behaviors in a fluid environment. The research will involve studies of the peer society, and faculty–student relations as well as naturalistic observations of relevant social settings in order to present a comprehensive view of the context of exploratory behavior.[1]

My interest in developing principles of intervention from an ecological conception of adaptation is derived from the conviction that most programs of individual or organizational change focus on either organizational behavior or the activities of specific individuals, with only slight consideration of the interdependence of individuals *and* the organization or the benefits and costs of any intervention for individuals *or* organizations. What this research is aimed toward is the creation of empirical knowledge of the interdependence of societies and their members. It is my belief that without knowledge of the process of adaptation to varied environments, it will not be possible to evolve a science of interventions. The remainder of these comments will focus upon some ideas about how the primary variables of the research can be defined in an a priori fashion as interdependent.

Individual Coping Styles
(Exploratory Behavior)

One of the interpretations of an ecological analogy is that the dominance of certain behaviors will be specific for social settings (Smith, 1966; Kelly, 1967). As has been mentioned, the general class of environments studied is high schools.

It has been assumed that the behavior of students in the high school will affect their behavior when they are not in school. It was also thought that life in the high school would have observable effects upon the socialization process of the adolescent, a critical data source for planning and evaluating interventions.

In concluding an analysis of sources of behavioral variance dealing with anxiousness, Endler and Hunt (1966, p. 345) conclude:

> The fact that interactions contribute approximately a third of the variance implies that personality descriptions can be improved by describing people in terms of responses they manifest in various kinds of situations.

The writer, in taking this mandate seriously, has asserted that male high school students who are high in their preferences for exploration are predicted to undertake more adaptive roles in a high turnover environment than in another. The research also is aimed to define the type of roles students will perform in the school setting as well as the type of behavior they will manifest in varied social settings.

Exploratory behavior has been identified as having different effects for the expression of social competence in varied environments. The term refers to preferences for participation in varied social settings and an attraction for novel or unique social situations, and is currently measured by a 30-item paper and pencil questionnaire with items such as "I like staying home and keeping friendships with people I've known a long time," and "I don't like it when a special TV program takes the place of the one I usually watch." On the basis of pilot studies, these scales have been found to be uncorrelated with social desirability, independent of measures of other coping styles, and positively related to Rotter's measure of internal-external control (Kelly, 1966; Rotter, 1966).

Preliminary findings have suggested partial validity since male high school students who were defined as high explorers had a higher probability of being nominated as deviant members in a high school with little population exchange than did students who preferred low exploratory activities (Kelly, 1966). It is hoped that one of the by-products of this approach to construct validation is to specify the diverse conditions for expression of exploratory behavior.

Conception of Adaptive Roles

The ecological analogy also assumes that as environments vary so do the adaptive and maladaptive behavior they generate. Defining adaptive roles for a particular social environment highlights two complementary issues: the relationship between the social settings and the type of adaptive behaviors that develop in such settings, and the second issue is the type of personality variables that are correlated with adaptive roles. For the present work, the prediction is that persons who prefer one coping style will fulfill comparable organizational requirements. For example, persons who have expressed a preference for high exploratory behavior will emerge as effective in performing the following activities: (a) assessment of alternatives for solving organizational problems (analysis): (b) proposing recommendations for organizational change (criticism): (c) defining new activities, new norms, or new modes of social control for that environment (planning); (d) identifying relationships of the present environment with other resources (scouting). Adaptive roles that the person with high preferences for exploration is not likely to value or take part in are: (a) implementing a solution for one specific activity or event (execution); (b) monitoring current activities, norms, or modes of social control for the organization (surveillance); (c) assessing the members' responses to the current environment (facilitation); (d) identifying obstacles limiting operation of the organization (confirmation).

While both kinds of behaviors are identified as essential for every organization, it is assumed that environments with a high exchange of members will generally reward and value the first set of adaptive roles rather than the second set. This latter set of roles will be viewed as more congruent for organizations with little exchange in their membership. It is expected that there is a selective process operating for each of these environments whereby high explorers will adopt the first set of roles and not the others. Postulating this distinction between differences in individuals and variations in organizations hopefully will generate data to clarify not only the varieties of adaptive roles within an organization but also the relationship between personality and organizational variables.

Social Setting

The measurement of social settings, the spatial locations for social interaction within environments, provides a definition for those aspects of the structure of the environment that are related directly to the expression of adaptive roles as just described. Again the interdependence of individual behavior and organizational roles is linked with the functional taxonomy of the organization and its environmental form.

Where 50% of the members of an environment come and go during any period of the life cycle of the organization, there will be a greater quantity of social settings than are expected for an environment in which only a small percentage of its members are new. The values attached to participation in social settings in the high-exchange environment is also expected to vary considerably over time, so that new settings will arise, have a short life history, and then be replaced by new modes of action correlating with the changing standards for that environment. Conversely, social participation and social interaction in the constant environment are predicted to have a smaller number of settings that are not expected to change over time. These predictions for the effects of population exchange complement Barker's findings on the effects of school size on social settings (Barker, 1964). He found that although there was a greater number of settings in the large schools, more students took part in the affairs of the small schools. The student body in the large high schools did not participate in the larger number of available activities. The present work suggests that a fluid environment can compensate for the negative effects of large size by generating new settings as a consequence of population exchange.

Another prediction for the effects of rate of population exchange upon the functions of social settings is the level of the formality of the settings. The social process in a high-exchange environment is as likely to occur in informal social interactions, on playgrounds, at football games, in the cafeteria, or at the favorite pizzeria. The settings at the constant school are expected to be almost identical with the formal settings such as the classroom, assembly halls, study halls, and at the meeting places for extracurricular activities. There is also expected to be differences for behavior expressed in school settings and those outside of school. For the fluid environment, what one does in school and on school property will be equivalent to the same wide range of behavior expressed off school grounds. An analysis of the social settings at the constant school will present more dichotomous behavior. More students will be doing the same things in the same way over a long period of time in school, yet will be doing quite different things in their leisure activity. It is a guess that the almost complete predictability of the constant environment for the students will function as a motivator for seeking uniqueness in new environments.

Wheeler (Brim & Wheeler, 1966, p. 78) has suggested two concepts for studying the structures of socialization settings that are also apt for making additional predictions for social participation in these contrasting environments. In discussing the idea that authorities in organizations vary in their response to recruits, he states that in *homogenizing settings* there is a tendency to reduce the relevance of prior experience for present adjustment. In *differentiating settings,* there may be an urging of recruits to give expression to the different backgrounds and interests they bring into the organization. In the present example, fluid environments would be expected to have more differentiating settings, while constant environments would be predicted to generate more homogenizing settings. On the basis of preliminary findings of organizational responses to newcomers in two Columbus, Ohio, high schools, this is the case (Kelly, 1966, 1967). New students at the fluid environment were actively welcomed, were informed of both acceptable and unacceptable activities going on at the school, and were given a mandate, "Try us out." New students not only perceived that the total resources of the school were available to them but they reported that their previous activities and experiences were utilized. New students at the constant school seemed compelled to make the first move and were judged, studied, and categorized according to the existing social order before any social relationships began and then only with persons in equivalent status positions.

Effects of Environmental Exchange

Before discussing the nature of the integrative tasks for this work and the implications for designing interventions, brief comments will be made on the predictive power of population exchange as a unit in the ecological chain. It is assumed that this variable will affect not only the number and range of social settings but the generation of adaptive roles and the socialization for exploratory behavior. This particular ecological variable was selected for study not only for its intrinsic value but because of the number of parallel predictions that can be generated for the effects of this type of environment upon a range of plant and animal populations (Smith, 1966; Levins, 1967). The other primary reason for the selection of this particular variable is that it should be possible to document the simultaneous effects of how individuals (explorers) respond (take adaptive roles) in varied environments and how organizations respond (generate social settings and adaptive roles) to varied rates of immigration and emigration.

Integrative Tasks

Interdependence of Variables

This work requires at least three distinct integrative tasks. One is the conceptual integration of the interdependence of variables, which has been mentioned. A second is the integration of methods and the third is the integration of theory with practice.

Specifying the environmental conditions for various forms of behavior can provide two sources of data for defining mental health. One is the effects of an organization upon specific coping styles, in persons performing specific adaptive roles. The second is an analysis of the consequences of adaptive performance in one organization as it relates for membership in a new organization. An adaptive member of a fluid environment may learn the rudiments of innovative behavior, but if faced with physical relocation may perceive himself to be in crisis. The adaptive member of a constant environment may learn a set of specialized roles and the rudiments of citizenship, but react in a maladaptive fashion in an organization when he is relocated or when his environment undergoes rapid changes. The provision for a cohort design in each of the selected high schools will be created to assess the profits and costs for high and low explorers who are living in these contrasting environments. If this kind of integration can be made, it will help to define the context for generating varieties of "healthy" behavior.

Utility of Multiple Methods

In the preliminary work, two methods have been used, a paper and pencil questionnaire to assess coping preferences, and naturalistic observations to document the type and range of social settings within each school. The next phase of this work will include additional methods to reduce the effects of method variance, and to represent the intricacies of the environment. Survey instruments will be created to assess the perceptions of the students and faculty regarding the normative rules within the school and the mode of faculty–student relations. Intensive case studies will also be conducted with a sample of high and low explorers in order to provide complementary information regarding their perceptions of the environment and their views of the socialization process.

One of the major methodological assignments is to create data collection procedures so that an estimate can be made of the research process on the natural life of the environment. On the basis of preliminary work, it was found that observing hallways in the fluid school seemed to have no noticeable effect on the students' behavior. The same observers, however, in a constant school were perceived by both faculty and students as an intrusion. For the present work we will recruit high school students from the host school to carry out observations in the schools and to employ videotape recordings to supplement these personal observations. Also, we will be responsive to document the effects of naturally occurring crises in the local communities and schools. The diversity of methods to be employed is intended to increase the precision of assessing the school societies as they respond to unplanned events.

Theory and Practice

The integrative task of linking theory to practice is provocative since it focuses on the utility of knowledge. The objective of this work is to contribute basic knowledge about relationships between social structures and individual coping styles in order to establish an ecological basis for deducing preventive services. One axiom of the ecologist is that an intervention in one part of the organization will affect the total organization. An ecological orientation is particularly apt for most community mental health services, because not only are preventive services usually imposed or added onto an ongoing program, but by the nature of preventive work, multiple agencies and organizations are usually involved as participants if not consumers.

Geertz (1963) reports an example, attributed to the ecologist Clarke (1954), that illustrates an ecological chain. Clarke tells of ranchers,

> who disturbed by losses of young sheep to coyotes, slaughtered, through collective effort, nearly all coyotes in the immediate area. Following the removal of coyotes, the rabbits, field mice, and other small rodents, upon whom the

coyotes had previously preyed, multiplied rapidly and made serious inroads on the grass of the pastures. When this was realized, the sheep men ceased to kill coyotes and instituted an elaborate program for the poisoning of rodents. The coyotes filtered in from the surrounding areas, but finding their natural rodent food now scarce, were forced to turn with even greater intensity to the young sheep as their only available source of food. (pp. 4–5)

While there is no intent here to equate mental health professionals with these ranchers, mental health programs do not always anticipate any adverse effects of their interventions for the resources of the community or the functions of key persons. A more prevalent view is to alter overt behavior with minimal assessment of organizational or personal side effects. One ethic for the ecologist is to assess the host organization in order to anticipate the effects of the intervention upon the functions of the organization.

Referring to constant and fluid environments as examples, it is predicted that reports of mental health problems in a constant environment will be quite different from the reported concerns from the fluid environment. In the constant environment with its value for absorption for its members, persons of this setting will be expected to ask for help for those persons who "criticize," who question normative structures, or who may "agitate for change." The treatment fantasies of the faculty will be to "fit" students in or exclude them. Faculties from the fluid schools who are oriented by necessity to develop and actualize their members will tend to see anybody who prefers "direction" as a person in "crisis" and will want advice from the consultant on how to motivate him.

These predictions about the effects of living in these two diverse environments and the generation of maladaptive behaviors lead to quite different proposals for interventions. For the remainder of these comments examples of interventions considered relevant for these two contrasting environments will be presented.

Contrasting Interventions

A change program for the fluid environment would be designed as a program aimed to improve the socialization for the students of the high school.[2] The change programs for the constant high school would be focused on the adult faculty and administration, with less attention to the student body. The purposes of these interventions are different, as are the methods and style of the change agents and the bases for evaluating program success.

Socialization Aid for a Fluid Environment

A tentative intervention for this setting is to supplement existing informal and formal social processes and promote the identity development of the students.

Older high school students, high school graduates, and a variety of formal and informal community resources could be involved to strengthen the existing life of the high exchange environment, without limiting the open-ended quality of the environment or creating new organizational structures. Change agents working in this program would be trying to facilitate the operation of the fluctuating activities of these multiple social units. For example, simultaneous programs, such as car maintenance, athletic skill development, vocational training, educational enrichment, could be interventions for school environments that are fluid and serving lower-class populations. Equivalent socialization programs relating to leisure-time activities, such as sailing clubs, as well as courses and seminars relating to personal development, would be the suggested content for students from fluid schools serving a higher socioeconomic class. Tutorial programs with informal supervision by peers and adults would characterize the relationship of the change agents and the clients in both types of fluid schools.

The time periods needed for developing these contrasting programs would vary as well. For instance, there would be a short period of preparation and a longer period of implementation for the fluid high school. Because this type of school is expected to define change as a way of life, the school authorities and students will not require long periods of orientation, warm-ups, clarification, and rationales; their thirst for action will lead to instant programming. To refine the intervention and to enable the program to become an integral part of the total society, a longer period of time would be required. This difference in the metric of the intervention is a consequence not only of the students' and faculty's unfamiliarity in coping with intact organizational structures but also because of the time required to establish functional communication for all the diverse and scattered units of this changing environment.

An evaluation of the interventions for this type of environment could be measured by phrasing questions such as: Will a person with preferences for exploration be able to develop a self-perception and self-esteem as a risk-taker? Does he emerge with a self-perception of a more integrated individual? If the interventions have been effective the high explorer, in addition to surviving in a chaotic society, should be able to differentiate himself in that society.

Faculty Development for a Constant Environment

This type of social environment could receive an equal number of services but in this case they are faculty-oriented, to allow the faculty to consider the expected personal costs for those students attending such an environment. The interventions could be provided by a variety of professional persons and could include various forms of human relations training and consultative services, including studies of the school environment. The goal of this program for this type of environment is to help the faculty of the school redefine the purposes of the school, and to create feedback functions so that the organization can begin to assess the effects of their environment upon its members. For this type of social organization the period of preparation for the change program would be expected to be longer than the period of implementation. Because of the absence of organizational diversity, long periods of time would be expected to be required to interpret the program, to receive sanction from the faculty for the program, and to communicate the goals of the program. Following interpretation, the operation of the program can be expected to be implemented in a shorter period of time. In fact, the change agents for this program will be alert to ensure that the services do not receive premature adoption, and the faculty absorbed and preoccupied with a newer ideology.

Evaluating the effects of interventions for the constant environment would assess the effects of the program upon the functions of the organization, particularly aspects of the school environment, such as use of resources, relationships to other community resources, how the organization plans for change, and how the school goes about developing mechanisms for increasing diversity.

Conclusions

The proposed interventions for these two types of schools are based upon a view of the social settings and the individual behavior of the members as interdependent. The interest in this work is in knowing as much about adaptive societies as adaptive persons. The approach to this integrative task is to study both processes in contrasting environments, and to learn how people emerge in changing societies, without limiting the development of either themselves or the evolution of the society.

W. Bennis cites A. N. Whitehead, who crisply sums it up:

> The art of free society consists first in the maintenance of the symbolic code, and secondly in the fearlessness of revision. . . . Those societies which cannot combine reverence to their symbols with freedom of revision must ultimately decay. (Bennis, 1966, p. 205)

Notes

1. See Orth, 1962; Mechanic, 1962; and Becker *et al.* 1961, as examples of studies of coping responses to social environments: Lazarus (1966) presents a review of the recent experimental and theoretical literature on the topic. Klein and Lindemann (1961) and Caplan (1964) provide excellent conceptions for preventive services.

2. See H. Bredemeier (1964) for a comprehensive socialization program that does not take into account diverse environments.

References

Ardrey, R. (1966). *The territorial imperative.* New York: Atheneum.

Barker, R. G. (1960). Ecology and motivation. In M. R. Jones (Ed.), *Nebraska symposium on motivation, 1960,* (pp. 1–49). Lincoln: University of Nebraska Press.

Barker, R. G. (1965). Explorations in ecological psychology. *American Psychologist, 20,* 1–14.

Barker, R. G., & Gump, P. V. (1964). *Big school, small school.* Stanford, CA: Stanford University Press.

Becker, H. S., Blance, G., Hughes, E., & Strauss, A. (1961). *Boys in white: Student culture in medical school.* Chicago: University of Chicago Press.

Bennis, W. G. (1966). *Changing organizations.* New York: McGraw-Hill.

Bredemeier, H. C. (1964). Proposal for an adequate socialization structure. In Group for the Advancement of Psychiatry (Ed.), *Urban America and the planning of mental health services* (pp. 447–469). Washington, DC: Group for the Advancement of Psychiatry.

Brim, O. G., Jr., & Wheeler, S. (1966). *Socialization after childhood: Two essays.* New York: John Wiley.

Caplan, G. (1964). *Principles of preventive psychiatry.* New York: Basic Books.

Clarke, G. (1954). *Elements of ecology.* New York: John Wiley.

Dyckman, J. W. (1967). City planning and the treasury of science. In W. R. Ewald Jr. (Ed.), *Environment for man: The next fifty years* (pp. 27–59). Bloomington: Indiana University Press.

Endler, N. S., & Hunt, J. M. (1966). Sources of behavioral variance as measured by the S-R inventory of anxiousness. *Psychological Bulletin, 65*(6), 336–346.

Geertz, C. (1963). *Agricultural involution: The process of ecological change in Indonesia.* Berkeley: University of California Press.

Katz, D., & Kahn, R. L. (1966). *The social psychology of organizations.* New York: John Wiley.

Kelly, J. G. (1966a). Ecological constraints on mental health services. *American Psychologist, 21,* 535–539.

Kelly, J. G. (1966b). Social adaptation to varied environments. Paper read at American Psychological Association meeting, New York, September.

Kelly, J. G. (1967). Naturalistic observations and theory confirmation: An example. *Human Development, 10,* 212–222.

Klein, D. C., & Lindemann, E. (1961). Preventive intervention in family crisis situations. In G. Caplan (Ed.), *Prevention of mental disorders in children* (pp. 283–306), New York: Basic Books.

Lazarus, R. S. (1966). *Psychological stress and the coping process.* New York: McGraw-Hill.

Levins, R. (1966). The strategy of model building in population biology. *American Scientist, 54,* 421–431.

Lewontin, R. C. (1958). The adaptations of populations to varying environments. *Cold Springs Harbor Symposium on Quantative Biology, 22,* 395–408.

Macfayden, A. (1957). *Animal biology: Aims and methods.* London: Pitman.

Mechanic, D. (1962). *Students under stress: A study in the social psychology of adaptation.* New York: Free Press.

Orth, C. D. (1963). *Social structure and learning climate: The first year at Harvard Business School.* Boston: Graduate School of Business Administration, Harvard University.

Pugh, D. S. (1966). Modern organization theory: A psychological and sociological study. *Psychological Bulletin, 66,* 235–251.

Rotter, J. B. (1966). Generalized expectancies for internal versus external control of reinforcement. *Psychology Monographs, 80,* 1 (All no. 609).

Simpson, G. G. (1967). Biology and the public good. *American Scientist, 55,* 165–175.

Smith, R. L. (1966). *Ecology and field biology.* New York: Harper & Row.

Sommer, R. (1967). Small group ecology. *Psychological Bulletin, 67,* 145–152.

Watt, K. E. F. (Ed.). (1966). *Systems analysis in ecology.* New York: Academic Press.

Williams, G. C. (1966). *Adaptation and natural selection: A critique of some current evolutionary thought.* Princeton, NJ: Princeton University Press.

2

Adolescent Boys in High School

A Psychological Study of Coping and Adaptation

Reflections

The selection included here was originally published as "Exploratory Behavior, Socialization and the High School Environment" from Adolescent Boys in High School *(1979). The book presents a significant amount of research carried out at the University of Michigan from 1966 and 1972. The research was a multimethod effort to understand the development of a coping measure (exploratory behavior of boys) from 8th grade through 12th grade in two contrasting high schools in the Detroit, Michigan, area. This exciting expedition revealed some differences between boys' exploratory preferences according to the high school they attended. Several chapters were unique and valuable as a report of research because they also document the experiences of the liaison persons and administrators from each school.*

In 1966, the first step with initiating this high school study involved the inclusion of doctoral students in the research planning. These students represented different areas of the department: Dan Edwards (clinical), Tom Gordon (developmental), Evie McClintock (social), Phil and Barb Newman (social-developmental), Dick Roistacker (social/statistics), and David Todd (clinical-organizational). Later Jim Hershey, Bill Jones, and Bob Weigl (clinical); George Gilmore (education); and Phil McGee (social) participated. There was also a Fulbright student from Germany, Reinhard Fatke. Carol Mowbray (developmental) also contributed later. Seven of these students reported on their doctoral dissertations in the book.

The work of these committed and talented individuals clarified information and observations during this six-year period. Some doctoral students were concerned with measurement of individual differences of the high school students

(Edwards, Gilmore, Jones, Roistacker, and Fatke). Others (Todd, Weigl, Hershey, McGee, and B. Newman) focused on the interdependence of the cultures of the two schools and the students. Still others attended to assessing the primary social settings of the schools (P. Newman).

The original plan was to include two suburban schools and two urban schools. The 8th-grade boys attending the feeder junior high schools for these four high schools were assessed in spring 1968. The assassinations of Malcolm X, Martin Luther King Jr., and Robert Kennedy during this time created heightened concern about white investigators doing research in African American communities. This concern was beginning to nag at me. In consultation with a new faculty member, James Jackson, the proposed research at the two African American high schools was transferred to him. While feeling a sense of loss, I believe that it was right to transfer the opportunity to symbolize an anticolonial belief about the way that research should be done.

With the approval of NIMH, the funding organization, the grant was divided between myself working with the two white schools and Jackson, who supervised the research at the African American schools. The report included here refers to the findings through the 10th grade at the two white schools. Dan Edwards carried out subsequent analyses, which are reported in "Coping and Adaptation: A Longitudinal Study" (1980). Boys with high preferences for exploratory behavior, measured by several methods, in either school had the most positive scores on adaptation measures. Wayne, the more "fluid" high school, had more students entering and leaving in a year, which predictably facilitated higher levels of exploratory behavior.

After the fact, we guessed that one of the consequences in administering a more fluid school is to impose more structure and clear norms for behavior. What seemed salient is that the qualities of the social environment of the high school generate different levels of satisfaction for students with varied degrees of exploratory preferences within each school. Although the findings did not pan out exactly according to the theory, enough clarity existed to tentatively confirm the level of interaction between exploratory preferences and the quality of the school environment. It was an engulfing enterprise that stimulated more thinking about person—environment connections. The final chapter from the 1979 book, included here, attempts to integrate the various findings during that time.

This volume has been concerned with an ecological analysis of the socialization of male high school students. Since young people spend a major portion of their time in school, the public school system is a critical setting for assessing how skills, beliefs, and dispositions to act are acquired (Brim & Wheeler, 1966; Clausen, 1968; Inkeles, 1968; Smith, 1968). Yet, despite the significance of the topic of socialization for the high school, there are few research examples that dig deeply and intensively into the social processes that determine how students acquire competences in a particular school setting (Inkeles, 1968; Smith, 1968).

At the 1965 Social Science Research Council's Conference on Socialization for Competence, Barbara Biber introduced her remarks with the following comments (Biber & Minuchin, 1965):

> Societies have long regarded their schools as primary institutions for the socialization of competence, created and sustained for the expressed purpose of inducting the child into his culture as a competent and skillful human being. As a crucial socializing force, the school shares its function with the family, the peer group, sometimes other institutions such as the church, but even more than the others its function is described directly in the realm of "competence"; to educate means, at the very least, to make competent.
>
> Within the consensus that the school's function lies in this realm, however, there is a range of viewpoint among educators and in the environments and methods they have created. If we approach education with a research stance, we need to begin with the understanding that schools vary in their vision of what they are trying to accomplish for the child—the scope of what they wish to undertake, the hierarchy of their goals, their cognizance of psychological development as it affects functioning, and the extent of their concern for the propensities, heritage and equipment the child brings with him into the learning situation. (p. 1)

The challenge of grasping the organizational life of a school system and defining how students learn to be competent in various roles is gigantic. The topic requires a focus upon multiple levels of the organizational life of the school and how topics such as decision making, communication patterns, and peer group structures affect the expression of individual coping preferences. To succeed in reflecting the organizational life of the school requires that the research develop a variety of methods and improvise approaches. Getting into the life of the school, then, involves defining research so that the methods reflect the life force of the environment. This particular research was initiated to reflect the varied relationships of how persons adapt to the school environment. In focusing upon the functions of the high school environment, we have taken into account such issues as differences in the administration of the two high schools, the variability within the school faculties, and variations in the economic and cultural values of the parents. Though such contextual factors were considered, still, our primary attention was to reflect the attitudes of students and faculty in the school setting.

Although the research has not been strictly ecological, an ecological perspective was present. The research reported here assumed that if we spend enough time in one place, we will acquire, not always with awareness, specific and unique ways of doing our work consistent with the setting. The ecological perspective has generated research to understand the interactions of high school students with the social environment.

In chapter 13 [of the original volume], Paul Gump presented a theoretical perspective that asserts that a change in the behavior of persons affects the environment, just as changes in the social environment may affect the life of individuals. This means simultaneously examining the reciprocal effects of persons and social settings, trying to locate those processes that affect social participation and the regulation of the environment. The spirit of the [other] chapters has been to grapple with these issues.

The Two High Schools and Their Impact Upon the Socialization of Students

The two high school environments were similar in many respects; yet they were also different, especially in their informal social structure. Gilmore, in Chapter 7, was interested in identifying the social competences of students with different levels of exploratory preferences. From Gilmore's data, the structured interview revealed that boys with high exploration preferences expressed their competences within the school and were more confident of their ability to influence their friends and parents. These findings offer partial validation of the self-report questionnaire measure of exploration preferences as a predictor of engaging and self-confident behavior. The fact that a large number of boys at Wayne reported more competences than did the boys at Thurston suggests that the Wayne community and Wayne High School foster a positive self-image, *or* that the greater number of reported competences may be an expression of feigned self-importance and bravado. Additional comments on this point are made later.

The relationships between exploration preferences and participation in school affairs found by Gilmore are strengthened by the results reported and summarized by Edwards in Chapter 5. The finding that high-explorer boys express more identification with the school, express more initiative, have higher self-esteem and self-satisfaction, and report that they know the school principal better than moderate- or low-explorer boys is a consistent pattern. The boys with high exploration preferences also report that they have fewer social problems, are less unhappy at school, chat with a fewer number of students at informal settings in the school, and feel less watched and less uncomfortable in group situations. The omega statistic (ω^2) employed by Edwards, however, keeps our vanity low. The foregoing relationships account for between 4% and 15% of the variance between exploratory preferences and the dependent variables.

A few qualitative comments can be made about the types of competences reported by students in Gilmore's sample. In response to Gilmore's question, "What are some of the things you are good at and like to do?", recreation and sports were reported by 61% to 71% of the boys. The relationships of exploration preferences and recreational competences for these boys was positive and linear (45%, low; 75%, mod; 92%, hi), whereas the relationship was more curvilinear at Thurston (83%, lo; 33%, mod; 67%, hi). These findings suggest that competences in sports at Wayne are much more pervasive and define the social conditions for being involved in the culture of school. The boys at Thurston, on the other hand, are involved in acquiring alternative competences via academic work, jobs, or hobbies. Of the first two competences mentioned at either school, only 6% at Wayne and 3% at Thurston were categorized as social competences. A question for future research is whether the more active social environment of Wayne will nurture social competences as the boys continue their high school careers.

The research of William Jones provides insights into questions about developmental levels, competences, and the implication of being a student at each of the high schools. Jones found in his experiment that pairs of boys with high preferences for exploration expressed more of the following behaviors than did matched pairs of boys with moderate or low exploration preferences: elaboration of solutions, giving information, using their partner as a resource, task involvement, and directing the interaction related to the solution. Additional validation data for the Edwards self-report measure of exploration preferences is again obtained. In addition, Jones offered the following testimony based upon an analysis of the transcripts:

> The High–High Exploration dyads seem to already have at hand cognitive maps of the school and to have already reached well-thought-out conclusions about such things as whether the vice-principal would bend a rule. The transcripts show that most of these students, like other adolescents, engage in preparatory and hypothetical problem solving. Most of them, for example, had previously thought about how to obtain driver's education as soon as possible (one of the problem stories) and had discussed it with friends. They appeared, especially the H–H dyads, to come equipped with at least elementary notions of problem solving: identifying a solution, evaluating and elaborating it, and selecting alternatives if the initial solution seemed inadequate. (Jones, p. 170)

Jones also provides an excellent discussion (pp. 170–171) of possible reasons for the different results obtained for boys attending Wayne and Thurston High Schools. Originally, it was predicted that the students attending Wayne, because of more opportunities for informal social interaction, would perform better than the students at Thurston, where there was some confusion about social norms. Jones found that the Wayne students were more enthusiastic participants but not better problem solvers.

Jones presents an interesting interpretation for what he refers to as the *school switcheroo*. He considers the following possibilities: not enough time in the experimental procedure to allow for the expression of school differences, latent cultural differences in the school populations, varied levels of psychosocial maturity of the boys at the two schools, the role of anxiety in reducing or enhancing problem-solving behavior, and the different socialization of coping styles. In commenting on this last hypothesis related to socialization, Jones suggests a useful clarification that relates to knowledge about the socialization processes at the two schools.

> In deriving the hypotheses, a case was made for Wayne being more likely to encourage exploratory behavior because of the school's clearer norms and greater flexibility. There is another way of looking at it, though. It may be easier to be a social explorer at Wayne, but it may also be less crucial. For instance, if information about norms is freely available, there is less need to acquire coping styles to help obtain it. Thurston provides a rigid but murky environment. Norms are not clear. Students are not as comfortable with peers or staff. There is tension and ambiguity. Under these conditions, a high explorer may get more mileage out of his coping style, in spite of the lumps he may take. In sum, the noxious environment of Thurston may actually provide greater rewards for exploratory behavior and with it develop greater capabilities for school problem solving. (Jones, p. 171)

Jones put these ideas about coping styles and environmental qualities into his experimental design, and he confirmed the construct of exploratory behavior while providing a new empirical basis for viewing the socialization media of the two high schools. Our view of the interdependence of personal preferences and social context is expanded and differentiated as a result of Jones's work.

What about the social structure of the high school environment and its functions for socialization? What settings for socialization are these schools providing? In a carefully selected representative sample of the faculty and students at both schools, Philip Newman, in chapter 11, describes consistent differences in the quantity and quality of social interactions mentioned earlier. Not only was the quantity of social interaction greater at Wayne than at Thurston, but the interactions between students and faculty also took place in more social settings, both informal and formal, at Wayne than at Thurston. With regard to differences in the quality of these interactions, students at Wayne perceived more personal interest from faculty and felt more comfortable in informal interaction with school adults than did the students at Thurston. Wayne also encouraged more active student involvement; norms were perceived as being clearer and consequences for norm violation harsher at Wayne than at

Thurston. Students at Wayne demonstrated a greater preference for the company of adults, whereas students at Thurston displayed a greater preference for the company of their peers.

These findings are also consistent with the work of Edwards, reported in chapter 6, who drew his data from a stratified sample in the longitudinal study. In his high-, moderate-, and low-explorer boys, Edwards found that the students at Wayne expressed more positiveness about the principal, believed they had greater influence over fellow students and student government, and felt that their school was better than did the students at Thurston.

Barbara Newman's work provides independent, complementary evidence of the difference in the cultures of the two high schools. As reported in chapter 8, she created an informal group setting in which nine boys at each school from Gilmore's sample—three high, three moderate, and three low explorers—met for eight discussion sessions. Her interest was in assessing the verbal and nonverbal behavior of boys within the group. Consistent with the findings of Edwards (chapters 5 and 6), Philip Newman (chapter 11), and Gilmore (chapter 7), Barbara Newman found that there was more diversity in the responses of the boys at Wayne. The boys at Wayne were also more expressive in their participation than the boys at Thurston. The one statistically significant finding, which differentiated between the behavior of the boys at the two schools, was that the Wayne boys asked the leader for information and sought her opinions more than did the boys at Thurston, who were more cautious in their approach to the group and the group leader. From the findings in this unstructured group setting, it was apparent that the cultures of the two schools *were* different. Wayne served as a more active and supportive environment for the socialization of students than Thurston.

One additional insight obtained from Barbara Newman's work regarding differences in the expression of exploratory behavior at the two schools was that high-explorer boys at Wayne were more expressive and involved in the group, whereas the low-explorer boys at Thurston were more expressive. The findings of relatively less expressive behavior on the part of the high-explorer boys at Thurston suggests that the assessment of emotional behavior at Thurston will be more difficult in the future; e.g., the school environment at Thurston does not encourage the expression of emotional behavior. If the boys with high exploration preferences at Wayne continue to be expressive, it will be a relatively easier task to learn about their adaptation.

One of the most striking findings in the work of Barbara Newman was the vast range of individual differences she observed in the boys. At both schools, the boys were different in physical size, interests, and verbal skills. From the wide range of responses in the discussion groups, it seems appropriate to subdivide the exploration groups according to developmental levels in the future. Exploration at a lower developmental level can be expressed via body movements. At more advanced developmental levels, exploration is more likely to be channeled into conceptual activities. If such distinctions can be made, the interaction of social forces and developmental levels can be further illuminated.

Todd, in chapter 10, reports an intensive study of the help-giving process in the two subcultures, which clarified the nebulous quality of the social structure of Thurston High School. Todd found that the nonschool affiliative group, whom he called the "tribe," reported more reciprocal help-giving acts than the group he referred to as "citizens" in responses to sample surveys. In these log reports of their helping behavior, the "citizens" engaged in more reciprocal helping transactions and were more often involved in receiving and giving help with girls than were the tribe members.

The differences in response to the two research methods were encouraging rather than disconfirming. A marginal subgroup such as the tribe could be expected to present an image of solidarity to an outside research investigator, whereas the opposite would be true for members of the citizen culture who took the "tests" more casually, yet were more dedicated when contributing autobiographical log reports for the "diary" of help-giving behavior. The increased appearance of girls in the lives of the citizens, as reflected in their log reports, was interpreted as reflecting the real significance of girls as friends by the citizens when they were forced to look closely at their personal accounts. The tribe members, on the other hand, seemed to live a more marginal life with girls as well. Girls are a commodity to be dealt with infrequently, but on their own terms. Todd's work provides a provocative approach of "funneling" down into the social structure of the school, without losing the authentic complexities of the environment. Through this approach, we have learned that the socialization of help-giving competences varies within subgroupings at one school.

Implications for the Ecology of Socialization and Competence

On the basis of the data reported in the preceding chapters, it is possible to discuss the social environment of the schools. At Wayne Memorial High School, there is a variety of informal settings in which students may actively express their ideas and participate in school affairs. Students can vary in their mode of accommodating to the school *if* they have the principal's approval, and *if* the extracurricular activities absorb the students. There is a definite social organization at Wayne that creates a forum that involves the school's resources. The social environment functions to provide intact social settings for informal and formal interactions and clear social norms that contribute to socializing new members. At the same time, it is not clear how tolerant the setting is, how rapidly organizational problems can be dealt with, how new extracurricular opportunities can be created, or how cognitive skills are learned.

At Thurston, there are diverse viewpoints within the school and the community, but this variety is not articulated for faculty and students. The social norms generated by the faculty operate to reduce the opportunity for outside resources to influence the school. Although the specific sources for this norm are unclear, one possibility is that the school policies reflect the concerns of the local school board and community leaders and that the school administration works to limit the influence of forces and demands that the faculty and administration cannot meet. One consequence of this condition is that the competences needed by the school, and that are present at the school and in the larger community, often go unnoticed. In the Thurston environment, it appears that the resources that are available are not fully utilized. Instead, the social norms of the larger community operate to reduce the degree to which external influences affect the school.

With regard to implications for the ecology of competence, our findings suggest that one school (Wayne) behaves as if it were a "scout camp," whereas the other school (Thurston) generates ambiguity. What are the consequences of students attending the two different schools? At Wayne, a future question is, what happens to students who are not congruent with the modal social norms of the "scout camp?" At Thurston, the concern is for students who care about their school but cannot locate the social supports for their development. These two requirements for adaptation will have divergent effects upon the students' participation in school activities and in the development of preferences for adult help-giving roles. The results of the study affirm that the quality and diversity of the social environment has a definite impact on the way in which the student learns to cope with environmental demands. To the extent that such effects are empirically demonstrated, this research can provide concepts for designing preventive interventions for varied social environments.

The ecological thesis affirms that the socialization of competences can succeed if the following criteria are met:

1. A diversity of formal and informal social settings encourages social interaction.
2. A variety of informal roles in the social environment allows for spontaneous help giving and for personal interactions across divergent roles.
3. Varied competences are valued, and persons contribute these competences to the larger community.
4. There are clearly recognized social norms for relating to the surrounding external environments.
5. There is a commitment to examine the impact of the social environment upon its members.
6. There exists the design of a social environment where the dominant activities take into account the diverse cultural values of the members.

On the basis of the research findings, our thinking about the ecology of competence suggests the following tentative conclusions:

1. Students at Wayne are expected to learn how to interact with adults in authority roles, initiate social interactions with strangers, and feel optimistic about their ability to influence the events of the school.
2. Students at Wayne are expected to participate in hierarchical relationships and to influence persons with power who are above them in social status.
3. Students at Wayne are expected to learn how to deal with and engage those with social influence.
4. Students at Thurston, on the other hand, are expected to move toward their individual life goals without deviating from their objectives and without participating actively in their immediate social settings. What the Thurston students have, they keep and parlay for new achievements at a future time.
5. Students at Wayne are expected to be involved and committed toward making their world effective, whereas students at Thurston are concerned primarily with ensuring that they maintain a current and valued position.

What are the potential strains for these different patterns of socialization? The students at Wayne are expected to be naive about realities of the social milieu that are different from their own. Consequently, their views of the world are expected to be cognitively more simple than the world view of Thurston students. In contrast, students at Thurston are expected to have a more realistic, if not cynical, view of how social institutions function and to have little emotional investment in actively participating to bring about change. On the basis of these ideas, boys with high preferences for exploration at Wayne would be expected to have more personally satisfying and adaptive high school careers than Thurston boys with high preferences for exploration. Furthermore, the high-explorer students at Thurston would be expected to feel more psychic strain as they attempt to engage and participate in a vague and unresponsive environment.

The ecological thesis is that competences will vary as a consequence of participating in different environments. A longitudinal study, hopefully, can clarify how natural features of different social environments affect their members. On the basis of the work presented in this volume, it is possible to offer some initial statements of principles. These five statements relate to the substantive findings as well as to the ecological perspective.

1. Tenth-grade boys in the two high schools vary substantially in their development.

The research reported by Edwards (chapters 5 and 6), Gilmore (chapter 7), Barbara Newman (chapter 8), and Jones (chapter 9) illustrates the wide ranges of response to life events, to the school regime, to such activities as going steady, and to beliefs such as trust of authority and commitment to maintain themselves in school. This variability, which reflects rich individual differences in development, forces the developmental researcher to suspend judgment on what is acceptable or normal behavior. It also prompts the formulation of a system of governance for secondary education in which small groups of students are encouraged to educate themselves at their own pace.

Increasingly, secondary schools are moving to decentralized modular scheduling. A developmental conception of adolescence as a period of variability and searching was popular several decades ago, and such a view may come back again. The contributions of Piaget, Erikson, and their followers receive support from the preliminary findings, which clearly articulate the transitional and variable nature of the developmental process.

2. Tenth-grade boys place strong emphasis upon personal athletic competences and bravado.

The repetitive theme running through the protocols, interviews, and responses to research instruments was the focus on—almost preoccupation with—self-expression via body movements. It was apparent that the young person who has excelled in athletics has it made. If the 10th-grade boy has tried nothing else, he will be tested by athletics; and only a few will be lucky enough to be encouraged to develop other skills and competences. This finding, which was discussed by Edwards (chapter 5), Gilmore (chapter 7), and Barbara Newman (chapter 8), has important implications for planning educational programs, as well as for a continued appraisal of this age period. If the performance of physical and athletic activities is germane upon entry at high school, then a variety of intramural and extramural sports, graded by difficulty level and readiness for performance, can become a dominant part of high school life for the 10th-grade boy.

Psychologists, both for research and action purposes, can increase their authenticity as observers of the high school period by understanding how sports and athletic competence are related to the identity, self-esteem, and self-regard of the tenth-grade boy. The prominence of energy and physical activity, along with the benefits of knowing how to use the body, are topics that are rich for extending the theoretical foundations for adolescent psychology. It would seem that the future coping potential of tenth-grade boys can be positively affected by the extent to which they understand and use the body in athletic competition and sports programs. Leisure activities and diverse sports programs can serve a preventive role for youth as they express their personal competences, first through athletic activities and then in other social and interpersonal activities.

3. Social exploration is an emerging behavior that is worthy of study in the 10th grade and beyond.

When the research began, emphasis was given to measuring social exploration as an individual difference variable that would illustrate how boys develop preferences for engaging social structures. Considering the difficult measurement and research tasks, definite progress has been made in developing a research assessment procedure that reflects preferences for social engagement from the 8th to the 10th grade. As an individual difference variable, the predictive validity of the exploration construct is encouraging. Boys who initially had high preferences retained them, and boys with low preferences did so.

Social exploration concepts, as operationally developed by the assessment techniques of Edwards (chapter 5), reliably assess an aspect of adolescent behavior that is divergent from other personality measures. Although further research will be required to determine how valid the scale is for diverse populations, the interview data (Gilmore), the observations of groups (Barbara Newman), and the experimental intervention (Jones) described in this volume affirm that the concept of exploration is alive and worthy of attention. It is a personality concept that is free of references to pathology and that refers to self-actualization preferences for active participation in the social structure of the school. Boys can vary in level of exploration and not be "sick." What is more important for boys who are high in this preference for exploration is the possibility of assessing the effects of their environments upon the expression of future exploration.

Will the boy with high exploratory preferences find new channels within the high school social structure, or will he be a "victim" of the socialization processes of nonsupportive environments? The questionnaire measure of exploratory preferences developed by Edwards seems quite appropriate to assess the differential effects of participation in contrasting environments. This measure can also help to focus on the developmental correlates of a behavioral disposition that seems likely to have an adaptive function for adulthood.

4. Multiple methods are preferred for research on adolescent development.

Given both the variability and surging growth of the adolescent, it is limiting to assess this particular period of life without using several different methods. The portraits of "Dave" and "Harold," revealed in the questionnaire data reported by Edwards (chapter 5), the interviews reported by Gilmore (chapter 7), and in Barbara Newman's observations (chapter 8), provide a generally consistent picture. Yet each of these methods also brings out and highlights facts that were not reflected in the other methods.

The reports from questionnaire, interview, and group observation data all conveyed "Harold's" lack of intensive involvement in the activities of the school. Each method also illuminated a possible source of this behavior. Though all three methods reported the intensive involvement of "Dave" in multiple settings and activities at Wayne, the three investigators all spoke of their concerns that "Dave" was moving too fast to be settled; and there seemed to be a feature of "flight" in "Dave's" adaptation to his environment. The three vignettes about these two students present a comprehensive view of the boys' general orientation to their social and academic world.

The combined effect of the independent reports of the behavior of these boys raises additional questions about the benefits and the limiting qualities of these boys being nonvisible participants in their high schools. "Harold" was involved only with the academic regime at Thurston; he returned to his junior high school associates or to friends elsewhere for his social contacts. Apparently "Harold" was not involved in school, and the Thurston environment was not actively engaging him. Is it possible for Thurston High School to involve an able and relatively engaging student? A question for the Thurston faculty is whether the school seeks out talent.

"Dave," on the other hand, is a very active and spirited person who is very much involved in the multiple opportunities at Wayne High School. All three reports of "Dave's" behavior, however, inquired if he was not unhappy and ill at ease in spite of this spirited activity. It is hypothesized that a "test" for students at Wayne is whether outgoing, energetic participation can be a "false-positive" sign of environmental mastery. An important task in differentiating the socialization process at Wayne lies in distinguishing between the realities of adaptive mastery and the signs of pseudomastery.

5. Social environments can be assessed in terms of their psychological effects upon individuals.

Multiple methods sharpen the analysis of the socialization process in different social environments. The development of the Environmental Assessment Inventory by Philip Newman (chapter 11) provides tangible data that the faculty and students at *each* high school agreed with each other in the perceptions of the quality of life in their schools. These reports also indicated that the settings for socialization and social interaction can be identified. The compelling and striking differences in the number and quality of social interactions at the two high schools—e.g., the number of settings for interaction among faculty and students and between students—provide a frame of reference for assessing the effects of participation in these demographically similar yet psychologically distinctive environments. If Wayne students do in fact have more occasions for social engagement and informal chitchat than the students at Thurston, will the Wayne students take with them more confidence and more ease in social interactions after graduation from high school? Will the high-explorer boys at Wayne emerge as more outgoing and competent because their surrounding environment was more congruent with their personal style?

The development of a multimethod study of both persons and settings is a comprehensive undertaking. The five topics noted above suggest different qualities about the two high schools that were evaluated and reflect some of the unique psychological properties of these varied social environments. It seems apparent that no single method, whether interview, survey, or field observations, can provide comprehensive answers to questions about person–environment fit. Each method can illuminate different facets of the student's expressive behavior that describe something unique about the individual, as well as reflecting the social structure of the environment. Each method, attending to varied levels and facets of person–environment interaction, adds clarity or suggests new dimensions, both of which are needed in ecological inquiry.

The research reported in this volume on the interaction of settings and persons was conducted within the context of a commitment to improvisation. Within this context, the authors have designed specific studies in accordance with our general research goals. We hope that we have given the reader a coherent orientation to our expedition.

References

Biber, B., & Minuchin, P. (1965). *The role of the school in the socialization of competence*. Working paper presented at the Social Science Research Council's Conference on Socialization for Competence. Puerto Rico, April.

Brim, O. G., Jr., & Wheeler, S. (1966). *Socialization after childhood: Two essays*. New York: John Wiley & Sons.

Clausen, J. A. (1968). Perspectives on childhood socialization. In John A. Clausen (Ed.), *Socialization and society*. Boston: Little, Brown & Co.

Inkeles, A. (1968). Society, social structure, and child socialization. In John A. Clausen (Ed.), *Socialization and society*. Boston: Little, Brown & Co.

Smith, M. B. (1968). Competence and socialization. In John A. Clausen (Ed.), *Socialization and society*. Boston: Little, Brown & Co.

3

Antidotes for Arrogance

Reflections

At the same time the high school research started, the American Psychological Association began to recognize community psychology as a new division. I was to have a role in the development of this new APA division, and Robert Reiff was drafted as its first president after the APA Board of Directors' approval at the New York annual conference. In 1968, elections were held for the next president, and I was elected. I was naturally very pleased. I was expected to give a presidential address at the APA meetings in Washington, D.C., in fall 1969.

Increasing tensions and concerns were developing about the relevance of current psychological approaches to research and practice. This was at the time of student activism, protests against the Vietnam War, and the height of national recognition of the civil rights movement. Various groups of students, including graduate students at the University of Michigan, were challenging the Department of Psychology and the university about the colonial nature of psychology and its insensitivities to women and nonwhite persons. Several meetings were held with the faculty and graduate students to clarify these issues. As developer of the Community Psychology Area, I was pleased that my views seemed congruent with the aspirations of those with interests to connect psychology and community. Several doctoral students were interested in my vision for community psychology training. Stephanie Riger and Sharon Rosen were especially supportive of my initial efforts.

All of these changes in the field of psychology were present. What was I going to say in my address? Sometime during the summer, I sat down at my dining room table to write a first draft of my comments. The words came easily. At no other time has the preparation of a presentation or publication been this effortless. The ideas and words flowed. It was almost like what I knew of automatic writing. I never experienced this again! The address gave me an opportunity to

state an ecological approach to training in the field. Right before the APA meet-
ings, speakers were anxious that their presentation would be disrupted by public
demonstrations. I was assured that I would not be interrupted. I gave the talk to
a full audience, and I remember becoming emotional when delivering certain pas-
sages. At the close, I received a standing ovation that seemed to go on for a long
time. I was blown away! I believe that I responded to concerns and interests of
the audience to have psychology more connected and responsive to the needs of
communities.

The thesis of this article is that if psychologists can broaden their definitions of therapeutic activities, expand their definitions for the criteria of competent helpers, become participants in their local communities, and alter their time perspective, then they can help to build a psychology *of* the community.

A redefinition of the psychologist's job is advocated, and a new set of criteria for the hallmarks for this profession is proposed. Being a community psychologist is more than being a good psychologist, for community psychology is a sufficiently different activity. To achieve valid training or able professional role models for this field, accommodations to the heritages, assumptions, and styles of previous training are sharpened and redefined. Developing competences for work in the community is a different task and requires new political alliances and new criteria for personal and joint accountability between the community and the psychologist.[1]

The spirit of the community psychologist is the spirit of a naturalist who dotes on his environment; of the journalist, who bird-dogs his story; and of the conservationist, who glows when he finds a new way to describe man's interdependence with his environment. The recommended way to prevent professional extinction is participation in the local community; the preferred antidote for arrogance is an ecological view of man.

Psychologists sneer and smart over the arrogances and disdain of radicals, militants, or the citizen with conservative reflexes. The most arrogant guys around are often we professionals who *analyze, position, reflect, study, commission, postpone, garble, intrude,* and *play with,* but rarely play out, the crosscurrents of community events. It is our quiet and sometimes folksy and affable arrogance that can interfere with colleagues' and students' opportunities to adopt tentative explorations and offbeat enterprises that are an integral part of psychology. For many of the younger generation, too often, psychologists have been models for community change that represents, at best, tokenism; sometimes in moments of haste, we have generated the seeds for alienation.

Elsewhere, the present author has stated how concepts from biological ecology can be applied to designing social interventions (Kelly, 1966, 1968; Mills &

Kelly, in press [1972]; Trickett, Kelly, & Todd, in press [1972]). If all of the stimulating ideas from biology are distilled into a single theme, it is a fondness, a commitment, a love, if you will, of the very community where you live and work; an involvement that engulfs your attention and draws your curiosity to make an adventure out of knowing all there is to know of its heritage, its conflicts, its people, its political forces, and its efforts to launch campaigns for social goods, as well as its failures when the status is quo. Few of us have been trained to cathect to a locale. I am confident that few psychologists have been taught to worry about our communities, and still fewer of us have given our time to see the promotion of a civic cause fulfilled.

How did psychology get into such a fix? One of the key events can be attributed not to the heritage of psychology, but to the reluctance of psychologists to chart a course of action that is around our roles, beneath our status, and beyond our scientific canons. Perhaps we psychologists have been too hung up with ourselves and have been able to see our world only through the mirrors of ourselves. How many articles or books on community psychology discuss the community? Klein's (1968) recent work is alone in this respect. How many conferences at professional meetings talk about the development or evolution of communities? Few, if any.

We certainly seem to be in a fix! Are we addicted? These charges may seem severe, undisciplined, and untestable. Perhaps they are! I would also like to take this opportunity to express some ideas on how we might right the fix and get ourselves spruced up for a campaign that can be, in William James's (1911) terms, a moral equivalent for war.

What follows is a recitation of some concrete ways in which psychology as a science and profession can create a point of view for training ourselves and our students as community psychologists. Then, psychologists can ask APA and our colleagues to come and see the crop; to do something other than yell at the APA Central Office for the fertilizer! The following are seven ideas for pulling ahead of social crises, for being professional *and* revolutionary without rhetoric and without arms.[2]

Each of these seven principles are offered as ways in which training for community psychology can be created and nurtured. The focus on training is not an emphasis on how to tinker with the curriculum, but refers to the socialization of a new profession. The initial premise is that since community psychology is different from other forms of psychology, then its socialization will need to be different. For the training of the community psychologist demands a critical period in which he learns the styles of work that are going to be relevant for his own future adaptation. If the differences in requirements are real, training programs will need to be designed to reflect these varied conditions.

In all of these comments, references to university-based training will be emphasized, particularly those relationships between the university, the community, and the training program. The following principles, however, also could apply with appropriate modification to field training centers and their relationships to the community.

Field Assessment and the Selection of Community Psychologists

I cannot decide whether my interest in community psychology is in spite of my training in psychology or in addition to my training in psychology. As I look back on my development, the most critical events seem to be the planned and unplanned experiences of working and dealing with the broadest range of persons. Some important occasions were related to the opportunities I had as a graduate student at the University of Texas in the late 1950s. Most of them, however, were not; they involved the people I worked with, the people I worked for, and the stress I dealt with as I tried to make and find my way. Persons I have known to be turned on about the excitement of community work also seem to be accidentally a part of psychology. I certainly do not know of any doctoral training programs in psychology that begin with the goal to train persons who are effective change agents and then proceed to select and train persons for that very purpose.

What I think we need as a start are ways to locate potential community psychologists as early as high school and provide a series of activities that can prepare them to be responsive to the tough tasks of community work. Rather than relying only on the Graduate Record Examination, Miller Analogies Test, testimonials from eminent psychologists, and matriculation at Ivy League schools, the new training program should expend its resources to create field tasks of moderate intensity and difficulty. Such assessment procedures would not be designed just to meet the requirements of a pass–fail situation, but would suggest the various combinations of skills that the applicant has developed up to a particular time. Such an assessment would be so designed to provide alternative ideas for obtaining training that can adapt to his needs. Under these conditions, universities could join together, create a national academy, pool resources, and encourage the student to enter the university that is most congruent with his developmental level. The new student would have the option to continue his training at other universities of his choice at a future point in his career.

Such a training program could provide the additional benefits of relating the university to additional resources, like undergraduate and high school instruction, and encouraging students to enter their graduate career when (a) their interest, (b) their competence, and (c) their field performance suggests, and *not* just when they have accumulated the necessary credit hours or meet the resident requirements. The field assessments, where the student tries to solve a community problem, can also include provisions for advisory committees, with representatives of the applicants, as well as community leaders and faculty, all helping to design the assessment procedures. Mechanisms could be worked out so that the criteria for performance can shift to accommodate changes in communities, generational shifts of interest, and the development of new knowledge by the faculty. What happens after selection?

Continuous Interdisciplinary Interaction

One of our hangups that must be resolved is our inability to work effectively with members of other professions. I am not preaching tolerance for all disciplines, nor am I suggesting that we create a multidisciplinary project that collects representatives from other disciplines, *nor* do I mean sending psychology graduate students across campus to pick up a course in anthropology or sociology *after* they complete all other requirements. I am affirming that the entering students should be given the chance to become involved with multidisciplines, both faculty and students, as they work toward the solution of a problem that lies outside the territorial boundaries of their discipline. Under these conditions, the student has the opportunity to work toward the resolution of complex problems in the presence of faculty and students outside his discipline, and he has the chance to learn the process of collaborating with other professions *by doing it.*

New settings can be created to assist the student in solidifying the collaborative skills that he is just learning. For example, the faculty member tutoring the student will be expected to have been through such an experience, or committed to go through it for the first time with the student. It also is assumed that the group of students going through such training will have a chance to view their own group process and reflect and achieve clarity about their own participation in that process. The premise is that listening and engaging others can be learned directly from the practice of working in natural field conditions. If the student uses such experiences, he will have acquired an internal resource that helps him generalize to new settings, and he has taken an essential step in learning how to be a change agent. The hypothesis is suggested that if the student can work effectively with other disciplines, he will be able to reach out and work with citizens, independent of their beliefs, even when they conflict with his own. He has learned how to make the resolution of personal conflicts and confrontations be generative for himself and others.

One of the important contexts for encouraging such work at the departmental level is the support from the university administration and the federal agencies; both must support more than the spirit of working across disciplinary boundaries. Working out all the right conditions for a collaborative enterprise at the local level is limiting if the federal agencies preach good deeds but are not able to make these deeds count and actively nourish interdisciplinary training. It may be completely naive to think that federal agencies can leave their catacombs, but universities must do a better job by encouraging, cajoling, and gigging federal officials to function as interagency ombudsmen.

One of the important by-products of the successful interdisciplinary process is that it devises a training ground for a generalist, a generalist who is not a dilettante or world traveler, but a person who has achieved a working perspective via direct and sustained experience in a local community. I also think the ability to collaborate implies a seasoned toughness of spirit, a point which reemphasizes the importance of the field selection for students entering the program. Here, the student first learns how to work on a problem with a group of nonpsychologists. Graduates of such a program with this type of socialization are expected to have a greater chance to be an effective colleague, even when the substance of community psychology changes and the problems shift.

The Longitudinal Perspective

The development of persons, like the evolution of communities, requires a view without restrictions on time. One of the most difficult tasks facing community psychology is to learn how to tune into a community and assess how transitory or how deep-rooted are the issues of the day. This task is critical for the survival of the community psychologist. *If he misjudges gossamer for grit, he is dead before he starts.* Mapping out the antecedent factors that have contributed to the current balance of political events is an exciting activity that forces the community psychologist to draw on professions and involves processes that may be unfamiliar to him. If such an effort is made as a cross-sectional analysis, the risk of making programmatic error rises sharply. A value for the longitudinal perspective is that it reduces the community psychologist from appraising effects of environmental conditions from being "good" or "bad." It allows him to hang loose and relate the processes that have appeared to be disruptive to processes which can contribute to community development at a future point in time. The longitudinal perspective also helps to make explicit ideas that are useful in dealing with complex events and cautions the packaging of monolithic formulations of the change process that are so pervasive and contagious. The longitudinal perspective also can give immense satisfaction in working with persons over time.

How does the university go about achieving this? To my mind, the criteria for training would be shifted from defining units of courses to creating segments of training. In sum, the student would participate in training until that particular activity is completed—when the particular segment is achieved. If a student is learning consultation skills, he may be working with a client system for a period of several years, depending on the particular characteristics of the client system. To view graduate training in an unstructured fashion requires efforts by both faculty and students to be accountable to each other and to be open and confrontable. Unless the curriculum can be replaced by the personal accountabilities between faculty and students, a program without credit hours and without courses could be anarchic or at least anomic. To start, the faculty must be prepared to get with an open-ended process. Such a longitudinal program also requires an unusual amount of documentation and archival recording of critical periods. Such an activity is expensive and involves supporting staff. Certainly, the typical departmental secretary is not enough of a framework for such a training program. Fulfillment of this principle requires new resources for the university, resources that are urgently needed if the community psychologist is to reorder his way and restructure his home environment.

Mixing Theory and Practice

The challenge of community psychology to me means that the psychologist puts aside all of his polarities and his hyphenated role conceptions and plunges right into a practice to create ideas that are pragmatic. This is what Reiff (1968) has been telling us for years. The essence of the task of the psychologist is to conduct himself so that his behavior expresses the integration that he has made of the development of his theoretical and his practical ideas. This does not mean assigning students to the classroom under one faculty member and then assigning them for a practicum under another faculty member, with the result that the student is left to cope with two supervisors and their idiosyncrasies. The ecological perspective affirms that acquiring competence for community psychology involves direct personal experience in building practice and theory, so that the two feed on one another and assist the community psychologist to become a generalist who is relevant, who can become an advocate, and who has a survival potential that lasts beyond several years. The guess is that the training program that creates such a mix assists the psychologist to be adaptive to changing environmental conditions.

As the student works toward the integration of these ideas for himself in the presence of other students and faculty, all learn in still another way to be accountable to each other for actualizing these values. The attainment of this integration for me implies something, if you will, that is precious, namely, that the conversations, confrontations, dialogues, and "rappings" are reciprocal. The faculty's participation is enhanced when they are able to say clearly and concisely how their efforts worked and did not work. The students' contributions are real when they can ask the searching questions. Such aspirations may seem like having counsel from a favorite uncle, niece, or nephew. This may not be so farfetched, for the frequency and quality of interaction approaches the definition of a community. It is these types of informal interactions that are the sources for personal and professional integration.

But this type of interaction asks a lot of both students and faculty—it means the professor drops his Socratic ways, his citations, and his defensiveness about being professional, and even says quite frankly that he does not understand a particular problem any better than anyone else. The student can no longer hide behind padded bibliographies, simulated silences, and he is not allowed to "cop out" and be uninvolved in his own graduate career. Shedding such role sets can make a whale of a difference to faculty and students independent of substantive interests. Such freedom from professional sclerosis can generate a whole new profession!

These thoughts are suggested not as a way of creating a club, or a new commune, but as settings to help develop disciplined and integrated professionals that the field demands. The criteria for seeing whether the theory and practice do mix *is* that the theoretical products are valid if they explain what is happening today; the practices are relevant if they help the community psychologist anticipate the effects of interventions for some future time. Working for such criteria affords a climate for students and colleagues to create a viable society. This is definitely a nice bonus.

Taking Advantage of Community Events

Another hangup that we professionals have is our tendency to structure our lives and fill our curriculum as if our pieces of knowledge were bits of honey in a beehive. We so preempt our lives with our definitions of professional practice that we allow little room for picking up a piece of the action, and we give ourselves few chances to move with the changing conditions. The community psychologist needs free hours for both faculty and students. Community events, whether they are crises or public holidays, represent our laboratory and require that we be in attendance to observe and participate and earn a right to contribute. It is on such occasions that persons who may be intensely involved and yet alienated from their communities can be noticed and persuaded to become new resources for the community. When the community psychologist is free with his time, he is free to replenish his energy that is so quickly spent when he involves himself in situations with persons who are strangers. The intellectual and affective resources involved when dealing with emergency events can be an exhausting experience—an experience that you must be up for. I personally have been impressed with the effectiveness of persons who perform in stress situations. When I have checked, one of the critical ingredients of their success is their lack of fatigue rather than particular novel or provocative words they have spoken.

Freeing the curriculum of structural requirements and replacing it with alternative ways to seed learning without a calendar is an essential hallmark when embarking on the training of the community psychologist. To try to model the training along the traditions of the university and the heritage of training in professional psychology is worse than shortsighted. It is fraudulent!

The adaptive tasks of the community psychologist are not to accommodate to the university; his tasks are to follow the life course of the community and to adapt to the community's environments. Advocating care for the locale means giving it the first option. Representing the university happens when the community psychologist acts; the academic side of the role is the presence of the community psychologist in the center of things. Accountability for this role must be shared, and it demands resources within the community and the university for this new joint accountability. It is likely that such resources will have to be identified and created; we have no clear roles for these functions in our society.

This is a difficult principle to see born, let alone keep alive, for it means that the university administration must see its faculty on detached service and not expect the faculty member to perform functions previously identified as marks of a university professor. I am not advocating a new elite, for the community psychologist should replace these deleted functions by involving colleagues in his work, by defining the validity of work via relating it to others. Such dialogues may require more tact, more tolerance, more clarity of purpose, and more humility than we would like. But what better training ground for the community psychologist than rapping with colleagues. Besides, we might learn something!

There is another facet of taking advantage of community events, namely, that it requires a sense of personal identity that is constantly tested. Being on the battlefield means that the psychologist does not call "foul" or does not go home mad when things get rough. In fact, his validity as a professional is reinforced when he remains involved, when he has a sense of how the battles are affecting him, what they are costing him, how his performance stacks up, and when he needs help. This sense of personal integrity cannot just be hoped for, and we cannot refer back to childrearing practices for an understanding of it. This personal integrity must be learned via the socialization of mastering community events, including those occasions when the community psychologist looks like a loser. It is this *kind* of laboratory where coping with unplanned events can generate the future development of the community psychologist and a psychology *of* the community.

Identification of Community Resources

The recitation of these ideas may sound like the community psychologist is either a guru, a saint, a mayor, a ward heeler, or a new kook. What has been intended is that as the effective community psychologist works, an initial premise is that he makes for himself a program of community development that depends on encouraging others to work with him. He turns over to others work that for him is a major investment. Being able to collaborate is a very high priority as he searches for persons who can replace his own activities. This coping style is a very infrequent part of the socialization of the psychologist, but a behavior that is vital for the psychologist who is going to be an effective community resource. I noted that when psychologists try to function in the community in the same way that they try to function in their departments or agencies, and play out the same political battles that are relevant there, they often fall flat. A particular city or town may operate like a university, but the operating guideline for the community psychologist is that *every* setting, organization, and subgrouping of society has a culture that is ecologically distinct and requires different channels for expressing social influence. A hedge against his own limited political idiosyncrasies is his effort to locate and develop resources out of the local culture.

If community psychologists are going to be open and resilient and draw on the resources of others, then they too will need help. The organization that sponsors the community psychology training must become involved with the surrounding environment, must be alert to identify and accommodate persons with talent, and must have a commitment for being involved in the exciting *and* the boring, the repetitive, *and* the ephemeral events that are the media for community change. We professionals too often sneak away from such daily chores. How often do we in psychology not only ask persons to change to fit our aspirations, but then add the additional burden that they march to our drum while they do it? Finding ways and having commitments to work with persons with varying ideologies is a tough, exhausting, but actualizing experience. It is an interaction, nevertheless, that is mandatory for the development of an effective community program.

For me, the social revolutions in our society mark the end of the professional as *the* policy maker! When I keep saying this to myself, I realize how incomplete, how fragile, and how invalid some of my own training has been. I begin to think how I can begin to create conditions so that the committed, the involved, and the curious student and citizen can find settings to create his own competence and enlarge his worldview. One thing I am convinced of is that our frame of reference must shift, and our training programs should be redesigned so that the settings for the personal development of the community psychologist are viable, coherent, and of the highest quality. One way to create a richer and more valid enterprise is by teaching the community psychologist to identify with *all* the people in his community and to become involved in the creation of *new* community resources.

Updating the Community Psychologist

If the community psychologist works toward implementing such principles, how is he himself going to generate new ideas and mobilize energy for adapting to change? Of all the people, he will most frequently need to revive his concepts, shift his perceptions, rotate his ideologies, and learn how to manage new environments. How can this be achieved? One idea is for the academy of training facilities, who were participating in the selection of new students, to work together again in creating a facility for the continuing education of the community psychologist.

I have been struck by the historical accounts of the role that the Marine Biological Laboratories at Woods Hole, Massachusetts, has played in the development in biology (Conklin, 1968a, 1968b). For many years, Woods Hole served as a social setting with a mixture of functions. It was a place where biologists could come to work; it was a place where the leadership attracted the stimulating and provocative minds. It was a place where faculty came with their students and, under very informal and casual conditions, worked, talked, and shared their ideas and hopes that so frequently do not appear in the final publication of scientific reports. Biologists with whom I have spoken are unanimous in their praise for this institution and for the major influence that the setting has had in the development of their own work.

The picture of Woods Hole, as sketched by those who have been associated with it, can take on the properties of a romantic South Sea island. Putting aside such reveries, the creation of an analogue to Woods Hole for the training of community psychologists seems to me to be an idea worth pursuing on its own merit. An idea that, if implemented, could play a critical role in the updating of the faculty and the generation of students who can become the eminent and accomplished innovators.

When I begin to consider the means by which a Woods Hole laboratory can be created for the training of community psychology, some features occur to me that are different than those of a research laboratory located in a scenic marshland along the Massachusetts coastline. Such a facility would not be in one place, but would be scattered in different parts of the country and would be located in geographical areas where there are varying political conditions, different opportunities for the delivery of community services, and where each of the laboratories would have contrasting styles of working with citizens. Such facilities could provide a node for regenerating community psychologists rather than creating totally new communities.

As I think about how social change occurs in the practice of professions, I am struck with the apparent need we have to identify with *new* bureaucratic structures. Social innovations seem to be symbolized only through the creation of new buildings, new departments, and new professions, with intact identifiable social structures. What also occurs to me is that the innovative life history of such social organizations is over almost at the time of the birth of the new institution. What we have been unable to do is to devise alternative social settings that relate to the workings of society, and then to consider how to use ad hoc and temporary groupings of persons to nurture the development process. Glidewell's (1968) ideas regarding the relevance of temporary societies as media for self-development are an intriguing set of ideas because they force community psychologists to focus on the form and style that is congruent and relevant for the change activity, rather than expecting that any new structure *or* formal social organizations will replenish us and our society. I am proposing that a loose collection of laboratories situated in strategic sites can achieve for community psychology what Woods Hole did for an earlier generation of biologists.

Conclusion

All of the aforementioned ideas are options we have. They are ideas that I think can make our commitments clear, our interventions long-lasting, and our knowledge adaptive. I hope that these seven points offer a set of conditions that spell out channels and opportunities for community psychology to make its way. The task of community psychology is to educate ourselves and our communities to the fact that social change does not *only* occur as a result of reactions to specific crises or demonstrable technologies, but can be a product of social processes—processes that have their origin in the design of social settings arranged for innovation *and* for change.

Notes

1. The final report of the Task Force on Community Mental Health suggests additional emphases for the psychologist working in community mental health (see Glidewell & Brown, 1969).

2. An important source for several of the following ideas is the report "Ecological Concepts and Mental Health Programs." Acknowledgment is expressed to George Coelho, Project Officer of the National Institute of Mental Health, for the contract to conduct this study. Appreciation is given to him and to the author's colleagues for their collaboration in this work (see Kelly, Goldsmith, Coelho, Randolph, Shapiro, & Seder, 1967).

References

Conklin, E. G. (1968a). Early days at Woods Hole. *American Scientist, 56,* 112–120.
Conklin, E. G. (1968b). M. B. L. stories. *American Scientist, 56,* 121–129.
James, W. (1911). From the moral equivalent for war. In *Memories and studies.* London: Longmans, Green & Co. (Also in *The philosophy of William James.* New York: Modern Library, 264.)
Glidewell, J. C. (1968). The professional practitioner and his community. Chairman's address, Mental Health Section, presented at the meeting of the American Public Health Association, Detroit, November.
Glidewell, J. C., & Brown, M. (1969). *Priorities for psychologists in community mental health.* Report of the Task Force on Community Mental Health, Division 27.
Graziano, A. M. (1969). Clinical innovation and the mental health power structure: A social case history. *American Psychologist, 24,* 10–18.

Kelly, J. G. (1966). Ecological constraints on mental health services. *American Psychologist, 21,* 535–539.

Kelly, J. G. (1968). Towards a theory of preventive intervention. In J. W. Carter Jr. (Ed.), *Research contributions from psychology to community mental health.* New York: Behavioral Publications.

Kelly, J. G., Goldsmith, R., Coelho, G., Randolph, P., Shapiro, D., & Seder, R. (1967). *Ecological concepts and mental health programs* (Final Report: Contract No. 67-1488). Chevy Chase, MD: National Institute of Mental Health.

Klein, D. C. (1968). *Community dynamics and mental health.* New York: Wiley.

Mills, R. C., & Kelly, J. G. (In press [1972]). Ecology and cultural adaptation: A case study and critique. In S. Golann & C. Eisdorfer (Eds.), *Handbook of community mental health.* New York: Appleton-Century-Crofts.

Reiff, R. (1968). Social intervention and the problem of psychological analysis. *American Psychologist, 23,* 524–531.

Trickett, E. J., Kelly, J. G., & Todd, D. M. (In press [1972]). The social environment of the high school: Guidelines for individual change and organizational redevelopment. In S. Golann & C. Eisdorfer (Eds.), *Handbook of community mental health.* New York: Appleton-Century-Crofts.

4

Quest for Valid Preventive Interventions

Reflections

In September 1967, soon after the formation of the Division of Community Psychology, the executive committee of the division appointed a Task Force on Community Mental Health. The task force had been instructed "to develop cogent positions on the current and critical issues confronting psychologists involved in research and practice in community mental health." Jack Glidewell and Mortimer Brown were appointed co-chairpersons. I do not recall the selection process, but Bernard Bloom, Lou Cohen, Herb Dorken, Will Edgerton, Ira Iscoe, Bob Reiff, and I were invited to prepare position statements at a conference that was held at Loyola University in spring 1968. The following September, the report was presented to the executive committee, revisions were made, and a book edited by Jack Glidewell was published with the title Issues in Community Psychology and Preventive Mental Health *(1971). The spirit of the times was to separate community psychology from community mental health, so the chapters reflect these distinctions.*

I saw that it might be valuable to offer a research attitude for understanding mental health consultation, organizational change, and community development. In my mind, each was a vital option for community psychology, yet they each suggested different research methods. The criteria used for assessing radiating effects of mental health consultation to the faculty of an elementary school would be different than when evaluating how organizational members are able to solve crises or even documenting a community development process to see if more ethnic minorities were added to the community planning process. Different problems require different methods in varied circumstances. Research should adapt to community needs.

These were my ideas for how to move beyond the individual to include organizations and communities. As I recall, the audience was respectful but anxious about what I was asking to be done. In the days before PowerPoint, I presented three rather complex overheads to try and illustrate the thoughts. One of my own personal pleasures was locating a quote from Henrik Ibsen that I used as an epigram to express the spirit of the ideas: "One should never wear one's best trousers to go out and battle for freedom and truth." Ibsen's pithy comment illustrates how my perspective shifted from the notion of research as contrived, neat, or controlled activities. Rather, I was suggesting that we dig into messy complex topics and abandon limited research procedures. I believed then (and still do) that more is to be gained if we free ourselves from the constraints of pretending that causal links exist between independent and dependent variables.

One should never wear one's best trousers to go out and battle for freedom and truth.

—Henrik Ibsen

Introduction

William James's legacy to psychology was remembered at the 75th anniversary meetings of the American Psychological Association in 1967 by a series of commemorative symposia focusing on humanism and the problem of will, the modern meaning of instincts, levels of awareness, and brain functions. In addition to James's substantive contributions to psychology and his eclectic and humanitarian concerns, he also began a quest for societal alternatives for social pathology that continues to speak directly to the emerging field of community psychology.

There is still much unfinished business for this legacy of William James. He challenged psychologists to create new social institutions with varied means and open ends. His own eloquence was expressed as follows:

I spoke of the "moral equivalent" of war. So far, war has been the only force that can discipline a whole community, and until an equivalent discipline is organized, I believe that war must have its way. But I have no serious doubts that the ordinary prides and shames of social man, once developed to a certain intensity, are capable of organizing such a moral equivalent as I have sketched, or some other just as effective for preserving manliness of type. It is but a question of time, of skillful propagandism, and of opinion-making man seizing historic opportunities. [James, 1911]

There are numerous current and visible illustrations of the functions of crises and social disruptions that take on the properties of miniature war-like confrontations. The wisdom of Loaste's aphorism, "In every crisis there is opportunity as well as danger," has eluded citizens, government officials, and most change agents. We have failed, for the most part, to identify and moderate the social forces in our communities that are responsible for the personal and organizational casualties of change. What type of society can mobilize social change? Where in the life cycle of change programs are there opportunities to effectively influence social movements? How do interventions facilitate the evolution and development of social organizations? These searches, stimulated by William James, are still beyond the grasp of systematic knowledge.

The emergence of community psychology as a relevant area of professional engagement comes at a time when historic opportunity is seizing *us*; we certainly have not been effective in offering even minuscule suggestions for turning naturally occuring crises into social reform. While community psychologists have been active in proselytizing for change, we have not held positions of influence that would permit us to help identify opportunities for facilitating change, nor have we been able to pass on to others pragmatic and valid ideas that they might act upon. Eighty years after William James's words, we find that the community psychologist has joined the policy planner, the action researcher, the community developer, the urbanologist, and various groups of citizens working at making new communities. In the midst of this new and fast changing mix, we must ask: "What can we contribute that is unique?" and "How do we know that what we do counts?"

The operational issues which face community psychologists include such questions as: "When is an intervention by an outsider constructive?"; "When are interventions initiated?"; "How should interventions vary from place to place?"; "What criteria are employed to evaluate interventions?" Answers to these questions, generated out of involvement with real-world affairs, suggest to the present writer that psychology must reorder its concepts for evaluating change and for conducting research, and must develop new methods of carrying out our work.

What is effective, useful, and sympathetic in the design of research for univariate laboratory studies is inappropriate for the observation and evaluation of social change in natural settings and uncontrolled environments. Building toward a systematic account of the evaluation of change in social settings suggests an approach which involves multiple methods, an improvised style that emphasizes continuous participation with the local community, and a commitment to generate criteria for change. I am assuming that the community psychologist will increase his individual adaptations to social change by developing knowledge in different settings and requiring himself to create contrasting methodologies. The spirit of this personal response to the William James legacy is that adaptable knowledge will be best derived from work that emphasizes alternate methods stimulated by and appropriate to the requirements of local natural settings.

In this chapter, I will present some personal views about these issues. Three approaches to preventive interventions are described in which methods are contrasted and aims are compared. In addition, examples are offered of the type of questions that these new methods generate for verifying knowledge about personal, organizational and community change. The main thesis is that the uniqueness of community psychology is in the verification of interventions that work in a variety of social settings. If we are ingenious enough to create ways to validate these ideas, we may eventually even contribute to a redefinition of scientific activity in psychology.

Three Methods for Preventive Interventions

The following comments focus on preventive interventions that are closely identified with three types of therapeutic programs. The clinical approach which focuses upon changes in individuals or small groups can be a setting for an intervention that radiates effects that result from services offered to relevant individuals. Programs designed to initiate systematic change in an organization can also provide the setting for creating interventions that can assist an organization to deal with future crises. Community organization techniques that focus on ways to mobilize community resources for community action provide a heritage for designing preventive interventions that can enable a community to plan for its future. For each of these prototypic approaches to personal, organizational and community change, I have selected one example to illustrate the relevance of preventive programming.

For the clinical method, I have selected mental health consultation as an example of how the behavior of a consultee can be altered to affect the immediate larger environment. While most organizational change methods focus on redesigning role assignments and communication networks, altering the form of an organization also has the advantage of providing a context for developing capacities within the organization to handle future crises. The assumption is that the lifestyle and ways of doing business of a social organization can be shifted to reduce the paralyzing features of an emergency which may face the organization. Community development is based on a dominant premise that the survival of a community depends upon its capacity to reach a new level of adaptation. Community development, with its tradition of multiple approaches and improvised formats, offers a setting for defining community change efforts which provide important guidelines for preventive intervention. In this case, the preventive intervention is developing criteria for the community to employ when setting goals for its own future.

When consultation services enable the immediate social environment to benefit from such help, this work contributes to an intervention that is preventive. If the organizational change program can rearrange the social fabric so that the new organization can deal effectively with internal and external crises, then the change program has been, by definition, a preventive intervention. Community development programs function as a preventive intervention when they enable the local community to plan for its future.

It is the present writer's view that these approaches to community change represent: (1) contrasting premises about the change process; (2) have quite different aims; (3) employ new types of data for evaluation; and, most importantly, (4) demand different principles for inferring verification of knowledge. While programs of personal and organizational change serve to generate goals that are valid as discrete accomplishments, new goals are required in order for such services to reduce expressions of maladaptive behavior. Viewing prototypic change programs as preventive interventions suggests different criteria for each evaluation. These criteria provide new options for linking change programs to social processes which may help them to become more directly related to the local host community.

Intervention I: Mental Health Consultation as a Radiating Process

Descriptions of mental health consultation methods are legion, including an increasing number of efforts at evaluation that are now appearing in print (see Cowen, Gardner, & Zax, 1967; and Iscoe, 1967). The work of Caplan (1964), Berlin (1962), Bindman (1959), Morse (1967), Spielberger (1967), White (1966), and others has been effective in contrasting the professional activities of a psychotherapist and a mental health consultant. All of these writings emphasize an implicit premise: The aim of the consultant is to improve the functional competence of the consultee; for example, to improve the teaching effectiveness of the classroom teacher, to assist the principal in administering his school, etc. The primary focus is the consultee's performance of occupational roles, and not necessarily the consultee's own personality structure or his overt expression of mental strain. The consultant's diagnostic task is to assess the consultee's competence and his ability to carry out his job in a natural setting. The assessment process differs from the diagnostic process that takes place with clients in mental health treatment facilities by including data from the immediate social environment.

The historic focus for clinical work has been the patients' or clients' feelings, perceptions and attitudes about his environment. Community mental health practice has emphasized the extension of clinical practice so that effort is expended to discuss feelings, attitudes and perceptions that relate directly to concerns about the occupational role. The type of intervention to be discussed here gives greater emphasis to clarification of how the individual copes with his environment and involves a more active, detailed exposition of the interrelationship between an individual's present behavior and his future relationships with the key persons.

If we take preventive intervention seriously, we need to derive new types of criteria for assessing its effectiveness. The payoff from a consultation program is not only an alteration in the feeling states, belief systems and aspirations of the consultee, but should also reflect a change in a person's relationships with those significant others who directly participate in his life setting. Therefore, evaluation studies should not measure changes in attitudes of consultees nor analyze samples of the interactions between the consultant and consultee, nor note changes in the consultee's self concept, for such attempts at evaluation are not congruent with a conception of consultation as a preventive intervention.

One of the early rationales for developing consultation techniques was that they allowed the professional to work with key resources in the community who in turn would have direct access to large segments of the population (Klein & Lindemann, 1961). If this rationale is taken seriously, we are faced with establishing new standards for verification. If, for example, consultation is effective in initiating a change process, then indices of effectiveness should be defined not only by changes in consultee performance, such as the classroom teacher, but by cumulative and successive changes in the behavior of significant others, for example, students in the classroom as well as the behavior of other teachers in the same school environment. The evaluation of such activities has not progressed, however, and new criteria for designing studies are in demand.

When considering research designs to document the effectiveness of consultation methods as a preventive intervention, it is essential to provide for the assessment of the radiating effects of the intervention. Since the creation of pre-and postgroup comparisons and control groups to verify radiation effects would be prohibitive, it will be necessary to take into account what Campbell and Stanley (1963) have termed "a quasi-experimental design" in which attention is given to time and spatial effects. This type of design permits periodic measurements of selected individuals, in this case both students and classroom teachers over a period of time, before and after the introduction of an intervention such as consultation. A schema for conceiving consultation as a radiating process is illustrated in Figures 4.1, 4.2, and 4.3.

In Figure 4.1, an example is presented for two classroom teachers where one teacher is the consultee (Teacher A). This design is relevant for assessing the radiating effects of the consultation process when the consultee has frequent interactions with other persons. The elements of this design which have been diagrammed indicate that the design provides for measuring changes in the behavior of the students in each teacher's classroom. It is expected that the changes in students' behavior in Teacher A's classroom ($SI_A \ldots SS_A$) are more salutary than those observed in the students in Teacher B's classroom ($SI_B \ldots$

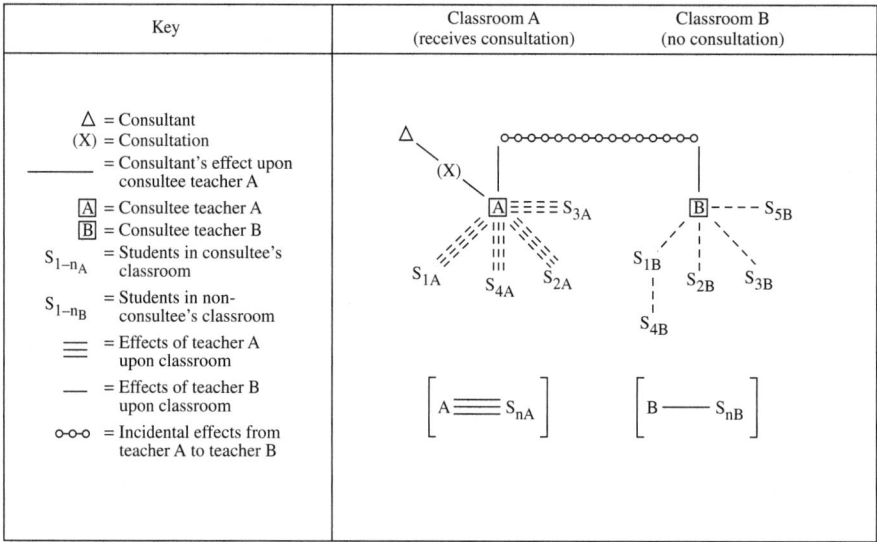

Key	Classroom A (receives consultation)	Classroom B (no consultation)

$\triangle$ = Consultant
(X) = Consultation
___ = Consultant's effect upon consultee teacher A
[A] = Consultee teacher A
[B] = Consultee teacher B
S_{1-n_A} = Students in consultee's classroom
S_{1-n_B} = Students in non-consultee's classroom
≡ = Effects of teacher A upon classroom
— = Effects of teacher B upon classroom
o-o-o = Incidental effects from teacher A to teacher B

Figure 4.1   Consultation as a radiating process

SS_B). Thus, the thesis is that an intervention such as consultation can be preventive if the consultee produces change in significant others.

Figure 4.1 illustrates that Teacher A, who receives consultation, is the medium for producing change in the students in her classroom.

Figure 4.2 diagrams a time-series design which involves repeated measurements of the students in both classrooms before and after the introduction of the intervention. Through the use of change scores and trend analysis, it should be possible to note the shifts in behavior of students in two different classrooms, one in which the teacher receives consultation, a second in which the teacher does not receive consultation. An additional feature of this design is that it permits documentation of the exact stages in the time sequence of the consultation process where its effects are seen in the behavior of students. Such work can clarify the meter of the consultation process and provide direct feedback for the practice of consultation.

Figure 4.3 presents examples of dependent variables which reflect the effects of the consultation intervention. In the rationale for consultation previously stated, an effort is made to influence the occupational role of the consultee. Criteria for evaluating consultation as a preventive intervention can be specifically related to occupational activity such as a teacher's ability to revise her teaching methods or the quality of teacher–student interactions. In the present example, the choice was to identify the number of changes in the teaching content of the teacher. The rationale for this example is that change in the content of the curriculum is a central behavior of the teacher and defines a major segment of teaching competence. In the example, Teacher A, who received consultation,

Key	Time Series Design
S_{1-n_A} = Observation of students in classroom A	Classroom A: $\left(S_{1-n_A}\right) T_1$ + $\left(S_{1-n_A}\right) T_2$ $X\left(S_{1-n_A}\right) T_3$ + $\left(S_{1-n_A}\right) T_4$
S_{1-n_B} = Observations of students in classroom B	
$T_1 \ldots n$ = Times for observations	Classroom B: $\left(S_{1-n_B}\right) T_1$ + $\left(S_{1-n_B}\right) T_2$ $\left(S_{1-n_B}\right) T_3$ + $\left(S_{1-n_B}\right) T_4$
X = Intervention of consultation	

Figure 4.2   Consultation as a radiating process

increased the number of changes in her lesson plan more than did Teacher B who did not receive this service.

The same type of predictions can also be applied to students in the classroom. If consultation has been effective as a preventive intervention, then students will be able to discriminate such effects as curriculum changes. Verification of the effectiveness of the intervention is derived from assessing changes in outcome patterns. Such quasi-experimental designs have been regarded as valid in the more successful sciences even though, as Campbell and Stanley have pointed out, they have been rarely accepted in the social sciences.

A source of uncontrolled variance that is intrinsic in this design is any unanticipated historical event which brings about a discontinuity in performance that is unrelated to one intervention. One approach to controlling this effect is to select and stratify teachers and students on the basis of the amount of contact with the consultee. As with most designs for interventions, concurrent field assessments of the local setting are also required in order to provide contextual evidence for changes in the performance of students and teachers that are inferred to be a consequence of the intervention. This type of research design reduces so-called progression effects and selection biases that often plague studies of behavior in natural settings.

With such designs, we then can test directly the effectiveness of consultation as a preventive intervention since we are no longer restricted solely to the behavior of the consultee as a criterion for outcome and can assess "fallout" effects of the consultative relationship via the performance of others in the consultee's immediate environment. This design can also include provisions for the assessment of intermediate effects, such as comparisons of consultant–consultee interactions and changes in the attitudes of a consultee regarding performance of work roles. Such observations help to establish an empirical basis for defining the process of carrying out interventions, and link outcome criteria to intermediate effects. This phase of the evaluation of intervention effects requires the identification of precise points in time where the intervention is affecting change. Suchman (1967) has an additional review of this topic in discussing outcome and process research designs.

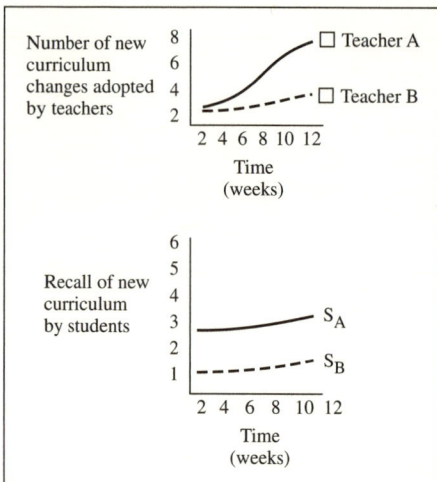

Figure 4.3   Consultation as a radiating process

Intervention II: Organizational Change as Environmental Restructuring

Recent work by Katz and Kahn (1966) and by Bennis (1966) presents a view of organizations, such as neighborhoods or communities, as open systems. These conceptions are based upon a premise that an organization is a series of interdependent units. Analogies have been drawn from cybernetics and general systems theory. The view of the organization is as a biological process, a view conspicuously missing in psychological treatises on organizational development. Most approaches have concentrated upon analyses in which individuals and the total organization are seen as aggregates of disconnected parts bearing little relationship to one another. The axiom of interdependent units provides a basis for a view of an organization that comes closer to the ways in which people and roles and organizational tasks are tied together under natural conditions. The behavior of people *in* organizations then is the focus of analysis in contrast to more abstract formulations of a model social structure. This point of view comes closest to an organic formulation of an organization which allows for simultaneous assessment of both organizational and personal behavior as they are portrayed through the performance of organizational roles *and* the performance of roles by individuals.

Interventions designed to affect the life of the organization can be validated via changes in the adaptive behavior of interdependent units, usually through a redefinition or realignment of various parts of the organization. If the creation of new organizational groupings, or the revision of existing social groupings, brings about overt changes in an organization's performance in coping with crises, then the intervention can be assessed by observing how the organization responds to crises. This thinking assumes that the restructuring of an organization is reflected in the total organization's ability to deal with emergencies without a significant loss of personal or operational effectiveness, and without a reduction in communication with other allied organizations.

In the same way that consultation can be used as a treatment rather than a preventive intervention, organizational change programs often deal with momentary personnel conflicts, such as, for example, issues of productivity and a variety of management–labor issues that do not involve plans for assisting the organization with long-term development. Kahn, in discussing the implications of organizational research for community mental health, commented that there have been a variety of methods to initiate change in organizations through

> various mixtures of cognitive input and peer group interaction. . . . These include T-group or sensitivity training (Bradford, Bibb, & Benne, 1964; Schein & Bennis, 1965); the managerial grid (Blake & Mouton, 1964); the earlier work as the Tavistock group (Jacques, 1951); and the feedback discussions in overlapping groups as developed by Mann (1957, 1964). [Kahn, 1968]

In commenting on these change programs, Kahn noted at least two generalizations that apply to all of these approaches; they all have been shown "to produce changes in interpersonal behavior in perceptions of self, and in attitudes toward others. Secondly, these changes are harder to produce, but more likely to endure, when they are generated in live, organizationally-embedded, ongoing groups."

It is one thing to observe that an organizational change program affects the behavior of individuals in organizations, but quite a different problem to determine whether current change approaches influence the performance of individuals and organizations under conditions of stress. Still another new question is how to relate change programs to role relationships in an organization which bear directly upon the performance of the total organization in dealing with planned and unplanned change. The present writer believes that change programs which help the organization deal effectively with its future must include criteria for judging effectiveness, and must focus on additional elements of the change process. More attention must be given to changes in social influence for the help-giving behavior of persons, independent of their roles, as well as help-giving behavior that can be added to the performance of key roles within the organization. Following Katz and Kahn's formulations, such changes should substantiate precisely how the organization is interdependent. If a change effort can increase the expression of spontaneous help-giving behavior in members of the organization and create social norms so that the performance of executive functions can include help-giving behaviors, there is a possibility that there will be increased interaction and support for a wide variety of help-giving acts. The assumption is that an appropriate "organizational climate" will provide a social structure which can generate adaptive solutions for dealing with internal and external events.

The creation of an experimental design to evaluate such change programs is complex and difficult to formulate. The use of pre- and posttest designs and controlled measures in the study of organizations is not generally feasible since the natural life of an organization does not coincide with the aperiodic and unanticipated social events indigenous to organizations. There is one type of design, however, that may be relevant for identifying changes in the adaptive behavior of an organization. This design involves the use of similar, yet nonmatched organizations, and is called, in the terminology of Campbell and Stanley [1966], "the Nonequivalent Control Group Design." For this design to be optimally effective the two organizations should be selected with attention to equivalence of their general function. This is desirable in order to provide measures to control for possible sources of "error," such as historical events affecting the organization and maturation of the organization, as well as the effects of the process evaluation. Such controls may be obtained by systematic or naturalistic observations prior to the onset of the intervention and further enhanced by continuous documentation of critical events in *both* organizations during the intervention. This operating procedure makes it possible to infer that any detected differences between the pre-and the post-tests in the adaptive behavior of the organization receiving the change program are not readily explained by the effects of extraneous variables. The possibility that differences in postintervention scores may vary directly with differences between the populations from which the selection was made can be managed by covariance analyses and other statistical techniques (Campbell & Stanley, 1963, p. 49).

The design for this type of intervention is illustrated in Figures 4.4, 4.5, and 4.6.

Figure 4.4 presents an illustration of a prototypic statement of directional influence in two organizations. At T_1, while the form of the influence varies for the two organizations, these influences are assumed to be equivalent in direction and magnitude. Following the preventive interventions, which has as its purpose the linking of directional influence, such as help-giving behavior and coping skills, organization A is expected to develop not only a quantum increase in levels of influence but also to increase the level of reciprocal influences in the organization. In sum, the aim of the intervention as a change program is to increase the interdependence of the members with each other. Figures 4.4 and 4.5 illustrate the structure of the design and the types of predictions that can be made in differentiating responses of the members of the two organizations before and after the intervention.

As an example of dependent variables that reflect an influence of the intervention, the members of organization A are expected to voluntarily devote more effort, that is man hours of work, to solve problems than the members of organization B who have not experienced such a change program. If such predic-

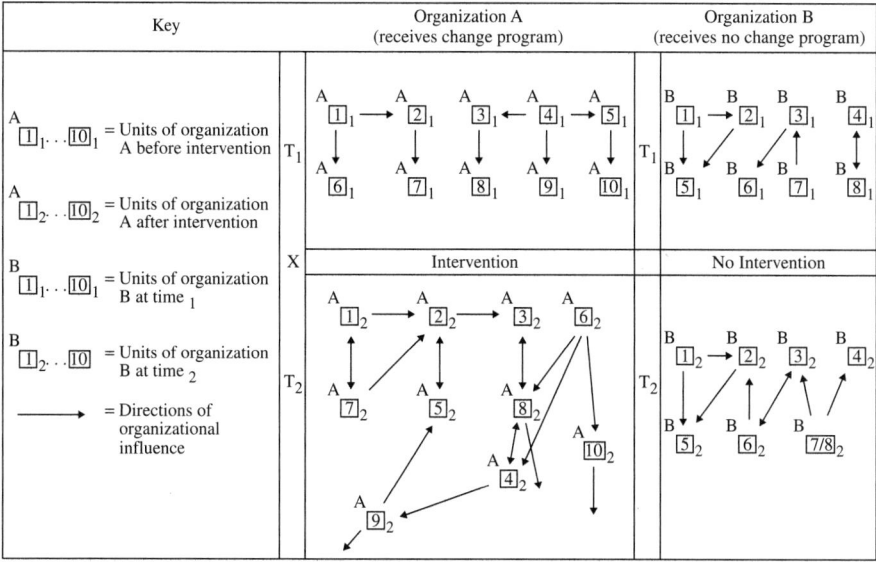

Figure 4.4 Organizational change as a process of restructuring the environment

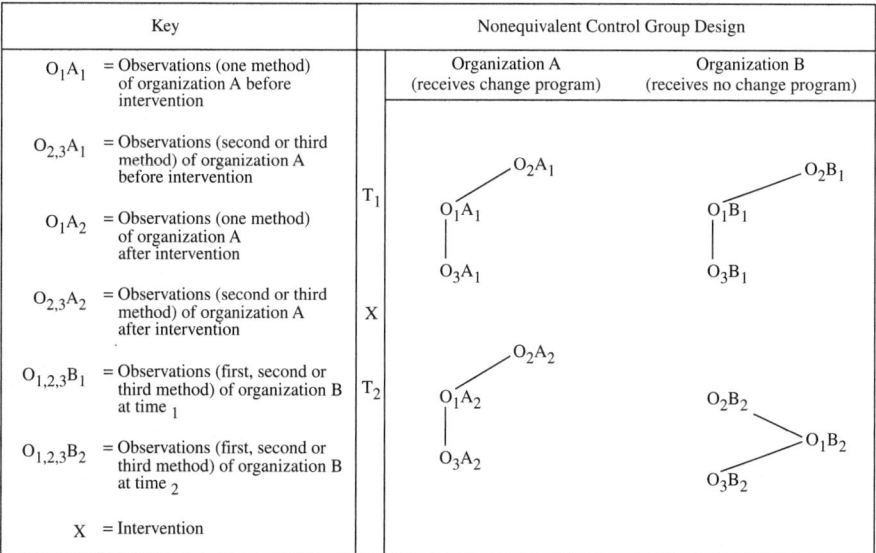

Figure 4.5 Organizational change as a process of restructuring the environment

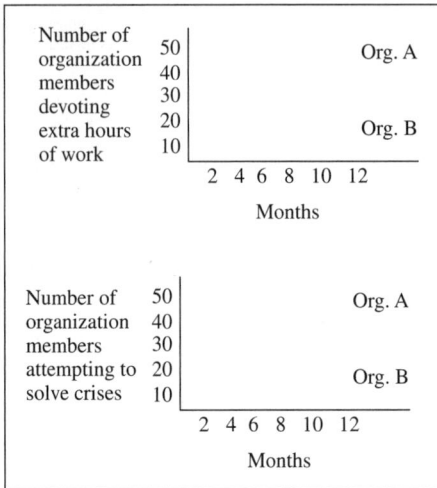

Figure 4.6 Organizational change as a process of restructuring the environment

tions can be made and verified, then the specific program has met the criteria of producing long-term effects for the organization as well as changes in perception, attitudes and role behaviors. The primary criterion for evaluating the change program is dependent upon identifying how *both* organizations deal with future crises. It is assumed that the organization hosting the change program will expend fewer resources, suffer fewer casualties, and revise more functions after coping with crises such as budgetary cuts, shifts in public support, or loss of decision makers, than will the "control" organization.

This type of design is relevant for the evaluation of community mental health programs. Many community mental health services have increased their liaison and visibility in their local communities, with the result that the public has increased demands for accountability for services, and this often poses a genuine threat to the mental health program. As a result of attempts to develop preventive programs, increasing efforts have been expended by the mental health program and citizens to create additional community resources. If organizational change programs are viewed as a lever for initiating change rearranging or redefining community services, with a decrease in specific *direct* mental health services, then an organizational change program for the community marital health center staff can be classified as preventive. Efforts at program evaluation will require coordinated and integrated studies which simultaneously assess intraorganizational activities along with morbidity rates for relevant population groupings outside the immediate organization which are directly influenced by the organization. For such community studies, the Non-Equivalent Control Group Design provides an important approach for specifying the fallout effects of interventions.

Organizational change programs with staffs of mental health programs have characteristically employed laboratory training methods (T-groups). Such programs designed as in-service training for the staff of community mental health programs often serve to realign staff resources and redistribute decision-making functions regarding patient care. One potential effect of such a change program is to make it possible for the professional staff of community mental health centers working inside the center to accommodate to criteria for relevant community services developed by citizens. As roles for community mental health practice respond to change methods such as the ones described above, criteria for community mental health programs will be expected to shift and new types of data will be required for verification.

A synthesis of intervention methods can eventually bring about a greater affiliation between the clinician and the action researcher in the development of methods for assessing personal effectiveness and organizational effectiveness as reciprocal processes (Kelly, 1968). Through a combined program of interventions, such as consultation and organizational change methods, interventions in a variety of settings can be more closely assessed as having positive and negative functions for the organization and for the broader community. Such interventions can describe these processes and how they mediate change, one of the most important substantive tasks for building a science of community psychology.

Intervention III: The Development of a Community as an Evolutionary Process

The previous interventions described in this chapter have been derived from contrasting premises about the change process. Consultation as a preventive intervention was viewed as a process of "radiating" change from the consultant to the consultee and to the consultee's clients. Organizational change programs were presented as examples of preventive interventions for restructuring the environment, with the goal of facilitating the organization to be more effective in dealing with crises. The third example of an intervention strategy which will now be presented is community development. This approach rests on the premise that social change is *not* a consequence of discrete man-made interventions, but rather that change occurs as a result of the evolution of the functions in a society (Biddle & Biddle, 1968). The goal for community development is to create opportunities for a community to plan for its own change. In this class of interventions, the change agent is neither a passive observer nor the final architect for plans, but a creative participant working with communities in the design and reorganization of their activities.

The term *community development*, like consultation and organizational change, can refer to a euphemism for Utopia or Pollyana, or it can be used to denote an ethnocentric enterprise. There are few examples to cite in which a professional change agent has been a "participant conceptualizer" in the collaborative work of a community.[1] More often we have been protagonists for change and have been invested in interventions without regard for the goals of the community. Our statements regarding community goals have been limited to our own entrepreneurial interests. In the present writer's opinion, until community psychology can formulate new definitions of professional practice for community development, we will not achieve the unfinished business which was so eloquently prescribed by William James.

Community development is a radical departure from most professional practice in community mental health. Community development commits the designer of an intervention to be quite clear about goals and values he elects himself and espouses for "his" community. It is one thing to mobilize citizens to fight for a cause; it is another to mobilize citizens to develop plans and actions to guide their own future. This distinction is very easy to articulate but very difficult to translate into reality, which is the heart of the matter. Biddle and Biddle [1964] have written at length on this theme and make the following observation:

> Most believers in democracy have advanced to the point of admiring controversy and stopped there. They are fighters for what they deem to be righteous. Some have advanced further to an admiration of compromise but the compromise they have in mind usually means a yielding of some demands when opponents will also yield a few—a type of horse-trading. Only a few have advanced to an appreciation of creative reconciliation, in which new and undreamed of solutions to problems arise out of cooperative thinking and working together. Here is the great need and opportunity in an age of increasingly complex problems and interdependent solutions. An encourager belongs in the company of the creative reconcilers.
>
> By accepting developmental goals, he does not reject political controversy. He merely leaves this necessary activity to someone else. His job is not to encourage attack upon rivals but to strengthen people's abilities to find creative solutions to conflict. He is not a political controversialist. He is a reconciler of conflict, to the end that people may become more competent to create their own solutions to problems.

This quotation could be interpreted as espousing special kinds of persons who can encourage community development. The intent of the statement can also mean, however, a value to expand and diversify resources from all segments of the population. As the above comments indicate, designs for documenting this type of change program are nonexistent. What little evaluation that has been accomplished is preserved in the accumulated wisdom of the change agent or in the archives of anthropological field notes.

The community psychologist has an obligation and a rare opportunity to contribute to the definition of criteria for community development. Designs for community change require momentum and the resources to sustain evaluations of the process over a long period of time. Asking any professional to think in terms of decades is unique and presents a series of taxing requirements for the research process. The dependent variables considered useful in the evaluation of consultation as a preventive intervention were the performance level of students and teachers in the classroom setting. The criteria suggested to assess organizational change were measures of coping with crises. In contrast to coping with change events, the type of dependent variables that will be required to evaluate community development are measures of *planning* for change. It is assumed that planning for change represents a higher level of organizational adaptation than either coping with crises or radiating change.

Campbell and Stanley (1963) provide a provocative initial suggestion for a design for community development known by the folksy title, "the patched-up design," or, if you prefer a more technical term, "the recurrent institutional cycle design." They describe this design as

> a strategy for field research in which one starts with an inadquate design and then adds specific features to control one or another of the recurrent sources of invalidity. The result is often an inelegant accumulation of precautionary checks which lacks the intrinsic symmetry of the "true" experimental designs but nonetheless approaches experimentation.

In this case the research design is selected to accomodate to the unpredictable and tentative events that are generic in mobilizing citizen groups to work toward goals for achieving change at the community level. Rather than an integrated attempt to reduce sources of error, this design defines a variety of procedures to maximize opportunities for specifying the conditions under which change takes place. In this sense it is an approximation to laboratory conditions, but only an approximation. The design requires that both longitudinal and cross-section studies be continuous. It also assumes that: (1) a variety of methods will be employed; (2) the research process will be flexible in spirit; and (3) the project will be bountiful in resources so that unanticipated, spontaneous community events can be assessed.

In the same sense that consultation and organizational change programs have intrinsic validity in their own right, community development, in its aims to mobilize citizens for change, also has intrinsic merit. The thesis here is that community development becomes a preventive intervention when aroused and motivated community groups work together to effectively plan for future unknown events. This assumes that the aroused citizenry is able to utilize current resources, create new resources, and link to a maximum number of constituencies. The elements of the design are presented in Figures 4.7, 4.8, and 4.9.

The design combines the longitudinal and cross-sectional approaches commonly employed in developmental research. It assumes that scheduling is such that, at one and the same time, a community *in* development and a community *prior* to development can be assessed, e.g., comparisons of observations can be

Key

$CAP_{1\cdots4_1}$ = Planning units (1–4) in community A before intervention

$CBP_{1\cdots4_2}$ = Planning units (1–4) in community B at time $_2$

$CAP_{1\cdots4_{2-4}}$ = Planning units (1–4) in community A after intervention

$CBP_{1\cdots4_{2-5}}$ = Planning units (1–4) in community B at time $_2$

——— = Univariate planning functions
═══ = Reciprocal planning functions
X = Intervention

Community A (intervention of community devel.)

Community B (natural conditions)

O_1 CAP_{2_1} CAP_{1_1} CAP_{3_1} CAP_{4_1} O_2

CBP_{4_2} CBP_{1_2} CBP_{3_2} CBP_{2_2}

X

O_3 CAP_{1_4} CAP_{2_4} CAP_{3_4} CAP_{4_4} O_4

CBP_{3_5} CBP_{4_5} CBP_{2_5} CBP_{1_5}

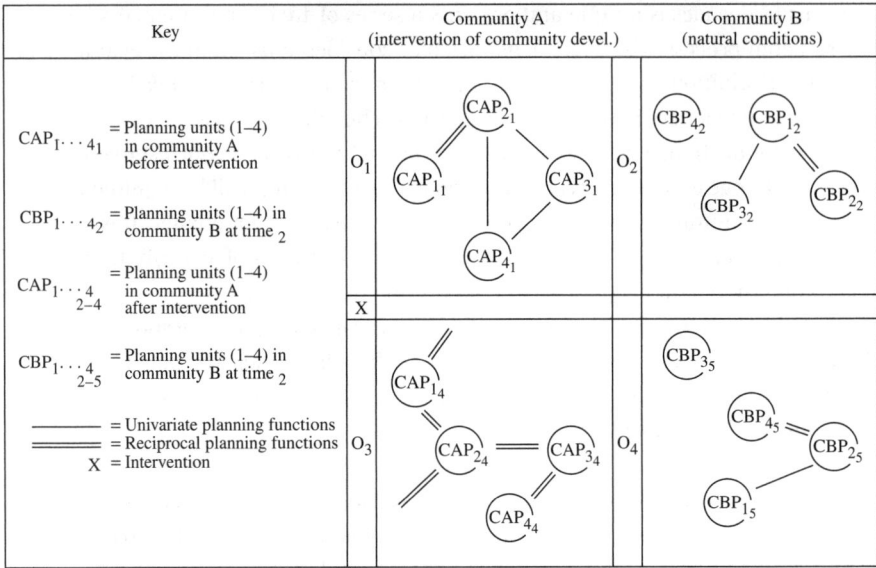

Figure 4.7   Community development as an evolutionary process

made at O_1 and O_2. As Figure 4.7 indicates, Community A, which is in the process of development, has similar planning functions to Community B early in the development cycle. The planning that is ongoing in each community is relatively autonomous, largely ad hoc, and likely to be tied to a few individuals in formal governmental positions. Measurements in this case might be surveys, naturalistic observations, in-depth interviews, participant observations, and other types of field work including attendance at formal and informal community functions. The measurements should include all that is possible and feasible in conducting a community study.

Following the community development program, observations are repeated so that a detailed evaluation of the planning process can be charted. If the program has succeeded, it would be expected that Community. A will have developed more viable reciprocal planning functions, created new resources, and included more new citizens in its planning. As Figure 4.8 indicates, this type of design allows for taking advantage of unexpected events to document critical unplanned occurrences in the life cycle of the program, such as at time O_3, as well as comparative data collection in both communities at other times such as O_4 and O_5. Observation points can be as close as several weeks, or only six months, depending upon when the real-life events take place. The total time period needed to evaluate and document the planning process per se may take several years.

Reassessing the functions of the two communities in their ability to plan for change provides a basis for many comparisons in the life of the change pro-

Key	Patched-Up Design

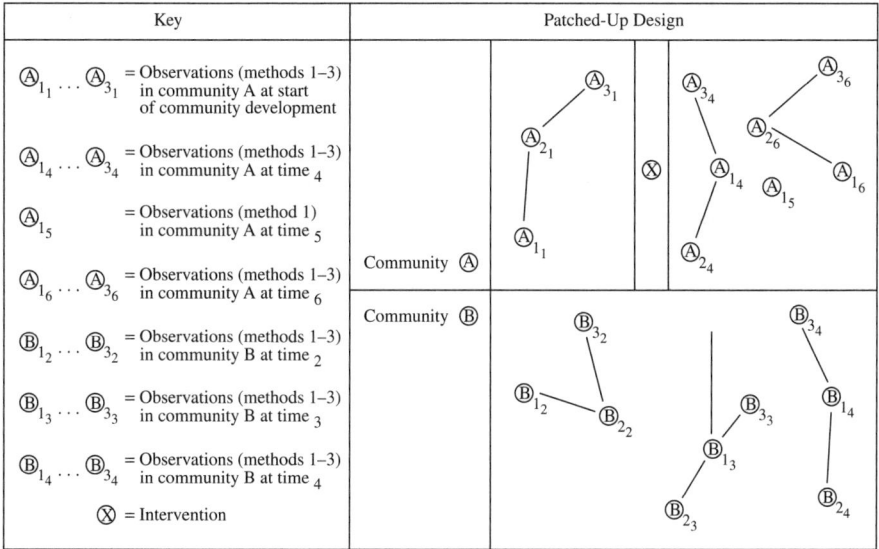

Figure 4.8   Community development as an evolutionary process

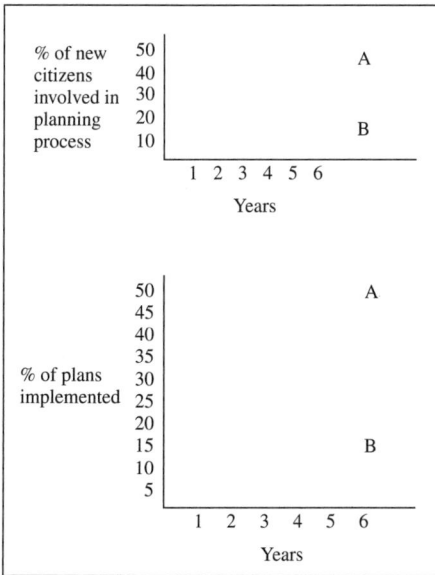

Figure 4.9   Community development as an evolutionary process

gram. While the design does not directly control for maturation effects over time, it can be extended to assess effects over time since maturation effects can be a basic part of the study. Figure 4.9 presents an example of two types of predictions that can be made in assessing community development. One example is a prediction of the different number of citizens involved in working directly on the formulation and implementation of community change. Of specific interest is the proportion of new citizens who were not previously a part of the community planning effort.

The basis for this prediction is that the community development process is effective when it can continously involve, over a period of time, different citizens. The criteria refers to the number of new citizens involved who have not been involved previously in such work. The criteria also refers to increasing the proportion of persons from minority groups who are otherwise not active in the development of their local community. The effort of the community development process as a preventive intervention is to increase the diversity of citizens who are influencing change in their community.

It is expected, for example, that such an effective intervention, with its accompanying social processes, would produce a community participation curve which is S-shaped. In contrast, the predicted curve for the number of persons involved and number of actions and plans implemented in control communities would not vary over time and would be only slightly positively accelerating. Such a positive acceleration is expected to reflect the effects of changes outside the community upon the local population.

Much of the emphasis in community work has been placed on the prevention of pathological conditions in individual and social settings. The prospect of obtaining knowledge about the positive development of persons in natural settings could be increased if psychologists worked to create empirical data about the ways in which communities evolve and how they establish criteria and norms. One of the important by-products of the evaluation of community development programs is the creation of a psychology of social change. How groups of persons are mobilized, how impediments to action are reduced, and how old investments of citizens are redefined and replaced by indigenous efforts are examples of discrete activities which combine to affect community goals. The evaluation of community development can also provide hypotheses about the success and failure of broader societal changes in that they provide a more restricted setting to observe the diffusion of change processes into local communities.

There is a critical need for research centers and universities to focus on the aspirations and interests of their local host communities. The contributions of the social sciences have limited relevance to understanding contemporary social problems in communities, and most public issues raise questions which go beyond the social scientists' traditional data source. We cannot expect to understand the problems of community conflict without attempting to understand the delights and the hazards of positive community change. Our present knowledge of community development comes largely from cultures beyond our own which illustrate our ideological and motivational constraints. It should be less difficult to work toward community change in the United States than in a Peruvian village, and thereby help our citizens to affect their own destiny. Community development work is thus offered as a critical area for psychologists to offer new commitments that are expressed daily and that are lasting.

Conclusion

The three contrasting approaches for preventive interventions that have been described suggest new criteria for change programs. Consultation methods as a preventive intervention as presented do not focus on the symptomatic or expressive behavior of the consultee, but rather upon the radiating effects of the consultee's clients. Organizational change methods are not concerned with the productive behavior of the members of an organization, but with the members' ability to handle crises. The verification of community development does not depend solely upon economic development, but also considers the communities' competence to plan for its future (Meier, 1965, 1966). These new criteria are required if community psychology is to contribute verifiable knowledge about the effectiveness of individuals in organizations and communities. The main thesis in these comments has been that the community psychologist views the development of knowledge as an ecological enterprise, an enterprise in which the conditions for verification are defined in terms of the specific host environment and its requirements for intervention (Barker, 1965; Kelly, 1966). A science of intervention encompasses a series of diverse and interdependent sciences, each with its unique requirements and principles for verification, and its own methods for the control of error. Psychologists can participate in this redefinition of the scientific process if we obtain for ourselves a liberal education. We can then contribute to social betterment without the hidden costs of social engineering!

Each of the three types of interventions which have been described involve unique experimental designs and methods of quality control that generate their own built-in ethics. These designs provide for the observation of naturally occurring events to help confirm or disconfirm the effects of interventions. This kind of research obviously requires a strong commitment to longitudinal studies as well as the development of research facilities that are organized to take account of unanticipated and spontaneous community events. The goals of the scientific enterprise presented have been simply stated by philospher of science Herbert Feigl, [1951]: "Scientific explanation is where more specific or more descriptive statements are derived from general or more hypothetical assumptions." The linkage between our general statements and our assumptions of the rate and direction of social change can permit the design of interventions in social settings to create a science of community psychology. For this adventure man is viewed in his natural setting, not as an atom in a smasher.

Notes

This chapter has benefited from the critical appraisal of Lenin A. Baler, Keith Smith, and Randolph Harper whose help is gratefully acknowledged.

1. The phrase "participant conceptualizer" has become an apt identification for the unique role of the community psychologist. For future archival value, this phrase was first coined by Forrest Tyler, then of the National Institute of Mental Health, now at the University of Maryland, in group discussions at the Boston University Conference on Community Psychology, Swampscott, Mass., May 5, 1965. One exception where there has been a report of a long-term collaborative work with a community is the Cornell-Peru Project (Holmberg & Dobyns, 1962; Dobyns, Carlow, & Vazquez, 1962; Lasswell, 1962).

References

Barker, R. G. (1965). Explorations in ecological psychology. *American Psychologist, 20*, 1–14.

Bennis, W. G. (1966). *Changing organizations*. New York: McGraw-Hill.

Berlin, I. N. (1962). Mental health consultation in schools as a means of communicating health principles. *Journal of the American Academy of Child Pyschiatry, 1*, 671–679.

Biddle, W. W., & Biddle, L. J. (1968). *Encouraging community development*. New York: Holt, Rinehart, & Winston.

Blake, R. R., & Mouton, J. W. (1964). *The managerial grid*. Houston, TX: Gulf.

Campbell, D. T., & Stanley, J. C. (1966). *Experimental and quasi-experimental designs for research*. Chicago: Rand McNally.

Caplan, G. (1964). *Principles of preventive psychiatry*. New York: Basic Books.

Cowen, E. L., Gardner, E. A., & Zax, M. (Eds.). (1967). *Emergent approaches to mental health problems*. New York: Appleton-Century-Crofts.

Dobyns, H. F., Carlos, M. M., & Vazquez, M. C. (1962). Summary of technical-organizational progress and reactions to it. *Human Organizations, 21*, 109–115.

Feigh, H. (1951). Principles and problems of theory construction in psychology. In *Current trends in psychological theory* (pp. 179–209). Pittsburgh, PA: Pittsburgh Press.

Holmberg, A. R., & Dobyns, H. F. (1962). The process of accelerating community change. *Human Organizations, 21*, 107–109.

Iscoe, I., Pierce-Jones, J., Friedman, S. T., & McHehearty, L. (1967). Some strategies in mental health consultation: A brief description of a project and some preliminary results. In E. L. Cohen, E. A. Gardner, & M. Zax (Eds.), *Emergent approaches to mental health problems* (pp. 307–330). New York: Appelton-Century-Croft.

James, W. (1911). The moral equivalent for war. In *Memories and studies*. London: Longmans, Green.

Jacques, E. (1951). *The changing culture of a factory*. London: Tavistock.

Kahn, R. L. (1968). Implications of organizational research for community mental health. In J. W. Carter Jr. (Ed.), *Research contributions from psychology to community mental health*. New York: Behavioral Publications.

Katz, D., & Kahn, R. L. (1966). *The social psychology of organizations*. New York: John Wiley & Sons.

Kelly, J. G. (1966). Ecological constraints on mental health services. *American Psychologist, 21*, 535–539.

Kelly, J. G. (1968). Toward an ecological conception of preventive interventions. In J. W. Carter Jr. (Ed.), *Research contributions from psychology to community mental health*. New York: Behavioral Publications.

Klein, D. C., & Lindeman, E. (1961). Preventive intervention in family crisis situations. In G. Caplan (Ed.), *Prevention of mental disorders in children* (pp. 283–306). New York: Basic Books.

Lasswell, H. D. (1962). Integrating communities into more inclusive systems. *Human Organizations, 21*, 116–124.

Mann, F. C. (1957). Studying and creating change: A means to understanding organization. *Research in Industrial Human Relations*, Industrial Relations Research Association (No. 17), 146–167.

Mann, F. C. (1964). Toward an understanding of the leadership role in forma organizations. In R. Dubin, G. Homans, & D. Miller (Eds.), *Leadership and productivity*. San Francisco: Chandler.

Meier, R. L. (1956). *Science and economic development*. Cambridge, MA: MIT Press.

Meier, R. L. (1965). *Developmental planning*. New York: McGraw Hill.

Morse, W. C. (1967). Enhancing the classroom teacher's mental health function. In E. L. Cowen, E. A. Gardner, & M. Zax (Eds.), *Emergent approaches to mental health problems* (pp. 271–289). New York: Appelton-Century-Crofts.

Schein, E. H., & Bennis, W. G. (1965). *Personal organizational change through group methods*. New York: John Wiley.

Spielberger, C. D. (1967). A mental health consultation program in a small community with limited professional mental health resources. In E. L. Cowen, E. A. Gardner, & M. Zax (Eds.), *Emergent approaches to mental health problems* (pp. 214–238). New York: Appelton-Century-Crofts.

Suchman, E. A. (1967). *Evaluative research*. New York: Russel Sage Foundation.

White, M. A. (1966). The mental health movement and the schools: Theory, evidence, and dilemma. In R. H. Ojemann (Ed.), *The school and the community treatment facility in preventive psychiatry* (49–68). Iowa City: University of Iowa Department of Publications.

5

Community as Teacher

Reflections

Teaching practical ways of designing preventive interventions was one of the ways I tried to give meaning to the ecological perspective. I experimented with the concept at Ohio State University and then expanded the point of view at the University of Michigan. At that time, the University of Michigan was an excellent host for interdisciplinary teaching. A social norm for communication and sharing perspectives flourished across the social sciences. Doctoral students were able to pursue opportunities to work with faculty and students in other departments. By and large, faculty from different departments welcomed students.

The Social Adaptation class provided an opportunity for doctoral students to participate in a team with students from other disciplines. Teams selected a topic and community that was considered important. Their shared and collective interests were also tapped. At the time, students were often catalysts or activists, so community work was not strange to them. The class was held in the Rackham Graduate Center in a large room where there was ample opportunity to have small groups working at the same time. One significant course requirement was to participate in a critique of the final product with community residents at the end of the year. This was one of the most instructive parts of the experience. The community participants reduced any unwitting arrogance and usually inspired all of us.

During one version of the class, I was very fortunate to work with two doctoral students who served as teaching assistants. The three of us met before and after each class at a local restaurant. One assistant was Ben Gottlieb, who later received his degree in social work and psychology. The other was Joe Dimento from Urban and Regional Planning. Ben is now a professor at the University of Guelph. Joe is a professor in the School of Social Ecology at the University of

California, Irvine. As I recall, we were a cordial and productive trio. It was great fun and a heady time.

Somehow Don Flournoy from University College at Athens, Ohio, heard about the course and invited the three of us to contribute a chapter, "Community as Teacher," to his book project. Our collaborative writing reaffirmed to me that it was possible to teach in a way that included opportunities for multidisciplinary teams of doctoral students to engage a community and make a useful contribution. The chapter also convinced me that thinking ecologically was valuable. The ideas were useful and overarching.

The ecological perspective had the added bonus of offering its own ethical principles that could express and anchor the work. The "Community as Teacher" chapter provided an important public statement about an approach to teaching community psychology as an interdisciplinary team enterprise. I discussed the teaching experience again at the Vermont Conference on Primary Prevention in 1987; the paper was published in 1992 as "On Teaching the Practice of Prevention." Frankly, the course was never as satisfying and unique as when I taught with Joe and Ben back in the late 1960s and early 1970s. I taught the course at the University of Oregon with some success and again at the University of Illinois at Chicago in the early 1980s. At that time, the Department of Psychology was not establishing social norms for doctoral students to go outside the department for their intellectual development. Some students were adventurous and went against the norms despite the active discouragement for students to have classes or seek out research experiences beyond psychology. The basic knowledge and skill in working collaboratively was lacking. I did not wish to teach the necessary basic skills because it meant counteracting the competitive culture between university departments. I am confident that with a supportive cross-disciplinary culture, the course could be salient once again. The contexts in the 1980s, however, were not right for such an ecological teaching expedition.

College teaching is less than it could be. Our teachers often work alone, textbooks are used as the primary resource for knowledge, and our teaching has been confined largely to classrooms. The three of us, a professor of psychology and two graduate students (one in urban and regional planning and the other in social work and community psychology), have been working as a team to go beyond textbooks so that the classroom reaches some pressing social problems. The course we describe, called Social Adaptation, is designed to help graduate students become acquainted with the needs and resources of communities and to give communities some help in solving a problem.

Several premises have emerged as we worked with communities and served as resources for graduate students. These premises represent working guidelines for the development of this course. First, we find that training in a single discipline does not help solve problems in a community. Most graduate training programs in the behavioral sciences reflect a single-discipline approach to problems. Neither the curriculum nor the field training of such programs will help the student understand and solve a problem as defined by the citizen. We advocate multidisciplinary training designed to help citizens solve a problem.

Second, the work group is a critical social setting for problem solving. In our experience, the momentum for change at the community level often results from a small group of people working hard to figure out how to solve a contemporary issue. In contrast, few students learn in classrooms to use a small group for problem solving or to experience the group as a supportive setting for doing community work. It is somewhat ironic that as participation in groups becomes a visible activity for many parts of society, the group as a medium for solving community problems is sparsely developed or nonexistent in professional training programs.

Our third premise is that the citizen is as learned as the professor. We have noted that credentials are not prerequisite for identifying or understanding social problems. There are, however, few opportunities for citizens to be welcomed as equals into the university, and no obvious mechanism exists for redefining the links between community and university. We feel strongly that mutual stereotyping of the university and citizenry will be overcome only if community workers trained in the university also learn from citizens. The university likewise must create ways for citizens to enter and contribute to the process of student training. Students need to learn how to enter a community and to become a resource for that community.

Finally, the ecological analogy is useful for assessing and working on community problems. As we tried to understand how persons adapt and cope within social systems, and wondered about the kind of data needed to see why persons make it or don't in different communities, we have been unimpressed with many theoretical ideas in the behavioral sciences that focus upon community process. In contrast, analogies from biological ecology are particularly apt for this task, for they derive from premises about person–environment interactions in natural conditions and seem useful for both assessing and changing social systems. Designing social interventions requires a dynamic view of the way people and settings are coupled.

These four premises have evolved from our field work, our research, and our efforts to offer students a classroom activity that is real and constructive. This mix of community work and theorizing is characteristic of the emerging field of community psychology, which requires a continuous interaction between the professional and the citizen. We hope Social Adaptation develops a closer understanding of the natural workings of communities.

The history of this course has been evolutionary: it was given twice at the Ohio State University and offered on four occasions at the University of Michigan. It is only now beginning to serve as a setting for multidisciplinary groups to design change interventions for a community problem. Not only does the growth of a teacher take time, but we need time to gauge student needs and to arrange supportive conditions for learning. Training students to work at the community level makes new and different demands on the professional. Though more detailed elaborations of this thesis are available elsewhere, the following comments sketch some attributes of the community psychologist which have contributed to the creation of social norms for our course.

The community asks the worker to have a defined and visible skill. The professional often substitutes jargon for performance, mistakes his social position for meaningful involvement, and fantasies his theoretical constructs as wisdom. The community can teach us precisely what competences we require to solve a problem and how to gain from the inductive process. The Social Adaptation course encourages the student to become sufficiently involved in a community to find out firsthand the skills required to manage a particular problem. The student discovers directly from his experiences what gaps exist in his training, rather than indirectly through a professor's evaluation.

The community worker must be able to identify with the total community. The total community can teach us how it is organized and how it works, who the real constituencies are, and where it is going. Many university courses restrict interaction with communities. The intellectual basis for university work has derived from values which are often disjunctive with nonuniversity resources. Students in our course receive wide exposure to a particular community; they not only view that segment which is most congruent with their own values but also appreciate those parts they never knew.

The complexities of community subsystems cannot be understood via a lecture in a classroom. To develop a working definition of the total community the student must sample multiple social settings and events and attempt to define how they all relate to each other. We expect the student to test his ability to understand divergent viewpoints and contrasting belief systems within multidisciplinary class teams and within the community at large. Appreciating these contrasts within a locale is a first step in learning to cope with cultural and ideological differences. As teams of students begin work on a problem, they spend much time reflecting, arguing, and weighing the pros and cons of going one way or another in their plan of attack. Having a social setting, such as the Social Adaptation course, forces students to explicitly express premises about what to do with a real problem. This process is often exciting, as students test their ideas with one another and with an actual community.

As the teams obtain substantial evidence for their particular solution, they begin to learn when to be energetic and when to be cool, when to move faster toward a goal and when they need to create new opportunities and new events to facilitate goal attainment. Community workers do not learn enough about the phasing of their work. While a semester is not long enough to provide a total view of this pacing and rate of change process, the students do have some experience in seeing how ecological principles and their own interactions with citizens teach them the importance of the metabolism of change.

A community worker must be able to make decisions and take positions under circumstances which have uncertain outcomes. We encourage students to struggle with the ambiguities and uncertainties in a local community and formulate plans which take into account the limitations of a specific situation, yet still help a community move beyond current constraints. We feel reassured to see that students with varied disciplinary backgrounds can learn to help each other and can cope with the uncertainties of a risky decision.

Much of what is done in community psychology is anonymous. Even when success has been achieved, the role of the professional worker may not be recognized, at least not in proportion to the effort expended. He is rewarded by seeing others emerge as leaders, witnessing at a distance deeds performed. Satisfaction is a reflected glow rather than the beam of a spotlight. As new professionals start their careers, they may have egocentric views of their accomplishments and wish for tangible signs of respect and acknowledgment. The Social Adaptation course tries to communicate how students can do something workable for a community yet not expect a community to give explicit recognition; when students do produce results, they may receive an extra bonus. The five work teams in the course have been very fortunate in receiving public recognition for their work. But we want students to understand that such a reward is not guaranteed or a right.

The development of these work teams is the heart of Social Adaptation. Several growth stages are recognizable, not only in the content of their work but also in the emotional atmosphere which prevails. Passivity is the first norm shattered. In the first class session, instead of reciting course requirements, the instructors engage the students in a brainstorm session to generate topics related to community problems which interest them. Small groups form, then, on the basis of interrelated subjects. While some students articulate only general interests, such as drug problems or unrest within the schools, others are concerned with such movements as Zero Population Growth or Women's Liberation. Still others discuss established programs and agencies such as Model Cities or community mental health. A few students know precisely what and where community problems exist and can state their interests operationally. From the very beginning, interest and a certain amount of anxiety are generated— especially when contrasted with expectations of "initial lecture passivity."

We require only that each group be composed of a wide range of disciplines. When the groups begin to congeal, this one guideline, this single vestige of structure imposed from above, becomes the focus of attention. As students struggle with the question, "Who are we?" they are often surprised to discover disciplines which, for them, never existed. Also their stereotypes are of little predictive value: Not all urban planners dream of sewers and gutters; not all social workers are women wearing fruit-bedecked hats; forest rangers are not the only professional products of natural resource departments; nor are all clinical psychologists "anal retentive." During this process of discovery all deny any disciplinary biases and present their personal selves. Exchange of background information serves to minimize the anxiety engendered earlier, leaving the security of shared insecurity.

Time constraints and the emergence of a task leader are forces which move the groups from their cocktail conversation to the search for a community. At this point the groups typically experience a phase of stage fright in which there is an unverbalized discomfort about leaving campus and contacting citizens out there. Heavy intellectual discussions ensue; complex hypotheses are developed; expansive theories are woven, but at last consensus is reached that empirical verification is essential. The group member who, all agree, in his appearance and behavior most closely approximates a citizen in the community is volunteered. His assignment: to make contact and facilitate entry. Following this, a scouting party ventures forth, having settled such grave issues as clothes, hair styles, and the appropriate balance of aggressive and inquisitive behavior. The myth of the entry trauma is quickly exploded, and most group members return to campus feeling comfortable about the community, if not totally infatuated.

From this stage of early contact until the final presentation, the group's methods can best be characterized as "flying by the seat of our pants." For the process of muddling through issues constitutes the essential learning involved in community work. The group provides a supportive setting in which important questions related to our task and our professional identity can be asked and jointly resolved. How do we define our relationship to the citizens? Are we learners or experts? What are our credentials? What are the media for help-giving? Do we attempt to supply answers or do we provide a methodology for self-help? How do our idiosyncratic styles facilitate or hinder our work in the community?

When group members first approach the community they feel quite uncertain about what they have to offer and how they will offer it. Although they wish to avoid the role of researcher, which they believe exploits the community, they do not want to take an active role which might serve both to identify them with a particular segment of the community and to usurp the prerogative of local initiative. This professional limbo—which provides neither the comfort of alliance nor the status of leadership—is the vantage point which maximizes student learning. Within the time constraints of a semester the goal is to help students tolerate this marginal status. We do not promote a situation in which students are at the center providing answers.

What, then, do the students contribute? In most cases they offer a methodology which the community can use to move more quickly toward its change goals. Indeed, the citizens often view the final presentations as useful vehicles for priority-setting, evaluating past efforts, and, most important, planning for the future.

Disciplinary biases, previously so strongly denied, emerge as the students work toward change in the community. The student in clinical psychology is frustrated: "Therapy with one individual is hard enough; with a community it's impossible." For him the community is nothing more than the sum total of the component personalities; the agency director is viewed as "overcontrolling." For the urban planner, on the other hand, the community may be seen as a system in which the agency head protects the organizational domain. These biases are most evident when they try to determine who speaks for the community. For example, one group was planning the implementation of a free medical clinic in a rural area. The clinic was to be set up jointly by citizens of the community, agency representatives, and medical personnel who wished to extend their activity beyond the university setting. The venture was undertaken in good faith by all parties, yet they disagreed over who would control and govern the clinic. These discrepancies were reflected in the student group. For the social work student, control should be held by the consumers of the service. The public health student envisioned a partnership between local agency heads and elected officials. The psychologist felt the clinic would not survive unless the doctors who provided services held veto power in all policy matters. The students' intervention consisted of a workshop design in which these discrepancies were made explicit and subsequently worked through. Through this project the students learned to recognize values implicit in their professional roles—values which emphasize differences between an advocacy and a service-delivery model; between a fee-for-service approach and a sliding scale fee; between community control and professional management.

The course is structured so that the student divides his time between attending lecture-discussion sessions in which ecological principles are presented and participating in the community work groups. The reading list is divided into sections on political influence, citizen roles in community change efforts, the dynamics of community change in response to interventions, and case examples of the application of ecological principles in community practice. Within these topics, we tried to provide a multidisciplinary perspective and a sampling of ideologies of change. At the end of the third week the groups submit brief outlines which delimit the problem they have chosen, describe the working relationship they have established with citizens, and present their preliminary notions on the design of an appropriate intervention. We then give our reactions to the outline and pose questions relevant to future planning and action.

A class session open to the public held during the fifth and sixth weeks of the semester provides ongoing feedback. Here we scrutinize the group's assessment of the community situation, challenging premises and action plans, and ask questions about the utility of ecological principles as a framework, for viewing the community. The last weeks of the course are devoted to comprehensive reports summarizing each group's work. Citizens from the host community react to each report, as do student peers, who also provide written evaluations. Criteria for these written evaluations tap such areas as the practicality of the proposed intervention and methods for determining its success; concern for the community's future following the group's departure; the clarity with which the ecological principles are applied; the degree to which the presentation format itself is coherent and actively involves the community residents. These evaluations determine grades, which are assigned on a group basis.

To accomplish its goal of sensitizing the audience to the community in which it was working, one group invited an elderly gentleman to offer in its final presentation a running commentary about the slides to be displayed. He recounted personal anecdotes related to the history, folklore, and social characteristics of the locality. His contribution emphasized aspects unique to the community, reserved for those who know it best. He communicated a depth of concern and attachment which involved the audience in a way that textbooks and classrooms would never do. So, as student groups develop a methodology which they hope to give the citizens, the citizens reciprocate with a feeling for the community, a respect and concern for its future.

There is no technology which specifies the norms, behaviors, and tools requisite to community change. As resources for graduate training in the helping professions, we have acted on what we have learned by promoting multidisciplinary teams whose focus is to help citizens identify and solve real problems. Our ecological perspective emphasizes continuous interaction of the helping professional and the citizen and a mix of classroom activity and field work in the community. With this model, and the learning it fosters about the intricacies and joys of working with people, we will continue to work so that the community serves as teacher.

6

Qualities for the Community Psychologist

Reflections

This particular article appeared in American Psychologist *in 1971 and is considered a companion piece to the "Antidotes for Arrogance" article. I did not conceive of them that way, but they do go together. I was invited to speak with the faculty of the Lila Acheson Wallace School of Community Service and Public Affairs at the University of Oregon in November 1970. The school was named after the primary benefactor and co-founder of the* Reader's Digest. *Its mission was to prepare undergraduate students for careers in community organizations and various local government agencies.*

I decided to speak on personal qualities of doing community work because it is essential yet discussed infrequently. From teaching, I had discovered that doctoral students were having understandable difficulties in moving from the frame of reference of social scientist to the framework of being a community resource. I also wanted to illustrate how ecological ideas could be translated into criteria for education. I believed then, as I do now, that ecological thinking serves as a framework for training as well as for research and practice.

I am not sure where it came from, but I developed a style of presenting ideas in units of sevens. The talk and the eventual publication had seven points that I thought were important to address. The emphasis was on the importance of having a diversity of skills when working in a community. Each individual would have specific skills; the key was to have more than one identifiable competence. Those skills could range from survey research, community organization, or interpersonal qualities. Because undergraduates did not have as of yet professional identities, it was important that they were competent in several areas rather than being assistants to the professional.

The most important point was "metabolic balance between patience and zeal." At the time, concerted community action was an emerging value. From my research, I learned the importance of recognizing that real change in a community takes time. The community worker could improve the quality of the work if the community resource could learn to moderate energy and allow pauses for development to take place. My effort was to share useful ideas based on my experience. I was advocating a broader role for doing community work than was the norm at the time. The conventional view was that community work was just another place to conduct professionally defined research or practice. Community psychology could be much more.

As the field of community psychology emerges, there are plentiful opportunities to develop new hallmarks for the roles of the psychologist as an active participant in developing community resources. Community psychology can have several reference points. It can be viewed as an extension of clinical psychology, where the role is a therapeutic resource to individual clients and treatment groups in a specific geographical community. Community psychology can also be viewed as equivalent to community mental health. Here the term refers to organizing existing community services and multiple levels of professionals and nonprofessionals for the prevention of mental disorders. This second definition emphasizes the mission and practices of public health in contrast to clinical medicine, as in the first example. Community psychology can refer as well to those psychological and social issues that can be studied by established methods in the behavioral sciences. In this instance, the term community psychology represents a set of topical issues for research and evaluation by a wide variety of psychologists, sociologists, and urban specialists. Community psychology also can represent a goal to create a social environment that offers for its members a sense of "community." Community psychologists include proponents for each of these ideas as well as still many other points of view. The evolution of the field no doubt will define which of these various approaches will mature, which will blend, and which will fade. As this process continues, still additional criteria for evaluating the profession should emerge.

Ideas that have stimulated the thinking of the present writer have evolved when community psychology is defined in relation to natural conditions of the community. As I have grappled with assessing a natural community, I have been stimulated by the aptness of analogies from biological ecology, which can offer new dimensions for viewing community work. What follows are seven qualities for the community psychologist that derive from personal experiences and that are enriched by the ecological analogy.

One of the touchstones of the ecological perspective is: The focus for work is the local setting. The premise of the ecological perspective is that intact community services as interventions in an ongoing community should contribute to the development of the community. What the ecological perspective boils down to is assessing a natural setting and then redesigning the context surrounding a social problem so that a specific community problem is altered as the host environment is changed. The ecological perspective offers some promise of not just dealing with effects but with systemic causes. The details and implications of the ecological perspective have been presented elsewhere (Kelly, 1966, 1968, 1969, 1970a, 1970b; Mills & Kelly, in press [1972]; Trickett, Kelly, & Todd, in press [1972]). The present comments focus on the fallout from such a perspective, those qualities that can make a difference in how the community psychologist behaves in carrying out community work.

It is hoped that by making these qualities explicit, the power of the ecological analogy is affirmed more clearly. For the present author, adopting the ecological perspective means shifting the focus in our communities away from our personal aspirations, our sponsoring institutions, and even the visible persons or institutions in town, and, instead, making the local conditions and the local events the forum for our work. To carry out such an expedition means doing new and different things; it means grasping the intricacies of the total community so as to identify talents and resources that are hidden yet present. It means locating the persons who care about their town. During the past decade of participating in the work of four varying communities, I am encouraged by the increasing number of persons that I find who do care about their town and wish to join an expedition.

Viewing a community ecologically means seeing how persons, roles, and organizations, as well as events, are interrelated. If we can view the community as a series of interrelated systems, we have a better chance of designing projects and services that approximate the needs of the total community. The new ecological program can be organic to the community and not restricted, for example, to just one group of professionals or one social strata. The ecological perspective affirms that if we place ourselves in the midst of a social setting, we are more likely to make an effort to solve a community problem rather than simply offering a formula congruent with our professional skills. One of the biggest impediments in the provision of human services is the reluctance of professionals to work on generic problems as defined by citizens. Certainly, the major problems of poverty, racism, and pollution go beyond most of our current competencies. The ecological development of a community means that the professional must be willing to develop. He must be able to leave his professional cocoon and affiliate with many and divergent persons and their resources. Doing ecological good means helping to develop the natural resources of a community. Good is not viewed as the absence of ill health in individuals; good is viewed as the development and creation of competencies within the community.

For the ecological perspective, criteria shift to the interrelationships of persons, how resources are maintained and strengthened, how subunits of the community can grow and evolve, how the community adapts to new influences, and how multiple and smaller communities succeed one another over time. Viewing the community as a complex set of resources offers a new dimension for where to begin looking at a particular locale; for example, what are the constraints that impede the development of the local community? Are those constraints related to affluence or poverty? How are attitudes of smugness or ambition limiting development? Is a constraint the instability of top leadership or the longevity of such leadership? The issue is what processes, what roles, what persons are limiting development? As an analysis is made, the various contexts within the community will unfold, and systemic problems of the community can be clearly seen. Designs for progress can be tailored not only to the problem as defined by the professional, and not only by the interests of one subgroup, but community programs can be developed that affect the lifestyles of the total community and its future development.

For example, a community mental health program could be created to provide direct mental health services to a particular population with the impetus originating from the members of the mental health professions. The same service program can be developed, however, with the specific purpose of creating *new* community resources simultaneously while services are provided for troubled persons. There are not too many examples of the nonprofessional as a resources for community development when they are an integral part of a community mental health program. Too often they are replicas of the professional with less status, yet have equal or more program responsibility. An ecological intervention then includes ways for the community to function as a better ecosystem as it solves a community problem, by focusing on two processes, solving a problem, and developing the community. Such a synthesis increases the satisfaction of both citizens and professionals and improves the vitality of the community. Ego trips by elite professionals are unacceptable, and citizens are clearly identified and involved as collaborators in this work.

How is an ecological perspective acquired? What are the desired behaviors when the community psychologist behaves as an ecologist? The following seven qualities offer a start for an ecological expedition. Putting these ideas into practice does, however, require some rearrangement of our contexts for learning. Acquiring these qualities certainly implies different, if not radical, approaches to training and involves new criteria for selecting persons for community service. These ideas require new types of social settings to supplement the classroom. Here then are some qualities for the community psychologist. These seven qualities are suggested not as a universal creed, but rather as guidelines for assessing the performance of the community psychologist.

A Clearly Identified Competence

The community psychologist must do at least one thing clearly and well. Using the reference points mentioned in the introduction, he must be able to be therapeutic with individuals, organize a community service, study a complex social problem, or create a community for others. He must deliver and be accountable to himself and others. Without a recognizable competence there are few opportunities for the community psychologist to be in a position to solve genuine problems in the community. The expression of competence defines how the community psychologist relates to the community, whether he is understanding the role conflicts of community organizations, helping with the selection of staff for an OEO project, or training community development workers. A visible competence is also an insurance policy; for when the ambiguities and stresses get tough, the community psychologist may be able to get another job.

This quality of competence is emphasized first because it is the quality from which other qualities build. I have observed a trend in the development of professionals where there is a reverence for far-ranging reflexes and a warm glow for acting as a self-actualized universal resource. I wonder if such a person can survive in an open market? Training for community work requires more than an endless number of self-development sessions. Communities require problems to be solved: there is a child to learn, a law to be repealed, a budget to be prepared; there is inevitably some decision to make. I affirm that process skills should be learned but, simultaneously, while learning a technical competence. The community psychologist seeks out the setting where his competence can be displayed and works hard to learn new ones. What the ecological perspective offers are some suggestions for picking the settings where the competence can be expressed.

There is still another value in learning a competence, namely, that it can and should be taught to members of the host community, thereby returning a skill to the locale. The ecological twist requires that the competence be taught, and not just prized. This also encourages the psychologist to learn how to translate and vary his competencies from place to place. Understanding how a context affects the expression of a skill makes a big difference, particularly if the skill is not being used. One of the very important demands for community work is to understand why talent is not used in a particular social setting. A common plight is to see a ready, willing, and able resource underused. Often it is because the style or manner of the resource does not match the social norms of a particular culture. If the features of the social environment go beyond the community psychologist's ability to cope with the demands of the particular setting, he will need to acquire new skills. The thesis of the ecological perspective is that the community psychologist adapts his competencies to the requirements of varied settings. It is not enough to be competent; he must express and communicate so that his competencies are adopted by local resources. To do ecological good, the community psychologist must care about the locale and not just the prized competence.

Creating an Eco Identity

After a competence is learned and some effort is made for members of the community to adopt it, the community psychologist can begin to develop the quality of identifying with the total community. The ecological perspective advocates that part of the community psychologist's own identity should be related to the natural community he is working with. His definition of himself is determined by his direct engagement with the community. Defining himself as having a professional role in the surrounding environment helps accelerate the type involvement that is needed to diagnose the various social settings that are a part of the community. If the primary source of identity is the community psychologist's professional role, he will not be able to move about easily and see the locale from various perspectives. The community psychologist, as ecologist, requires emotional involvement to carry him on his expedition to the diverse social settings within the community. The open and direct expression of care, plus the equity he has achieved by his competence, can enable him to become a helpful resource. Certainly, to decide where to be helpful in a community requires a lot of love to carry the helper over the rough spots.

Some further comments should be made about how care is expressed. Building an eco identity certainly does not mean spilling positive regard for every niche and corner of the environment. It refers more to caring enough about the community so that all of the various sectors are explored, observed, and digested. The community psychologist, so goes the ecological thesis, cannot understand what problems to work on unless he sees the various geographical areas and knows something of how these areas affect the political process and how each of the subcommunities are interrelated. Love for the community is expressed by his moving about and by his trying to grasp the intricacies and subtleties of the community. To paraphrase a greeting card commercial, "he has to care enough, to move the very most." This quality affirms that the very complexity in the life of the community is similar to the intricacies of a pond or stream adapting to its surrounding environment. The community psychologist is interested in grasping this complexity.

Learning how to assess a community adds another feature, namely, how to meet, relate, and care about people who are unlike the community psychologist. This moving about the community is conceived to have an adaptive function, for it provides still another way for the community psychologist to increase his own competencies. This is particularly salient when the community psychologist is in a community that is very different from his or her personal background. It certainly takes a lot of personal toughness to make it through a community, to sense the range of behavior, styles of life, and conflicts, without becoming immune to the diversity and seeing only chaos. Coping with the ambiguities of the environment requires that the worker be sustained and carried by his commitment to understand the locale.

Tolerance for Diversity

When the community psychologist moves into a locale with a sense of competence and an emerging love for the locale and begins to move across and through the settings of the community, he is likely to meet many variations in how people express kindness and how they respond to strife. This can be confusing and most often contradictory. To grapple with these inconsistencies will demand a great deal of perspective in knowing how to contrast and compare various cultures and how to obtain more information about their histories and expected future outcomes. The quality of appreciating differences between persons and groups refers to an active searching out of what these differences mean. Seizing and understanding this variety is important because it offers ways to estimate the direction for the future development of the community. Being able to see variety in the way persons cope with tragedy, how they confront social inequities, initiate legal action, and celebrate good times is the measure of the community psychologist. The axiom that defines the psychologist's movement through the community is: There is something valid in each example, yet something incomplete in all of them. Another important element relating to the movement through the community is the basis for which diverse resources or groupings relate to each other and how such resources can be related directly back to the community. Diverse resources that are contained have some chance of contributing to the development of the community, but as in all organic systems, resources must be managed. This quality of the community psychologist represents his effort to understand how these resources are managed and how they are related. If the couplings or potential relationships of these diverse resources can be understood, then there is some merit in figuring out how to involve these untried resources and help them to create a new authentic role in the community. If current and diverse resources can be worked with, it is likely that new resources can contribute to the locale.

This quality asks the community psychologist to seek out as many different opportunities as possible in order to see what diversities are contributing to the community. This quality represents a commitment to understand, for example, in which social settings adults can relate to youth, what community services can work together to solve a problem, and which distinct parts of the community can be expected to work on specific issues. Tolerance of diversity is not expressed passively as a spongy attitude; tolerance for diversity is the quality of putting the resources to work to help secure options for the long-term cultivation of a locale. Diversity represents an active effort to mobilize the community to plan for its future.

Coping Effectively With Varied Resources

It is not enough to be tolerant of variety. The community psychologist actively deals with these various resources so that they will contribute to the total community. The community psychologist works to develop a repertoire so he can respond to an array of divergent persons and to minimize his negative contributions to the community. This quality is closest to what might be termed empathy, for it means that the community psychologist can take the role of others and move beyond the expressive roles and postures persons often display. The community psychologist also must be able to rise above a stereotyped role and not be stopped by the defensiveness of persons, but go beyond and search out skills and talent. This quality, more than the others, speaks directly to the interpersonal effectiveness required of the community psychologist. He must be able to quickly assess persons in their natural setting and relate to them with ease and respect. This quality certainly means that the community psychologist is a part of the world of events and not only the world of ideas. It means that the community psychologist is aggressive and involved and has access to his own psyche. It means that he can recover from social slights, brush-offs, stalls, confrontations, flatteries, and payoffs, and keep going on to the location of talent. This quality represents living day in and day out with the events of the community, and includes being able to be a resource with unknown persons about unexpected events. The ecological perspective directs the community psychologist to focus on the relationship of informal and formal roles that characterize social settings in order to figure out how these contexts affect the expression of needed resources. Identifying the talents and skills that are needed for a community is the gutsy work of community development. For many community psychologists, this quality represents an exciting attribute of trying to go beyond the uptight veneers, the defensiveness of fellow professionals, and helping to create a social setting where professionals and citizens can learn how to work together and, by example, can learn how to cope effectively with each other. Coping effectively with varied resources is not superhuman work; it also involves, for the community psychologist, knowing when to call for help, when to request rest and rehabilitation, and when to disengage from combat.

Effective coping with varied resources defines the operational role of the community psychologist by focusing on the local situation and then bringing together available resources. Performing this role involves an important and rare activity, namely, linking available resources to the solution of a community problem. Creating such linkages is the first step in determining what new resources are required for the future development of the community. Expressing this skill provides a role model for problem solving in the community and sets the tone and direction for the adaptation, if not the survival, of the community psychologist.

Commitment to Risk Taking

The previous four qualities have derived from participating in community work blended with the insights from the ecological perspective. These four qualities, representing a clearly defined competence, an identity that is related directly to the local environment, a tolerance for diversity, and effectiveness in dealing with varied resources, provide the context for the role of the community psychologist. The next three qualities represent values more than concepts and suggest examples of internal guidelines that the community psychologist can set for himself.

The quality of commitment to risk taking is particularly troublesome for most professionals, but it is critical if the community psychologist is, in fact, to be a resource for the community. Risk taking does not refer to impulsive acts or expressing whims. Risk taking in this context refers to being an advocate for a real cause and helping the community move beyond its present steady state. It means participating with citizens in social programs that may fail. It means working with persons who would be strangers were it not for present circumstances. Risk taking means going to bat for a marginal person; it means taking a personal position on a controversial issue and working hard to behave in such a way that persons with low status, who are now economically and politically weak, have as much influence on how the community psychologist spends his day as the more fortunate and self-contained.

Affirming this quality derives from the premise that the maladaptive strains in a local community provide important choice points for the future development of the community. Citizens stating demands and requesting help can mean that certain resources are no longer available to them. By being able to respond to these signs of maladaptive functioning, real support can be given to the total community. This interdependence of resources is seen as critical for the development of a community. If real support can be given to a marginal group, a greater chance of linking known but invisible resources to both the host and the marginal community is expected. The value of a commitment to risk taking means putting aside the need achievement of the professional and the aspiration to bet only on winners. A commitment to risk taking affects not only personal issues but also includes a commitment to participate with the community in an "iffy" enterprise. The community psychologist's resolution of the commitment issue, if communicated to citizens, can generate new options even if the project fails. There is often a sizable benefit that emerges during a temporary collapse of a project, and a momentary failure can define the cause for energizing new communities into thrusts of activity; if the community psychologist is clear in his position, he is ready for a new risk.

Commitment to risk taking then requires that the psychologist participate in community work when the rewards are indefinite and when there may be a loss of group affiliation when projects fail. If the community psychologist thinks that there is even some chance for the community to get itself together, then he must define a helpful role, however offbeat. The history of effective and successful community development is related to the viability of indigenous movements launching risky activities.

Metabolic Balance of Patience and Zeal

This quality, perhaps, is more related to mood and health status. The importance of the idea comes from observations of the process under which communities make a difference in the way persons are helped. Being really helpful involves a cycling of patience for achieving long-term goals with a zeal for pursuing short-term objectives. The present author has seen that too often the style of community worker is either overly patient or overly zealous. In this situation, the worker misses the opportunity to be zealous or patient when the situation warrants one metabolism but not the other. Learning how to balance these energies means that the worker must create a perspective to help himself see how to get from one part of his objective to the other. It is not simply a matter of being able to be fast or slow, or to know when to balance the expression of both skills; the community psychologist must be able to communicate this metabolism to others and to have influence when other community resources express their point of view.

One way to help clarify how to balance the expression of very active or passive responses to community work is to have a clear conception of the various constraints affecting a particular activity. The community psychologist needs to have a realistic idea of the obstacles that lessen change. It is important to know how much energy is required to alter the problem. Knowing when to mobilize and when to lay back is an "art" in community work. This type of judgment is also very important to express to citizens. This judgment involves, in part, learning how to get from one goal to another; it involves knowing the types of resources that are needed at any one particular time to solve a problem; and it involves an ability to define the issue upon which energies should be focused. By assessing the complexity of factors that impede the development of the community, there is an opportunity to define priorities more clearly and to organize energies.

Because community work is uncertain and lacks the definiteness that usually accompanies many work roles, it is often helpful to celebrate examples of successful achievement for the persons doing community work. Community work can be sustained much better if the participants are involved in a regular sharing of successes and triumphs and for supporting one another during the blues and blahs. The community psychologist in this way supports those who have performed, and also has a better understanding of the constraints and joys he experiences in his work. One of the most distressful situations is to see a well-trained professional caught with his cycling of metabolism down, when he is either too defensive, too proud, or too alienated to initiate a supportive environment for others and himself. Without a supportive environment, the community psychologist's own metabolism will get low. If the community psychologist is unable to create a nutrient environment for himself or hasn't access to such a setting, he probably should post-pone his community work until he can build it. Those community psychologists who are actively involved in the training of the next generation of community psychologists have an opportunity and a responsibility to create workable and active social settings that help the helpers.

Giving Away the Byline

The last quality refers to how satisfaction is enjoyed when community work is done. The hallmark of a community psychologist is that he works to achieve the first of these six qualities and enjoys the development of people and communities without seeking visibility and public applause for his service. Too often professionals have a frail vanity about making sure that they get the credit for what they do. This need for explicit recognition for work too often means that professionals seek out the easy and short-range problem that satisfies a neat and finite result. When the community psychologist is able to work on the tougher and troublesome issues, it is too often done in silence, with some ambivalence, and as a citizen. I am proposing that a new flag be carried, namely, the flag for community service. Community service for the present writer means that the criteria for success are not personal, but the criteria refer to how work is received, what it contributes to a locale, and how it leads to the evolution of the community. A vita and a newspaper feature article reporting good works too often are signs of a value for consumption, a consumption for the proclamation of deeds. By themselves these items do not reflect deeds performed. What needs to be affirmed is that a new set of criteria for scientific work is needed, criteria for the assessment of natural environments that lead to useful and real help for community resources. Here again the community psychologist is showing his commitment if he focuses on the consequences of his work rather than the work itself. The task is to develop resources for the community and not to seek hierarchical relationships in which the community psychologist expects that by being one up, he is therefore up on the problem. The community psychologist, so this quality states, acts by working as an equal and as if the byline for his work is a community story.

By encouraging equivalent interactions and worrying about what happens with these interactions, the community psychologist is validating for himself what many citizens already know, namely, that the community must have a final say in what is judged to be "good." The rewards for the effective community worker will come when he is invited to work on still tougher problems. Doing good work also means being available during times of trouble. The presence of the community psychologist on such occasions allows him to have the humble and enriching experience of seeing the raw constraints on development, and if he is present, and does something, he can have the satisfaction of making a difference during a crisis. If we take the heat of such events, we can also enjoy the reflection, and our colleagues will enjoy and value us as well.

Conclusion

The thesis for these comments has been ecological and affirms that the community psychologist survives as he does good works in different settings and copes with diverse persons and real issues. The seven qualities presented are suggestions for redefining the behavior for the community psychologist and for revising our methods of training. It is proposed that the hallmarks for community psychology are met when the locale is the primary source both for the energies and the work of the community psychologist.

Acknowledgments

The present article is a revised and edited version of comments made at the Lila Acheson Wallace School of Community Service and Public Affairs, University of Oregon, November 19, 1970. The author has benefited from the comments given by the following persons who cared enough to help sort out the good thoughts from the garbled prose: Randolph Harper, Peter Mattis, David Todd, and Ben Gottleib. To Dave Share goes thanks for his careful scrutiny of the ideas.

References

Kelly, J. G. (1966). Ecological constraints on mental health services. *American Psychologist, 21,* 535–539.

Kelly, J. G. (1968). Towards an ecological conception of preventive interventions. In J. W. Carter Jr. (Ed.), *Research contributions from psychology to community mental health.* New York: Behavioral Publications.

Kelly, J. G. (1969). Naturalistic observations in contrasting social environments. In E. P. Williams & H. L. Raush (Eds.), *Naturalistic viewpoints in psychological research.* New York: Holt, Rinehart & Winston.

Kelly, J. G. (1970a). Antidotes for arrogance: Training for community psychology. *American Psychologist, 25,* 524–531.

Kelly, J. G. (1970b). The quest for valid preventive interventions. In C. D. Spielberger

(Ed.), *Current topics in clinical and community psychology* (Vol. 2). New York: Academic Press.

Mills, R. D., & Kelly, J. G. (1972). Cultural and social adaptations to change: A case example and critique. In S. Golann & C. Eisdorfer (Eds.), *Handbook of community psychology*. New York: Appleton-Century-Crofts.

Trickett, E. J., Kelly, J. G., & Todd, D. M. (1972). The social environment of the high school: Guidelines for individual change and organizational redevelopment. In S. Golann & C. Eisdorfer (Eds.), *Handbook of community psychology*. New York: Appleton-Century-Crofts.

7

Tain't What You Do, It's the Way That You Do It

Reflections

During 1978 to 1979, I was in Osnabrück, Germany, as a Fulbright Scholar. Right before I left the United States, I learned that I had received the Division of Community Psychology's Award for Distinguished Contributions to Community Psychology and Community Mental Health. This honor would involve a talk at the American Psychological Association meetings in Toronto in August 1978. I started to brood about what I was going to say. My experiences over the past 20 years made me think that the topic should be the process of doing work. Over and over again, I discovered that not only did the content of a research or preventive program matter but also the steps taken to build a working relationship with community members. The lyrics of a song written by Trummy Young and Sy Oliver with the Jimmie Lunceford jazz band in the 1930s strongly resonated with the project. The title rang true and motivated me.

One of the major points I wanted to make was that the processes of implementing research should vary according to each community. I started to mull over how the processes would differ in a responsive versus a resistant community. Once again the ecological premise was used: so goes the community, so goes the processes of doing the work. The talk gave me another chance to focus on the resources necessary for working in various communities. This led me to deal with local cultures and how the host culture was an important topic before doing the work. In 1978 considering the local ecology as a critical subject for community research was still a novel (if not heretical) idea.

I recall starting to write the paper at a small desk in a rented house in Blaubauren, Germany, while fellow Fulbright faculty and students were learning the German language. Being in a different culture further intensified my learning and commitment to the essential qualities of focusing on cultures and adapting to the local ecology. My own adaptation to the German culture made it

*all real for me. I struggled to reconcile my values as a professor with the domi-
nant value at the time for the German professor to have the highest social status. The consequences were that the professors were inaccessible and doctoral
students were seldom given coauthorship opportunities because they were
rarely considered colleagues. I was very glad that I had my own values. However, the German professors at this university devalued me. I was not a traditional scientist. There were many examples of the German culture that required
my adaptation, but this role expression was certainly central.*

*I flew back to Toronto for the APA meetings. Dave Todd and Ed Trickett pre-
pared a wonderful introduction with humor and panache. There was a nice
crowd. The audience seemed to be refreshed by the ideas, and I was satisfied that
I had done both the award and myself justice. It is also true that the very opportunity to make those comments in public was motivating for me to keep on
the ecological expedition. A nice touch was that my daughter, Maureen, agreed
to translate the musical script into an epigram in the publication that appeared
in 1979.*

The 1978 Division 27 Award for Distinguished Contributions to Community Psychology and Community Mental Health: James G. Kelly

Editor's Note: James G. Kelly was honored at the 1978 annual meeting of the
American Psychological Association in Toronto, Canada, on August 30, 1978,
receiving the Division of Community Psychology Award for Distinguished Contributions to Community Psychology and Community Mental Health. The selection was made by an Awards Committee composed of all the past Presidents
of the Division. Dr. Kelly was introduced by David M. Todd of the University of
Massachusetts, and Edison J. Trickett of the University of Maryland.

Introduction: *James Gordon Kelly, a Tribute*

James Gordon Kelly has been a thoughtful, energetic, creative, and compassion-
ate contributor to Division 27 throughout its history. We are honored today to
highlight Jim's contributions to community psychology and to participate in
the Division's recognition of their distinction. Consistent with the way Kelly has
helped us learn to think, we understand these accomplishments as a result of a
dynamic, reciprocal interaction of the person, Jim Kelly, with a variety of set-

tings, through time. We have received generous accounts of this process from many significant people in Jim's life. There is not time to mention all of these people, but we will try to convey the caring, respect, and appreciation which they expressed.

Jim was born 48 years ago in Cincinnati, Ohio, the only child of Cosmo Belle and James G. Kelly. Many of the qualities which characterize his professional contributions were evident in his early years. Jack Glidewell, for example, refers to Jim's "zestful openness." Zest and a preference for exploratory behavior have apparently been long-standing qualities of Jim. For example, his mother reports that as a child Jim was so hard to keep track of on shopping trips that she had to get a harness for him, and that a schoolteacher once threatened to tie Jim to his seat. With a Midwestern pragmatism that seems to have rubbed off on her son, Mrs. Kelly told the teacher, "If that's what it takes, O.K."

Jim's preference for action and exploration was linked early with a value for ideas. His father placed a strong emphasis on the importance of education and when he got home from work, often read to young Jim. He also introduced Jim to a setting in which his passions for ideas and action found strong expression: baseball. Through their Sunday trips to Crosley Field, Jim developed an understanding of baseball which began with a thoroughly scientific mastery of facts, but extended far beyond to an appreciation of the system dynamics, esthetics, and human drama of the sport. While still in grade school, Jim was interviewed by the Cincinnati Reds' announcer Dick Bray in a program called "Fans in the Stands." When Bray found out the boy wanted to be a sportscaster when he grew up, he handed the microphone over and had him interview other kids. While Jim ultimately chose an alternative career, his description of one of his heroes, sports announcer Red Barber, has strong resemblance to Jim's approach to psychology. Kelly admires Barber, he says, "for his scholarly approach to baseball broadcasting, for succeeding to transmit knowledge in an easy, informal way, for getting inside the game, and relating to his audience as neighbors and peers. For making something unique and personal out of a career."

Charlie Lamb, recalling a conversation with Jim in Cooperstown, New York, at the time of the annual Hall of Fame inductions, captures some of Jim's love of and involvement in the human side of the sport. "So I ended up," says Charlie, "sitting in the bar of the very elegant Otesoga Hotel while Jim, who turns out to be a veritable encyclopedia of baseball trivia, told me more about the various baseball 'personalities' in the room than a person really needs to know. 'There's Joe Shinguard, who caught for the Black Sox in 1898 and batted .307' he would say of some doddering old codger, and of course you had to *believe* him. He would even point out the *widows* of baseball players—because he has that manner about him."

Since a major focus of Jim's research has been on the high school, it is interesting to seek out the origins of his person and career in his own high school experience. Several qualities stand out. First of all, Jim learned during this time, to cope with adversity and, despite setbacks, to count on your environment. His father died in 1945 while Jim was a sophomore in high school, and Jim received important support and encouragement from friends and their parents. He, in turn, pitched in to help his family by going back to work at the Alberta Food Shop. Second, Jim learned during this time to handle and appreciate diversity, in part as a member of an informal peer group which called themselves "13 hits and a miss." Kelly, as the only non-Jewish member of the group, was the "miss." (We are surprised, given his interest in baseball, that he wasn't called the "error.") Jazz, social perceptiveness, humor, and limit-testing seemed to be shared qualities of this group. Finally, Jim's way of actively and creatively engaging settings is evident in his high school experience. He participated in some formal activities, including a performance of *Arsenic and Old Lace*. But more often he seemed to create new activities.

To quote Lew Keck, Jim's best friend during that time, "he managed—how he managed I'll never know—to talk that fool principal into allowing him to be a D.J. He was going to play, of all things, jazz records before school started each morning to wake everybody up." Getting approval may have required a strong measure of persistence and logic, since Jim's mother remembers being called into the principal's office more than once.

Fortunately for us, Jim Kelly chose to channel his energy and talents into psychology, where he has participated in a wide array of settings. Jim obtained his BA from the University of Cincinnati, during which time he married Sue Rombach—then a student nurse at Good Samaritan Hospital in Cincinnati. Jim's life and career from that point have been strongly nurtured by Sue and their children—Jim III, Maureen, Sharon, Anne, and Kay.

Jim received his MA from Bowling Green in 1954 and moved to the University of Texas at Austin for doctoral work in clinical psychology. Ira Iscoe, in recalling Jim's clinical skills and personal qualities at that time, remembered Jim as "giving a fair Wechsler, a mean TAT, his Bender-Gestalt was a little wavy, but his Draw-a-person was right on."

At Texas, Jim's clinical interest were shaped toward the emerging field of community mental health, and he took a "post-doc" at Mass General, where he was supervised by Don Klein, and then a master's in Public Health at Harvard where he worked with Eric Lindemann and Gerald Caplan. Jim then became the chief of the community projects section, Mental Health Study Center, at NIMII, and has held faculty positions at the University of Maryland, Ohio State University, the University of Michigan, and the University of Oregon, where he served for six years as Dean of the Lila Acheson Wallace School of Community Service and Public Affairs. He has just begun a sabbatical at the University of Osnabruk, Germany, as a Fulbright Hays Fellow, after which he will return to Oregon as a Professor of Psychology.

Throughout his career, Jim has been an active participant in the profession; President of Psi Chi at Texas, member of six APA divisions, President of our own

Division as well as the Division of Psychologists in Public Service, President of the Oregon Psychological Association, and participant in numerous review panels and committees of the American Psychological Association and National Institute of Mental Health.

Jim's professional work is marked by many of the same qualities we already described, but several qualities and contributions should be highlighted as the basis for this award.

Many of Jim's colleagues cite his unique appreciation and talent for attending to the process of a setting; he combines the qualities of contributor, Dutch uncle, clarifier, and mediator. Ira Iscoe describes Kelly as a graduate student who was unusually involved in the activities of the program: "He has great communication skills and sensitivity. He was an ideal person to ameliorate ideological and other types of quarrels between faculty. When we had an important decision to make, Kelly was inevitably consulted."

Charlie Spielberger captures many of the same qualities in Jim's subsequent professional career: "His sensitivity and skill, getting at the essence of a problem, identifying the available resources for solving the problem, and alternative courses of action are unparalleled in the field. He also has great courage in facing difficult problems head on and dealing with these problems constructively in terms of the long-term best interests of the people and systems with whom he works."

Jim also combines a strong dedication to his settings with a capacity to adapt his style to the unique qualities and needs of the environment. Jack Glidewell compares two such person–environment interactions:

> At the NIMII study center he was the young Turk scientist, bent on a compelling demonstration that an ecological epidemiology was not only possible but especially enlightening. As the Dean of a professional school . . . he was the passionate leader–reformer bent upon a compelling demonstration that participatory decision-making was not only possible but especially enabling . . . in both settings he designed a special niche, using special resources particularly useful to him, finding those resources where they were readily available, and processing the resources by a constantly developing strategy, attuned to the setting. . . . Each setting grew with him; each became more actively and creatively adaptable to a changing environment.

In like fashion, Bill McKeachie, Harold Raush, and Rick Price all describe Jim's persistence, patience, and adaptability as essential conditions for the establishment and endurance of a community psychology program at the University of Michigan. Jim's contributions to this division further reflect these qualities, for it is fair to say that he has participated in every major event in the creation and evolution of the Division of Community Psychology—from Swampscott to Vail to Austin, from the decision to form a division to the decision to stress the role of students in its governance. He has brought a special consciousness and caring to this task, for which we are particularly grateful.

The final qualities we wish to stress are Jim's continuing commitment to integrating theory and practice and his passion for ideas and knowledge that make a difference. He has drawn heavily on the rich biological framework of ecology to help us understand the complexity, pattern, and development of persons in settings. In so doing, he has, as a professional style, concurrently immersed himself in the arena of action *and* the world of ideas. His intellectual career exemplifies Seymour Sarason's contention that social action *is* an indispensable vehicle for learning; indeed, Jim credits this theory *and* practice stance with providing the gist for much of his talk today. In his writing, Jim has applied his ideas to such diverse areas as policy and service delivery in his paper, "Ecological Constraints on Mental Health Services," training, in his Division 27 presidential address, "Antidotes for Arrogance," criteria for the profession in "Qualities for the Community Psychologist," and to research reported in several papers and a forthcoming book on varied high school environments and adolescent coping. He is currently completing a book coedited with Muñoz and Snowden on *Research in Social Contexts: Bringing about Change.* As readers of Jim's work, we have come to see Jim as a person who knows how to find the phrase, the language which expresses precisely what he wants to say—there is a flow, a clarity of intent, and precision of meaning which strengthens and makes more vivid the impact of his ideas. And Kelly's colleagues have no trouble evaluating the importance of his ideas to the field: Seymour Sarason reflects a broad consensus when he says that of the few people who "represent a distinctive point of view, Jim represented the most distinctive . . . in that he endeavored to interrelate psychological and ecological concepts." Sarason's conclusion dignifies this occasion: "You cannot talk about the field of community psychology without paying serious attention to the ideas and research of Jim Kelly."

Through all of these activities and accomplishments, Jim Kelly has given of himself to the field of community psychology. Cowen embellishes it well and without exaggeration: "There are Kelly nuances," he writes, "which, if missed, lose the hue and tones of a rich color portrait: (1) the special care and attention he brings to events and life circumstances that are important to *others;* (2) his uncanny ability to adapt comfortably to multiple, diverse groups and circumstances; (3) his relaxed style; (4) his ability to laugh at himself; (5) his (even 'under fire') remarkably nondefensive way of interacting with others; and (6) the fact that he has never, for all of his many splendored achievements, lost his humility."

Effectiveness, adapting strategies to reflect local conditions, persistence in seeing tasks through, energy, caring, thoughtfulness, and humor. These qualities recur in descriptions of how Jim Kelly has "made something unique and personal out of a career." "Making a difference" is a helpful phrase—in the ideas and lives of students, his place of work, and his profession. His career has clarified the critical differences: between being busy and being productive; between being well-meaning and being effective; between testing limits and being creative; and, to use Jim's words, "between playing *with* and playing *through*" commitments, relationships, and ideas that are important for the development of community psychology.

In his 1971 paper, "Qualities for the Community Psychologist," Kelly, in a section titled "giving away the by-line," writes that the community psychologist "enjoys the development of people and communities without seeking visibility and public applause for his service" (pp. 902–903). Today, on this elegant and affectionate occasion, we have the privilege of publicly asserting to our friend and colleague that—in the judgment of his peers—he may not give away the by-line any longer.

David M. Todd
Edison J. Trickett

Taint What You Do, It's The Way That You Do It

The process of our work is as fully important as the content! Community psychology can achieve and sustain a valid and unique place within the science and profession of psychology to the extent that we empirically test ideas about how we do our work. If we are successful in defining and communicating our knowledge of process, citizens will be able to put into action their plans for community development. Much is demanded when describing any process. For example, the continuing search for process variables for the psychotherapeutic relationship shifts from confusion to momentary clarity when studies report findings for the relationships between therapist–client interactions and outcomes (Lambert, De Julio, & Stein, 1978). Observations about the process of evaluation research and organizational development have independently directed attention to the client–practitioner relationship including properties of the setting where the work is done (Cotton, Browne, & Golembiewski, 1977; Franklin, 1976; Kaplan, 1978; Riecken, 1977). Disciplines outside of psychology are becoming invested in the topic of process. In the field of architecture, for example, an architect is giving attention to the process of design and includes as topics: qualities of the architect, qualities of the client, the architect–client working relationships as well as properties of imagery (Zeisel, 1978). So far, it is not clear just what proportion of variance relates to the characteristics of the consultant, the designer, the client, or the setting, when organizational development, program evaluation or architectural design is successful. Each of the recent half-dozen publications I have read on the topic of process point to the absence of a conceptual framework. I offer the following ideas as a start.

What do I mean by process? *Process* refers to the following acts of induced change: (a) *new* expectations for both us as community psychologists and for clients as to how change will begin; (b) *new* forms of social interaction between us and clients; (c) *new* guidelines for how the social norms of induced change will be defined. Attending to these three criteria of process guides the application of our methods. Whether our preferences are for such methods as goal attainment scaling, variations of mental health consultation, community development, or program evaluation, the methods by themselves do not produce tangible impact unless there is a directed effort to understand the relationships between the community psychologist, the method of choice, and the setting in which the work is done. The procedures and techniques about which we write and publish are given authentic meaning by the processes we create.

Methods and processes are particularly interdependent for community psychology since there are less personal resources, yet more uncontrolled variables, more directed and undirected political and social influences, more constraints and detours than when doing clinical or organizational psychological tasks. The societal sanctions that are available and make it possible to define the therapeutic process for the work of clinical and organizational psychology are as yet not available for community psychology.

There are several benefits when we define and elaborate the topic of process. There is a pragmatic benefit, which makes the application of our methods easier. There is an ideological benefit, which increases the occasions for citizens to absorb and redefine community development for themselves. And there are also egocentric benefits. One such benefit is that knowledge of process improves the quality and effectiveness of our work by encouraging us to create meaning from diverse and conflicting experiences. Another is that such knowledge helps transmit our worth and expertise to the next generation of community psychologists. The question students ask me most frequently is not, "What is community psychology?"; colleagues ask that question. Students ask "How do you do community psychology?", "When is it better to do this activity rather than that?", "What do you say at this point, and why?"

I have a premise: elaborating process is dependent upon the personality and the professional competences of the community psychologist. To presume to offer this observation affirms the validity of common sense! The field of community psychology in focusing so much upon external environments has put aside questions of our personal qualities. In doing so, we have avoided those features of ourselves, including our foibles, that in fact emerge as central defining elements when doing our work and as pivotal elements when conceptualizing what we do. Our personal qualities are the foundation for the choices we make when we select our tasks and give time to our work. Why is this so? It is so, because our work is largely unpredictable, certainly ambiguous, often tentative, and even indeterminate. Under such working conditions, we are compelled to rely on what we give and project into the tasks. We rely upon our qualities and quirks and our premises about other people, for better or worse, to get us through when there are no set or clear guidelines.

What are some of the personal qualities that intrude? (a) A work orientation that takes time away from participating in the informal chitchat of the communities in which we work. (b) A personal identity solely restricted to one's career as a community psychologist, eclipsing our other selves. (c) Low curiosity, a preference for a restricted life space, missing the chance to be in diverse settings. (d) A nonegalitarian style of relating to others that prohibits our personal relationships becoming reciprocal.

What are some conceptions of human behavior that don't help? (a) A view of people as "subjects" who perform for us. (b) Explanatory concepts that focus only upon here-and-now causes and effects. (c) Diagnostic perceptions that exclude the often subtle and supportive contributions that people give to each other and their organizations when we psychologists are not around to observe or intervene. (d) A dim view of the world's conditions derived from our professional life space, a view that can be cynical and spawn paralysis.

Guidelines for Defining Process

Until recently our searches for guidelines about "know how" have been unavoidably individual enterprises. Many of us, I am sure, have sketched out a temporary set of hunches to help us through what often seems to be disorganized, cumbersome, and muddling activities. We then begin to realize a basic axiom, that in the design of a preventive intervention there is an orchestrated interdependence of personal qualities, relationships with people in the community, and the methods and process of the intervention itself. There is incompleteness, if not error, if we overemphasize the individual and focus our attention away from the role of social forces. Here, erroneously, we may put aside the essential task of defining the values and goals for doing our work as H. Warren Dunham (1977), Art Pearl (1974), and Seymour Sarason (1978) have been asserting. There is incompleteness, if not error, if we over-emphasize community dynamics and put aside ourselves. We are just beginning to think it important, and useful, to identify as a topic personal qualities. Bill Fairweather and colleagues, for example, have called attention to persistence and capacity for team-building (Fairweather, Sanders, Tornatsky, & Harris, 1974).

What follows are ideas for elaborating the process of intervention. The guidelines for the processes are: Creating Resources for Ourselves, Expressing Competences in Diverse Settings, and Committing Time and Energy. For each of these three guidelines comments will be made about the community psychologist as a person and about our role when managing the entry process. Managing entry—those multiple demands and opportunities when we first begin—is as diagnostic of ourselves as it is of clients. The discussion of entry will be developed for two types of social settings: a responsive setting and a setting resistant to change. A *responsive* setting consists of a group of persons who want to improve their setting and are willing to work with an outside resource. A *resistant* setting consists of a few persons within a group who have decided to improve their setting, and have ambivalence about beginning the task, plus there is palpable opposition from others about stimulating any change as well. In the resistant setting, the persons who are active for change are vulnerable to attack, to loss of social status, and certainly are at epidemiologic risk for the new stresses they will soon assume. While most of the settings in which we work are composites of both responsive or resistant social organizations, I have chosen the dichotomy, responsive versus resistant, to sharpen the discussions and to illustrate more definitely the contrasting processes when doing the work.

How we go about designing the initial stages of entry will determine how useful the work will be for clients. Adaptations of method and process are required when working in each of these settings, and the criteria for success and failure also will vary. Achieving initial success is easy to visualize in a responsive setting, yet true success consists of working for more long-term maintenance of change. While failure in working with a resistant environment is much easier to accept personally, extra attention must be given in the resistant setting to understand the factors—both within the setting and within ourselves—that restricted the change.

The analysis of process expands and clarifies our definitions for successful work in community psychology. We are obligated to move beyond the easily managed and often inconsequential interventions produced when working with a responsive environment. In contrast, we elevate ourselves from depression or projecting rancor when working with a resistant environment.

The source for the following three guidelines is the ecological analogy.[1] I continue to believe that this analogy stimulates deeds that are both compatible and intrinsic with the goals of community psychology. First, the ecological analogy directs our attention to the development and evolution of persons and social settings. We and our settings are conceived of as moving and changing over time. It is possible to perceive ourselves in a phase of development: We are a product of an explicit past, and we are moving in a future in and out of concert with our settings. Second, by definition we and our settings are interdependent. We cannot consider ourselves without being a part of social contexts; likewise our social contexts are affected by how we behave in them. There is a mutuality between our acts and the activities of our social settings. Causes and effects between us and our social contexts are reciprocal. Third, priority is given to understand the dynamics of the social relationships between us and our social contexts. Activities, occasions, and the structure of our settings integrate us within social contexts and connect us with one another. Social structures are of interest because they affirm which traditions of the recent and remote past give meaning to the total social context. Fourth, the stated ethic for studying ourselves and our settings is to identify the salutary forms of social interactions that create personal and social integration. There is a defined "good" to search for those personal and social characteristics that contribute to life-enhancing qualities for ourselves and our settings. Fifth, attention is given to assess the impact of any new person and any new activity intruded into an ongoing social setting. There is conspicuous attention to the consequences of planned and unplanned interventions. The ecological analogy affirms that every new intrusion has some effect, even though not always direct, and not always observed, and not always good. The impact of externally initiated change is attentively appraised. These five hallmarks of the ecological analogy are the premises for the three guidelines about the processes of doing community psychology.

Creating Resources for Ourselves

This guideline asserts that we community psychologists begin first by activating a social support system for ourselves. Doing useful community psychology is not for the lone entrepreneur! The presence of social support reduces the stressful impact of the work, and makes it possible for us to seek help when our personal competences have been tested. It is best when doing community psychology that we ourselves be fully integrated members of a functioning social unit. Our membership anchors us: we can then express our vexation, be nudged, called to task, encouraged, and even loved. However, being a contributing member of a social support system is not easy for us professionals. Certainly the interpretation we give to life in the University and Human Service Organizations does not make it easy for our work space to serve as a primary locale for giving and receiving support. In fact, being a successful faculty member or community practitioner can encourage solitary activities. Such behavior conflicts with the requirements for being a good member of a support group. There are exceptions to this general condition. When we are fortunate to be a part of a supportive setting, we revere the setting and our friends. It is because our professional work space often is without such properties that we must be assertive in building a healthy environment for ourselves.

There are personal prerequisites when creating resources. For example, one ability is to understand what makes us angry. This is a very tough life task, but if managed, it will not only bring joy to our friends, but also give inspiration to our clients. Anger can be displaced upon the ambiguity of our work and move us to apparent good deeds, but only with a veneer of commitment that too often is seen for what it is: role taking, simulating helpfulness, but without any "gut" excitement. Anger and its disguises produce a dead-end detour for the work of community psychology, and its indirect and disguised expression prevents us from being an example to our clients of what induced change requires. Creating resources demands the expression of energy, clear assertiveness, and an active effort to initiate a variety of interpersonal exchanges. Certainly included are making our needs known to strangers, finding out if, in fact, we and others have a common and mutually satisfying basis on which to develop a working relationship. Creating resources depends upon our knowledge of how we are perceived by others and our knowledge of our own needs when being a working partner, how we respond to stress and how well we can give and receive help. Anger dissipates such abilities, it consumes us and then deadens.

What are some ways to create resources for ourselves when working with two kinds of settings: one that is responsive and one that is resistant? The primary task we have when we create resources within a responsive environment is to *expand communications and relationships with other organizations*, to create new resource opportunities within the larger surrounding environment.[2] In working with a responsive setting, we are certainly helped if we know something about the processes of creating resources for ourselves. If we are familiar with these processes we can appreciate the emerging commitments clients are making for themselves as well as their settings. The task then is to expand the adaptive capacity of the organization, so that ideas and know-how from other organizations can be introduced into the host setting.

What are some skills that are involved here? Three skills are suggested as important for this particular environment: (a) developing an active working relationship with influential persons, which involves expressing appropriate etiquettes and courtesies, (b) creating alliances, and (c) monitoring fantasies about success particularly stimulated when working in a congenial setting. Expressing these skills also assists us in the management of the entry process within a responsive environment. Some brief comments about these skills: Influential persons expect deference. They also expect that if we really know anything we will quickly see who has power and then work to establish rapport with those who have it. In doing so the entry process is further enhanced to the extent that we are sensitive to influential persons' preferences for getting work done. Getting answers to such questions as the following help: When meetings take place how long should they last? How is confidentiality preserved? In what public places is it either an asset or a liability for an influential person to be seen with a community psychologist?

The entry is managed when autonomous groups within the organization, unaware of the proposed work, do not feel threatened by our presence. But most important in working with a responsive environment is the following. When initial success seems imminent, the celebration of accomplishments is circumspect. We devote conspicuous energy to ensure that the impact of an initial success will be maintained. *The* salient criterion when working with a responsive environment is whether we have created something substantial that can and does evolve over time.

In working to create resources within a resistant environment, the entry task is different. Here the task is to *form, then mold, a small group of persons into a work group and to begin the difficult initial tasks of creating a resourceful setting.* Any visible signs of group formation within the organization, particularly for inter-personal problem solving, will be questioned, most often privately. There is likely to be persuasive resistance within the organization against such a group forming.

In working with a resistant organization the entry tasks call forth such skills as: (a) Being able to offer emotional and technical support so as to bind a fragile, tentative group under conditions of uncertainty and covert attack. (b) Being observing and then accessible to reduce self-destructive behavior and to enhance adaptive performance as a result of the predicted and inevitable frus-trations related to doing work as a marginal group. (c) Creating explicit sanc-tions from the various leadership groups of the host environment for the work to get underway. (d) Reducing anxiety about the consequences of failure of the work, particularly for the small group planning for change. These skills repre-sent political "savvy." The community psychologist is a steadying, calming in-fluence upon the work group while expressing needed competences so that the work group has confidence in the community psychologist's opinions and skills. There is a clear mandate to be tough-minded yet sensitive to the stresses related to the work and the personal risks that the small group has assumed. The common task in creating resources within both types of organizations is to help create new social norms for how resources are used, managed, and then developed.

There are also risks when there is success. Working with a responsive envi-ronment may lead the organization to become colonial rather than egalitarian. An entrepreneurial zeal may dominate! What originally seemed like a potential for resources to be perceived as an outcome of reciprocal relationships may end with new resources collected, used, and then unreplenished, consistent with past social norms. Within the resistant organization, the risk is that success may mean that a new nucleus of persons, a new clique, has been formed and congealed, and they have adopted the values of the community psychologist. Their very success has been accompanied by a limitation, e.g., inadvertent and implicit cooptation by the community psychologist. This phenomenon is a corollary of Gerald Caplan's law that the initial consultee is deviant in social status within the organization. An unwitting consequence of success in work-ing with a resistant organization may be creating a new tightly formed, mutu-ally supportive, yet deviant group. One of the major risks of success occurs when both settings propagate only humanistic values and a strictly psychologi-cal orientation. Such values adopted, and expressed too quickly or too emphati-cally, can be maladaptive within many organizations. Being open and confronting can be self-defeating. Ground rules for survival in many organiza-tions reward competitiveness and solitary zeal. Instead, performing concrete tasks, clarifying and being explicit about purposes of the group, plus creating operational goals and then achieving them, may have more impact than reaf-firming just a psychological perspective.

Creating resources within the work setting sets the change process in motion. Much time is spent getting our feet wet. Staff, at all levels, are talked with to assess how persons can work together, to learn what topics and issues have some basis of consensus. Ample time is spent with executive leadership to define which activities are most apt to initiate change at the time within the organization. The entry process is managed to the extent that natural social settings can be modified so the talents and problem-solving abilities of persons in different parts of the organization can be brought together. Managing entry includes assessing both the formal and informal settings within the organization and having ideas for how settings can serve as resources for the future development of the larger organization.

In the responsive environment, the visible presence of the community psychologist in various settings signals that there is a serious effort underway to improve the quality of the setting. In a resistant organization, on the other hand, the presence of the community psychologist may stimulate anxiety, retard change efforts, and aggravate suspicion. Completing a successful entry process results in assessing resources without intimidating persons who are politically antagonistic to the community psychologist or embracing too quickly those who express values similar to our own. Creating resources involves giving support to those who are working for change, helping them acquire new competences and social power, without risking the loss of already gained influence.

Expressing Competences in Diverse Settings

The entry process involves then entering new social settings and assessing them well enough so that it is clear how our competences as community psychologists can be expressed. To the extent that the lifestyle of clients and their settings diverges from the settings in which we ourselves work, we devote time and energy to understand the antecedents for the expression of responsiveness or resistance. Implicit within this guideline is the belief that we can accommodate to diverse settings. There are at least two benefits for doing so: (a) we learn how varieties of social organizations affect the expression of both healthy and unhealthy behavior; (b) by investing ourselves in different settings we can learn new competences as we go through our own processes of entry. The combined effect of these two benefits is to understand varieties of personal and cultural adaptations. Most important, we are obliged to be clear about our own personal work preferences and are ready to see how we can or should revise preferred ways of working. This process requires a blend of clarity and assurance, plus tentativeness and moderation, as we meet and talk with persons in work roles we have never known and see for the first time expectations for styles of work that are different from our own. While developing clarity about the processes for change, we work to understand how the clients carry out their work. In going through these steps, we are alert to see how being different is, in fact, better, and how our ideas about helping can be and should be modified when working in this particular yet different setting.

Responsive and resistant organizations offer contrasts in how they acknowledge and develop diverse settings. A comparison of the two settings high-lights some differences. Within the responsive environment the question is: *Can a positive result obtained within one setting, hold for all of the settings?* For the resistant setting the question is: *Will a negative result in one of the settings limit work that is attempted within other settings?*

Some of the skills involved in working within a responsive environment are: (a) integrating what we have learned from the different settings; (b) clarifying how sanction is given for new work, and how tangible support is expressed for doing new work at the multiple decision-making levels of the setting; (c) testing out an evolving portrait of the organization so that the principles learned from this portrait can be translated into a plan for daily activities of the organization; (d) organizing some of the varied parts of the setting to initiate new activities when there are no precedents to do so. These various skills are directed to understand the latent variety within the setting, and how the diversity of working styles contributes to the socialization of competences. The community psychologist tries to find out whether the variety reflects different ways to achieve the same goals or whether the variety represents individual efforts to be expressive, in the absence of any clear expectations for shared values.

In working with a resistant setting, there is a contrasting opportunity to test our methods and ideas about process. Working to express one's competences in a resistant setting, particularly one that is divergent from our own, is an adventuresome activity as we attempt to learn new competences under limiting and often unflattering conditions. Some of the qualities that are involved are: (a) persistence, sheer persistence, in expending energy to create a work setting for the preferred activity to be done; (b) an ability to deflect and not be intimidated by hazing from different subgroups within the setting, developing a tough hide; (c) an ability to understand the psychological, economic, and social determinants affecting a subgroup's resistance to change, avoiding stereotyping; (d) explaining the rationale and hopes for change activities to different subgroups within the setting, while expecting minimal feedback. The skills required when working with a resistant setting are indeed subtle and taxing. The integration of these observational and diagnostic skills coupled with persistent probings, is no doubt like learning to be an informed observer and interpreter of other cultures. But the eventual gains are worthwhile. If we community psychologists are successful, then we have definitely learned something about the evolution of social change.

In working with both responsive and resistant settings, the community psychologist attends to the differences within the settings, differences in goals, style, and opinions about change, so that the differences, whether expressed in

dichotomies or expressed as perceived complementary relationships, can stimulate the evolution of the setting. In both settings the community psychologist
encourages members to recognize and be self-conscious about their skills, and
to value learning new competences from each other. In a responsive environment, the task is to note explicitly the resources and how they vary, so that the
members can see how there may be personal and organizational advantages in
being mutually dependent upon each other. This awareness in itself can become
a new social force within the setting. In a resistant setting, the task is to establish enough rapport and trust with key individuals and subgroups, so that new
personal redefinitions of each other can begin to take place. This is expected to
be difficult since members of a resistant organization are likely to be private and
not accustomed to express openly their most valued skills. The opportunity to
develop a social innovation within a resistant setting is limited to the extent that
such fears are reduced.

When we are successful in noting and developing diverse competences
within settings, we can feel that we are indeed effective. We give ourselves
credit. We worked hard, at great odds, and made it. Those of us who have a
strong need to dominate may be tempted to celebrate these accomplishments as
our personal achievement. Fortunately, such foibles are predictable both by us
and by our clients. Our friends, along with clients, can temper any tendency to
follow us as "true believers." Working to learn new and diverse competences
and to develop them with clients, has as an extra benefit preventing us from becoming complacent and arrogant.

Committing Time and Energy

A third guideline to clarify the know-how of community psychology is committing time and energy to the entry process. The entry process inescapably demands time and energy to initiate, to probe, to clarify, and then to establish the
conditions for work. What integrates the entry process is our personal belief
that our work is important to do. Personally committing time and energy makes
it possible to take advantage of the unplanned and natural opportunities that
occur as the new working relationship unfolds.

How does this principle apply when working with responsive and resistant
environments? In a responsive environment, the community psychologist, devoting time and expressing energy, can be an effective role model when the latent energy within the setting is noted and given direction. It is a truism: when
clients see us give our personal time and energy they will follow our example.
Our commitment of energy can increase the self-esteem of clients while giving
of our time creates an exponential benefit to accelerate the organization's commitment to change.

Expressing such commitments within a responsive environment can be very
satisfying. Four examples are: channeling current resources and energy so that

there is more efficient use of energy, serving as a "thermostat"; self-protection against overidentification with the organization, working to maintain an independent view of the organization; assisting the organization to be specific in setting goals, preventing the warm glow of a congenial relationship to abide by untested and global generalities; coaching the organization about the value of conserving energy, being explicit and persistent that wasting energy is "harmful to our health." *All of these skills relate to preserving a balance between the expression of time and energy by the community psychologist and the conserving use of that energy by the setting.* The selective use of energy is a preferred hallmark for change.

When working with a resistant environment, giving energy and time improves the diagnostic process by clarifying how personal, social, and organizational constraints limit or enhance the expression of energy. The goal of the diagnostic process is to see how the organization can free up energy. The risk in managing entry with a resistant organization is that the consultant's own energy may be consumed. *The task centers upon conserving the psychologist's resources while attempting to identify how the setting not only can conserve its resources but also redirect them to create a more active and responsive environment.* Examples of four skills involved here are: an assessment of the organization's ability to use both personal and economic resources, identifying how the setting integrates and balances a value for people and for tangible possessions; creating guidelines for the use of resources for each of the major social groupings within the organization, promoting the idea that subgroups can maintain autonomy by having independent yet connected goals; an assessment of how persons and settings within the organization can sanction a redirection of energy, identifying the blend of persons and settings that will be needed to help propel the process; determining how the resources and the energy now devoted to resisting change can be redirected to initiate change, having ideas about the recycling of resources and the relationship of recycling to change. The role of the community psychologist is to minimize threat within the organization while creating a new context for constructive change.

One of the expected outcomes for devoting time and energy is the likelihood that a positive atmosphere for change is set in motion. The psychologist's availability and accessibility during the entry process and the accumulation of social relationships while working on entry creates an atmosphere that some accomplishments are possible. In the resistant environment, there is an added proviso that the positive tone reflects that all subgroupings are involved in the proposed work and that there is at least explicit neutrality about the prospects for some good being accomplished. In the responsive environment, the task is easier, as the work effort encourages members' feelings of well-being and self-confidence.

As mentioned for the other two guidelines, there are also potential negative consequences for a successful management of entry in these two settings. This is also true for committing time and energy. In terms of success in a responsive environment, members can enjoy both the tasks and processes of change so well that they can become advocates for change just for the sake of being for change. Such a perspective may not help the organization to evolve. In a resistant organization, a consequence of successful work is that the community psychologist and the work group, as a result of their mutual commitments, expressed under difficult conditions, become personal friends, and political allies. Working under these crisis conditions can reduce their chances to be accurate observers of the organization. They may have spoiled a chance for themselves to be a resource for the next occasion. By being aware of these consequences, the community psychologist can enjoy the satisfactions of seeing commitments fulfilled in a newly competent setting, whether it is responsive or resistant.

In the resistant organization, continuous, watchful probing ensures that energy is not diffused or absorbed while frequently checking the members' commitment to work on the topic. Knowing how much energy we stimulate and how much energy is generated within a setting is essential for managing entry. In both of these organizations the energy of the outside community psychologist is a useful, a catalytic force. One hallmark for managing entry is to mobilize and generate energy within the organization without the psychologist's energy and commitment either dominating or being wasted.

Conclusion

Here then are three initial guidelines for managing the entry of community work. They are offered as a source of ideas for systematic inquiry. I believe that clarifying these topics can contribute to the unique professional status of community psychology. There is also one other guideline that can serve as a foundation for the other three. It could be termed the *dignity of problem solving*. Carrying out the entry process and attending to these guidelines is aided by a point of view which asserts that problem solving is fun and helpful. Believing that this is so creates a force for implementing these ideas. This belief is energizing. An induced change process is successful when the community psychologist self-consciously verbalizes this problem-solving process and makes it possible for clients to see what problem solving is like and how change comes about. Then both the client and psychologist create a co-joint understanding of what has been accomplished, and certainly *how* it has been accomplished. Mystery and myth are replaced by less comforting but more long-lasting interpretations of events. The community psychologist takes the lead in reflecting, integrating, and communicating the informal efforts at interpersonal and organizational change. The latent power of a problem-solving perspective is visible within a responsive setting. It is possible for problem solving to be explicitly identified by persons in varied roles within different parts of the organization, as members see and benefit from the newly emerging interdependences between each other and their organization.

In the resistant setting, these three guidelines define the preconditions for the *next* effort at working on the dilemmas of the setting. Success, real success, in working with a resistant organization, may not be whether a problem has been solved, but instead noting whether a representative group of people have agreed to work on the problem. The community psychologist's legacy in working with a resistant setting is having persons in the setting committed, poised, and ready to work.

These three guidelines embraced by a problem-solving attitude are offered as activities that will increase our ability to know how to do and to model what we do. I believe that what really transpires when change occurs is that first our methods allow us to frame the problem and give the problem structure, give us our start. *Then our knowledge of process is the medium for change.* If our knowledge of process reflects the anxieties and aspirations of our clients, they adopt our notions of process, and we are permitted to work. As we understand the processes of entry, and the way we impact the settings in which we work, we increase our chances of being perceived, as in fact we wish to be perceived, as reasonable, caring, perceptive resources to the community. These guidelines have been presented with my genuine belief that both the settings in which we work and the persons residing there are the natural resources for change. Our task, when it comes down to it, is to help both open up and then conserve these resources.

The wisdom expressed in the first three lines of a lyric by Sy Oliver and Trummy Young, popularized by the Jimmie Lunsford Orchestra in the mid-1930s, says it best:

> 'Tain't what you do, it's the way that you do it . . .
> 'Tain't what you do, it's the time that you do it . . .
> 'Tain't what you do, it's the place that you do it . . .
> That's what gets results!

Thank you very much for being here. I appreciate very much this honor and the occasion you have given me to think some more about, and say some more about, the field of community psychology.

Notes

An abbreviated version of these comments was presented upon receiving the 1978 Award for Distinguished Contribution to Community Psychology. Many drafts of the initial manuscript were patiently typed by Mrs. Susan Evans, Secretary to Dean, School of Community Service and Public Affairs, University of Oregon. Initial drafts also benefited from the thoughtful and critical comments of Christine Axelrod, Larry Baker, Rick Brown, Pollyann Jamison, Kathy Finnell, Jack Glidewell, Bart Hirsch, Ricardo Muñoz, Paul Schlueter, Lonnie R. Snowden, Julie Steinmetz, Dave Todd, Norm Sundberg, and Marc Zimmerman. Their investment not only improved the manuscript, but encouraged me to keep improving it. Final preparation of the manuscript was completed while a Fulbright Guest Professor, University of Osnabrück, Federal Republic of Germany. Sue R. Kelly plunged in, took time from her own sabbatical, and working from green marks of marginal penmanship on yellow sheets, prepared a typed revision. Mrs. Gudrun Chafik, the multilingual Secretary of Fachbereich 3, Universitat Osnabrück, produced a final manuscript under the pressure of other commitments, in record time, while gently probing me to improve my German and English.

1. The meanings and interpretations I have given to the ecological perspective have been influenced and stimulated by the empirical research, essays, and conceptions of many. Persons whose published work and, in some instances, personal conversations with me have had a compelling attraction are: Roger G. Barker, Gerald Caplan, René Dubos, Clifford Geertz, John C. Glidewell, Walter Goldschmidt, Robert L. Kahn, Daniel Katz, Erich Lindemann, David Mechanic, Eugene P. Odum, Howard T. Odum, Harold L. Raush, Seymour B. Sarason, and Robert W. White.

2. John C. Glidewell (1976), in an enlightening essay, presented three criteria for induced social change, one of which focused on communication (linkages) with other organizations. I believe that this criterion is particularly apt for describing the entry process with a responsive environment.

References

Cotton, C., Browne, P. F., & Golembiewski, R. (1977). Marginality and the OD practitioner. *Journal of Applied Behavioral Science, 13,* 493–506.

Dunham, H. W. (1977). Community as process: Maintaining the delivate balance. *American Journal of Community Psychology, 5,* 257–268.

Fairweather, G., Sanders, D., Tornatsky, L., & Harris, R. (1974). *Creating change in mental health organizations.* New York: Pergamon Press.

Franklin, J. L. (1976). Characteristics of successful and unsuccessful organization development. *Journal of Applied Behavioral Science, 12,* 471–492.

Glidewell, J. C. (1976). A theory of induced social change. *American Journal of Community Psychology, 4,* 227–239.

Kaplan, R. F. (1978). States in developing a consulting relation: A case study of a long beginning. *Journal of Applied Behavioral Science, 14,* 43–60.

Lambert, M. J., De Julio, S. S., & Stein, D. M. (1978). Therapist interpersonal skills: Process, outcome, methodological considerations and recommendations for future research. *Psychological Bulletin, 85,* 467–489.

Pearl, A. (1974). The psychological consultant as change agent. *Professional Psychologist, 5,* 292–298.

Riecken, H. W. (1977). Principal components of the evaluation process. *Professional Psychologist, 7,* 392–410.

Sarason, S. B. (1978). The nature of problem-solving in social action. *American Psychologist, 33,* 370–380.

Zeisel, J. (1978). *Designing: Images, presentations, tests.* Unpublished manuscript.

Netherlands Institute for Advanced Study in the Humanities and Social Sciences, Wassenaar.

Publications of James G. Kelly

Books

With Baldwin, J. A. (1962). *Community mental health and social psychiatry: A reference guide.* Cambridge, MA: Harvard University Press.

With Grosser, C. E., & Henry, W. F. (Eds.). (1969). *Nonprofessionals in the human services.* San Francisco: Jossey-Bass.

With Muñoz, R. F. (1975). *The prevention of mental disorders.* Homewood, IL: Learning Systems.

[1978]. *Adolescent boys in high school: A psychological study of coping and adaptation.* Hillsdale, NJ: Lawrence Erlbaum Associates.

With Muñoz, R. F., & Snowden, L. R. (Eds.). (1979). *Research in the community: Methods, processes and outcomes.* San Francisco, CA: Jossey Bass.

Articles

[1964a]. Graduate training in community mental health. In *Pre-conference materials* (Prepared for Conference on the Professional Preparation of Clinical Psychologists). Washington, DC: American Psychological Association. Also appears in Lubin, B., & Levitt, E. E. (Eds.). 1967. *The clinical psychologist: Background roles and functions.* Chicago: Aldine.

[1964b]. The mental health agent in the urban community. In Group for the Advancement of Psychiatry (Ed.), *Urban America and the planning of mental health services.* New York: Author. Also appears in Bindman, A. J., & Spiegel, A. D. (Eds.). (1969). *Perspectives in community mental health.* Chicago: Aldine.

[1965]. The community mental health center and the study of social change. In J. R. Newbrough (Ed.), *Community mental health: Individual adjustment or social planning?* (NIMH, U.S. Public Health Service Publication No. 1504). Washington, DC: U.S. Government Printing Office.

[1966]. Ecological constraints on mental health services. *American Psychologist, 21,* 535–539. Also appears in Bindman, A. J., & Spiegel, A. D. (Eds.). (1969). *Perspectives in community mental health.* Chicago: Aldine; and Cook, P. E. (1970). *Community psychology and community mental health: Introductory readings.* San Francisco: Holden-Day.

[1967]. Naturalistic observation and theory confirmation: An example. *Human Development, 10,* 212–222.

[1968]. Towards an ecological conception of preventive interventions. In J. W. Carter Jr. (Ed.), *Research contributions from psychology to community mental health.* New York: Behavioral Publications. Also appears in Adelson, D. E., & Kalis, B. L. (Eds.). 1970. *Community psychology and mental health.* Scranton, PA: Chandler.

[1969]. Naturalistic observations in contrasting social environments. In E. P.

Willems & H. L. Raush (Eds.), *Naturalistic viewpoints in psychological research.* New York: Holt, Rinehart & Winston.

[1970a]. Antidotes for arrogance: Training for community psychology. *American Psychologist, 25,* 524–531. Also appears in Denner, B., & Price, R. H. (Eds.). 1973. *Community mental health, social action and reaction.* New York: Holt, Rinehart & Winston.

[1970b]. The quest for valid preventive interventions. In C. D. Spielberger (Ed.), *Current topics in clinical and community psychology* (Vol. 2). New York: Academic Press. Also appears in Division of Community Psychology (27) of the American Psychological Association. (1971). *Issues in community psychology and preventive mental health.* New York: Behavioral Publications.

[1971a]. The coping process in varied high school environments. In M. S. Feldman (Ed.), *Buffalo studies in psychotherapy and behavioral change.* No. 2, Theory and research in community mental health. Buffalo: State University of New York at Buffalo.

[1971b]. Ecological programs go beyond clinical services. In J. S. Cohen (Ed.), *Confrontation and change: Community problems of mental retardation and development disabilities.* Ann Arbor, MI: University of Michigan.

[1971c]. Training in community psychology at the University of Michigan. In N. J. Matulef, K. E. Pottharst, & P. J. Rothenberg (Eds.), *The revolution in professional training.* St. Louis, MO: National Council on Graduate Education in Psychology.

[1971d]. Qualities for the community psychologist. *American Psychologist, 26,* 897–903.

[1972a]. Coping and adaptation to the high school environment. In W. S. Mitchell (Ed.), *Environmental design: Research and practice.* Los Angeles: University of California.

[1972b]. Moving to a psychology for community service. In I. Iscoe (Ed.), *Mental health in the Americas.* Austin, TX: Hogg Foundation for Mental Health.

[1975]. Community psychology: Some priorities for the immediate future (invited editorial). *Journal of Community Psychology, 3,* 205–209.

[1976a]. In honor of John Calvin Glidewell. *American Journal of Community Psychology, 4,* 222–227.

[1976b]. Synergy: Making it happen. In B. Boldt et al. (Eds.), *Synergy '76.* Eugene, OR: Center of Leisure Studies.

[1977a]. Community psychology: Ecological approach. In B. B. Wolman (Ed.), *International encyclopedia of psychiatry, psychology, psychoanalysis, and neurology* (Vol. 3). Boston: International Encyclopedia.

[1977b]. In honor of Ira Iscoe. *American Journal of Community Psychology, 5,* 132–137.

[1977c]. The search for ideas and deeds that work. In G. W. Albee & J. M. Joffe (Eds.), *Primary prevention in psychopathology.* Hanover, N.H.: University Press of New England.

[1977d]. Varied educational settings for community psychology. In I. Iscoe, B. L. Bloom, & C. D. Spielberger (Eds.), *Community psychology in transition.* Washington, D.C.: Hemisphere Publishing.

[1979]. Creating power and reducing constraints. In S. Cooper & W. F. Hodges (Eds.), *The field of mental health consultation.* New York: Human Sciences Press.

[In press]. Some "learnin's" from doing community work. In T. R. Vallance & R. M. Sabre (Eds.), *Society's stepchildren: Mental health services in transition.*

With Blake, R. R., & Stromberg, C. E. (1957). The effect of role training on role reversal. *Group Psychotherapy, 10,* 95–104.

With Dimonto, J., & Gottlieb, B. H. (1972). The community as teacher. In D. M. Fluornoy (Ed.), *The new teachers.* San Francisco: Jossey-Bass.

With Edwards, D. N. (in press). Coping and adaptation: A longitudinal study. *American Journal of Community Psychology.*

With Ferson, J. E., & Holtzman, W. H. (1958). The measurement of attitudes toward the Negro in the South. *Journal of Social Psychology, 48,* 305–317.

With Gelfand, S. (1960). The psychologist in community mental health: Scientist and professional. *American Psychologist, 15,* 223–226. Also appears in Bobbs-Merrill Reprint Series in the Social Sciences (Xerox XIP) *Readings in Psychology,* p. 458.

With Gelfand, S., & Glidewell, J. C. (1961). Santé mentale et éducation des parents aux Etats-Unis. *Informations Sociales, 12,* 35–38.

With Henry, W. E., Friedman, A. S., & Mitchell, H. E. (1967). The American Psychological Association Committee on Relations with the Social Work Profession, 1950–1966: A summary report. In B. Lubin & E. E. Levitt (Eds.), *The clinical psychologist.* Chicago: Aldine.

With Mills, R. C. (1972). Cultural and social adaptations to change: A case example and critique. In S. Golann & C. Eisdorfer (Eds.), *Handbook of community mental health.* New York: Appleton-Century-Crofts.

With Newbrough, J. R. (1962). A study of reading levels in a population of school children. In J. Money (Ed.), *Reading disability: Progress and research needs in dyslexia.* Baltimore: Johns Hopkins Press.

With Snowden, L. R., & Muñoz, R. F. (1977). Social and community interventions. *Annual Review of Psychology, 28,* 323–361.

With Trickett, E. J., & Todd, D. M. (1972). The social environment of the high school: Guidelines for individual change and organizational redevelopment. In S. Golann & C. Eisdorfer (Eds.), *Handbook of community mental health.* New York: Appleton-Century-Crofts.

Reviews

[1967]. Concepts of community psychiatry: A framework for training, S. E. Goldston (Ed.). *Contemporary Psychology, 12,* 485–486.

[1968]. Mental health volunteers: The expanding role of the volunteer in hospital and community mental health services, P. L. Ewalt (Ed.). *Contemporary Psychology, 13,* 138–139.

[1970]. Handbook of psychiatric consultation, J. J. Schwab. *Contemporary Psychology, 15,* 361–362.

[1971a]. Career guidance, who needs it, who provides it, who can improve it, E. Ginsberg et al. *Monthly Labor Review, 94,* (11), 75–76.

[1971b]. Community dynamics and mental health, D. C. Klein. *Community Mental Health Journal, 7,* 78–79.

[1971c]. The nonprofessional revolution in mental health, F. Sobey. *Monthly Labor Review, 94*(2), 81.

[1971d]. People in context: Measuring person-environment congruence in education and industry, G. G. Stern. *Contemporary Psychology, 26,* 320–323.

[1972]. An introduction to social psychiatry, R. J. Arthur. *Contemporary Psychology, 17,* 540.

[1974a]. Community mental health consultation and crisis intervention, R. K. J. Singh. *Community Mental Health Journal, 10,* 475–477.

[1974b]. Practical aspects of mental health consultation, J. Zusman & D. L. Davidson. *Community Mental Health Journal, 10,* 475–477.

[1975]. Qualities of community life, R. G. Barker & P. Schoggen. *Contemporary Psychology,* 1975, *20,* 193–195; and (1974). *American Journal of Community Psychology, 2,* 399–403.

[1976]. The practice of mental health consultation, F. V. Mannino, B. W. Maclennan, & M. F. Shore (Eds.). *Contemporary Psychology, 21,* 838–839.

[1978]. Psychology and community change, K. Heller & J. Monahan. *Contemporary Psychology, 23,* 296–297.

8

Seven Criteria When Conducting Community-Based Prevention Research

A Research Agenda and Commentary

Reflections

In 1986, the Prevention Research Branch at NIMH was created under the direction of Mort Silverman. Silverman and Jane Steinberg, a psychologist in the branch, brought together 18 scholars to focus on the methods and strategies for doing prevention research. The scholars represented various points of view from a range of disciplines. A summary of the presentations was included in a U.S. government publication, "Preventing Mental Disorders." I was asked to be a contributor to the conference and the publication.

I chose to emphasize topics the investigator focuses on before doing the prevention research. As Silverman and Steinberg say in their introduction, "James Kelly's perspective is one of a seasoned community-based researcher who champions the necessity of knowing your audience before you intervene. His contributions provide practical methods for initiating and maintaining community involvement in preventive intervention research." This is an accurate characterization of what I attempted to do in my comments.

In her book One Writer's Beginnings, *novelist Eudora Welty had recently published three of her lectures to the Harvard University Graduate Program in the History of American Civilization titled "Listening," "Learning to See," and "Finding a Voice." I thought that these ideas were terrific departure points for my presentation, so I anchored my presentation to them. I do not know if she would have agreed with my translation to prevention, but I referred to listening as the capacity to dig into the lives, events, and social settings of participants before the preventive intervention. By "learning to see," I advocated that the professional grasp the interdependence between the status of individual's lives and their contexts. And for "finding a voice," I meant the commitment to follow up to assess the impact of the intervention. These were ecological ideas without explicitly employing the ecological words. This paper derived from Eudora Welty's thesis.*

My concern was not just with the style of the work but also the processes of community-based research, especially with tackling topics that are often beyond the current reference point of the investigator. At the time, social scientists and most health researchers were operating from a positivistic frame of reference, rather than viewing research as a potential resource to the host community.

The ideas expressed then were a continuation of the concepts presented in the award address several years ago and mentioned in chapter 7. I felt confident about these ideas because I was seeing them bear fruit in my own work. Without a trusting and educated relationship with the host community, any intervention was likely to be limited, fragile, and ephemeral. Our task as prevention, community-based scientists was to include issues of process along with content, methods, design, and analysis. At the time, phrases like the "research relationship," "trust," and the "research process" were not yet part of research, professional practice, or conventional wisdom.

There is more appreciation of these ideas today. I was grateful for the invitation to be present at this conference and for the opportunity to speak with colleagues about issues I considered helpful to the aims of prevention research. As I recall, the audience had an uneasy response to my comments. Linking a novelist's ideas to scientific research was questionable, no doubt. Yet I felt that I was on the right track. The seven criteria still have merit today. My colleagues and I developed these ideas further in a book titled A Guide to Prevention Research: First Steps, which is not excerpted here but can be referred to for further detail.

Prevention research is compelling and challenging and relatively new in the mental health professions. Doing prevention research creates the opportunity to develop a genuine science of community mental health. To develop such a science, however, mental health research will need to be carried out differently.

The following seven criteria are proposed as agenda to develop knowledge that can contribute to the design of community-based preventive interventions.

One of the major generalizations, emerging across several disciplines, that bears directly on the topics of community mental health and prevention is the relationship between social support and self-direction and health. With options for self-direction and social support, persons have a predictable increase in health (Berkman, 1984; Brownell & Shumaker, 1984, 1985; Cohen & Syme,

1985; Cohen & Wills, 1985; House, 1981; Kahn, 1980, 1981; Kelly et al., in press; Kohn and Schooler, 1983; Whittacker & Garbarino, 1983).

The following guidelines are presented on the assumption that research that continues to elaborate the empirical meaning of personal and social-setting factors as they relate to social support and social direction provides a major watershed for the creation of preventive interventions.

Certainly, promoting *mental health* is a uniquely different activity from preventing *mental illness*. Both self-direction and social support increase the likelihood that the individual can withstand stress. Ideally, prevention research selects variables and conducts inquiries that enhance our understanding of these topics. Doing research that illuminates the qualities of persons and social settings that promote or facilitate social support is appealing, because it affirms that empirical inquiry can be useful to individuals and can serve as a basis for public education. The assumption I am making is that the study of social support and self-direction is enriched by close and sustained relationships between the research staff and the participants.

Prevention research in the field of mental health, with a simultaneous commitment to assess personal and environmental variables, and with an allegiance to and search for both scientific quality and public benefit, is likely to be perceived as divergent and unorthodox. Designing empirical inquiries for variables that affect health status require *new* methods of inquiry, *new* modes of analysis, *new* styles of communicating and working with participants, and *new* criteria for evaluating research findings. Prevention research is not just a new topical interest or a new way of doing applied research; it is very much a new paradigm for doing basic research. I believe the agenda presented below provides an optimistic meaning of prevention research. These attributes are my response to the challenge of conducting prevention research.

Ideas initiated by Eudora Welty, the novelist and story writer, inspired my rationale for the paradigm. She gave three lectures to the Harvard University Graduate Program in the History of American Civilization titled *Listening, Learning to See*, and *Finding a Voice* (Welty, 1984). While these titles referred to her personal growth as a writer, I believe these concepts are also central to the evolution of prevention research.

Listening can refer to the capacity and commitment of the research community to dig into the lives, events, and social settings of participants before developing or designing a research agenda. Prevention research depends upon engaging, tuning into, and attending to the lifestyles, aspirations, and plights of citizens in the communities where the research is to begin.

Learning to see can refer to grasping the interdependence between the status of individuals' welfare and the context in which individuals live. This concept can also guide our understanding of the relationship between social policies and the plight of individuals, and help us appreciate the necessity of articulating for the research staff and the participants the stages of the research process.

In prevention research there is validity in "seeing" relationships between the research staff and those activities that are initiated to clarify and integrate the entire research activity, e.g., to enrich the rapport between the scientific activity and the research participants in their natural setting.

Finding a voice can represent a commitment to follow up the research activity with explicit efforts to clarify the impact of the research process on policies and outcomes, e.g., how a collaborative process between the research staff and participants will increase the chances of both short- and long-term benefits for the participants, their kin, friends, and support group members.

For me, these three concepts of Eudora Welty present the essence of the concept of prevention research and relate to the following guides for conducting community-based prevention research.

1. Select Variables That Illuminate Developmental Processes for Individuals, Groups, and Organizations

Preventive interventions depend upon knowledge of how persons, groups, and organizations evolve over their life span. Preventive interventions can be misguided and misplaced if this knowledge is inadequate. This guideline recommends more inquiries about growth and maturation processes, especially more longitudinal research, which specifically assess the *processes* of development as well as the qualities of individuals over time. A critical feature of such longitudinal research is developing, prior to data collection, an explicit framework to assess changes over time. Research related to preventive interventions cannot depend simply on the collection of descriptive data at different times, but instead must ascertain which qualities of social settings and which developmental life tasks are salient for persons of different genders, ethnic backgrounds, and social status positions at different times.

This point goes to the heart of the concept of preventive interventions. Developmental and organizational processes over time must be considered in order to select evaluation criteria congruent with the individual's gender, ethnic background, and social status in the future. A preventive intervention is expected to have an impact at some time in some specific social setting.

One of the deficiencies in formulating goals for prevention research is that interventions are often planned to be salient for *all* persons, independent of gender or ethnic status. I'm arguing that we need to know more about the varieties of developmental processes before affirming any particular intervention as valid or useful.

A related aspect of studying developmental processes is choosing specific attributes that are salient for specific groups of persons. Resiliency, for example, is considered basic for assessing mental health functioning at various stages of the life cycle. Other attributes may be salient for specific developmental phases. For example, *tolerance of ambiguity* may be important for the early adolescent who is challenged to respond to a variety of social situations with a minimum of experience to provide a frame of reference. The validity of such terms as "resiliency" and "tolerance of ambiguity" should be specified not only by conventional means, but also by elaborating how intrapersonal, interpersonal, family, and organizational variables contribute to their meaning—how antecedent events contribute to the validity of a specific term at a particular time for a particular person. This point reaffirms the concept of representative design expressed by Egon Brunswik three decades ago (Brunswik, 1956).

Eudora Welty's concept of listening is particularly apt for community-based prevention research, which must identify the experiences of nonwhite and foreign-born persons in the United States who, as a necessity rather than an option, have had to construct both white and ethnic cultural perspectives. In order to understand the origins of later adaptive behavior, prevention researchers need to understand the socialization processes that enable persons to learn several potentially competing value systems. Different cultural origins may create both different constraints and different opportunities to elaborate the meaning of a particular psychological construct. For example, loyalty to family versus career may be a particular source of anguish for nonwhite persons attempting to improve their social status. Adopting this principle helps to ensure that no single standard of research or research paradigm should prevail. Incorporating what we learn about the antecedent processes of social development can counter criticisms that prevention research is potentially intrusive, elitist, or prescriptive.

The main idea I am expressing here is that individuals should be assessed in terms of how they work through life events. Prevention efforts cannot even implicity suggest that certain behaviors are preferred without clarifying the varied routes and steps that persons take in development. Prevention research thus depends upon a rigorous, culturally sensitive analysis of the diversity of developmental stages for individuals.

2. Assess Social Settings and Persons Simultaneously

The legacy of public health plus the increasing amount of environmental research suggests that social factors *do* impact the behavior of individuals (Stokols & Altman, in press). Organizations and social settings can stifle and limit individual initiative and reduce motivation and morale. For prevention research, this means that social settings should be assessed simultaneously with the assessment of individuals. One implication of this idea is that investigators cannot restrict their work to a variety of assessments of individual differences, but rather are obliged to anchor empirical inquiry about individuals with assessments of these individuals as they function in social settings.

A conceptual framework is necessary to generate hypotheses about which qualities of social settings will affect which persons differently. Because the aim of prevention work is to carry out activities that have potential positive impact upon individuals and groups, we must develop knowledge about how the behavior of individuals in different social settings can affect the quality of social interaction. In particular, prevention research staff should look for those person–setting interactions that affect opportunities for self-direction and that affect the quality of social support.

Opportunities for informality within organizations provide the energy for persons to perceive each other as resources, for group barriers to break down, and for social norms of cohesiveness to anchor the groups' behavior. Informality may also engage persons who otherwise would be perceived as shy or marginal. Informal social settings make it possible for everyone to know one another independent of social status. Settings with social norms for informality can generate positive socialization outcomes for members of the group. Informal groups are expected to be satisfying and are able to take advantage of individual preferences and unique qualities. These qualities cycle back to the group and thereby acknowledge the values of self-direction and social support.

From the point of view of prevention research it is important and useful to know what personal qualities contribute to the emergence and maintenance of informality in social settings. For example, what personal variables relate to behaviors that nurture and sustain informal group norms? Are different individual variables salient for different genders and ages and ethnic perspectives? How do concepts like resiliency and tolerance of ambiguity contribute to the expression of informality? What additional qualities of persons contribute to generating an atmosphere of informality? What about such qualities as "presence," affability, sense of humor, and ability to engage authority? Are such qualities indeed complementary with the informal qualities of groups? What events within informal transactions are particularly catalytic when creating a social norm of informality? How do spontaneous or planned celebrations affect the expression of informal contagion? How can such occasions be understood as opportunities to enhance commitment to group goals? These questions are examples of trying to specify the interdependence between persons and social settings.

Another important aspect of environmental assessments of social settings is determining how resources are made available to increase options for innovation within the organization. The resourceful organization is expected to create socially supportive settings for members to pursue their work roles with a spirit of self-direction. Social settings that include social support, where there is evidence of reciprocal exchanges of emotional support and tangible aid between members, increase the opportunities for the participants to invest in their work roles. Persons are expected to seek self-direction when they have autonomy to do so.

One long-term contribution of prevention research is to point to qualities of persons and social settings that make it possible for *both* individuals and social setting to develop. To achieve this aim, more specific knowledge is required about how individuals and organizations can be coupled to engage in this mutual enterprise. Without empirical verification, the risk is that such values can be absorbed quickly into the culture and end up as enunciations of a preferred personal philosophy, idea, or hypothesis. A challenge of prevention research then is to provide clarity for how persons and social settings mesh.

3. Develop Methods to Assess Reciprocal Effects Between Persons and Social Settings

Community-based prevention programs can thrive, i.e., can increase social opportunities for acquiring interpersonal competencies, to the extent that the participants are embedded in a milieu that supports such goals and where the social networks are operative and lasting. Designing community-based prevention programs depends upon knowing precise ways to ascertain how the chain and sequence of interactions between individuals, and between individuals and social settings, affect each other in a reciprocal manner. More understanding is needed about the personal or social-setting variables that affect or maintain qualities such as "trust," "initiative," "assertiveness," and "sense of humor." It is not yet known, however, how such individual qualities influence such behaviors, or under what social conditions these individual qualities can be expressed, or how organizational qualities can either strengthen or reduce the expression of these qualities. How these qualities affect, stimulate, and activate informal peer groups and other interpersonal and social relationships is a basic datum in prevention work.

An important topic for understanding reciprocal effects is the extent to which personal qualities are susceptible to social influence. How are personal qualities like resiliency affected by friends, peers, or persons in authority? To what extent can group norms enhance the expression of resiliency? How many persons in a chain of interdependent relationships can affect the resiliency of the network? What properties of the structure of friendship and social support groups affect the staying power of a resilient reciprocal network? Answers to such questions can help explain not only the operation of informal group structures and how such structures evolve to create a resource group, but how the quality of informality affects the initiation and preservation of other social support functions. Some close-knit reciprocal units may be convoluted and preoccupied with their own internal worlds while others may guide their mutuality toward other aspects of the larger culture. A latter group, with its outward perspective and inward solidarity, may be a social force for generating personal and group self-efficacy and thereby attract new members with high levels of self-direction.

These ideas when tested can evaluate the unique qualities of preventive interventions to stimulate self-initiated, self-help movements for personal and community development. Testing these hypotheses will require prevention research to create new methods to assess concepts of individual and social settings that are stated in compatible terms. It is important to know not only how people are tied to one another, but how they are coupled and integrated within a social setting. Such exploration may enable us to redefine qualities such as commitment of the individual to the social setting and the social settings' commitment to the individual. How are members of an organization interdependent so as to generate shared values and social norms for commitment? How does social support increase personal commitment to a social setting? Studies of only organizational values or personal leadership are not sufficient. Rather the suggestion here is to identify the social structures that are needed by both individuals and organizations to instill energy and engagement. New members will be able to emotionally commit themselves to the organization to the extent that key leaders of local organizations themselves and other members who are testing their commitment to the organization are members of active reciprocal support systems.

Self-direction and social support are expected to be valued and visible in how members assume informal roles as they pass on their reciprocal ties to the next generation of members. The effect on the chain is that opportunities are then available for new forms of reciprocity to be communicated as solidarity is being established. Reciprocal social units are expected to be the source of untapped resources and energy for self-direction and social support. Knowledge of reciprocal ties is proposed as the watershed to learn how individual and group competencies emerge and develop.

4. Create Social Settings for Participants to Contribute and Benefit From the Research

Listening to participants is a continuous process that includes investment of time by the research staff prior to the design of the research. Creating informal social occasions for the participants to be active and thoughtful "consultants" gives the research staff occasions to learn about the unique and salient aspects of the participants' culture. A second benefit is that the research staff can demystify the research activity and help the participants understand standards for interpretation for error and bias of data. Third, the participants can work with the research staff to create or adapt research methods to the particular setting. These discussions with participants can ensure that the key topics and variables have been grounded within participants' milieu. Fourth, the research staff along with the participants can then develop a set of ground rules so that the research findings will be useful in generating mental health policies, e.g., helping to improve conditions related to the quality of life of the participants. Participants should not be "subjects" but persons who share choices about the research agenda and the potential significance of the work.

Such social settings initially may be awkward and delicate. The research staff's behavior is critical in affecting the tone and spirit of the occasion. Staff will need to consider the culture of the other party in the dialog when discussing research topics. By being openly expressive and seeking out participants, any status differences will not become part of the formal or hidden agenda.

Implementing this guideline may inconvenience the research staff by expecting them to give time and effort to interpret, and most of all, understand the points of view of the participants. Nevertheless, this particular principle for prevention research is essential because the research style supports and is congruent with qualities that affect well-being, e.g., self-definition, self-direction, and empowerment. When the research staff increases options of collaboration, the words and spirit of prevention research are consistent. The researchers, with the help of a community advisory board, should select a topic for investigation *that derives from the needs and priorities of the people providing the data.* The best of all possible conditions occurs when citizens seek out the prevention research staff to focus upon a topic that they believe is central to their needs.

One important feature of this collaboration is that the research staff is in a unique and valuable position for identifying how the participants evaluate the concept of prevention. For example, if participants have intense physical symptoms that require immediate treatment, their overriding expectation may be for the research staff to help locate high-quality medical care. After the crisis is passed, opportunities can be created to explore options for prevention efforts focused on the crisis. For those persons with little opportunity to pursue self-direction, the search for health may be premature, as they will understandably want their particular plight addressed. As the research staff works with such participants, the staff can increasingly determine how cultural, gender, and age expectations either limit or enhance the expression of competent behavior as well as illustrate the salience of prevention work.

Prevention work is indeed done within a whirlpool of personal, cultural, and social expectations. If communicating and accommodating with citizens is initiated, then the research will be compatible with the long-term goals of prevention, namely to illuminate qualities of persons, social settings, and social events that promote the expression and interpretation of self-direction and social support.

5. Assess the Direct, Indirect, and Side Effects of Interventions

A major opportunity in designing prevention research is to create methods that can verify the efficacy of interventions. The outcomes of the preventive intervention may not be different from what was expected, but they may be indirect and are expected to generate unknown and unanticipated sequelae. The rationale for this point of view is the thesis that every intrusion by an outside resource to influence an ongoing social system will generate some indirect effect (Kelly, in press). Less developed are research procedures and monitoring devices that look at side effects (Kelly, 1971).

A preferred examination of preventive interventions then is to probe the variety of effects generated from various services or treatments not initiated by the research design. To what extent are preventive interventions intrusive activities? By being self-conscious about the process of prevention research, a framework is provided to examine direct, indirect, and side effects. The penetration or radiating quality of the intervention is clarified by assessing such effects.

During the operation of Head Start programs, besides the direct effect of children increasing their learning skills, occasional mention was made of unintended effects, interpreted as positive events (Kelly, 1977; Fiske, 1975). For example, parents began to assume more leadership in being informed about school policy and began to express preferences to influence policy in contrast to previous nonexistent participation. At the time, this phenomenon was considered as a side effect. Today, with increased attention given to key aspects of the culture of communities, this same result may be considered a direct effect.

What is salient about this example is that increasingly prevention researchers can predict how the participants will be affected by the intervention. The principal investigator can specify the social context and the key members of the participants' setting and envisage both direct and indirect effects of the preventive intervention. Most importantly, the challenge for the principal investigator is to suggest how different persons will be affected differentially by the intervention. To accomplish these aims, the research team must think in terms of not only individuals or organizations, but larger social systems, e.g., not only how various persons and organizations are coupled, but how various social systems are linked together. More knowledge is certainly needed on how persons are interrelated, how role functions are interdependent, and how social processes define how persons *and* roles *and* policies are all tied or not tied together.

Unraveling such connections can have a hidden benefit for the development of prevention theory. Just think how much more we could know about social supports if we could empirically specify just how far social support effects extend. Is social support only a perception of two persons in a dyad? If so, what and how do others in the persons' immediate social world benefit from one dyadic bond of intimacy? How can a person's participation in clubs, voluntary associations, and larger celebrations feed back and influence feelings of well-being and empowerment? How does a socially supportive employer affect the worker and his or her family relationships? How do the spontaneous generosities of neighbors and co-workers influence a personal sense of efficacy? To the extent that prevention research shifts from a study of individuals to the study of reciprocal effects of persons and social settings, it will be possible to grapple with the question of the vitality, staying power, and regenerative quality of an intervention. One criterion then for assessing the effects of an intervention is to assess the *future* performance of social support structures, to examine how the intervention can be assessed as a reservoir for the quality of social *structures* that facilitate or impede the flow of community development. It will be necessary then to predict how social systems "host" interventions and how communities respond with help.

A diagnostic question for future preventive interventions is: To what extent is it possible to know the various processes by which communities embrace, deflect, ignore, or actively resist the implantation of community-based preventive interventions? Most importantly, it is critical to know just how community social structures adapt to externally initiated change, and what factors are involved in resisting or embracing the planned intervention.

A possible outcome in following this principle is that the focus for a preventive intervention can be defined as a common agenda for both scientific and practical purposes by members of different disciplines and members of the local community. The work of applied anthropologists, community organizers, and organizational development resources offer plentiful anecdotes of less apparent, but long-standing effects. Such effects over time can engender in the primary social setting qualities intrinsic to the values of the community without the original intervention being planned to do so. This argues for looking beyond the focal beneficiary and viewing key segments of the community as benefactors. The community and its substructures are looked to for diffusion and fall-out of the intervention. By documenting such effects, it is possible to determine just how much impact the intervention has actually produced.

6. Establish Social Settings to Appraise the Ethics of Interventions

Prevention research can be interpreted as a significant next step in the evolution of mental health services. One risk when engaging in such enlightened activities is that the work can take on an aura of both conventional and unquestioned validity. No matter how thoughtful or well-intentioned prevention research may be, both the research staff and participants need to be aware that *all* prevention activities are interventions.

In a working relationship between the research staff and participants, taking stock of the risks of interventions can be viewed as a natural extension of ongoing work. When this is not the case, where an atmosphere of collaboration and mutual investment in the research enterprise is less apparent, a special citizen-research review group can be created to consider the risks to participants. A particular function of such a review group is to examine the impact of direct and indirect side effects. A side effect of the participants' involvement in such a review group may be that the participants become more conscious of their own health status and education. If a citizen review group adopts the values of the research staff, then it is important to assess how the review group can be encouraged to develop more critical scrutiny so as to reduce premature acquiescence.

A particularly important ethical issue is whether the planned research, either its content or its process, inadvertently makes the participants feel less adequate, or more guilty, or less appreciative of their own culture. An achievement orientation and entrepreneurial bias is often latent in psychological research and interventions. A citizen review process is needed to assess if the research work is unwittingly demeaning or subjugating for the participants.

Subtle forms of mutual accommodation are suspect unless both research staff and citizens work to define just where the values of the participants and research staff clash. Since no tradition has been established for such community review procedures, it will take goodwill from the research staff to stimulate a variety of mutually beneficial procedures. One possible procedure is to form citizen/scientist teams to determine if the research procedures meet the standards of scientific quality and ethnic validity. A possible side effect of this procedure is that team members may become more informed about each other's perspectives and work to integrate their views without grappling with the intrinsic issues of the research.

A potential *positive* side effect of working as a team is that new insights are talked about, new topics for study are cited, and new insights and recommendations are generated for the research staff to consider. In this sense, the review process serves both as quality control and advance planning. The goal of such ethics reviews is to affirm that the research activity is without obvious restrictions and limitations for the participants. In working on these formats to initiate and then preserve ethical inquiry, it is also essential to define ways to protect the research staff so that they can follow their individual intuitions and have the freedom to nominate research topics that meet the primary requirements of scientific merit.

A *negative* side effect of implementing checkpoints for ethics is that the research staff may perceive the review as an irritating requirement. However, as the research staff identifies the theoretical as well as practical benefits, an ethics review can become a source of shared support and equity as the research staff and community participants take on the next study.

7. Create New Organizational Forms for Doing Preventive Research

Conducting research according to the above principles requires a capacity to (1) carry out longitudinal research on developmental processes for individuals, groups, and organizations; (2) create and test hypotheses in terms of the qualities of social settings; (3) develop methods to assess how persons influence and affect each other as well as how persons and social settings are influenced by each other; (4) initiate and then sanction the creation of advisory groups to review the ethics of the particular research activity, with safeguards to ensure that the effects of being participants in the research are not directly injurious or limiting; (5) assess indirect and side effects of the research upon the participants; and (6) devote time and resources to increase opportunities for participants to influence and benefit from the research relationship as well as the research findings.

Two organizations can serve as examples. Each offers a history of accomplishments to assist the development of research enterprises in prevention. The Woods Hole Marine Biological Laboratory has hosted a variety of applied and basic research efforts in biology with the following unique features (Carter, 1967; Conklin, 1968a, 1968b; Kelly, 1970; O'Rand, 1986, 1987; Thomas, 1974). During the summer months, full-time staff convene with visiting scholars in informal conversations about each other's work. The permanent research staff and the visiting research staff report continued benefit from these exchanges. Some of the major directions in biological research over the past four decades were nourished if not initiated in conversations and informal gatherings at Woods Hole. The combination of basic and applied researchers gathered to engage in informal conversations over several months is particularly attractive for the multifaceted work of prevention research in mental health.

A second example is the Framingham Heart Disease Research Project (Brody, 1985). For nearly four decades, this longitudinal research effort has played an influential role in conducting multidisciplinary community-based field trials relating to the correlates of heart disease, as well as the characteristics of persons free of major cardiovascular complications (Castelli, 1981; Kannel, 1978; Phillips, 1983; Savage, 1983). Here the contribution to prevention research is the operation of a research organization designed to carry out a series of multidisciplinary research activities to integrate a variety of multiple assessments of individuals.

Other examples are also appropriate, such as the Midwest Research Station in Oscaloosa, Kansas, where Roger Barker and colleagues have worked over four decades to develop knowledge about social settings of children and adults in one community (Barker & Schoggen, 1973; Barker, in press).

Each of these research organizations shows how a group of investigators can work together to develop new methods. The topic that these organizations stimulate is how the social organization of a research laboratory can be designed to assist the staff to be productive in a social setting in which the social setting itself has been a unique contribution to scientific exploration.

One implication of the above six guidelines is that prevention research requires *new* types of organizations. There is "preventive" value in considering the unique organizational needs of the members before the research is actually planned. There is merit in examining the sources of stress in this type of research so that the research staff are not themselves casualties of this promising but difficult effort.

A substantive issue for prevention research is to document the types of organizational structures that are particularly helpful in carrying out specific research tasks in different communities. The development of prevention research as a scientific enterprise depends on the capacity of the research organization to nurture and facilitate agendas like those outlined above in a variety of locales.

A primary task of prevention research organizations is to orchestrate and harness multiple research activities to ensure that the activities can become a resource for communities. The research leadership in the laboratory should also be aware that different staff working on divergent topics may be unwittingly competitive. In an equally important way, the novelty of the organizational structure and its operation should not create so much ambiguity that the research staff spends their energy on reducing ambiguity rather than emphasizing the substance and process of the research.

Conclusion

Prevention research is different from laboratory investigations of individuals. I have suggested a point of view that includes seven items that specifically focus upon research topics that emerge out of the community. Prevention research differs from other types of research by giving equal attention to issues of scientific merit and community acceptance, and to the various processes of adapting the research enterprise within the community.

Prevention research is an intervention. Interventions require a review process that is self-conscious and deliberate. Prevention research attends to basic variables like the impact of social support and self-direction upon health. Prevention research seeks outcomes where the participants can themselves see the significance of social support and self-direction, not only as salient concepts in reducing negative features of stress, but in enhancing competencies to promote personal well-being for different subgroups within a community.

I have reasoned that prevention research is a new form of basic research addressing such fundamental topics as theories of personal and organizational development, measurements of social settings, and methods for the analysis of side effects.

Since at the present time there are few examples to follow, a period of testing can verify these ideas in new research settings. The research process as well as the various outcomes of the research can be evaluated for their capacity to be accountable to both research peers and participants. The merit of the work can be judged by its capacity to offer insights about relationships between persons and social settings; by its capacity to offer criteria for how ethical standards articulate with research methods; and its capacity to show how a theory can have practical benefits. Each of these efforts is aimed at developing informed citizens and just policies.

References

Barker, R. G., & Schoggen, P. (1973). *Qualities of community life.* San Francisco: Jossey-Bass.

Barker, R. G. (in press). Prospecting in environmental psychology: Oskaloosa revisited. In Stokols, D., and Altman, I. (Eds.), *Handbook of environmental psychology.* New York: John Wiley.

Berkman, L. F. (1984). Assessing the physical health effects of social networks and social support. *Annual Review of Public Health 5,* 413–432.

Brody, J. E. (1985). Heart disease: Big study produces new data. *New York Times,* January 8.

Brownell, A., Shumaker, S. A. (1984). Social support: New perspectives in theory, research, and intervention. Part I. Theory and research. *Journal of Social Issues* 40.

Brownell, A., & Shumaker, S. A. (1985). Social support: New perspectives in theory, research, and intervention. Part II. Intervention and policy. *Journal of Social Issues* 41.

Brunswik, E. (1956). *Perception and the representative design of psychological experiments.* Berkeley: University of California Press.

Carter, L. J. (1967). Woods hole: Summer mecca for marine biology. *Science* 157, 1288–1292.

Castelli, W. P. (1981). *The filter cigarette and coronary heart disease: The Framingham study.* DHHS Publication No. 0-341-030/709. Washington, DC: Supt. of Docs., U.S. Govt. Print. Off.

Cohen, S., & Syme, S. L. (Eds.). (1985). *Social support and health.* New York: Academic Press.

Cohen, S., & Wills, T. A. (1985). Stress, social support, and the buffering hypothesis. *Psychological Bulletin* 98:310–357.

Conklin, E. G. (1968a). Early days at Woods Hole. *American Scientist* 56, 112–120.

Conklin, E. G. (1968b) M. B. L. Stories. *American Scientist* 56, 121–129,

Fiske, B. (1975). Head Start: After 10 years, planning experiments. *New York Times,* June p. 40.

Gonzales, L., Hays, R. H., Bond, M. A., & Kelly J. G. (1983). Community mental health. In Herson, M., Kazdin, A. E., Bellack, A. S. (Eds.), *The clinical psychology handbook* (pp. 735–758). Elmosord, NY: Pergamon Press.

House, J. S. (1981). *Work stress and social support.* Reading, MA: Addison-Wesley.

Kahn, R. L., Katz, D., & Adams, J. S. (Eds). (1980). *The study of organizations.* San Francisco: Jossey-Bass.

Kahn, R. L. (Ed.) (1981). *Work and health.* New York: John Wiley.

Kannel, W. B. (1978, Febuary). Ad hoc committee on cigarette smoking and cardiovascular diseases. *American Heart Association 57*(2): 406A–407A.

Kelly, J. G. (1968). Toward an ecological conception of preventive interventions. In Carter, J. W. (Ed.), *Research contributions from psychology to community mental health.* New York: Behavioral Publications.

Kelly, J. G. (1970). Antidotes for arrogance: Training for community psychology. *American Psychologist 25,* 524–531.

Kelly, J. G. (1971). The question for valid preventive interventions. In Spielberger, C. D. (Ed.), *Current topics in clinical and community psychology* (Vol. 2). New York: Behavioral Publications.

Kelly, J. G. (1977). The search for ideas and deeds that work. In Albee, G. W., & Joffee, J. M. (Eds.), *Primary prevention in psychopathology* Hanover, NH: University Press of New England. 1977.

Kelly, J. G., Dassoff, N., Levin, I., Schreckengost, J., Stelzner, S., & Altman, E. (in press). *A guide to conducting prevention research in the community: First steps.* Washington, DC: Supt. of Docs., U.S. Govt. Print. Off.

Kohn, M. L., & Schooler, C. (1983). *Work and personality: An inquiry into the impact of social stratification.* Norwood, NJ: Ablex Publishing.

O'Rand, A. M. (1986). Knowledge form and scientific community: Early experimental biology at the Marine Biological Laboratory. In Stehr, N., & Bohne, G. (Eds.). *Sociology of the sciences yearbook.* Dortrecht, Netherlands: D. Reidel.

O'Rand, A. M. *Microtubules and macrostructures: Social circles and organizations of biological science.* Manuscript under review.

Phillips, G. B. (1983). Association of hyperestrogenemia and coronary heart disease in men in the Framingham cohort. *American Journal of Medicine 74:*863–869.

Savage, D. D. (1983). Hypertrophic cardiomyopathy and its markers in the general population: The great masquerader revisited: The Framingham study. *Journal of Cardiovascular Ultrasonography 2:*41–47.

Stokols, D., & Altman, I. (In press). *Handbook of environmental psychology.* New York: John Wiley.

Thomas, L. (1974). *Lives of a cell.* New York: Viking Press.

Welty, E. (1984). *One writer's beginnings.* Cambridge, MA: Harvard University Press.

Whittaker, J. K., & Garbarino, J. (1983). *Social support networks: Informal helping in the human services.* New York: Aldine.

9

Generating Social Settings for a Public's Health

Reflections

Erich Lindemann was affiliated with Massachusetts General Hospital from 1954 to 1965. He pioneered concepts in community mental health, consultation, and preventive interventions. The Human Relations Service of Wellesley was one of the earliest community mental health programs, which Lindemann founded in 1948. He was one of the most creative persons I have ever known. I had the pleasure of being a postdoctoral fellow with him from 1958 through 1960. He died in 1974. David Satin, Elizabeth Brainerd Lindemann, and Jean Farrell organized a series of lectures in his honor at the Harvard Medical School. I was asked to give the 10th lecture in 1987. This was a major event for me. I wanted to say something in the spirit of his thinking. The preparation for this event allowed me to extend my thinking to focus on the essential power of social settings for the delivery of preventive mental health services.

I felt good about what I had composed. I was able to emphasize the importance of process when constructing relationships between professionals and citizens as they work together to establish meaningful social structures for services and programs. I presented six ways the concept of social setting could be useful in establishing a social structure for designing preventive services. The ideas, I hoped, paid tribute to the research and thinking of Roger Barker and Seymour Sarason, who had created the groundwork for understanding how communities could be strengthened to withstand stress.

The presentation took place in the Harvard Medical School Library. From the walls hung pictures of Harvard Medical School luminaries, which were rather intimidating. Without using the ecological thesis explicitly, I mentioned the value of professionals being interdependent with citizens to create meaningful social structures and social places for aid and personal validation to take place. Creating communities to reduce casualties was the essence of the com-

munity perspective. Although this may seem idealistic even in today's terms, it is a premise I have carried with me and owned as I have done my work. Linde-mann's ideas have contributed to my silent epistemology for the content and focus of my work. Given the contexts for the loss of a community perspective, I felt the necessity of reminding the mental health professions in attendance that it was not impossible; professionals could commit themselves to genuinely en-gage in collaborative efforts with citizens. This was the heart and soul, as I un-derstood it, of Lindemann's efforts and dreams. I felt as if I was paying him back in a modest way for his inspiration. Today, evidence in the field of community psychology shows that collaborative work with citizens is viable if not vital. I feel redeemed.

A public health approach to mental health services includes a commitment by the mental health professions to explicitly and honestly seek the participation and involvement of citizens. When public health services have been imple-mented there has been clear and tangible evidence that the effectiveness of these programs derives from the quality of the collaborative relationship be-tween professionals and citizens. However, the history of public health ap-proaches in community mental health suggests that most preventive services have been largely dropped upon or applied to the community rather than devel-oped with the community. The unsettling fact is that the substantial benefits of a collaborative relationship are still not recognized either as a core value or as a style of work.

I am in the process of defining the elements and process of a collaborative re-lationship. I am presenting the main ideas here for the first time. These ideas are yet to be tested. I believe that when they are tested they will provide a practical framework for designing, delivering, and evaluating community-based preven-tion programs.

The key concept I offer for creating a collaborative relationship is the concept of social setting. This concept is stimulated by the research of Roger Barker and his colleagues[1] and the writings of Seymour Sarason.[2] The significance of Barker's research for the concept of social setting is that the places where we in-teract have meaning for us and affect our behavior. Sarason argues that the places where we interact become resources for our development. Social settings are means by which we develop relationships, affect our social structures, and stimulate personal, organizational, and community change. They also serve as resources to develop a collaborative relationship between the mental health professions and citizens.

My ideas have benefited from involvement in mental health consultation, which I first learned at the Human Relations Service under the guidance of

Erich Lindemann and Gerald Caplan. My work and that of others demonstrate that the consultative relationship, when it works, is firmly grounded when consultants collaborating with consultees create social settings. Such settings make it possible to create resources for the consultees' organizations and their members.

The six concepts for social settings that I will present focus upon what professionals do when forming collaborative relationships. I assume that the professionals take the initiative.

In using the term *citizen*, I refer to those community residents who are not members of the mental health professions or behavioral sciences, yet are interested in addressing particular social issues or community problems. They are concerned and wish to promote a better climate or condition for themselves, their families, and their communities.

In using the term *professional*, I refer to those members of the mental health professions—psychiatrists, psychologists, social workers, nurses, and others—who are interested in developing community-based mental health programs.

The six concepts address the fact that most professionals are not trained, not socialized, to work in a collaborative mode. Implementing these concepts assumes that professionals, before the collaborative relationships begin, have clear professional identities and wish to expand or revise a particular style of work. Because of the novelty and ambiguity related to the processes of creating social settings, the professionals who engage in this collaborative work are expected to have invested in developing an explicit value system. To cope with the uncertain outcomes, unexpected events, and interpersonal, organizational, and community processes involved in creating settings, professionals require a frame of reference that enables them to be open to collaboration, yet remain clear about and anchored in their personal standards and ethics.

The Concept of Social Setting

By *social setting* I refer to the places and occasions essential to create and symbolize meaningful and satisfying collaborative working relationships between professionals and citizens. I believe that community-based preventive mental health services derive from a collaborative relationship, and not solely from the techniques or methods created by professionals or chosen by citizens to promote mental health. I believe that the very process of creating social settings is a process that can be empowering and thereby preventive. When professionals initiate processes with citizens actively codesigning service delivery, citizens are validated for taking action consistent with good mental health practice. They identify resources, receive support while creating resources, and have the autonomy to use these resources for the development of their own needs and aspirations. Most importantly, the collaborative experience in creating social settings is a resource to develop new social settings in their communities.

Social setting is significant in several ways:

1. A social setting illustrates the power of informal occasions to provide a sense of identification for participants.
2. It derives from a creative process that encourages participants to have a shared experience in doing something new.
3. It illustrates the impact of the constructive and positive qualities of social environments upon participants.
4. It provides an opportunity to reduce ambiguity as professionals and citizens work to form a new relationship.
5. It gives meaning to the collaborative activities of professionals and citizens and validates their working relationship.
6. It facilitates the working relationships without the constraints of only dyadic interactions.
7. It sanctions professionals and citizens to become informed about their community.
8. It encourages others to emulate this collaborative work.
9. Finally, a social setting is a historical marker for the collaborative relationship, defining the work of the participants.

These nine contributions of social settings point to the importance of creating a meaningful structure when professionals and citizens collaborate. The creation of social settings is not just another technique within the practice of community mental health. Such settings derive from the explicit needs and aspirations of the community, as was the case with the successful Rough Rock Many Farms Project, a health care delivery demonstration project undertaken by Cornell University and the Navajo tribe. The findings of this project do not emphasize the techniques used, but the quality of the relationship created between the physicians and anthropologists and the tribe (see J. Adair & K. W. Deuschle, *The peoples' health: Anthropology and medicine in a navajo community* [New York: Appleton-Century-Crofts, 1970]). The basic challenge for the collaborative relationship is for the professional and citizens to know enough about the community so that the social settings generated are clearly derived from the community.

I propose six concepts to facilitate the communication between the two "cultures" of professional and citizen. Each concept addresses the processes that assist the collaborative relationship as well as the generation of social settings for a public's health. They reflect the evolutionary nature of the collaborative relationship. The first three processes refer to beginning the relationship: (1) engaging the citizen world and appreciating its settings, (2) receiving sanction to explore the formal and informal settings of the citizen's community, and (3) redefining some functions of current social settings. The next three processes relate to the collaborative working relationship: (4) creating new social settings, (5) validating and celebrating social settings, and (6) creating social settings to exchange resources. The six processes act synergistically to create a social process to establish and embed a social structure for community health.

The Engagement Process: The Ability to Appreciate the Social Settings of Citizens

The first important social setting is one that makes it possible for professionals to interact with citizens interested in creating a community-based prevention program. A key to the engagement process is that the professionals spend time in the citizens' communities to gain information about them. By devoting an expenditure of time and effort in key social settings of the community professionals thus begin to know the citizens and learn about their unique values, norms, and working style. Most importantly, professionals learn the cultural, social, and economic constraints and pressures that face these citizens. The initiative taken by the professionals to engage the social settings communicates concretely the professionals' wish and ability to collaborate. They are not behaving as part of an elite class, even though there may be differences in formal education, technical training, or past socialization between them and some citizens. The professionals thus learn that the citizens have a commanding and privileged view of their own culture. The engagement process is genuine and not merely another "technique" for gaining trust and credibility to facilitate the professionals' preferred agenda.

As the professionals engage they seek a place to define the collaborative relationship. Some qualities of such a setting are: (1) Nominations of the place come from citizens. (2) The place selected is convenient and accessible for citizens. (3) There is opportunity for private and informal conversations. (4) It is supportive for all participants. (5) It facilitates rapport between professionals and citizens. In sum, the place should be purposely comfortable for the citizens. Professionals adapt to the community to learn about it and confirm the value of a community-based enterprise.

In moving out of a university, research institute, community organization, or government department, professionals are open and attentive to learning about the various social settings in the community that will be involved in developing collaborative relationships. As they engage they study the way citizens define resources and the criteria employed for using settings in their communities. If the citizens already understand and value the creation of resources it will be easier to create social settings where collaborative relationships can begin.

For professionals to take this step—to engage citizens who may not be academics, who may not have extensive formal education—requires that they pay heed to one of the key elements in defining a consultation relationship: to be alert that citizens will have stereotypes about who the professionals are and what they stand for. When engaging, professionals can draw upon the process of dissipating stereotypes, a process that has been eloquently written about by Gerald Caplan in *Principles of preventive psychiatry* (New York: Basic Books, 1964).

A stereotype can protect citizens from becoming too invested too soon in the collaboration. To enhance collaboration, professionals make explicit their purposes and agendas. They take the initiative in reducing the ambiguity of the engagement process. Frequent citizen concerns are that the professionals are there to use the community, will not be practical or appreciate constraints, will not be interested in what citizens have to say, cannot be counted on if there is trouble, or can't be counted on for time-consuming political negotiations.

Before becoming engaged, professionals think through these possible stereotypes and evolve for themselves positions on these topics. Professionals also should be prepared and capable of tolerating the ambiguity of this process, while also being responsive. The engagement process may be felt as a new and different social relationship, one that is unusually subtle and complex. The frustrations and disappointments over the impact of unpredictable and often uncontrollable events impinging upon the work are aggravated when there are few social settings to help give it structure and meaning.

The engagement process is important because it helps set the tone for developing the working relationship. Professionals' frustrations can be reduced when the work is defined as a relationship with recognition of the process involved in relationship building. Self-consciousness helps anchor the engagement process and prevent anxieties and frustrations. For example, in the collaborative role there isn't immediate feedback for the professionals' work, not all agendas are clear, and not all of the influential actors are known. Professionals are certainly outsiders or at least guests, and unknown quantities. They have to earn acceptance by the citizens.

The engagement process pulls from the professionals personal qualities that may not be engaged in other roles. When they communicate where they stand and listen and learn with humor and fallibility, the collaborative relationship can begin. Most importantly, social norms can take hold for activating the collaborative process.

Getting Sanction to Identify the Informal Settings of the Community

This concept rests on the premise that places that promote and encourage informality, where people can relate to each other outside of their primary occupational roles and in a relaxed manner, are important determinants of effective working relationships. Informal settings facilitate collaborative relationships. Professionals identify those settings that the citizens define as informal.

One bit of expertise that professionals bring to the collaborative relationship is knowledge of the impact of informal settings on individuals and social groups. The concepts of social support, social integration, group cohesiveness, community development, and effective coping can illuminate the influence of informal settings, informal communication and informal relationships upon the satisfaction and effectiveness of individuals and groups. Awareness of informal settings as an important variable assists professionals to encourage citizens to acknowledge those informal occasions, events, and settings that are meaningful for them. In this way professionals and the citizens together can develop a working concept of how social structures affect behavior. As professionals and citizens begin to develop their working relationships and create informal settings for themselves, their collaboration gives the concept of informality genuine meaning. The significance of informal settings for health may not be apparent to citizens. Professionals' ability to emphasize their significance can help establish the health potential of social settings. The very process of discovering the meaning of informal settings adds to their collaborative process. In this, as in the processes in developing settings, professionals take the initiative. They are the reference point in clarifying the various meanings of informality and the ways it can be expressed.

In elaborating this process professionals deal with initial entry, so familiar to consultants and so essential for establishing collaborative relationships. In addition to knowledge about the meaning of informality, professionals are knowledgeable about establishing informal working relationships. They are sensitive and informed about the qualities of persons and settings that help to create a context of informality.

Why is informality important for entry? Informal interactions reflect the level of commitment and interest the participants bring to their primary roles and settings. In many communities the places where informal interaction takes place may not be apparent to the casual observer, as pointed out in the observations regarding work with the Navajo tribe.

Questions about informal settings can allow professionals to serve as resources to citizens by explaining that they are trying to learn about informal occasions. This helps create a relationship in which the citizens are not stereotyping the professionals by believing that they "read minds." In developing answers to questions professionals and the citizens work out shared answers as another dimension of their collaborative relationship.

Some of these questions are: Is being open valued? In what ways do citizens spontaneously kid, banter, joke, tease, laugh with each other? When and in what settings do citizens address each other in more personal ways than their job titles would suggest? How do citizens express joy together? When do citizens walk, talk, and sit together in relaxed ways? Does the conversation include physical gestures and body movements for emphasis? Do the citizens actively listen and respond to each other? Do the citizens want to maintain informality? Do the citizens express—verbally and through gestures—a variety of ways of supporting each other? Are there shared and understood norms sanctioning informal interaction among the participants and the host organization? Do citizens acknowledge that they know something about other relationships? Do the citizens express tolerance for the quirks and idiosyncrasies of others? Do citizens express concern when other citizens are absent? What are the qualities of the persons and settings that make the occasion informal? What factors create opportunities for informal interaction? What are the common needs and incentives that bring people together?

While these questions are not exhaustive, they are guides to phenomena that are important in learning about the informal exchanges among citizens in the community. As professionals engage with citizens and share questions like these, the collaborative relationship can take hold and professionals and citizens define for themselves what is important in knowing about and appreciating informal occasions.

If it becomes apparent that the number and variety of informal social settings is inadequate, professionals work to identify those traditions, styles of interaction, and personal histories that constrain informal behavior. With an appreciation of both the supports and constraints professionals and citizens once again define their relationships to include informal settings. Such informal settings can be a shared reference point for them while they go about the task of creating social settings in the community at large.

The Process of Redefining Social Settings

The first two processes make it possible for professionals to initiate collaborative relationships by engaging the participants in building working relationships and obtaining sanctions to identify an important quality of social settings— their informality. The third process is making it possible for the participants to redefine their space and the way in which settings work, and to create more opportunities for social support and autonomy within their social settings.

This process is an index as to whether the entry process has been completed. During successful entry, citizens and professionals develop a shared appreciation of the citizens' culture and have the sense of integration that derives from experiencing informality. Then citizens and professionals are able to examine the ways in which the settings in which they live and work can be redefined, changed, and adjusted to be more responsive to the participants.

The significance of this process lies in the shared experience of altering a social structure and set of norms that previously had guided the behavior of the participants. It can be an enlightening if not empowering experience when the citizens are able to alter the very social processes in which they engage. The impact of this experience is that the citizens become more invested in collaboration and see its potential benefits.

Redefining new settings is coping with the entropy and inertia that inevitably develops within any group or organization. The process of redefining settings creates opportunities for citizens to generate new roles and new occasions to fill them, in contrast to perpetuating past or current traditions. This process develops the awareness that citizens can be flexible and self-corrective. They recognize that social settings, as well as individuals, can become resources.

In starting a new working relationship people often agree quickly on a given procedure in order to reduce the anxiety from the ambiguity of new relationships, the desire not to offend anyone, to present oneself in a favorable light, and to achieve positive status as a group member. Redefining settings makes it possible for people not to agree or be obliging so fast. Citizens are aware that it is possible to make changes in their social milieu. When they review their own situations and redefine their physical space they have reached the point where they can be comfortable in questioning and revising what they are doing in collaborative relationships. Negotiating this stage suggests that the collaborative process is working.

Here again professionals set the tone by trying out notions, taking the risk of understanding how social settings work, and asking whether there is now sufficient shared experience for the participants to examine what they do need from their settings and from each other. Professionals serve as facilitators for citizens as they define and create resources.

In carrying out this evaluative role professionals can draw upon two major research findings that identify the conditions for facilitating personal effectiveness—the presence of social support and opportunities for autonomy and self-expression. Professionals can also determine the degree to which these findings are salient for a particular group at a particular time.

While professionals and citizens are discussing these functions and revising their activities, they can experience the pleasure of developing new role relationships within the group, both among citizens and between citizens and professionals. The participants have become aware of the hazards and limitations of being trapped in roles or traditions that are not beneficial to them. As they learn how to define, create, use, and expand resources, they acquire a shared understanding of constructing social relationships that are mutually satisfying and add to group effectiveness. An élan can emerge as they see and experience the benefits of trust and self-confidence that come from revising and modifying social practices and roles.

This process of redefining settings generates new energy and therefore new resources for the collaborative relationship. There is now a shared understanding that change is possible. There is now enough structure and interdependence for the participants to create new settings and new opportunities for new role relationships among themselves and with other members of the community. As this third process gets under way, stereotypes have been dissipated and the anxieties of developing new roles and settings reduced. The meaning of a social setting has been experienced by professionals and citizens.

The Creation of New Settings

This is the defining process for generating a public's health. As professionals and citizens explore the promotion of mental health in the community and the prevention of mental illness, the focus is the creation of new social settings.

What new places, what new occasions can be generated to provide actual and symbolic recognition that citizens in the community can create resources for themselves? What are some examples of new settings? When consultants create opportunities for consultees to meet, that can become a social setting because the consultees are challenged to generate relationships among themselves and with consultants. Together they create ways to respond to community issues. Similarly, when the collaborative team of professionals and citizens meets in a church basement to take action to improve crime protection in their neighborhood, that meeting can become a social setting when it provides a supportive structure for the participants to identify their needs and creates an opportunity for them to be a collective resource for themselves. Similarly, when a group of persons invested in policy reform meets regularly to develop a strategy to improve health care delivery, the meetings become a social setting when the participants give public recognition to their shared agenda and serve as a resource to themselves for problem solving. When a group of professionals and citizens agrees to create a new playground, the playground becomes a social setting as it emerges as a place for community interaction as well as a protective site for children's play. *It is a social setting when the physical space takes on multiple and interdependent social, personal, and community functions.* The children's play place has meaning for adults as well as a place to converse and develop a sense of community while identifying shared resources for child care.

In the above four examples the place becomes a social setting as the participants create a new form of social interaction and meaning for themselves around some salient community issue. In this sense people not usually connected to each other create an opportunity to be together and a new social structure for themselves. When a place becomes a social setting there is an expectation that the very act of coming together will generate a social process that enables the participants to identify common needs, to develop a common agenda, and to create a common response.

One difference between a meeting and a social setting is that in a social setting there is self-conscious and shared understanding by the participants about their process. As citizens get together they interact with a recognition that there is a value in helping each other, in combining resources, and in developing an action plan for their future development.

Meetings are often one-time occasions. Generating social settings, by contrast, is part of a community development and organizing process that involves a variety of settings. Social settings give an added meaning to the physical space. It becomes a social space. The notion of space is important because physical space documents the meaning people give to the assigned social space. The social processes involved in the creation and maintenance of the social setting make it possible to activate and maintain the prevention program.

There are some significant by-products generated from the creation of a setting. Some of these are (1) the experience of participatory decision making; (2) the experience of understanding the benefits of a variety of roles to be performed; (3) the experience of developing themes, agenda, and issues for the total group, rather than for any individual or subgroup; (4) the experience of team building; and (5) the experience of engaging and resolving conflict. These by-products provide a shared sense of the change process and a framework for understanding personal experience in creating a social setting.

Techniques provide the content, people provide the skills, and the social setting provides the integration and the validation for the work.

At this point in history there is a compelling need for people to be active participants in a milieu that works for them. Many social structures are only places that confine, limit, restrict, fragment, isolate, and alienate, and are not social settings. Newly created social settings can be an antidote for past experiences of limited self-expression and undeveloped personal integration. Social settings can make it possible for people to be connected in meaningful ways to others while working on tasks that have immediate and long-term benefit for the participants. Social settings can generate a shared belief that people can give and receive support, that they can take action, and that the support they express and the action they take can lead to something. The collaborative relationship between professionals and citizens is activated and confirmed as social settings are generated. During the process of creating such settings participants learn the value of small victories, setting manageable goals, and developing an incremental and sequential frame of reference when developing resources. (See Weick, [1984].) During the process of creating social settings participants experience the self-confidence of personal and group accomplishment that comes from creating new relationships and a new social structure.

My thesis is that new social settings can encourage people to value being resourceful in creating activities and policies that are preventive. New social settings can validate the belief that people have the capacity to address the constraints that limit their development.

The Validation and Celebration
of Settings

Creating a new social setting is a complex, subtle, demanding, and artistic enterprise. The principles for the formation of social settings derive from the unique ecology of the situations in which the participants are living. Because of the uniqueness and special qualities involved in creating social settings there is a need to validate and celebrate that process and the new social setting. Working from the premise of small victories, the participants realize that such victories need and deserve celebration.

If participants do not take time to acknowledge each other and what they have created together, the new social setting may degenerate into a social structure—a place whose original meaning has eroded and where activities take on a predictable, empty, and routine quality.

As part of the collaborative relationship professionals advise citizens to take note of the importance of their work and affirm that the significance of their work resides in the very process of acknowledging it, of taking time out to appreciate, integrate, and applaud what they have created. It is expected that the process of celebration not only makes it possible to symbolically acknowledge their work but also sets the stage for the participants to identify new activities. The social setting then can help generate these new functions. Since there is often a tendency for us to stay with our successes, celebrating provides an occasion to consider the new demands, the new opportunities, the new ecology.

There is more to a celebration than having a party. A social setting for celebration can be an opportunity to assess the collaborative process and the styles of work and problem solving that the participants engaged in to achieve their present status. When the participants generate social norms that encourage a review of past work this consolidation can facilitate the next phase of work. In this phase the participants can explore the reinvestment of their energy and how they can build upon what they have achieved to create resources for their continued development. They can develop informal roles for planning and carrying out the celebration.

The important feature of this celebrating process is that explicit sanction is given to summarize and reflect upon what they have experienced, where they are in their own personal developments, how they view their social settings, and how these evolved. What is examined are the values, the social norms, and the roles that have contributed to the creation of the new setting, reflecting consciously on the elements, events, or processes that have contributed to the group's accomplishments now being honored.

The comments up to this point have focused upon how the participants create social settings. This process is incomplete unless it includes an assessment of settings in the existing community that are serving important "prevention" functions. In fact, the efficacy of the collaborative relationship for preventive work depends upon understanding the value of these "natural" places. While the participants actively create their own process it is essential that they seek out, observe, note, and understand how the natural settings in the community function. Conversations with the members and creators of these natural settings can help identify functions analogous to those the participants are already familiar with. The persons involved in such natural settings can then serve as resources to the participants in the collaborative relationship to help them realize that there are spontaneous processes going on that accomplish the same ends. In this way citizens and professionals in the collaborative process can be less stuffy and self-important, and can put aside the notion that they are unique in their skills in activating settings. Recognizing that there are places and activities ongoing in the community that can create resources for the collaborative relationship *and* noting how these places can become social resources gives real meaning to the concept of social settings.

Celebrations, for both the spontaneous and the generated settings, provide opportunities to revise the collaborative relationships. Acts are celebratory when they are genuine, spontaneous, and derive from the shared experiences accumulated during the creation of the social setting. Celebrations are then integrative. All concerned can have a deep, shared, and explicit occasion to acknowledge that they now realize what they have done: they have created a social place that is unique, palpable, congenial, and validating.

Creating Settings to Link and Exchange Resources

This sixth process clearly reflects the evolution of the collaborative relationship. A criterion to evaluate its effectiveness is the emergence of the previous milieu as an identifiable and coherent social setting. Then the participants of the social setting can create ways to exchange resources with other settings. As they become involved in activities related to the first five processes, they are able to gain power by relating to and influencing other key resources and key social settings.

In this exchange process there is a subtle temperance to be preserved. A likely outcome of the process of creating social settings is that in their self-confirming experience the participants develop an understandable pride in their accomplishments. They can then become complacent, self-absorbed, or even arrogant. Linkage with other resources is an antidote for such hubris, making it possible for them to moderate pride in their own setting and accomplishments.

Another purpose in the creation of resources is to increase opportunities for these resources to be reinfused into the social setting. To make this happen the participants in the collaborative relationship must be willing to think about how resources can be donated or exchanged. This thinking process in itself requires a keen understanding of the workings of social settings. A process must be developed to both facilitate the transfer of resources and incorporate them. In essence there needs to be a ready recipient, a ready donor, and a medium of exchange.

This exchange process requires substantial commitment to understand the meaning and maintenance of social settings without becoming overimpressed with the unique validity of the setting. It is expected that the socialization process that has made it possible for citizens and professionals to evolve their social setting has also developed an appreciation of a diversity of resources. A social setting's capacity to exchange resources contributes to an understanding of adaptation and survival.

The process of creation of social settings is most useful for those who are without resources and the supportive structures to acquire them. A preventive program—engagement, creating informal settings, redefining settings, creating new settings, celebrating, and linking settings—can be initiated as a collaborative process between those who are without these resources and those who have them.

The significance of generating social settings is not just in developing potentially precious relationships between professionals and citizens, but as a practical resource for community development. The process of creating settings can be used to design community-based programs. Those citizens and professionals who have participated in the collaborative relationship and created social settings can now be authentic resources for a larger community development process.

Each of these six processes, then, focuses on the development and empowerment of persons and settings, and the connections of settings as resources. It is expected that the experience that the citizens and professionals gained in generating these various settings can become a resource to other persons and other settings.

Creating social settings for the prevention of mental illness does not just meet the needs of individuals by offering individual solutions. They meet the needs of networks of individuals by creating social supports and social processes that replenish undeveloped or depleted resources.

It is this sixth social setting concept that makes it possible for citizens and professionals together to form a confederation of new resources—other professionals and other citizens—to address important issues of policy reform and formation. A goal for the entire collaborative process is to create a grounded, embedded, connected, and informed group of people who can create social policy for the prevention of mental illness. Such a process develops a variety of resources that can fulfill a "bill of rights" for the mental health of citizens: the activation of sufficient opportunities for social support and social integration.

An Ecological Caveat

Before concluding, I'd like to affirm what is obvious: creating social settings is not simple, predictable, or always fun. There are likely to be some negative side effects. I want to mention a few of them.

The excitement of experiencing meaningful social relationships can be heady and can create an illusion of change. The tough tasks of the process require a resourcefulness and persistence that often staggers or drains us. The pleasure of being in informal settings does not mean that the participants are casual, relaxed, and unreflective. Designing social settings, while invigorating, is intellectually demanding and requires all the inventiveness that professionals and citizens can bring together. Also, the spirit that accompanies the process can be threatening to those observing it from a distance. The response of the participants to others who are not a part of their process can exaggerate this sense of threat or create an appreciation of the experimental nature of the process.

Creating settings also reallocates resources from other activities and reduces the time, money, or energy available to them. Pulling people together to create settings pulls them away from other valid activities. The participants consciously and continuously appraise the benefits and hazards of being involved in creating settings. Each of these limiting or potentially negative effects is anticipated and addressed. At each of the six steps of creating the settings the participants review and reflect upon what has transpired. They consider the possible positive and negative consequences of their work on themselves, their kin, and their friends in their own and other settings.

Conclusion

These ideas represent one approach to the continued development of community-based preventive mental health programs. They are presented as practical and consistent with a public health approach. The unique feature is that mental health professionals work *with* citizens to create places and occasions which then are sources of personal identification, social integration, and community empowerment.

These ideas are derived from a basic conviction that participation in a development process is essential for the well-being of people and organizations. These ideas call for professionals to be resources for the creation of social processes in addition to creating methods and techniques.

A collaborative approach to the design of social settings is corrective to the contemporary plight of fragmentation, isolation, and alienation. By focusing on the social setting, people and social structures are joined, and the shortcomings of individual and societal approaches to prevention are avoided. In creating social settings professionals and citizens are interdependent. The collaborative process not only creates public services but provides communities with networks of public resources.

Notes

This lecture was presented April 24, 1987 at the Francis A. Countway Library of Medicine, Harvard Medical School, Boston, MA.

1. See R. Barker & P. Gump, *Big school, small school* (Stanford, CA: Stanford University Press, 1964); R. Barker & P. Schoggen, *Qualities of community life* (San Francisco, CA: Jossey-Bass, 1973).

2. See S. Sarason, *The creation of settings and the future societies* (San Francisco, CA: Jossey-Bass, 1972).

Suggested Readings

Kelly, J. (1986). Context and process: An ecological view of the interdependence of practice and research. *American Journal of Community Psychology* 14:581–589.

———— (1987). Seven criteria when conducting community-based prevention research: A research agenda and commentary. In *Preventing mental illness: A research perspective*. Washington, DC: U.S. Government Printing Office.

Kelly, J., Dassoff, N., Levin, I., et al. (1988). *A guide to conducting prevention research in the community: First steps*. New York: Haworth.

Kelly, J., & Hess, R. H. (1987). *The ecology of prevention: Illustrating mental health consultation*. New York: Haworth.

Rubenstein, R., Kelly, J., & Maines, D. (1985). The interdisciplinary background of community psychology: The early roots of an ecological perspective. *Newsletter of the Division of Community Psychology, American Psychological Association* 18:10–14.

Schoggen, P., ed. (1987). *Ecological psychology*. Stanford, CA: Stanford University Press.

Weick, K. (1984). Small wins: Redefining the scale of social problems. *American Psychology* 39:40–49.

10

A Contextualist Epistemology for Ecological Research

Reflections

In September 1988, two faculty members from DePaul University, Pat Tolan and Len Jason, with Fern Chertok of Roosevelt University and Chris Keys of the University of Illinois at Chicago organized a conference on research methods and issues. Forty-one scholars plus doctoral students in the Chicago area participated in this event. I was invited to present a paper. I had been thinking more about the underlying philosophical assumptions of ecological thinking. Fortunately, I met Cindy Kingry-Westergaard, a doctoral student in clinical psychology at the University of Illinois at Chicago. She had recently received a master's degree from the Philosophy Department there and transferred to the Clinical Psychology program to work on mind/body topics. She agreed to work with me on preparing the paper for the conference. She was enthusiastic about the philosophical assumptions of ecological thinking and began to bring me treatises that were not just compelling but inspiring. These works persuaded me that I was developing ideas that were philosophically germane.

As I began to draft the ideas for a contribution to the conference, she brought into our discussions material that became the philosophical scaffolding. It was an enriching experience. As a background document she prepared a 100-page statement (edited down to 31 pages) about various philosophical positions and their shortcomings for community psychology. This document was circulated to the participants and received many positive comments. The conference was a highly intellectual occasion with much energetic discussion and debate expressed by participants. I presented the outlines of the ideas in my scheduled 15 minutes, which was frustratingly little time. There was, however, a positive response from the audience.

Then it came time to prepare written comments for the proposed book to be published by the American Psychological Association. The editors, already mentioned, lobbied to have the APA publish the book. It was a real event of acceptance. The first draft of our contribution was twice as long as page length would allow. There were several painful conversations between Cindy, the editors, and me as we boiled down the ideas to the point where I became concerned that there might be no "nutrients" left. The chapter you will read is that abbreviated version. However truncated, the ideas are preserved. Some readers have had difficulty with the compressed nature of the arguments. I hope that the passage of time and the currency of the ideas make it easier to read.

The chapter enabled us to make connections between biology and community psychology as examples of contextualist principles. We were also able to point to connections between ecological and feminist perspectives. One outcome that I had not produced until that time was the 10 theoretical propositions for the interrelationships between persons and settings. Essential elements of an ecological perspective include connections to constructionist premises, collaborative style, and social processes. In spite of its brevity, I believe that these few pages put the ideas together. They are still useful as a framework for ecological thinking. Looking at these ideas again after 16 years, I believe they have merit as asserting the essence of ecological premises. I am also aware of how difficult it is to shift paradigms, especially in the field of psychology with its long-standing emphasis on the study of individuals outside of contexts. I am fortunate that we were given the opportunity to make the statement back then.

We welcome the opportunity provided by this conference to examine the criteria for choosing between different methodologies and conceptual frameworks in Community Psychology. Psychologists, as well as philosophers of science, are now calling for a critical analysis of the theories and methods of empirical research in psychology (Altman & Rogoff, 1987; Ash & Woodward, 1988; Cronbach, 1986; McGuire, 1986; Meehl, 1986; Walsh, 1987). For example, at a 1985 American Psychological Association symposium in celebration of the 1965 Swampscott Conference (Bennett et al., 1966), Altman concluded that:

> Community psychology now needs to reflect on the philosophical issues that are central to any world view—units of analysis, time and change, and philosophy of science. By doing so, the field can enter its next stage of its life with a conscious understanding of its philosophical underpinnings. (1987, p. 627)

Making our philosophical assumptions explicit will facilitate the understanding of multifaceted phenomena in Community Psychology. Without explicit assumptions, researchers run the risk of tacitly endorsing assumptions that they themselves may not consider to be valid, authentic, apt, or robust for conducting research in Community Psychology.

In this chapter, we argue for an *Ecological* approach to community psychology. The guiding force of the Ecological approach is in its commitment to *Contextualism*. Contextualism is the epistemological theory that knowledge is relative to a given empirical and theoretical frame of reference and that we are implicitly embedded in the world we observe. Contextualism acknowledges the responsibility of the observer in choosing a given frame of reference and in justifying the chosen frame of reference. Contextualism requires that one be deliberately aware of the multifaceted nature of the conditions and motivations for the expression of behavior across environmental conditions. Contextualism also requires that observers be flexible in their selection of alternative or complementary methodologies when conducting research across different environmental conditions. Because of their commitment to the human responsibility of the construction of knowledge, contextualists are often called *constructivists* or *pragmatic realists* (Efran, Lukens, & Lukens, 1988; Giere, 1988). The Ecological approach advocates the use of alternative or complementary frameworks and methodologies when conducting community research. We hope to show that such an approach provides the most appropriate postpositivistic framework for characterizing the robust properties of community systems.

Epistemological Theory and Methodology: The Value of Having an Explicit Epistemology

It is now generally agreed, across a wide array of disciplines, that it is impossible to escape the implications of adopting a specific scientific method: The choice of method instructs us to record particular kinds of facts by using certain recognized procedures. Even if we are unaware of our own theoretical biases, we live with their effects. It is now recognized that "the nature of science in different periods has been determined by the methods employed in collecting facts and reasoning about them, and by the prevailing approach to the study of natural phenomena" (Hall, 1966, p. 159).

The history of philosophy of science contains many examples in which epistemological assumptions have affected the practice of science and shaped the evolution of human knowledge (Feyerabend, 1975, 1987; Giere, 1988; Gilligan, 1982; Hall, 1966; Hare-Mustin & Marecek, 1988; Keller, 1987; Lott, 1985; McGuire, 1986; Rose, 1987; Rosnow & Georgoudi, 1986; Suppe, 1974).

Epistemology is the analysis of the weighted importance of the observations, assumptions, and inferences that we make and of the justifications that we give for what we claim to know (Giere, 1988; Kornblith, 1985; Pappas & Swain,

1978; Quine & Ullian, 1970). More often than not, however, scientific disciplines have functioned with only an implicit knowledge of their epistemological assumptions. This has often had the consequence of generating "scientific paradigms" that contain principles or assumptions with which many researchers would disagree, if those principles or assumptions were made explicit. It also creates a narrowly focused worldview, or way of doing science, which precludes consideration of alternative metaphysical or epistemological assumptions in the practice of a given field of research.

The importance of epistemological techniques and assumptions, implicit or explicit, is not a concern that is specific to or even arises only out of community psychology inquiry. Contextualist epistemologies have emerged forcefully in several disciplines. Two examples are presented from the biological and psychological sciences. A further contribution comes from feminist epistemology.

Contextualism in Biology and Psychology

Kauffman (1971) and Wimsatt (1974) have independently argued for an explanatory model in the biological sciences that consists of a multivariate, multidimensional analysis of a given system. Kauffman and Wimsatt argue that there are multiple frames of reference for the observation of a given system (or subsystem) and that there is no preferred method. The researcher's role is to delineate the boundaries of his or her frame of reference, given personal interests, questions, and concepts of what is relevant to the research. Within such boundaries, certain things are "knowable," and some are inaccessible or excluded.

Kauffman (1971) showed that "an organism may be seen as doing indefinitely many things, and may be decomposed into parts and processes in indefinitely many ways." Then, given a chosen description of the organism as doing some particular thing, "we will use that description to help us decompose the organism into particular parts and processes which articulate together to cause it to behave as described." Kauffman argued that the descriptions of parts and processes of an organism from one theoretical or methodological frame of reference "need only be compatible with, and not deducible from, the descriptions of parts and processes articulated by a different decomposition" (Kauffman, 1971, pp. 258–259). His decompositional analysis allows the researcher to self-consciously choose the boundaries that frame what is to be observed or investigated in a specific context.

Kauffman and Wimsatt argue that examining the integration and interconnections of the many functional parts of a given system can provide the researcher with a more robust and ecologically valid interpretation or representation of an individual and the system(s) within which the person is embedded (Kauffman, 1971; Wimsatt, 1974, 1981). According to Wimsatt, "robustness" measures the reliability of the theories and methods of science. Because we have no absolute or a priori criteria with which to validate our theories, models, observations, or values, we must check them against each other. In doing so, we discover contradictions in the assumptions and techniques that produce them.

The Ecological approach to Community Psychology shares Wimsatt's belief in the "robustness" of human knowledge that does not appeal to the "fixed" or "objective" properties of objects themselves to distinguish knowledge from illusion or false belief. Instead, the Ecological approach relies on the logical and empirical coherence of the information obtained by multiple methods and observations, each considered in context. "Robustness" in terms of the Ecological approach implies an analysis of the discriminant and convergent validity of concepts.

Consistent with the contextualist and multivariate, multilevel, and systemic analysis of the Ecological approach, Shadish (1986) argues that *critical multiplism* will enhance research in psychology. Critical multiplism acknowledges the unique set of biases associated with a given research design or analysis. It acknowledges that no single approach provides the true characterization of a system and that researchers are "constantly engaged in a battle against the partial validity of the methods that are available" (Shadish, Cook, & Houts, 1986, p. 43). Multiple methods and analyses complement each other, compensating for the limitations of each other, to contribute convergent and discriminant validity of our claims to knowledge (Shadish et al., 1986). Planned critical multiplism provides "tools to help scientists explore the boundaries of their knowledge" (Shadish et al., 1986, p. 43), that is, to help them identify the specific assumptions, methods, values, and biases which constrain research and which produce claims to knowledge (Shadish, 1986).

Congruent with these Contextualist analyses, many feminists are also reevaluating the validity of claims to knowledge made from a positivistic, value- or observer-free perspective.

Constructivism and Contextualism in Feminist Epistemology

The contributions of a feminist epistemology, although complementary to those of Kauffman and Wimsatt, differ in that they advocate the recognition, authenticity, and importance of a distinctly female point of view, a distinctly female sociopolitical unit (structure, construct) in a community setting, and the structural and functional roles defined for those units (Flax, 1983; Gilligan, 1982; Harding, 1987; Harding & O'Barr, 1987; Hare-Mustin & Marecek, 1988; Harstock, 1983; Hoffman, 1981; Keller, 1983, 1987; Lott, 1985; Luepnitz, 1988a, 1988b; McVicker-Clinchy & Belenky, 1987; Riger, this volume [1990]; Wallston, 1981; M. R. Walsh, 1987).

For example, Belenky, McVicker-Clinchy, Goldberger, and Tarule (1986) saw that this feminist constructivist viewpoint had important implications for epistemology. First, the women they interviewed in their work were not just considered "subjects," but "key, active participants" who felt "empowered" by being understood and represented. Second, the need to develop a capacity to listen beyond traditional interviewing techniques was understood and appreciated. Third, according to McVicker-Clinchy and Belenky (1987), connected knowers are not dispassionate unbiased observers. Connected knowers try to see the phenomena examined from another point of view. The epistemology of the connected knower focuses on data not just as evidence to support a given hypothesis but as a guide to the experiences of the knower (McVicker-Clinchy & Belenky, 1987, p. 12). Feminists have shown that there is flexibility in our choice of "units of analysis" in a given system or setting; hence, they too are committed to a constructivist or contextualist theory of knowledge.

From a contextualist perspective, the choice of research methods is greatly influenced by the interests, values, and assumptions of the researcher (Belenky, et al., 1986; Falicov, 1988; Fish, 1983; Gilligan, 1982; Harding, 1987; Harding & Hintikka, 1983; Hare-Mustin & Marecek, 1988; Lott, 1985; McVicker-Clinchy & Belenky, 1987; Parlee, 1981; Ruback & Innes, 1988; Wallston, 1981). The assumptions of an Ecological Contextualist approach create interests and activities that diverge from traditional, positivistic research models.

A Contextualist Epistemology for Ecological Research in Community Psychology

The topic of ecology has had several key proponents who have helped shape and define a contextualist understanding of behavior. The works of Roger Barker and colleagues (Barker, 1960, 1968, 1987a, 1987b), Gregory Bateson (Bateson, 1972; also Luepnitz, 1988a), and Urie Bronfenbrenner (Bronfenbrenner, 1977, 1979, 1986; also Falicov, 1988) stand out in particular. The ecological approach of Bateson and colleagues has emphasized the various levels and types of communities in community research (Kelly, 1966, 1968, 1979a, 1979b, 1986, 1987; Kelly et al., 1988; Kelly & Hess, 1987; Kelly, Ryan, & Altman, in press; Trickett, 1984; Trickett & Birman, 1988; Trickett, Kelly, & Todd, 1972; Trickett, Kelly, & Vincent, 1985; Trickett & Mitchell, in press [1993]; Vincent & Trickett, 1983).

The Ecological approach defines the relationship between the observer and the observed (participant) as the source for the construction of meaning about the phenomena to be studied. Thus, persons and systems become understandable when they are considered a part of a multilevel, multistructured, multidetermined social context. Moreover, persons and systems may appear less tangible in virtue of the multifaceted ways in which their boundaries and complexity can be articulated.

The Ecological approach affirms that it is not possible to understand the meaning of persons or systems in context unless the observer and persons to be observed develop mutual criteria for their definition of *context*. The various multiple features of the context are considered to affect both the observer and participants. Both are considered to be part of the particular context where observations take place. The relationship between the observer (scientist or researcher) and the observed (participant) itself becomes a topic of research. A further definition of the process of understanding phenomena is that the observer is dependent on the creation of a reciprocal working relationship with the persons(s) or system(s) observed, not only to select a preferred topic for research, but also to define their own working relationship. Four facets can be identified as constituting the Ecological approach.

Facet One: Theoretical Propositions

Ten theoretical propositions affect the expression of constraints and resources in contexts and characterize the interrelationships of persons and settings:

1. Concepts about persons and settings are derived from the observer and participants appreciating their own contexts and constructing a mutual understanding of their shared context.
2. Persons in context are observed in terms of their role performance in creating resources and coping with personal, organizational, and community constraints.
3. Social settings are observed in terms of the operation of social norms as they affect the definition, use, and response to resources and constraints.
4. Social settings define the shared meaning and experience of persons and include being a member of a context where occasions, places, and events define and maintain social norms.
5. Adaptive behavior is defined in terms of the resources that persons and settings create, use, maintain, and replenish.
6. Adaptive behavior and the criteria for adaptive behavior may vary from place to place and from time to time.
7. Relationships are reciprocal: Persons affect settings, and settings affect persons; persons influence other persons, and one setting affects another setting.
8. Events, settings, and persons outside the immediate social setting affect the expression of structures, roles, and norms inside social settings.
9. Person–setting transactions in one setting indirectly produce tangible effects for the interactions of other persons in other settings.
10. Social processes can facilitate or inhibit the interdependence of persons and social settings and the interdependence of roles and social norms.

Facet Two: The Social Construction of Ecological Knowledge

The ecological approach focuses on the behavior of persons in social settings related to the social construction that the participants, both observer and observed, create of their own context. It is assumed that different participants may create different constructions of their context. Observations are bound by space, time, and the histories of role relationships of the participants.

What becomes essential in the elaboration of the Ecological approach is that the participants are able to consciously articulate the unique constraints and opportunities that affect their own context. A requirement for initiating a construction of their own context is that the researcher and participants must invest themselves in the ambiguity of the discovery process. Whatever understanding of phenomena is developed has an explicit bounded quality that communicates and denotes the nature of the observations in their sociopolitical, spatiotemporal context.

What is theoretically construed about persons and social settings comes about as the researcher learns about and experiences the events and processes related to the social construction of his or her contexts and the context(s) of the participants. The social construction of context frames the observations about roles, norms, and their interdependence in social settings.

According to this Ecological approach, theoretical propositions are tested, measured, and understood by the meaning that the propositions have for the participants who are experiencing the phenomenon. Understanding the expression of social roles and social norms requires that the participants develop a process and a plan to be informed about each other's community or system of study, and about their own working context.

Facet Three: The Collaborative Style

Under the ecological approach, the style of work is collaborative among the participants. The process of collaborative work involves both the researcher and the other participants defining a working relationship for the integration of research and practice. The researcher and other participants are expected to appreciate the value of their work together in redefining the research activity. The collaborative style reaffirms that research hypotheses are derived from the collaboration of the participants in the context of their working relationship. This working relationship focuses on a shared understanding of the operation of social structures, roles, and norms as they occur in given contexts. The assumed benefit of the collaborative style is that the discovery of information about the structures, roles, and norms expressed in context will enhance the authenticity, the validity, and, therefore, the usefulness of the research.

The epistemological significance of the collaborative relationship is that it occurs in a context in which ideas are tested, elaborated, redefined, examined, reexamined, and evolved. The collaborative relationship becomes a social structure by which the processes of discovery and understanding can take place. The observer (researcher) and the observed (participants), in this relationship, then create together a shared agenda to discover and to understand community contexts.

Facet Four: Social Processes

The validity of Ecological research is realized only if the participants understand their context or agenda-specific interests and roles in the collaborative enterprise. Understanding the processes of collaboration and the stages and sequences involved in the design of research and interventions is necessary for creating contextual knowledge.

This facet is concerned with how techniques and methods are interdependent with settings. Social settings become meaningful because of the sequences of social interactions that they set in motion. The study of social processes makes it possible to understand how roles and social norms create social structures, how social structures make roles and norms interdependent with persons and settings, and the processes of constructing knowledge. The ecological approach gives attention to the sequence of stages, steps, and activities that gives unique meaning to any particular social context.

Implications of a Contextualist, Ecological Epistemology

The Ecological approach emphasizes a sequence of activities in which the researcher understands, learns, and becomes informed about phenomena in context. The researcher is prepared to develop and to revise his or her concepts as the collaborative relationship evolves. What is not consistent with the Ecological approach is for the researcher to recruit or to persuade the participants to help test out concepts or hypotheses that are developed or selected solely by the researcher. In that case, the researcher is denying or not attending to the participants' own context. Research activity according to the Ecological approach is inductive, exploratory, improvisational, and requires constant testing and feedback; testing of ideas occurs by going back and forth between the concepts and the experience of the researcher and the participants. These activities must all take place before the official, public, or "real" research or intervention(s) can begin.

The four facets of the Ecological approach are interdependent; as each facet is addressed, meaning is given to each of the other facets and to the total context. Appreciating context allows the researcher to listen to the voices of others and provides the opportunity for understanding and empowering others. For both researcher and participants, "gaining a voice" presupposes dialogue, networking, and empathic listening and intervention. The ecological approach also acknowledges that the research process is constructed and influenced by its spatiotemporal and sociopolitical parameters, agendas, or frames of reference (Fish, 1983; Hare-Mustin & Maracek, 1988; Katz & Kahn, 1978; Kelly, Altman, Kahn, Stokols, & Rausch, 1986; Lott, 1985; Parlee, 1981; Ruback & Innes, 1988).

The Ecological approach adapts research styles to incorporate initial uncertainty and ambiguity as the collaborative enterprise is initiated. In this sense, research becomes an "open" process, because there is tolerance for checking the validity of assumptions, the efficacy of actions, and the very definition and meaning of research. The Ecological approach is empiricist, exploratory, collaborative, and contextual in its theoretical and methodological assumptions. Research that is ecological can provide an opportunity to understand what is complex and unique about a given setting or context.

Conclusion

It is our view that research performed under the philosophical assumptions and methodologies of Positivism has had the effect of reducing our knowledge about the complex and unique constraints and qualities of a given "system" and that such a research style is outside the aspirations of the field of Community Psychology. We propose that a contextualist, Ecological epistemology provides the freedom to pursue lines of inquiry more congruent with the philosophical and sociopolitical interests of Community Psychology.

In this chapter we have argued that an Ecological approach may provide a useful theoretical framework for the development of research strategies in Community Psychology. Our aim has been to show the value of alternative points of view and alternative investigative techniques. We believe such an approach is more congruent, compatible, and logically consistent with the aims and aspirations of the field of Community Psychology.

In closing, we recall Cronbach's comments, made in response to a 1983 conference on the potentialities for knowledge in social science. This chapter has been written with a feeling of intellectual kinship and the shared spirit of Cronbach's affirmations:

> The style and procedures preferred for one inquiry can be ill-suited for another topic or at another stage in the evolution of knowledge or for an investigator in different circumstances. With that caveat, I recapitulate a few preferences I have suggested: for more exploratory work, for less emphasis on the magnitude and statistical significance of "effect sizes," for more effort to record concomitant and intermediate events that help explain local variation, for more discussion of research plans and interpretations with peers having disparate

backgrounds. Each piece of research should be an effort to give an unimpeachable and reasonably full account of events in a time, place, and context. Multiple interpretations of information already in hand will often be more instructive, at less cost, than additional data gathering. I have encouraged critical analysis of research methods and their further development, along with substantive criticism of extrapolations. To advocate pluralistic tolerance of alternative accounts is in no way to advocate tender-mindedness.[1]

Note

1. From the chapter "Social Inquiry by and for Earthlings" in *Metatheory in Social Science: Pluralisms and Subjectives*, edited by D. W. Fiske and R. A. Shweder. University of Chicago Press, 1986. Reprinted with permission.

References

Altman, I., & Rogoff, B. (1987). World views in psychology: Trait, interactional, organismic and transactional perspectives. In D. Stokols & I. Altman (Eds.), *Handbook of environmental psychology* (pp. 7–40). New York: Wiley.

Ash, M. G., & Woodward, W. R. (Eds.). (1988). *Psychology in twentieth-century thought and society*. New York: Cambridge University Press.

Barker, R. G. (1960). Ecology and motivation. In M. R. Jones (Ed.). *Nebraska Symposium on Motivation* (pp. 1–49). Lincoln: University of Nebraska Press.

Barker, R. G. (1968). *Ecological psychology: Concepts and methods for studying the environment of human behavior.* Stanford, CA: Stanford University Press.

Barker, R. G. (1987a). Explorations in ecological psychology. In R. G. Barker, *Midwest Psychological Field Station*. Lawrence: University of Kansas.

Barker, R. G. (1987b). Prospecting in environmental psychology: Oskaloosa revisited. In D. Stokols & I. Altman (Eds.), *Handbook of environmental psychology* (pp. 1413–1432). New York: Wiley.

Bateson, G. (1972). *Steps to an ecology of the mind*. San Francisco: Chandler.

Bateson, G. (1979). *Mind and nature: A necessary unity*. New York: Bantam.

Belenky, M. F., Clinchy, B. M., Goldberger, N. R., & Tarule, J. M. (1986). *Women's ways of knowing: The development of self, voice and mind*. New York: Basic Books.

Bennett, C. C., Anderson, L. S., Cooper, S., Hassol, L., Klein, D. C., & Rosenblum, G. (Eds.). (1966). *Community psychology: A report of the Boston conference of the education of psychologists for community mental health*. Boston: Boston University Press.

Bronfenbrenner, U. (1977). Toward an experimental ecology of human development. *American Psychologists, 32,* 513–531.

Bronfenbrenner, U. (1979). *The ecology of human development*. Cambridge, MA: Harvard University Press.

Bronfenbrenner, U. (1986). Ecology of the family as a context for human development: Research perspectives. *Developmental Psychology, 22,* 723–742.

Cronbach, L. J. (1986). Social inquiry by and for earthlings. In D. W. Fiske & R. A. Shweder (Eds.), *Metatheory in social science: Pluralisms and subjectives* (pp. 93–107). Chicago: University of Chicago Press.

Efran J. S., Lukens, R. J., & Lukens, M. D. (1988). Constructivism: What's in it for you? *The Family Therapy Networker* (September/October).

Falicov, C. J. (1988). Learning to think culturally, In H. A. Liddle, D. Breunlin, R. Schwartz (Eds.), *The Handbook of family therapy training and supervision* (pp. 335–337). New York: Guilford Press.

Feyerabend, P. (1975). *Against method.* London: New Left Books.

Fish, V. K. (1983). Feminist scholarship in sociology: An emerging research model. *Wisconsin Sociologist, 20,* 45–56.

Flax, J. (1983). Political philosophy and the patriarchal unconscious: A psychoanalytic perspective on epistemology and metaphysics. In S. Harding & M. B. Hintikka (Eds.), *Discovering reality: Feminist perspectives on epistemology, metaphysics, methodology, and the philosophy of science* (pp. 245–281). London: Reidel.

Giere, R. N. (1988). *Explaining science: A cognitive approach.* Chicago: The University of Chicago Press.

Gilligan, C. (1982). *In a different voice.* Cambridge, MA: Harvard University Press.

Hall, A. R. (1966). *The scientific revolution 1500–1800: The formation of the modern scientific attitude* (2nd ed., pp. 159–185). Boston: Beacon Press.

Harding, S. (Ed.). (1987). Introduction: Is there a feminist method? In S. Harding (Ed.), *Feminism and methodology.* Bloomington: University of Indiana Press.

Harding, S., & Hintikka, M. B. (1983). *Discovering reality: Feminist perspectives on epistemology, metaphysics, methodology, and the philosophy of science.* London: Reidel.

Harding, S., & O'Barr, J. F. (1987). *Sex and scientific inquiry.* Chicago: University of Chicago Press.

Hare-Mustin, R. T., & Marecek, J. (1988). The meaning of difference: Gender, theory, postmodernism and psychology. *American Psychologist, 43,* 455–464.

Hartsock, N. C. M. (1983). The feminist standpoint: Developing the ground for a specifically feminist historical materialism. In S. Harding & M. B. Hintikka (Eds.), *Discovering reality: Feminist perspectives on epistemology, metaphysics, methodology, and the philosophy of science* (pp. 283–310). London: Reidel.

Hoffman, L. (1981). *Foundations of family therapy: A conceptual framework for systems change.* New York: Basic Books.

Katz, D., & Kahn, R. L. (1978). *The social psychology of organizations* (2nd ed.). New York: Wiley.

Kauffman, S. A. (1971). Articulation of parts explanations in biology. In R. S. Cohen & R. C. Buck (Eds.), *Boston studies in the philosophy of science: VIII* (pp. 257–272). New York: Humanities Press.

Keller, E. F. (1983). Gender and science. In S. Harding & M. B. Hintikka (Eds.), *Discovering reality: Feminist perspectives on epistemology, metaphysics, methodology, and philosophy of science.* London: Reidel.

Keller, E. F. (1987). Feminism and science. In S. Harding (Ed.), *Sex and scientific inquiry* (pp. 233–246). Chicago: University of Illinois Press.

Kelly, J. G. (1966). Ecological constraints on mental health services. *American Psychologist, 21,* 535–539.

Kelly, J. G. (1968). Toward an ecological conception of preventive interventions. In J. W. Carter Jr. (Ed.), *Research contributions from psychology to community mental health* (pp. 75–99). New York: Behavioral Publications.

Kelly, J. G. (1979a). *Adolescent boys in high school: A study of coping and adaptation.* Hillsdale, NJ: Erlbaum.

Kelly, J. G. (1979b). Tain't what you do, it's the way that you do it. *American Journal of Community Psychology, 7*, 239–261.

Kelly, J. G. (1986). Context and process: An ecological view of the interdependence of practice and research. *American Journal of Community Psychology, 14*, 581–589.

Kelly, J. G. (1987). Beyond prevention techniques: Creating social settings for a public's health. The Tenth Erich Lindemann Memorial Lecture, Boston, MA, April 24.

Kelly, J. G., Altman, B. E., Kahn, R. L., Stokols, D., & Rausch, H. L. (1986). Context and process. *American Journal of Community Psychology, 14*, 573–605.

Kelly, J. G., Dassoff, N., Levin, I., Schreckengost, J., Stelzner, S. P., & Altman, B. E. (1988). *A guide to conducting prevention research in the community: First steps.* New York: Haworth Press.

Kelly, J. G., Ryan, A. M., & Altman, B. E. (in press) [2000]. Understanding and changing social systems: An ecological view. In J. Rappaport & E. Seidman (Eds.), *Handbook of community psychology* (pp. 133–159). New York: Plenum.

Kornblith, H. (Ed.). (1985). *Naturalizing epistemology.* Cambridge, MA: MIT Press.

Lott, B. (1985). The potential enrichment of social/personality psychology through feminist research and vice versa. *American Psychologist, 40*, 155–164.

Luepnitz, D. A. (1988a). Bateson's heritage: Bitter fruit. *The Family Systems Networker* (September/October), 49–53.

Luepnitz, D. A. (1988b). *The family interpreted: Feminist theory in clinical practice.* New York: Basic Books.

McGuire, W. J. (1986). The vicissitudes of attitudes and similar representational constructs in twentieth century psychology. *European Journal of Social Psychology, 16*, 89–130.

McVicker-Clinchy, B., & Belenky, M. F. (1987). *Women's ways of knowing: A theory and an intervention.* Speech delivered at the Day Grant Award Presentation. Smith College School of Social Work, July 23.

Meehl, P. E. (1986). What social scientists don't understand. In D. W. Fiske & R. A. Schweder (Eds.), *Metatheory in social science* (pp. 315–338). Chicago: University of Chicago Press.

Pappas, G. S., & Swain, M. (Eds.). (1978). *Essays on knowledge and justification.* London: Cornell University Press.

Parlee, M. B. (1981). Appropriate control groups in feminist research. *Psychology of Women Quarterly, 54*, 637–644.

Quine W. V., & Ullian, J. S. (1970). *The web of belief* (2nd ed). New York: Random House.

Rose, H. (1987). Hand, brain, and heart: A feminist epistemology for the natural sciences. In S. Harding (Ed.), *Sex and scientific inquiry* (pp. 265–282). Chicago: University of Illinois Press.

Rosnow, R. L., & Georgoudi, M. (1986). The spirit of contextualism. In R. L. Rosnow & M. Georgoudi (Eds.), *Contextualism and understanding in behavioral science: Implications for research and theory* (pp. 3–22). New York: Praeger.

Ruback, R. B., & Innes, C. A. (1988). The relevance and irrelevance of psychological research: The example of prison crowding. *American Psychologist, 43,* 683–693.

Shadish, W. R. (1986). Planned critical multiplism: Some elaborations. *Behavioral Assessment, 8,* 75–103.

Shadish, W. R., Cook, T. D., & Houts, A. C. (1986). Quasiexperimentation in a critical multiplist mode. *New Directions for Program Evaluation, 31,* 29–46.

Suppe, F. (1974). *The structure of scientific theories* (2nd ed). Chicago: University of Illinois Press.

Trickett, E. J. (1984). Toward a distinctive community psychology: An ecological metaphor for the conduct of community research and the nature of training. *American Journal of Community Psychology, 12,* 261–279.

Trickett, E. J., & Birman, D. (1987). Taking ecology seriously: A community development approach to individually based preventive interventions in schools. In L. Bond & B. Compas (Eds.), *Primary prevention and promotion in the schools* (pp. 361–390). Beverly Hills, CA: Sage.

Trickett, E. J., Kelly, J. G. & Todd, D. M. (1972). The social environment of the high school: Guidelines for individual change and organizational development. In S. G. Golann & Eisdorfer (Eds.), *Handbook of community mental health* (pp. 331–406). New York: Appleton-Century-Crofts.

Trickett, E. J., Kelly, J. G., & Vincent, T. (1985). The spirit of ecological inquiry in community research. In E. Susskind & D. Klein (Eds.), *Community research: Methods, paradigms, and applications* (pp. 5–38). New York: Praeger.

Trickett, E. J., & Mitchell, R. E. (in press) [1993]. An ecological metaphor for research and intervention in community psychology. In M. S. Gibbs, J. R. Lachenmeyer, & J. Sigal (Eds.), *Community psychology: Theoretical and empirical approaches* (2nd ed.). New York: Wiley.

Vincent, T. A., & Trickett, E. J. (1983). Preventive interventions and the human context: Ecological approaches to environmental assessment and change. In R. D. Felner, L. A. Jason, J. N. Moritsugu, & S. S. Farber (Eds.), *Preventive psychology: Theory, research, and practice* (pp. 67–86). New York: Pergamon Press.

Wallston, B. S. (1981). What are the questions in the psychology of women? A feminist approach to research. *Psychology of Women Quarterly, 54*(4), 597–617.

Walsh, M. R. (Ed.). (1987). *The psychology of women: Ongoing debates.* New Haven, CT: Yale University Press.

Walsh, R. T. (1987). A social historical note on the formal emergence of community psychology. *American Journal of Community Psychology, 15,* 523–529.

Wimsatt, W. C. (1974). Complexity and organization. In K. F. Schaffner & R. S. Cohen (Eds.), *Proceedings of the meetings of the Philosophy of Science Association, 1972.* Dordrecht, Netherlands: Reidel.

Wimsatt, W. C. (1981). Robustness, reliability, and over-determination. In M. Brewer & B. Collins (Eds.), *Scientific inquiry and the social sciences* (pp. 124–163). San Francisco: Jossey-Bass.

11

Wellness as an Ecological Enterprise

Reflections

In 1996, several prominent community psychologists who studied with Emory Cowen—Dante Cicchetti, Julian Rappaport, Irwin Sandler, and Roger P. Weissberg—arranged for a celebration in his honor at the University of Rochester. This was followed up with a request for others to contribute to a book in his honor. Julian Rappaport invited me to contribute a chapter, which I was very pleased to do. I had been an admirer of Cowen's work and had known him for over 30 years. At the time, I was grappling with some issues that I believed were important for the study of community psychology. The theme for the book was to be "wellness," which was a topic that warranted ecological analyses. I developed a draft that was too long with too many ideas. Julian was helpful to me in selecting the most appropriate themes and issues. Preparing the comments gave me an opportunity to cite major influences on me that were apt for an ecological approach to wellness.

One of the most delightful opportunities was to refer to the work of the anthropologist Ed Wellin. I read his contribution, "Water Boiling in a Peruvian Town," when I was a student at the Harvard School of Public Health in 1959. I tracked him down and videotaped an interview with him. The written report and his comments nearly 50 years later contained several important concepts and principles. His work highlighted the value of in-depth participation in the life of a community to understand the array of forces that establish wellness. Second, his work emphasized the value of interdisciplinary work for understanding community support systems for wellness as well as the intricacies, both personal and community, that can impede establishing wellness behavior. I had seen few studies that approached the acumen and clarity of Wellin's work published in 1955. The enthusiastic response of doctoral students made it a treasured intellectual experience.

The invitation provided an opportunity to address topics that I had covered before, but to do so in a much more focused and substantive way. I also had the benefit of referring to recent work by Rebecca Campbell, Ken Maton, Vonnie McLoyd, and Robin Miller. Having contemporary work to refer to as exemplars for my ideas also made me feel good. I also enjoyed referring to classic sociological research and recalling for the reader the sage perceptions and views of people like Lee Cronbach, Sigmund Koch, and John Tukey.

I found the research and analyses of Dan Katz and Bob Kahn still fresh. As community psychologists, we still needed to embrace the power of such social psychological concepts as social norms and boundary spanning. By not understanding the application of such concepts, we were missing good research opportunities. Like the concept of trust, they provide a substantive reference point for designing and implementing community-based prevention programs. I felt that I had created interconnected proposals for approaching inquiry and conducting research in community settings. I hope that the reader will find some merit in what has been expressed and presented here.

Emory Cowen has persistently and persuasively refocused prevention efforts away from illness, away from disorders, and beyond deficits. He has advocated for an understanding of the social conditions and personal qualities of health, of positive well-being, and of resilient coping. He has invited us to shift our ways of thinking and our ways of doing research. Martin Seligman's reference to psychology as a positive social science gives the Cowen treatise more visibility and more sanction (Seligman, 1998).

The Wellness topic has significance for the analysis of risk and protective factors—currently of interest to prevention research investigators. The long-standing tradition of emphasizing epidemiological research for risk factors, such as abuses of substances, limited educational achievement, and the pernicious influences of various forms of social and racial discrimination, has established connections between the above factors and the expression of psychological maladies. However, this research tradition may not be as appropriate to examine protective factors. Devoting time and energy to the study of wellness is not simply a scrutiny of the absence of illness. Since the study of illness has been such a priority and so commanding of our attention for so long, it will take some doing to begin anew.

The following five ideas are presented to assist this shift in point of view. These five ideas reconceptualize how inquiries can be conceived and carried out. New criteria and new premises are employed; a different epistemology is invoked. This new enterprise could be referred to as the province of the Wellness scholar, a contextual scholar who focuses on situations and their impact on individuals. The Wellness scholar creates a pluralistic set of methods to examine the diversity of persons acting in a variety of situations.

These five ideas are:

1. Contextual thinking: an agenda for situated inquiry;
2. New disciplinary connections and pluralistic methods;
3. Learning with others rather than assessing others;
4. Learning about resilient and competent communities;
5. The analysis of variety and quality.

With these topics, the Wellness scholar embarks on an expedition to enlarge our understanding of the sources of healthy behavior. The five ideas underlying the paradigm of the Wellness scholar assert a different definition of what is "good" science.

The First Idea: Contextual Thinking—An Agenda for Situated Inquiry

One resource in the search for knowledge is the increasing need to attend not only to the states or traits of individuals, but to the various extra influences that impact, impinge, and affect the expression of individual behavior. Some extra individual influences are: the local economy and the impact on the wage earner, particularly for child care; the presence of supportive employers who can work out staggered work schedules; the presence of friends, neighbors, and kin who can both contribute tangible aid and share rituals and ceremonies and traditions; the sense of public safety that enables the person to travel alone and at night; "user-friendly" community service organizations that are accessible and responsive; the availability of mentors and/or more experienced persons who can provide help on coping with personal and organizational issues. Each of these topics represents constraints and/or resources that, when present, can aggravate or ease plights and close down or open up new opportunities. But these types of factors and forces are not usually within the purview of data collection. The range of topics for psychological investigation is often limited to just those factors that bear directly on the individual without considering that the individual is nested and situated in a milieu. These milieus are the sources of effects and influences that bear directly on the individual.

To shift paradigms is a challenge, for it requires the investigator to be involved with the individual informants long enough and deeply enough to become familiar with the less frequently examined ways in which local cultures define, limit, and/or promote the well-being of individuals. It is possible that new questions can be addressed: How do persons know when they are appreciated? How are persons in authority addressed without feeling the risk of recrimination? How do persons in a particular community express regard for others? How are differences of opinion addressed without anyone being stigmatized? How does a social setting foster creativity? How do groups become resources for their members? The answers to these questions not only arise from studying the qualities of individuals. The answers also derive from an analysis of the traditions, social norms, and expectations for behavior established within and across specific social settings. This is what is meant by the ecological enterprise: inquiry focuses on the person–environment fit of different individuals and varied settings (Kingry-Westergaard & Kelly, 1990). Understanding wellness is as much a topic of our contexts, our surroundings, as it is our personal qualities; an ecological enterprise is salient.

McLoyd, in an elegant review, focuses on the impact of poverty. "The link between socioeconomic disadvantage and children's socioemotional functioning appears to be mediated partly by harsh, inconsistent parenting and elevated exposure to acute and chronic stressors" (McLoyd, 1998, 1985). Most often, social scientists do not get close enough or listen attentively or seek out those who could inform us of the details of those circumstances and surroundings that limit skillful parenting or reduce various stressors in different communities. Contextual premises and thinking can point to the concrete and specific array of variables that may come into play. Most importantly, the ecological mission clarifies how different systemic factors come into play in different communities. To understand how "good parenting" may vary from community to community means acknowledging and defining how local customs and social norms contribute to the expression of behavior and the definitions of what behaviors are desirable. This realization of differences between people living in two different communities suggests that any reported differences may reflect variations in the very nature of the social structure of communities, so that what is being assessed is the lack of salience of any specific measure of good parenting. An ecological premise suggests that as communities differ, different conceptions of community are also salient for each of the different communities.

A challenge is to review our causal premises. To understand the expression of "good parenting" in a particular community means that the causal premises of the investigator as well as the informant must be considered. Some investigators may have as their causal premise "inconsistent parenting." Another investigator may focus on the "chronic stressors." McLoyd's point is that it is the combination of *both* factors that is essential, not simply one or the other.

Middle-class white investigators may operate on the belief that agency, efficacy, and the ability of the individual to rearrange environmental conditions is salient and feasible; their previous life experiences have validated their causal systems. Some other investigators may be more fatalistic, while still others may believe that a higher authority is a major causal force in their lives. Situated inquiry requires analyses of linguistic and cognitive styles and how these premises affect everyday constructions of topics that in turn affect the relationship of informant and investigator.

Situated inquiry gets at the linguistic and cognitive constructions that persons use in everyday acts. Such an inquiry can illuminate both the social constraints and the social resources within various milieus. How people define being "well" and being "sick," and how their immediate kin and confidants support or do not support these beliefs, can make the difference in whether prevention efforts are useful or fail. Situated inquiry focuses in on these microsocial processes (Seaburn, Lorenz, Gunn, Gawinski, & Mauksch, 1994).

Another defining feature of situated inquiry is the research relationship between the person inquiring and the person providing information. Situated research that is contextually based requires attending to the expression of trust in the research relationship.

Can people of a different social class trust a researcher who is different than they are? One community informant suggests that African American citizens may respond to white investigators by saying what they think the investigator wants to know (Bagby, 1996). Dave Todd once described the research process as peeling an onion (Todd, personal communication, 1968). It is a process of building levels of trust so that the informant is willing to not just fill out a questionnaire or even consent to an interview, but perhaps to disclose in that interview deeper reflections about themselves.

A recent report of persons responding to audio computer-assisted self-interviewing (audio-CASI) technology for measuring sensitive behaviors, such as male-male sex, injection drug use, and sexual contact with intravenous drug users reported these behaviors to be higher by factors of three or more. It is laudable and a significant methodological contribution that a more anonymous computer-assisted method can facilitate persons disclosing behavior that otherwise could be perceived as unacceptable. Yet, the availability of such technology may further erode researchers getting more closely and more personally in touch directly, without a computer interface, with the people and topics of interest. More effort is needed to assess the impact of persons participating in audio-CASI research, particularly on the informant's level of trust in the research process (Bloom, 1998; Turner, Ku, Rogers, Lindberg, Pleck, & Sonenstein, 1998). Understanding concepts of informants' causal systems can also point to what is important to the participants in their social environments and whether responding to audio-CASI methods enhances or diminishes their level of trust.

One of the potential contributions of an ecological endeavor is that such inquiries may illuminate the factors that come into play for some individuals and not others, as pointed out in the implications of McLoyd's discussion of parenting. Maton and colleagues (1998), for example, have commented on understanding the variables contributing to the high educational achievement of

African American males. They state: "Rearing academically successful African American sons requires the simultaneous presence of a constellation of promotive factors, encompassing socialization goals, parenting practices, parenting style, and community connectedness." If a study assesses one or two of these factors only, the lack of inclusion of the other critical factors may preclude strong findings from emerging. For instance, "strict discipline and community connectedness without determined parental academic engagement, *or* educational engagement and community connectedness *without* nurturance and strict discipline, may not be sufficient in many cases to counteract the negative contextual factors facing black youth" (Maton, 1993; Maton, Hrabowski, & Grelf, 1998).

Persons who express a religious orientation may make the church and related church activities a source of inspiration and solace. Persons who are seeking social contact and are not churchgoers may turn to bookstores, bars, beauty parlors, exercise clubs, or a variety of other settings and activities as significant sources of stimulation and connection. It may be that in their preferred settings persons' causal beliefs become more ingrained through their social contacts and their personal relationships in these settings.

One of the features of social milieus is to solidify the meaning persons subscribe to everyday events. Understanding these personal and social meanings about life, and the views and beliefs about one's personal power to change negative factors, enhances or limits the desired effects of an imported prevention program.

Some of the connections between social context and the behavior of individuals have been established. For example, there is available information about how social environments impact our mood. George and Brief (1992) present a thesis for how organizational variables, for example, may influence behaviors like spontaneity. Spontaneity is defined as making constructive suggestions and spreading good will. Several decades of research in organizational psychology affirms that social environments *do* impact our behavior both within and outside of the work environment. The qualities of our everyday work environments impact our sense of optimism, our humanitarian acts, our civility, and our generative thinking in addition to our mood (Katz & Kahn, 1978; Taylor, Repetti, & Seema, 1997).

Living in a community where there is dilapidated or boarded-up housing, poor illumination, or infrequent police visibility makes residents vigilant and fearful (Glidewell, Kelly, Bagby, & Dickerson, 1998; Tandon, Azelton, Kelly, & Strickland, 1998). The tradition of community organizing aims to affect a change in mood by making it possible for citizens who live in less attractive and decaying communities to address the systemic factors that are limiting the quality of life in the local community (Kahn, 1982). By direct action, they then can create the possibility that, through their actions, the members of the community will improve the conditions that are limiting their mood and the quality of their life. This is an essential point about an ecological thesis: people can influence the social conditions that are limiting their freedom, their dignity, and their opportunities for growth. They can also preserve the traditions and rituals that are health engendering. The Wellness scholar can play a potential role in being a resource for enhancing and preserving social systems.

Understanding the varieties of ways in which persons cope to change noxious physical or psychological environments is a salient topic. Knowledge from organizational and environmental psychology of how social environmental factors contribute to the expressions of health engendering behavior is a beneficial intellectual resource (Katz & Kahn, 1978; Stokols & Altman, 1987; Stokols, 1992). Contextual thinking is clearly interdependent with intradisciplinary and interdisciplinary thinking. The validity of the Wellness scholar is dependent upon contextual understandings of people and their ties and relationships to their social settings.

The Second Idea: New Disciplinary Connections and Pluralistic Methods

Situated knowledge is knowledge derived from appraisals of persons in terms of the specific locales, settings, and situations in which they are participants; the emphasis is on understanding the social dynamics of specific times and places and the impact of these temporal and community contexts on the individual.

New ways in which universities are organized, *new* ways in which doctoral students are educated, and *new* criteria for how research funds are allocated can ease the mission of the Wellness scholar. Wellness research, as situated research, depends upon thriving interconnections across disciplines.

For the past four years I have taught a doctoral level course on the history of community psychology (Kelly, 1996). The course reviews social science research, social movements, and policies that helped to create the field of community psychology.

The most stimulating and rewarding reading, as reported by students, is work conducted in a small village in Peru in the early 1950s by the anthropologist Ed Wellin (Wellin, 1955, 1998). This work examined the microsocial structures of this community and pointed out the personal, small group, and community factors that contributed to some persons boiling their water and others not doing so. Reasons *for* boiling and reasons for *not* boiling water were often the same. The power of this work attests to not only the subtlety of community structures, but also the complete insensitivity to these factors by the government physicians who were advocates for better health status for the residents. Wellin's work is a compelling example of the value of depth analyses of the communities in which preventive interventions are to be implanted. Wellin's work also attests to the value of psychologists working with persons in other disciplines.

Sources of health are expected to be learned and nourished and maintained in natural groupings of people as Wellin's work so graphically illustrates. Out of family traditions, ceremonies, and ritual occasions derive the opportunities for social bonds that give us our identities, sense of community, and our construction of our place in time and our history (Bell, 1997). These issues are also the province of other social scientists (Ochs & Capps, 1996; Payne, 1995). While sociologists of science have affirmed that knowledge is situated, the commitment to carry out explicitly situated inquiry is still undeveloped (Geertz, 1995; Lave & Wenger, 1991; Neisser & Jopling, 1997; Pollio et al., 1997; Shapin, 1994). This is even after the research and thinking of investigators such as Barker, Bronfenbrenner, Kelly, Maton, Moos, Trickett, and Raush (Barker, 1965, 1968; Bechtel, 1990; Bronfenbrenner, 1979; Kelly, 1979; Moos, 1973, 1976, 1979; Moos & Insel, 1974; Raush, Dittman, & Taylor, 1959; Raush, Farbman, & Llewellyn, 1960; Schoggen & Fox, 1989; Trickett, 1984, 1989; Trickett, Trickett, Kelly, & Vincent, 1985).

Many scholars have advocated for some time the utility of pluralistic methods to address the issues of situational effects (Cronbach, 1986). Cronbach quoted Mary Hesse's challenge as she expressed it 20 years ago: "What progresses is the ability to use science to learn the environment" (Hesse, 1978; Cronbach, 1986, p. 4). Cronbach has been a consistent voice in suggesting that inquiry is open-ended, and that the validity of measures is enhanced when there are multiple methods employed, and the research enterprise is conceived as a pluralistic process where a range of methods and data sources are invoked to enhance the understanding of phenomena (Cronbach, 1986). The topic of external validity is recast. To the extent that psychologists' theory of mind is embedded in a white culture, the psychologist getting ready to adopt ecological thinking examines the cultural premises under which he or she is working and then considers how these premises may be resources or constraints. Lillard describes these issues in detail (Lillard, 1998).

The Wellness scholar is prepared to develop a working thesis to consider multiple causal systems when appraising behaviors such as socioemotional functioning. Ecological thinking focuses on the array of personal-social-historical factors that may impact on behavior in contrast to the direct nonreciprocal causal connections implied in some forms of psychological research. White presents a helpful treatise advocating for an analysis of the causal inferences put in use by the layperson (White, 1990). This is a potentially useful effort when the informants vary in race, ethnicity, gender, lifestyle, sexual orientation, and social class.

Koch expressed alarm about the vitality of the dominant research tradition back in 1959 (Koch, 1959). His five points were recently summarized by Wertheimer and Robinson:

> First, the intervening variable paradigm for theory construction is deeply flawed; in short it does not work. Second, the range of potential generalization

of the psychological "laws" that have been discovered to date is pitifully limited. Third, the link between theoretical constructs and operational definitions of these constructs usually is, at best, anemic and so loose as to be epistemologically unacceptable. Fourth, quantitative formulations of systematic relationships in empirical data are premature and often carried out to ludicrous degrees of presumed precision, when that degree of precision is totally unwarranted by the poor reliability and validity of the underlying measurements. Finally, the hypothetico-deductive model of scientific practice is incomplete, misleading, and ultimately not feasible. In short, it does not work either. (Wertheimer & Robinson, 1998, p. 9).

So established are these emphases in psychology that Koch criticized that the primary role of the researcher is still a distant, detached, objective observer. The controlled experiment, the questionnaire, the systematic sample survey, or the structured interview are cynosures. Such methods, while initially valid choices, soon, however, became commonplace and sacred conventions. The dominant use of these methods are self-defeating when the research mission is to be knowledgeable about what behaviors are health sustaining and how the qualities of social environments and social groupings nurture positive, prosocial behaviors.

The premises of the Wellness scholar shifts: topics now reside outside the traditional definitions of inquiry. It is certainly a challenge to realize an ecological expedition since research conventions seem so ingrained. What is needed are adventuresome investigators who chart new approaches and design new methods to fit the requirements of the situation rather than first choosing the statistical or research method and *then* finding a topic that matches the method (Tolan, Keys, Chertok, & Jason, 1990).

To dig into the microsocial systems that illustrate and define integrative and self-validating occasions requires that we attend to the everyday events and interactions of people and do so in concert with other disciplines. To understand why, in the above example, some people in a small Peruvian village boiled water and others did not, Wellin lived in the village for four years and, as a result, was able to understand the intricacies of water boiling because he developed a multifaceted understanding of the daily lives of the people and the cultural and group norms that were operating on individuals (Wellin, 1998). To fulfill the Wellness challenge, we increase our efforts to anchor communication, interaction, and collaboration with other investigators who are also invested in natural communities. Interdisciplinary and cross-disciplinary enterprises seem apt, and attractive.

While universities are not generally creating bridges across departmental structures that traditionally define disciplines and set boundaries on inquiry, there are exceptions. At the University of Illinois at Chicago (UIC), for example, the Office of Social Science Research for the Social Sciences and the Great Cities Institute for the entire university are providing incentives for faculty in different departments to engage in research and to communicate about ideas that may over time create new ways of doing research.

Facilitating cross-disciplinary conversations is not easy or straightforward (Jason, Hess, Felner, & Moritsugu, 1987) John Gardiner, Director of the Office of Social Science Research at UIC, comments:

> Bringing faculty together from different departments had mixed results. Some were so deeply nested in the vocabularies, funding systems, and publication outlets of their disciplines that presentations based on other disciplines seemed unrelated to their own work. Others, however, seemed genuinely fascinated by the insights or alternative starting points and sought out advice on how to learn more, and some contacts led to joint projects using multiple approaches. (Gardiner, 1998)

Wim Wievel, founder of the Great Cities Program at the University of Illinois at Chicago, states the potential of interdisciplinary thinking:

> Increasingly, universities engage in partnerships, in linkage with external organizations to pursue knowledge. For a business, a city government, or a community organization, problems are usually holistic. Working with them thus requires universities to be more holistic. While we need the deep expertise that specialization can bring, we also need people who can bridge across these specializations. It is amazing how excited faculty can get when they have an opportunity to get outside of their narrow field, and how creative they can be in discovering how the concepts of one field can be used in another.
> The Great Cities program takes the urban and metropolitan environment as its field, and thus draws on people from many disciplines. It encourages an interdisciplinary, not just a multidisciplinary approach: we have to do more than involve disciplines in their own ways, we have to get them to talk to each other to let their insights be influenced and enriched by those of others, (Wievel, personal communication, June 1998)

NIH and other groups are encouraging ways to foster more interdisciplinary research (Azar, 1998). Norman B. Anderson, Director of NIH, Office of Behavioral and Social Science Research, supports the aphorism that "health problems do not organize themselves to be congruent with university departments" (Azar, 1998, p. 18). Knowledge domains may become more interdepartmental with the possibility of sharing current methods. As more and more ways are created to facilitate cross-disciplinary investigations, the promise of establishing situated knowledge may be realized.

The new opportunity for the Wellness scholar is to participate in the appraisal of methods and techniques that are developed by investigators representing different professions and with varying premises about scientific validity. This challenging opportunity depends on the local ecology of the participating investigators as they create their own social setting for interdisciplinary communication.

The Third Idea: Listening With Others
Rather Than Assessing Others

Psychology's research tradition has been dominated by a commitment to rigorous and cumulative empirical investigations with tests and scales and experiments. To gain insight about the sources of everyday caring and respect as sources of wellness, new ways of doing our work are needed. This means that caring about the informants and creating trust to work with them emerges as a high priority. Feminist investigators have been paving the way for this type of work for several decades (Lieblich & Josselson, 1994; Oakley, 1981). To appreciate the legacies of family, and peer contributions of social support and social networks, more detailed investigations of everyday life are essential. Anderson's ethnographic analyses of conjoining white and black cultures in a Philadelphia neighborhood is a revealing look at the everyday events that impact the lives of the residents in these two cultures (Anderson, 1990).

The Wellness scholar changes not only research venues, but also portfolios of techniques and criteria for truth. The Wellness scholar adopts new directions and listens to the stories of persons as they describe the people, occasions, and events that have made it possible for them to become more socially developed, competent, and effective in their coping; the Wellness construct is enhanced by including narratives and oral histories.

Scholars interested in autobiography, oral histories, and narratives represent a variety of disciplines and perspectives including sociologists, anthropologists, cognitive psychologists, feminists, and linguists. Each of these investigators expresses a desire to understand the ways in which stories and personal tales illustrate major themes and topics in lives (Conway, 1998; Denzin & Lincoln, 1994; Ross, 1991; Sarbin & Kitsuse, 1994; Schwartz & Sudman, 1994; Wolke, 1997). Even though these research activities may not represent a major thrust or paradigm within psychology, there is long tradition for this type of inquiry (Buss, 1985; Gergen, 1993; Hatch & Wisniewski, 1995; Linde, 1993; McAdams, 1996; Polkinghorne, 1988); more investigators are joining this tradition (Bruner, 1990; Goldman, 1996).

One consequence of this increased investment in an oral history/storytelling tradition is that new questions are being raised about the relationship between the scientist and the informant. Literature is increasingly defining oral history as initiating a dialogue between informant and interviewer rather than as a unidirectional investigation (Barone, 1995; Coles, 1997).

The significance of oral histories as a legitimate form of inquiry makes explicit that there are in fact different ways to understand phenomena, an issue that has been difficult to recognize. The topic of validity expands to consider the relationship between the investigator and the informant and not simply the level of the correlation or the differences in reported means. In the ecological expedition, the heart of the matter *is* the context in which the work takes place.

Tyler, Pargament, and Gatz in 1983 presented a rationale for research to be undertaken where the investigator and the person providing the information are seen as reciprocally influencing each other in decisions about what to assess and how to assess it (Tyler, Pargament, & Gatz, 1983). Sarason and colleagues have invested in the same type of enterprise emphasizing the role of resource networks when generating community service programs (Sarason & Lorentz, 1989, 1998).

The author has also invested in a collaborative process in documenting the development of African American community leaders (Glidewell et al., 1998; Kelly, 1992a; Tandon et al., 1998). When an inquiry is viewed as a reciprocal exchange between two people or two groups, the findings from such an inquiry become dependent upon the quality of the working relationship between the person stimulating the dialogue and the person who is relaying the information.

Engaging in this type of research emphasizes the personal values of the investigator. Too often, these topics are not considered when training research investigators. While personal qualities may vary with the community and the topic, some examples of those qualities that may facilitate collaborative inquiry are: openness to new experiences, investment in learning about new concepts, an ability to expend energy in the beginning of the working relationship; creating informal occasions where both parties can listen to each other; and creating social support groups for the investigator to help interpret unpredictable crises, etc. Certainly, such qualities as being a good listener define how well the obtained information will be salient, deep, and reflect the informants' stories; the present author has noted other generic qualities (Kelly, 1971). Here again the role of the distant, detached, objective observer is replaced by the investigator who expresses a genuine interest and cares about the informant.

The topic of Wellness is elusive and subtle and cannot easily be grasped from a predesigned questionnaire. Yet more clarity about wellness can be derived from dialogue between investigator and informant. The Wellness scholar learns to converse rather than to just label or categorize. Listening includes a variety of discrete skills, as mentioned above, that can become a substantial resource to validate the person who is telling the story. Categorizing and labeling evolves, a conjoint process between the Wellness scholar and the informant, where the first priority is to understand the behavior of persons in situ. The listener can consolidate the storyteller's sense of self in these exchanges and relay back to the storyteller the listener's impressions for more reflection. The Wellness scholar is an attentive and well-prepared listener and learner.

This third idea specifically asserts that the Wellness scholar defines inquiry as a relationship; that without that working relationship of trust, the social intricacies that affect how innovations evolve or stagnate will not be clearly understood.

The Fourth Idea: Learning About Resilient and Competent Communities

Listening to the reports of persons as they express their own health-engendering experiences is also a rehearsal; a rehearsal to listen to the collective stories of resilient groups and communities. Some communities and groups engage each other and generate workable solutions for those social issues that confront them (Iscoe, 1974). At this larger level of analysis, insights can be gained about the social norms and traditions of how groups and communities organize their personal, organizational, and community resources to create a culture that affirms such core values as participation, justice, and dignity.

Decades ago, the topic of community studies was a significant part of sociological and anthropological research. A premise for this tradition was that communities were essential to social life and influenced the behavior of individuals. The works of W. Lloyd Warner (1949), William Foote Whyte (1943), Floyd Hunter (1953), Robert Dahl and C. E. Lindblom (1953), and Herbert Gans 1962, (1962, 1967) are reference points for this tradition (Clausen, 1956). Working on the Wellness Concept is an opportunity to reinitiate such activities. If the role of community structures and processes in affecting wellness behavior can be clarified, then the underlying social fabric can be illuminated as potential positive sources of health engendering behavior. The climate of communities can either enable or diminish opportunities for individuals to feel engaged and active and purposeful and validated. The mediating roles of the small group, organizational, and community structures in facilitating wellness behavior can then be addressed.

When research data are collected from field experiments on participant democracy, the results are not always consistently positive (Feder, 1998). As with all "real" system innovations, some things work, others do not. But the legacy of such efforts is to give representatives from different levels of an organization an opportunity to reinvest their talents and energies. This is one criteria to ascertain whether a collaborative or participative enterprise is judged to be worthwhile: "Would representatives from all levels of the organization or community do it again?" When such participative projects are productive and a reservoir of social norms are established, communities may establish conditions of trust and cohesiveness. Such conditions may in turn promote standards for the expression of wellness behavior. It is thought that when cohesiveness and trust are operative, there are more opportunities to discuss what matters and to then establish norms that enable the desired behavior to be expressed. The topic of community capacity has been a focus of the research of Wandersman and colleagues, as well as the community development work of McKnight (Fetterman, 1996; Wandersman & Florin, 1990; McKnight, 1995). The Centers for Disease Control and Prevention convened a symposium in December 1995 to examine this topic. Social and organizational networks and a sense of community emerged as two of the nine topics that participants recommended for further study (Goodman et al., 1998) The Project on Human Development in Chicago Neighborhoods has employed the concept of collective efficacy that describes the informal controls that are potentially operable in local communities. These include such activities as "monitoring of spontaneous play groups among children, a willingness to intervene to prevent acts such as truancy and street-corner 'hanging' by teenage peer groups, and the confrontation of persons who are exploiting or disturbing public space" (Sampson, Raudenbush, & Earls, 1997, p. 918). Locating these activities and behaviors in specific communities requires attentive listening, dialoguing, and reconnaissance. The various listening skills acquired and tried out with individuals can be expanded to multiple levels of analysis at the community level (Kelly et al., 1988). Campbell and Ahrens created a multiple case study using qualitative interviews with rape victims, rape victim advocates, and workers from the human service organizations to assess at different levels and from different perspectives how to change the community response to rape. This is an excellent example of multiple levels analyses (Campbell & Ahrens, 1998).

Two concepts from social psychology and organizational psychology can nourish these tasks: *social norms and boundary spanning*. These venerable terms have immediate appeal. Knowledge of social norms can clarify the shared values and informal standards of behavior that affect how wellness behavior can be promoted, honored, and maintained in specific communities.

Murray Levine addressed the topic of social norms in terms of initiating prevention programs. Levine pointed out that if we understand the process of establishing norms, we have a basis to understand the processes to establish a sense of community. Rather than viewing preventive interventions as a technique of inoculation, he advocated, "Prevention efforts change norms . . . an effective preventive intervention will go beyond affecting individuals" (Levine, 1998).

Social norms reflect the guiding standards that in turn affect the expressions of behavior in that community.

Opp has provided three criteria to investigate the significance of social norms: (1) The communication opportunities between people in a social group that make it possible to pass the norm to others; (2) The cohesiveness of the group and the extent to which shared or uniform behavior is valued; (3) The importance of the norm for the group (Opp, 1982). A situated understanding of how these criteria are expressed can contribute to the analysis of specific microfactors that operate to facilitate the norms being shared. This is particularly so when understanding the descriptive norms of what people actually do in any given situation (Cialdini & Trost, 1998). These authors have pointed out: "Recent meta-analyses indicate that the most successful prevention programs for adolescents not only teach resistance skills, but also modify the social proof for using drugs: the programs change the descriptive norms about the prevalence of use among students and are delivered and reinforced by similar others, their peers (Tobler 1986, 1995)" (Cialdini & Trost, 1998, p. 157). A recently published example of the power of social norms is the work of Miller, Klotz, and Eckholdt (1998). In an intervention with gay male prostitutes, the effectiveness of the intervention was enhanced because it directly and specifically targeted key leaders and respected friends to spread the word about HIV prevention, thereby changing the social norms from unprotected to protected sex. Approval by others is a powerful source for norm creation.

What is often missing is to "hunker down" into the daily lives of people to understand and appreciate the subtle ways in which the social norms set the tone, if not the basis, for the criteria for approval. Finding out who is most important to an individual and assessing how the informant thinks that these important people prefer him or her to behave points to the potential power of situated knowledge. The empirical literature on the emergence and transmission of norms is small, as Cialdini and Trost point out (Cialdini & Trost, 1998). However, the significance of norms for understanding wellness behavior seems apt, timely, and long overdue.

The concept of boundary spanning can lead to understandings of how the community or group makes contact and encourages reciprocal connections to other groups and organizations. Boundary spanning is a construct most identified with organizational psychology (At-Twaijri & Montanari, 1987; Katz & Kahn, 1978). The notion is that the boundary of an organization is a key location between an organization and its surrounding environment (Dollinger, 1984; Jemison, 1984). Persons who function in roles that influence communication between the host organization and other organizations are considered to be in boundary roles and are referred to as boundary spanners (Kelly, Altman, Ryan, & Stelzner, 2000). If information and the exchange of resources can contribute to the health or efficacy of a group or organization, then the active nature of boundary spanning and the status of the person who activates these roles are of some significance. If the concept of Wellness can be conceptualized as a process to identify and exchange personal, organizational, and community resources, then boundary spanning activities are salient. Laumann et al. (1977) have stated that exchanges of communication and information is necessary in community decision making if local issues are to be resolved (Azelton, 1994). This makes boundary spanning a particularly appropriate concept to understand the group or organization's ability to adapt.

A topic for future investigation is whether the various ways in which interdependence can develop between groups and organizations increase the vitality of these organizations. Vitality—reserve energy for coping with crises, for example—may impact the positive socialization processes for future leadership behavior and further promote the capacity of members of organizations to carry out activities that promote wellness behavior, such as norms for sharing information and commitments to establish organizational values to increase trust and dignity. Emphasizing such concepts may expand options so that the study of wellness will not be restricted to the study of individuals! The point of emphasis is that the study of wellness is an interdisciplinary and multidisciplinary enterprise; an ecological expedition for Wellness depends upon the contributions of multiple research traditions.

The concepts of social norms and boundary spanning applied to the analysis of resilient communities can test the notion of whether personal growth and development can be enhanced when the places in which we live and work have linkages to other groups and organizations. An ecological premise is that the adaptive capacity of individuals and organizations can be enhanced when exchanges of information and resources between two organizations are a part of the everyday life of participants. The Wellness scholar works to understand how groups and communities identify whether personal and organizational resources do or do not facilitate institutional forms of coping.

The Fifth Idea: The Analysis of Variety and Diversity

Null hypothesis significance testing (NHST) has limited our understanding of research topics (Cohen, 1994). The reverence for the analysis of differences between individuals and groups has been ritualized.

There are other options. In 1962 John Tukey emphasized "detective work" as the metaphor for statistical analysis rather than "sanctification" (Tukey, 1962). He later detailed this thesis in his classic book *Exploratory Data Analysis* (Tukey, 1977). More recent sources for these ideas are represented in the work of Behrens and Loftus (Behrens, 1997; Loftus, 1996). Cortina and Dunlap have summarized their review of NHST with the following comment: "The abuses of NHST have come about largely because of a lack of judgment or education with respect to those using the procedure. The cure lies in improving education and, consequently judgment, not in abolishing the method" (Cortina & Dunlop, 1997).

The limitations of null hypothesis testing has been acknowledged as timely and needed by the APA Board of Scientific Affairs, with the creation in 1996 of the Task Force on Statistical Inference (Board of Scientific Affairs, APA, 1997).

To quote from the interim report of the task force:

> It is the view of the task force that there are many ways of using statistical methods to help us understand the phenomena we are studying (e.g.,

Bayesian methods, graphical and exploratory data analysis methods, hypothesis testing strategies). We endorse a policy of inclusiveness that allows any procedure that appropriately sheds light on the phenomenon of interest to be included in the arsenal of the research scientist. (Board of Scientific Affairs, APA, 1996)

Adopting Tukey's detective metaphor and applying it to Wellness investigations enhances the possibilities of finding diverse patterns of Wellness. It seems that what is more informative is seeing how many *different* patterns of wellness are prevalent in any community in contrast to focusing on what are the modal patterns of wellness.

Rapkin and Luke expressed this issue directly for community psychologists:

Quantitative methods focus on central tendencies; means, main effects, regression lines, discriminant functions, structural models. These techniques yield the best results when all cases conform to a given model and literally fall in line. However, models that emphasize uniformity seem inconsistent with the appreciation for diversity that community psychologists value. (Rapkin & Luke, 1993, p. 249)

They continue with a detailed exposition of the uses of cluster analysis to describe diversity in a sample.

Linear lines of concordance in traditional analyses can communicate that "outliers" are deviants rather than sources of potential feedback for further "detective" work. Other visual displays of data, by the use of box plots and scatter plots, can communicate the arrays of responses (Tufte, 1983, 1998). Campbell, in an analysis of the rape victim's experiences with a state legal, medical, and mental health system, used cluster analysis to clarify the experiences of rape victims with these large social systems. Using cluster analytic techniques, she discovered that there is no monolithic experience; there are only diverse experiences that vary by race and social class (Campbell, 1998).

Premature celebration of modal patterns of wellness behavior can inadvertently communicate a monolithic, unintended preferred standard for behavior rather than expressing the variety of potentially valid wellness behaviors. This is particularly so when the persons providing the data are from different social classes or ethnic groups and do not represent the usual reference point of college students as informants for psychological inquiry.

This fifth idea has additional meaning. It has long been observed that persons at the margin often are the sources of innovation and have the motivation for constructive change (Katz & Kahn, 1978). The marginal person, whose behavior deviates from the norm, may be a valid resource of generative action (Kelly, 1992b). Persons at the margin become potential sources for revitalizing groups and communities (Angelique & Campbell, 1998). Increasing consciousness about differences and variety, accompanied by methods of analysis that reflect patterns of variety, is a potentially useful approach to reduce any premature promulgation of a preference standard for desirable wellness behavior (Trickett, Watts, & Birman, 1994).

Examining patterns of diversity in wellness behavior can be a constructive force to limit the reification of the Wellness concept. In employing this fifth idea, individuals are not considered as a part of a homogeneous group but rather as a set of individuals who share qualities that they may not share with others. Not all people are considered equally well for all conditions or situations. An ecological perspective views some persons as "well" for one particular situation or setting, but not another. Exploratory data analysis techniques are particularly apt for understanding patterns of behavior as they are expressed on "the ground," where there may not be an apparent prior theoretical rationale or basis for predictions. Since interpretations of variance are sometimes conceived as "noise" or "error" rather than as a source of information, patterns of variability can provide an alternative frame of reference.

One implication of focusing on the variety of responses is that multiple types of interventions for varied forms of wellness can be created. This is in contrast to the dominant intervention protocol that assumes that any one intervention is universally applicable.

Conclusion

Emory Cowen has been a major exponent for redefining the focus for psychological inquiry, particularly inquiry that involves designing prevention research or evaluating preventive interventions. Emory's manifold examples have helped to redirect research to topics of positive sources of interpersonal and social relationships. I am pleased to offer some ideas that were stimulated from his original and continuing impetus.

I am suggesting that one point of view for generating Wellness inquiry is to create an ecological expedition. Five ideas were offered to begin the expedition that could potentially establish a new domain, that of the Wellness scholar.

The five ideas are heuristic topics of how ecological thinking can influence the type of information to be sought and found. These ideas were presented under the following five headings: Contextual Thinking: An Agenda for Situated Inquiry, New Disciplinary Connections, and Pluralistic Methods; Listening with Others Rather than Assessing Others; Learning about Resilient and Competent Communities; and The Analysis of Variety and Diversity.

The framing premise for these five ideas is that knowledge about Wellness is a process of inquiry that is cross-disciplinary and is a process that defines research as a personal relationship. This is so because to understand Wellness means understanding the varied ways in which persons construct meaning, create social ties, and establish a workable culture. In this sense, the Wellness scholar also has the potential to be a resource for healing when understanding the various sources of social cohesion.

Acknowledgments

The following persons read drafts of the chapter and/or offered useful substantive and editorial suggestions. I have appreciated their comments on this chapter: Becki Campbell, Paul Dolinko, Caroline Leopold, Robin Miller, Tony Orum, and Julian Rappaport.

References

Anderson, E. (1990). *Street wise: Race, class and change in an urban community.* Chicago: University of Chicago Press.

Angelique, H., & Campbell, R. (1998). Diversity among women: The need for visibility, dangerous dialogue and action. *Community Psychologist, 31*(1), 30–32.

At-Twaijri, M. I., & Montanari, J. R. (1987). The impact of context and choice on the boundary-spanning process: An empirical extension. *Human Relations, 40,* 781–798.

Azar, B. (1998, May). Federal agencies encourage more cross-disciplinary work. *APA Monitor, 18,* 18.

Azelton, L. S. (1994). Boundary spanning and community leadership. Unpublished manuscript. University of Illinois at Chicago.

Bagby, M. (1996). *Documenting community leadership.* Videotape recording. University of Illinois at Chicago, Department of Psychology.

Barker, R. G. (1965). Explorations in ecological psychology. *American Psychologist, 20,* 1–14.

Barker, R. G. (1968). *Ecological psychology: Concepts and methods for studying the environment of human behavior.* Stanford, CA: Stanford University Press.

Barone, T. (1995). Persuasive writings, vigilant readings, and reconstructed characters: The paradox of trust in educational storysharing. In J. Hatch & R. Wisniewski (Eds.), *Life, history and narrative* (pp. 63–74). London: Falmer Press.

Bechtel, R. (Ed.). (1990). The Midwest Psychological Field Station: A celebration of its founding. *Environment and Behavior, 22*(4). New York: Sage.

Behrens, J. (1997). Principles and procedures of exploratory data analysis. *Psychological Methods, 2*(2), 131–160.

Bell, C. (1997). *Ritual: Perspectives and dimensions.* New York: Oxford University Press.

Bloom, D. E. (1998, May). Technology, experimentation, and the quality of survey data. *Science, 280,* 789–968.

Board of Scientific Affairs, American Psychological Association. (1996, December 14–15). Task force on statistical inference initial report (draft). Available [online] at www.apa.org/science/tfsi.html.

Board of Scientific Affairs, American Psychological Association. (1997, March/April.) Task force on statistical inference identifies charge and produces report. *Psychological Science Agenda,* 9–10.

Bronfenbrenner, U. (1979). *The ecology of human development*. Cambridge, MA: Harvard University Press.

Bruner, J. (1990). *Acts of meaning*. Cambridge, MA: Harvard University Press.

Buss, F. L. (1985). *Dignity: Lower income women tell of their lives and struggles*. Ann Arbor: University of Michigan Press.

Campbell, R. (1998). The community response to rape: Victims' experiences with the legal, medical, and mental health systems. *American Journal of Community Psychology, 26*, 355–379.

Campbell, R., & Ahrens, C. (1998). Innovative community services for rape victims: An application of multiple case study methodology. *American Journal of Community Psychology, 26*, 537–572.

Cialdini, R., & Trost, M. (1998). Social influence: Social norms, conformity, and compliance. In D. Gilbert, S. Fiske, & G. Lindzey (Eds.), *The handbook of social psychology* (pp. 151–192). New York: McGraw Hill.

Clausen, J. A. (1956). *Sociology and the field of mental health*. New York: Sage.

Cohen, J. (1994). The earth is round (p < .05). *American Psychologist, 49*(12), 997–1003.

Coles, R. (1997). *Doing documentary work*. New York: Oxford University Press.

Conway, J. K. (1998). *When memory speaks: Reflections on autobiography*. New York: Knopf.

Cortina, J., & Dunlap, W. P. (1997). On the logic and purpose of significance testing. *Psychological Methods, 2*(2), 161–172.

Cronbach, L. J. (1986). Social inquiry by and for earthlings. In D. W. Fiske & R. A. Shweder (Eds.), *Metatheory in social science* (pp. 83–107). Chicago: University of Chicago Press.

Dahl, R., & Lindblom, C. E. (1953). *Politics, economics and welfare: Planning and politico-economic systems resolved into basic social processes*. New York: Harper & Row.

Davis, A., Gardner, B., & Gardner, M. R. (1941). *Deep south: A social anthropological study of caste and class*. Chicago: University of Chicago Press.

Denzin, N. K., & Lincoln, Y. S. (Eds.). (1994). *Handbook of qualitative research*. Thousand Oaks, CA: Sage.

Dollinger, M. (1984). Environmental boundary spanning and information process on organizational performance. *Academy of Management Journal, 27*, 351–368.

Feder, B. (1998, February 21). The little project that couldn't: Others learn from a failed test in worker democracy. *New York Times, Business Day*, B1–B3.

Fetterman, D. M., Kaftarian, S. J., & Wandersman, A. (Eds.). (1996). *Empowerment evaluation: Knowledge and tools for self-assessment and accountability*. Thousand Oaks, CA: Sage.

Gans, H. J. (1962). *The urban villagers: Group and class in the life of Italian-Americans*. New York: Free Press.

Gans, H. (1967). *The Livittowners: Ways of life and politics in a new suburban community*. New York: Columbia University Press.

Geertz, C. (1995). *After the fact: Two countries, four decades, one anthropologist*. Cambridge, MA: Harvard University Press.

George, J. M., & Brief, A. P. (1992). Feeling good—doing good: A conceptual analysis of the mood at work—organizational spontaneity relationship. *Psychological Bulletin, 112*, 310–329.

Gergan, K. J. (Ed.). (1993). *Refiguring self and psychology*. Hants, UK: Dartmouth Publishing.

Glidewell, J. C., Kelly, J. G., Bagby, M., & Dickerson, A. (1998). Natural development of community leadership. In R. Scott Tindale, L. Heath, J. Edwards, E. J. Posavac, F. B. Bryant, Y. Suarez-Balcazar, E. Henderson-King, & J. Myers (Eds.), *Social psychological applications to social issues: Theory and research on small groups* (Vol. 4) (pp. 61–86). New York: Plenum.

Goldman, A. E. (1996). *Take my word*. Berkeley: University of California Press.

Goodman, R. M., Speers, M. A., McLeroy, K., Fawcett, S., Kegler, M., Smith, P. R., Sterling, T. D., & Wallerstein, N. (1998). Identifying and refining the dimensions of community capacity to provide a basis for measurement. *Health Education and Behavior, 25*, 258–278.

Hatch, J. A., & Wisniewski, R. (Eds.). (1995). *Life history and narrative*. London: Falmer Press.

Hesse, M. (1978). Theory and value in the social sciences. In C. Hookway & P. Pettit (Eds.), *Action and interpretation: Studies in the philosophy of the social sciences*. Cambridge: Cambridge University Press.

Hunter, F. (1953). *Community power structure: A study of decision makers*. Chapel Hill: University of North Carolina Press.

Iscoe, I. (1974). Community psychology and the competent community. *American Psychologist, 29*, 607–613.

Jason, L. A., Hess, R. E., Felner, R. D., & Moritsugu, J. N. (1987). *Prevention in human services: Vol. 5. Prevention: Toward a multidisciplinary approach*. New York: Haworth.

Jemison, D. (1984). The importance of boundary spanning roles in strategic decision-making. *Journal of Management Studies, 21*(2), 131–152.

Kahn, S. (1982). *A guide for grassroots leaders: Organizing*. New York: McGraw.

Katz, D., & Kahn, R. (1978). *The social psychology of organizations* (2nd ed.). New York: Wiley.

Kelly, J. G. (1971). Qualities for the community psychologist. *American Psychologist, 26*, 897–903.

Kelly, J. G. (Ed.). (1979). *Adolescent boys in high school: A psychological study of coping and adaptation*. Hillsdale, NJ: Lawrence Erlbaum.

Kelly, J. G. (1992a). *Ecological inquiry and a collaborative enterprise: A commentary on "The Chicago Experience."* Unpublished manuscript, University of Illinois at Chicago.

Kelly, J. G. (1992b). Gerald Caplan's paradigm: Bridging psychotherapy and public health practice. In W. P. Erchul (Ed.), *Consultation in community, school and organizational practice: Gerald Caplan's contributions to professional psychology* (pp. 75–85). Washington, DC: Hemisphere Publishing.

Kelly, J. G. (1996). The history and varied epistemologies of community psychology: Describing the UIC course. *Community Psychologist, 29*(1), 14–17.

Kelly, J. G., Dassoff, N., Levin, I., Schreckengost, J., Stelzner, S., & Altman, B. (1988). *A guide to conducting prevention research in the community: First steps*. Binghamton, NY: Haworth.

Kelly, J. G., Altman, B. E., Ryan, A. M., & Stelzner, S. (2000). Understanding and changing social systems. In J. Rapapport & E. Seidman (Eds.), *The handbook of community psychology* (pp. 133–159). New York: Plenum.

Kingry-Westergaard, C., & Kelly, J. G. (1990). A contextualist epistemology for ecological research. In P. Tolan, C. Keys, F. Chertok, & L. Jason (Eds.), *Researching community psychology: Issues of theory and methods* (pp. 23–31). Washington, DC: APA.

Koch, S. (Ed.). (1959). *Formulations of the person and the social context.* New York: McGraw-Hill.

Laumann, E., Marsden, P., & Galaskiewicz, J. (1977). Community-elite influence structures: Extension of a network approach. *American Journal of Sociology, 83,* 595–631.

Lave, J., & Wenger, E. (1991). *Situated learning: Legitimate peripheral participation.* Cambridge, UK: Cambridge University Press.

Levine, M. (1998). Prevention and community. *American Journal of Community Psychology, 26*(2), 189–206.

Lieblich, A., & Josselson, R. (Eds.). (1994). *Exploring identity and gender: The narrative study of lives* (Vol. 2). Thousand Oaks, CA: Sage.

Lillard, A. (1998). Ethnopsychologies: Cultural variations in theories of mind. *Psychological Bulletin, 123*(1), 3–32.

Linde, C. (1993). *Life stories: The creation of coherence.* New York: Oxford University Press.

Loftus, G. R. (1996). Psychology will be a much better science when we change the way we analyze data. *American Psychological Society,* 161–171.

Maton, K. I. (1993). Moving beyond the individual level of analysis in mutual help group research: An ecological paradigm. *Journal of Applied Behavioral Science, 29,* 272–286.

Maton, K., Hrabowski III, F., & Grelf, G. L. (1998). Preparing the way: A qualitative study of high achieving African American males and the role of the family. *American Journal of Community Psychology, 26,* 639–668.

McAdams, D. P. (1996). Personality, modernity, and the storied self: A contemporary framework for studying persons. *Psychological Inquiry, 7*(4), 295–321.

McKnight, John. (1995). *The careless society.* New York: Basic Books.

McLoyd, V. (1998). Socioeconomic disadvantage and child development. *American Psychologist, 53*(2), 185–204.

Miller, R., Klotz, D., & Eckholdt, H. (1998). HIV prevention with male prostitutes and patrons of hustler bars: Replication of an HIV preventive intervention. *American Journal of Community Psychology, 26*(1), 97–131.

Moos, R. H. (1973). Conceptualizations of human environments. *American Psychologist, 28,* 652–665.

Moos, R. H. (1976). *The human context: Environmental determinants of behavior.* New York: Wiley.

Moos, R. H. (1979). Social climate measurement and feedback. In R. Muñoz, L. Snowden, & J. Kelly (Eds.), *Social and psychological research in community settings* (pp. 145–182). San Francisco: Jossey-Bass.

Moos, R. H., & Insel, P. (1974). *Issues in social ecology.* Palo Alto, CA: National Press Books.

Neisser, U., & Jopling, D. A. (Eds.). (1997). *The conceptual self in context: Culture, experience, self-understanding* (pp. 3–285). Cambridge, UK: Cambridge University Press.

Oakley, A. (1981). Interviewing women: A contradiction in terms. In H. Roberts (Ed.), *Doing feminist research* (pp. 30–61). London: Routledge.

Ochs, E., & Capps, L. (1996). Narrating the self. *Annual Review of Anthropology, 25,* 19–43.

Opp, K. D. (1982). The evolutionary emergence of norms. *British Journal of Social Psychology, 21,* 139–149.

Payne, C. M. (1995). *I've got the light of freedom: The organizing tradition and the Mississippi freedom struggle.* Berkeley: University of California Press.

Polkinghorne, D. E. (1988). *Narrative knowing and the human sciences.* Albany, NY: SUNY Press.

Pollio, H. R., Henley, T., & Thompson, C. B. (1997). *The phenomenology of everyday life.* Cambridge, UK: Cambridge University Press.

Rapkin, B., & Luke, D. (1993). Cluster analysis in community research: Epistemology and practice. *American Journal of Community Psychology, 21*(2), 247–277.

Raush, H. L., Dittmann, A. T., & Taylor, T. J. (1959). The interpersonal behavior of children in residential treatment. *Journal of Abnormal and Social Psychology, 58,* 9–26.

Raush, H. L., Farbman, L., & Llewellyn, L. G. (1960). Person, setting and change in social interaction: II. A normal-control study. *Human Relations, 13,* 305–333.

Ross, B. M. (1991). *Remembering the personal past: Descriptions of autobiographical memory.* New York: Oxford University Press.

Sampson, R. J., Raudenbush, S. W., & Earls, F. (1997). Neighborhoods and violent crime: A multilevel study of collective efficacy. *Science, 277,* 918–924.

Sarason, S. B., & Lorentz, E. (1989). *The challenge of the resource exchange network.* Cambridge, MA: Brookline Books.

Sarason, S. B., & Lorentz, E. (1998). *Crossing boundaries: Collaboration, coordination, and the redefinition of resources.* San Francisco: Jossey-Bass.

Sarbin, T. R., & Kitsuse, J. I. (Eds.). (1994). *Constructing the social.* London: Sage.

Schoggen, P., & Fox, K. (1989). *Behavior settings: A revision and extension of Roger G. Barker's "Ecological Psychology."* Stanford, CA: Stanford University Press.

Schwarz, N., & Sudman, S. (Eds.) *Autobiographical memory and the validity of retrospective reports.* New York: Springer-Verlag.

Seaburn, D. B., Lorenz, A. D., Gunn, W. B. Jr., Gawinski, B. A., & Mauksch, L. B. (1994). *Models of collaboration* (pp. 3–350). Oakland, CA: New Harbinger Publishing.

Seligman, M. E. P. (1998). President's column. *APA Monitor, 29,* 2–5.

Shapin, S. (1994). *A social history of truth.* Chicago: University of Chicago Press.

Stokols, D. (1992). Establishing and maintaining healthy environments: Toward a social ecology of health promotion. *American Psychologist, 47,* 6–22.

Stokols, D., & Altman, I. (Eds.). (1987). *Handbook of environmental psychology* (Vol. 1). New York: Wiley.

Tandon, S. D., Azelton, L. S., Kelly, J. G., & Strickland, A. (1998). Constructing a tree for community leaders: Contexts and processes in collaborative inquiry. *American Journal of Community Psychology, 26*(4), 669–696.

Taylor, S. E., Repetti, R. L., & Seeman, T. (1997). Health psychology: What is an unhealthy environment and how does it get under the skin? *Annual Review of Psychology, 48,* 411–47.

Tobler, N. S. (1986). Meta-analysis of 143 adolescent drug prevention programs: Quantitative outcome results of program participants compared to a control or comparison group. *Journal of Drug Issues, 16,* 537–568.

Tobler, N. S. (1995, June). *Interactive programs are successful: A new meta-analysis findings.* Paper presented at the Society for Prevention Research Meeting, Scottsdale, AZ.

Tolan, P., Keys, C., Chertok, F., & Jason, L. (Eds.). (1990). *Researching community psychology.* Washington, DC: APA.

Trickett, E. J. (1984). Towards a distinctive community psychology: An ecological metaphor for training and the conduct of research. *American Journal of Community Psychology, 12,* 261–279.

Trickett, E. J. (1989). Taking ecology seriously: A community development approach to individually based interventions. In L. Bond & B. Compas (Eds.), *Primary prevention in the schools* (pp. 361–390). Hanover, NH: University of New England Press.

Trickett, E. J., Kelly, J. G., & Vincent, T. A. (1985). The spirit of ecological inquiry in community research. In E. Susskind & D. Klein (Eds.), *Community research: Methods, paradigms, and applications* (pp. 331–406). New York: Praeger.

Trickett, E. J., Watts, R. J., & Birman, D. (Eds.). (1994). *Human diversity: Perspectives on People in Context.* San Francisco: Jossey-Bass.

Tufte, E. R. (1983). *The visual display of quantitative information.* Cheshire, CT: Graphics Press.

Tufte, E. R. (1998). *Visual explanations: Images and quantities, evidence and narrative.* Cheshire, CT: Graphics Press.

Tukey, J. (1962). Analyzing data: Sanctification or detective work? *American Psychologist, 24,* 83–91.

Tukey, J. (1977). *Exploratory data analysis.* Reading, MA: Addison-Wesley.

Turner, C. F., Ku, L., Rogers, S. M., Lindberg, L. D., Pleck, J. H., & Sonenstein, F. L. (1998, May). Adolescent sexual behavior, drug use, and violence: Increased reporting with computer survey technology. *Science, 280,* 867–873.

Tyler, F., Pargament, K., & Gatz, M. (1983). The resource collaborator role: A model for interactions involving psychologists. *American Psychologist,* 388–397.

Wandersman, A., & Florin, P. (1990). Citizen participation, voluntary organizations and community development: Insights for empowerment and research [Special issue]. *American Journal of Community Psychology, 18*(1).

Warner, W. L. (1949). *Democracy in Jonesville.* New York: Harper.

Wellin, E. (1955). Water boiling in a Peruvian town. In B. D. Paul & W. B. Miller (Eds.), *Health, culture, and community* (pp. 71–103). New York: Sage.

Wellin, E. (1998). *Exemplars of community psychology* (video). Chicago: University of Illinois at Chicago.

Wertheimer, M., & Robinson, D. (1998). Two views of psychology: A study of a science. *Contemporary Psychology, 43*(1), 7–12.

White, P. (1990). Ideas about causation in philosophy and psychology. *Psychological Bulletin, 108*(1), 3–18.

Whyte, W. F. (1943). *Street corner society*. Chicago: University of Chicago Press.

Wolke, B., Gershkovich, I., & Polo, M. (1997, August). *Examining the complexity of most memorable autobiographical experiences*. Paper submitted to the American Psychological Association, Chicago, IL.

12

Contexts and Community Leadership

Inquiry as an Ecological Expedition

Reflections

This chapter, published originally in 1999, was the address I gave at the American Psychological Association meetings in San Francisco in 1998. The address was in response to receiving the APA Award for Distinguished Contributions to Psychology in the Public Interest in 1997, which I felt really honored to receive. On previous occasions community psychologists Seymour Sarason, Stanley Sue, and Emory Cowen were recipients. I remember the occasion very well. Beyond colleagues, the audience included former students as well as my wife, members of her immediate family, and four of my five children. Several people from the community I was working with in Chicago were also present. We gave a symposium on our work at these meetings, so they were able to be in the audience for this award. Lonnie Snowden introduced me. Chris Keys arranged a reception in my honor, and Ken Maton organized a dinner sponsored by the Society for Community Research and Action.

I selected this publication as an exemplar of a decade's worth of work devoted to documenting community leadership. The work had several features illustrated in my comments. I described the work as an ecological expedition because it was intimately connected to the community and the methods were derived from the local culture. I also meant that research needs time to develop a trusting relationship with the community. Deriving methods from local culture is still an unorthodox idea. Spending 10 years engrossed with one community is still an unconventional effort. I took advantage of the occasion to argue for some key features of thinking ecologically.

I also enjoyed talking about ideas that were not usually referred to when discussing community research. The core of my work was determined by shared metaphors with the community organization, the Developing Communities Project, serving the greater Roseland area in Chicago, Illinois. The metaphor of leadership as making a soup gave the project a solid foundation. We had a common meaning about leadership that was based on joint community university discussions. A second metaphor was thinking about leadership as a tree, which referred to presenting findings in keeping with the frames of reference of the Developing Communities Project. Leadership as a tree was a way to present data that was not from the point of view of the researcher but consonant with the aspirations of the community group. I really felt good about these two metaphors being so explicitly central to the work. They were not just implicit ideas in the background but conceptual terms to represent the unique goals of the research and community organization.

This was a very important project for me. It enabled me to test out ideas much as I had done with the high school study some 30 years before. The work gave me a chance to really invest in a community and to embrace their goals of citizen and community development. It also gave me an opportunity to work with doctoral students and provide an in-depth research experience that was community-based. I felt comfortable and consistent about my ideas presented at this APA award ceremony because of an integration of my values and my work.

Citation

For important contributions to the public interest as a rigorous scholar, an examiner of values, and a respecter and protector of the rights and needs of public consumers of psychology. James G. Kelly, in his articulation of the ecological thesis, has been in the forefront of opening up the social context for psychologists to explore through research, intervention, and policy. During his entire career, he has been committed to understanding behavior in the natural social environment, not for its own sake but as a foundation to tackle the most pressing and difficult social problems. Kelly's research on the social ecology of high school demonstrates the crucial role of context in adolescent development. His current work examines cultural and environmental characteristics that promote the development of African American community leaders. Kelly's thoughtful treatise on conducting prevention research specifies issues to consider and steps to take to develop a research program that values the community and its members as well as the phenomena under study. He has given public-interest minded students a set of conceptual tools and practical examples that enable them to enter the world of action research armed with clear ideas as well as ideals and energy. In addition to his scholarship, Kelly has been a leader in the public sector, the university, and the community for more than three decades. By inspiring through example, his teaching, and his ecological perspective, Kelly has been instrumental in leading psychologists beyond the subject pool and into the community to address, ameliorate, and prevent important social problems.

Community leadership is a compelling topic for study because it illuminates the connections between ordinary citizens as leaders and the contexts of the communities in which they live. A nine-year ecological expedition documenting the development of African American community leaders on the south side of Chicago is described. The collaborative research process between the University of Illinois at Chicago and the Developing Communities Project generated the topics and methods of inquiry. Examples are given of how the collaborative process enhanced the quality and salience of the documentation. The role of metaphors is also discussed, which helped to further elaborate the shared meanings of expressed leadership. Examples are presented of methods (leadership trees) created to present the findings of interviews with 80 community leaders. These leadership trees are examples of context-specific methods derived from the ecological expedition.

> Once we've acquiesced in concealing our agency from ourselves and others, we've lost our moral moorings.
>
> Conway (1998, p. 179)

> But cultivation of that voice—the power of speaking for oneself—is a prerequisite for maturity, because until we've found our own voices we can't settle down to ask ourselves and others probing questions about life in the present.
>
> Conway (1998, p. 180)

Ella Baker was, from the 1940s through the 1970s, an influential leader in the civil rights movement. During the Montgomery, Alabama, bus boycott of 1955–1956, she made some trenchant observations about leadership. As her biographer, Joanne Grant, describes it,

> Baker had been thinking of the nurse she had met who would work all night at a hospital, but who was there in the morning to do whatever needed to be done. On one occasion, after the boycott was over, [Martin Luther] King was arrested and Baker was in a demonstration outside the jail. The nurse was there too, despite having worked all night. "Now that kind of dedication could have been utilized," Baker said. She spoke of the woman who baked pies and sold them and brought the proceeds to the Montgomery Improvement Association each week. "That woman may never have developed to the point of being a leader of a workshop, but she could have been integrated into a program and her talents could have been developed," Baker said. When asked, "What do you suppose happened to all of those people?" she replied, "Nothing. That's the tragedy of it." (Grant, 1998, p. 108)

Ms. Baker's appraisal is still a challenge to community organizations, community organizers, community foundations, and community psychologists who investigate the topic of community leadership.

The psychological inquiries of White, well-educated males working in large corporations could benefit from Ella Baker's observation that ordinary people are underutilized. Psychologists typically emphasize assessing individual traits of these formal leaders and do so with standardized questionnaires and surveys that are analyzed away from the actual settings where leadership is expressed. This type of research also has been carried out in a hierarchical relationship with the investigator as expert and the informant in a passive role. Although there are some investigators who do view leadership as a shared influence process, the dominant point of view has considered leadership to be a specialized role or the expression of specific skills, interests, and traits (Yukl, 1998). Therefore, the research literature on psychological studies of community leadership, particularly the expressed leadership of ordinary citizens, is not a major resource for guidance or hypotheses about understanding community leadership.

Ed Hollander, in his chapter in the third edition of the *Handbook of Social Psychology*, made a compelling case to assert that leadership was not a person but a process (Hollander, 1983). His viewpoint, however, is not widely shared. The dominant preference for the study of individual traits has continued. Over 5,000 studies of organizational leadership exist. However, these studies do not reveal how ordinary people become involved in improving the quality of their own lives in their own communities (Yukl, 1998). Fortunately, psychologists and scholars in other fields are providing insights about how ordinary people are involved in the leadership process. The following scholars have contributed to the work that I discuss in this address: the psychologists Bill Berkowitz, Dan MacAdams, Abe Wandersman, Paul Florin, David Chavis and colleagues, Ken and Mary Gergen, Ann Colby, and Bill Damon; feminist scholars Shlamit Reinharz and Kim Marie Vaze; educators Thomas Barone and Bill Ayers; sociologists Charles Payne and Anne Goldman; historian John Dittmer; psychiatrist Robert Coles; linguist Charlotte Linde; and many biographers, like Robert Caro and David McCullough and certainly Studs Terkel.[1] Each of them has gone beyond the past traditions of inquiry and devoted time and creativity to understanding the contributions of ordinary citizens for the development of their communities.

These investigators have not subscribed to the previous heritage of psychological inquiry where there is a clear demarcation between researcher and informant. Instead, the scholars just mentioned have defined the task of scholarship and inquiry as follows: to understand the topic of leadership by engaging the informant as an active partner in the inquiry. The work I will mention today is in the tradition of inquiry as collaborative activity with ordinary citizens (Brydon-Miller & Tolman, 1997; Tyler, Pargement, & Gatz, 1983).

Documenting Community Leadership in Chicago

Since 1990, a small group of graduate students and I at the University of Illinois at Chicago (UIC) have documented the development of community leadership on the south side of Chicago (Glidewell 1998; Kelly, 1992; Tandon, 1998). The community leaders are trained by the staff and board of the Developing Communities Project (DCP). The DCP, founded in 1986, is a church-based community organization concerned with improving the quality of life in the community through a variety of efforts to increase literacy, to increase the capacity of schools to support and draw on parent and citizen advocates, and to support projects such as the development of young female leaders (Obama, 1995).

What I report in this address are two ideas that I have found to be useful in thinking about and documenting community leadership. These ideas have shaped the work that I refer to as an *ecological expedition*. An ecological expedition represents efforts to reflect on the qualities of the community rather than to sanctify the methods of social science. An ecological expedition is an open-ended process of discovery where the very nature of the work, the spirit of the work, and the methods of the work are interconnected. An ecological expedition creates social settings so that the various contexts can be explicitly considered, where metaphors for the work can be expressed and guide the selection of methods to illuminate the particular contexts. An ecological expedition is not an elitist or a colonizing activity. The researcher is not in the privileged position of expert and sole owner of the process and the content of the activity. A potential tangible benefit of such an expedition is that the informants become invested in documenting their own specific leadership skills for themselves.

So far, the DCP-UIC expedition, although challenging and uncertain, is helping to generate some novel methods, provocative concepts, and, most important, insights about the topic of community leadership that may be of direct and immediate benefit to the DCP community. The two ideas present in this address are (a) context is not just something, it is the heart and soul of the matter and (b) metaphors are resources to create a psychology of community.

Idea 1: Context Is Not Just Something, It Is the Heart and Soul of the Matter

Background. John Hartford wrote a song back in 1962 called "I Would Not Be Here" in which he made an exquisite statement about how everything is related to everything else. His lyrics artistically illustrated how one person's current activity was inextricably connected with a concatenation of accidents, opportunities, and windfalls that involved a cascading list of happenstances. The UIC-DCP work is in this tradition of paying attention to how social inquiry is embedded in a particular time, place, and set of circumstances. These various events, opportunities, and influences become the very substance of community inquiry, because paying attention to them requires constant reflection and at least some reciprocity between the partners.

Following the lead of John Hartford, I will list a few of the contextual factors that have influenced this UIC-DCP collaboration:

- A community coping with a loss of jobs
- The ever-present demand on community organizations with small staffs to locate funding for community development activities
- The Division of Community and Prevention Research in the Department of Psychology at UIC—the organizational host for this work—whose faculty and students value doing community-based research
- Norms for graduate education that sometimes help and sometimes constrain creativity and adventuresome inquiry
- The risk taking of both community members and graduate students to engage in a partnership when it is not always known what the outcomes will be
- The length of time it takes to initiate and develop working relationships between university faculty and staff and community organizations and community residents
- The investment of time and energy and the responsibilities of both community persons and research staff in doing research as a collaborative enterprise

This is a starter list. Each of these conditions and settings has affected the development of this work.

The importance of paying attention to such examples of context seems self-evident (Shapin, 1994). Yet, as Elliot Mishler wrote 20 years ago,

> This ordinary and common sense understanding of meaning as context dependent has been excluded from the main tradition of theory and research in the social and psychological sciences. As theorists and researchers, we tend to behave as if context were the enemy of understanding rather than the resource for understanding which it is in our everyday lives. (Mishler, 1979, p. 2)

What are the benefits of paying attention to contextual influences? Here is another starter list:

- There are more opportunities for both researchers and communities to ask meaningful and penetrating questions.
- There is increased possibility for informants to reveal personal and authentic information.
- There is some chance that topics of common concern between researchers and community residents can be identified and examined.

- There is a definite possibility that researchers and community residents will grow and expand their understanding of their preferred topics.
- There is some likelihood that the results of the work will be shared, owned, and used by the community residents.

Being explicit about contextual inquiry is then not a job—not even a career, a duty, or an obligation—but an experience of shared learning and an adventure of understanding, detective work, and discovery.

An Example.   The immediate context of this work was the DCP's desire to receive state funds to try out a community-organizing approach to the prevention of substance abuse. The state required an evaluation. After several meetings of the state staff, DCP staff, and me, we established a working agreement to focus on the development of community leaders in contrast with assessing the incidence and prevalence rates of abuse (Kelly, 1992).

To begin this work, I asked the executive director of the DCP, John Owens, if he would agree to having a member of the board serve as a liaison between the DCP and our research group. He agreed. Margaret Bagby served in that position from 1990 to 1997. Since then, Mamie Thomas, secretary of the DCP board, has been the liaison. This role is an opportunity for the DCP and UIC to be informed of mutual interests and those constraints that may reduce the quality of the collaborative effort. I conceived the liaison role as being that of a "boundary spanner," facilitating communication and understanding between the UIC and DCP groups (Katz & Kahn, 1978). Creating this liaison role symbolically and concretely affirmed that the interests of the UIC research staff and the aspirations of the DCP were viewed as potential resources and an example of contextual thinking in practice. Margaret Bagby and Mamie Thomas have provided vital communication links between the DCP and the UIC research group and have helped to clarify expectations, respond to suspicions, and create the ground rules for mutual education and respect.

I also suggested that a panel of community members be composed to work with the UIC team (consisting of me, Lynne Mock, and Cecile Lardon) to review possible research and documentation methods and topics. An eight-member community research panel was established by John Owens. This panel met 19 times over 18 months between January 1991 and July 1992. Sandra Scheinfeld transcribed each of the 19 meetings (Scheinfeld, 1992). Epiphanies did occur.

For example, at the third panel meeting, after a discussion of the research literature on leadership, one of the panel members, Verna Worsham, commented,

> Our leader (Ms. Carr) always draws people in. I keep people in line—I'm like the policeman. I help with the transportation, getting people to meetings. I'm quiet, behind the scenes. I'm President of the Local School Council but Ms. Carr does the speaking. She's good at speaking. So she does that and I'm a supporter. (Worsham, as reported in Scheinfeld, 1992; Glidewell et al., 1998)

This is a nice example of what Fred Bales discussed some years back about the salience and efficacy of informal roles in groups (Bales & Cohen, 1979). Verna's comments also illustrate something else: A person in the most visible role with a title is not the only resource in any group; instead, all group members are resources to each other. Verna Worsham's example defined leadership behavior as it is naturally expressed in this community.

This illustration is significant because the past emphasis in psychological research on assessing the qualities of individual leaders implied that some people have more skills and talents than others. Psychologists may not explore the specific skills and talents of individuals whose performance on any single measure is lower than the modal responses of others. We may inadvertently communicate that we believe a life goal is to achieve perfect scores on tests rather than to appreciate the unique qualities of any one person. In contrast, in community work the challenge is to mobilize groups of people and then to embrace their talents. Certainly Verna Worsham pays attention to the unique qualities of herself and others.

If leadership can be viewed as a multidimensional concept, there is potentially shared meaning between empirical findings in cognitive psychology and the views of leadership as expressed by Verna Worsham, Ella Baker, and Ed Hollander: Leadership is a process involving different types of skills and talents emerging as a collective enterprise (Neisser et al., 1996). The essence of activating leadership may be attending to contexts, performed roles, and working relationships between people with varied skills.

At that same meeting Verna Worsham's comments stimulated Linda Bond, another panel member, to say,

> You know I often get visual pictures—like a bowl of soup. It depends on the ingredients that go into the soup—that gives it its taste. If there's too much of one thing it doesn't taste so good; if you have a lot of ingredients it tastes better. You see what everyone has to offer—that makes the best soup. It makes it taste good. (Bond, as reported in Scheinfeld, 1992; Glidewell et al., 1998)

Verna Worsham's comments about the essential interdependence of people in a group and Linda Bond's analogy that creating leadership is like making soup became the grounding ideas for the remainder of the meetings and provided a shared agenda for the UIC-DCP deliberations. The 19 community research panel meetings were a series of settings not only for tapping the shared perspectives of the panel but also for anchoring our collaborative work. The comments of Verna Worsham and Linda Bond helped to solidify the group and established that the work of the panel was indeed congruent and supportive of the DCP's purpose to develop a constituency of people with varied skills.

By accepting these ideas, both UIC and the DCP began to work together toward a common goal. The format of the community research panel was especially relevant given that the participants were new to each other and represented contrasting histories and life experiences. The panel meetings were social settings that provided opportunities for all of us to contribute our ideas that had been stimulated by our divergent histories and our previous contexts (Kelly, 1994).

Idea 2: Metaphors Are Resources to Create a Psychology of Community

Background.   The analogy of leadership as a soup gave the UIC group a cognitive map for developing an interview schedule with 80 community leaders. We defined our expedition to represent the varied ways in which community residents can and do assume leadership roles in community activities. We were less concerned with establishing measures to identify a hierarchy of specific skills but more concerned about identifying the unique ways each of the 80 persons expressed their leadership. Consistent with the views of Ed Hollander and Ella Baker, we viewed leadership as a collective process involving a combination of different people rather than noting individual achievements of a few people. The concept of the diversity of community leadership is pivotal for both inquiry and action.

An Example.   The UIC team tape-recorded and transcribed interviews with 80 DCP members. The four main topics of the interviews generated from the panel meetings were (a) family and community support for doing community work, (b) the skills applied and skills learned to carry out community leadership, (c) relationships with other organizations, and (d) personal visions for the future of the community. The interviews were conducted and transcribed in consultation with DCP staff and board members. A coding process similar to the process presented by proponents of grounded theory was carried out (Azelton, 1996; Glaser & Strauss, 1967; Strauss & Corbin, 1994; Tandon, 1996). Fifty-six initial codes were generated. At the point when three of us—L. Seán Azelton, Darius Tandon, and I—finally began grouping the codes, the utility of a metaphor became evident. Here's why.

We wanted to analyze and present the interview information so that the findings could be compatible with the philosophy of the DCP and be visually appealing. We believed that the information could be visually descriptive if it was presented as a tree. Information about the 80 persons and their unique leadership skills could be communicated, as could the overall DCP concept of leadership expressed by the total number of persons (Figure 12.1). Because the DCP is concerned primarily with the development of community leaders, the metaphor of a tree seemed apt. As a sapling develops, its branches spread and grow until it can be distinguished from other trees. As persons develop they con-

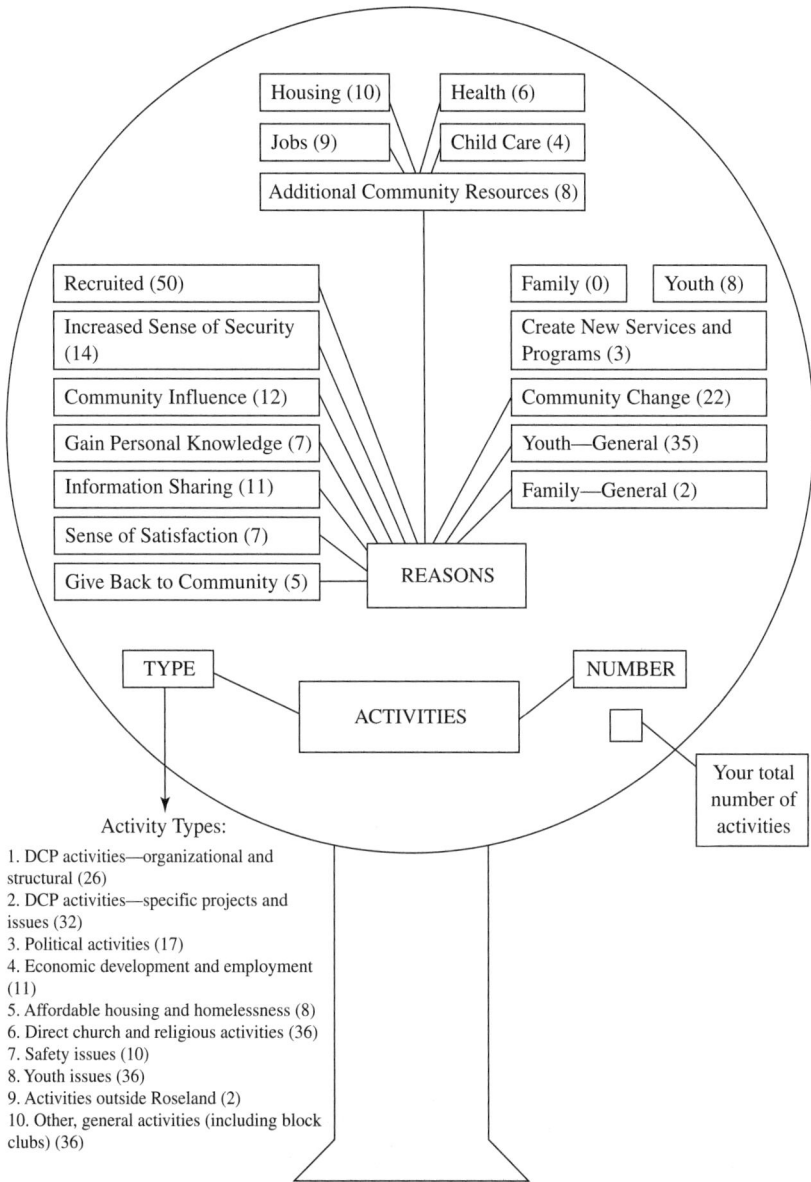

Figure 12.1   Community involvement tree template for DCP leaders.
Note: The numbers in parentheses indicate how many DCP leaders (out of 80) gave that response. The average number of activities DCP members are part of is 4.2. From "Constructing a tree for community leaders: Contexts and processes in collaborative inquiry," by S. D. Tandon, L. S. Azelton, J. G. Kelly, & D. Strickland, 1998, *American Journal of Community Psychology, 26,* pp. 669–696. Copyright 1998 by Plenum Publishers. Adapted with permission.

tribute in varied ways to a larger community (Rival, 1998). If leadership is thought of as a collective process, a forest represents the leadership in any specific community. The forest is made up of different trees.

As the coding process emerged, part of the DCP forest contained 80 different trees for each of the five dimensions of community leadership.[2] These five dimensions are community involvement, DCP influence on community leaders, facilitators for continued and active involvement in the DCP, religious beliefs affecting community work, and personal visions of DCP community leaders. Each of these five dimensions contains detailed information about each of the concepts. The visual presentation of the data identifies which of the 80 persons has expressed a response to a particular branch on any one of five leadership concepts. A person could have five trees of different shapes depending on his or her unique experiences and interests. The metaphor of leadership as a tree seemed to capture both the process of leadership for the total DCP community (all five trees for all 80 persons) as well as a view of the variety of activities and interests for each of the 80 persons.

The tree concept appealed to the DCP panel members and a new group of DCP participants, the DCP action task force, which was established as a way to present information with explicit attention to the culture and foci of the DCP group. The acceptance of the metaphor was crucial given the long history of African Americans being studied with little role or opportunity to extract the meaning of the obtained information that they themselves generated. During the entire coding process and the development of the tree metaphor, continuous exchanges with DCP staff encouraged us to push on.

Each of these five trees represents a major defining feature of community leadership for these 80 persons in this particular community, as revealed in the interviews. An individual looking at any one tree can identify his or her responses to each of the five dimensions and see a tangible report of his or her own components of community leadership. The DCP staff and board have pointed out that this information is potentially useful to identify changes in DCP members' development as leaders.

Each tree also can be a metaphor to reduce a sense of fragmentation; the persons realize when they view their personal trees that they are living their religious ideals and expressing their spiritual views very directly. Each tree can represent the interdependence between the internal coherence within their lives and their community. The tree metaphor is also apt for organizational issues facing the DCP, in that, just like a tree that loses branches, the organization that loses its "branches" can lose its vitality and effectiveness. Future analyses will continue to emphasize how varying styles of leadership can be recognized and disseminated. For example, Jill Williams from the University of Illinois at Urbana–Champaign has helped give the results of our collaboration back to the community as well as add to the general knowledge of community leadership. She used three quantitative methods (cluster methods, multidimensional scaling, and principal component analyses) to examine the association among the nature of reasons for community involvement, the first tree (Williams, 1997).

Jill Williams's analysis illustrates two complementary ways in which leaders expressed their community involvement. The members of one group (Group 1) were involved in community work to improve the quality of their community by doing things such as renovating housing or aiding the homeless. Members of a second group (Group 2) expressed more varied interests, such as to share skills, strategies, or information about community needs and problems; create additional community resources; or gain personal knowledge and give back to the community. More members of Group 2 expressed interest in creating programs for youth than did members of Group 1. Except for Group 1's interests in housing and the homeless, there were few other differences in the range of activities. Group 1 appears to have a greater level of activity and has maintained the high activity level over time.

There were also interesting demographic differences between these two groups. Group 1 members were more likely than Group 2 members to be DCP board members, serve on the board longer, participate in three or more DCP committees, be active in the DCP four or more years, and attend at least five training events. Conversations and dialogue with DCP staff and board enable alternative hypotheses and interpretations of these quantitative findings to be considered as we have done with the qualitative data.

The metaphor of the tree has helped focus on the diversity of types of community leadership and the varied ways they express their leadership. The tree metaphor suggests that the DCP board and staff can continue to realize their philosophy to involve, reward, and promote each person's unique talents.

The UIC group is continuing this type of analysis with the contributions of Mary Murray and Dave Henry (Henry, 1999; Murray, 1999). Specifically, they are trying out other cluster analytic and categorical methods to reflect the variety of expressed leadership styles and the diverse interests of these 80 community leaders. Initial analyses suggest wide variation in the configurations of plans, visions, and influences of the DCP on the individual. The future challenge is to carry out analyses that can reflect the philosophy of the DCP, the concepts of the earlier community research panel, and the spirit of the collaborative inquiry.

To complement the quantitative analyses, I am conducting oral histories, including videotaped interviews, with a small number of DCP community leaders. Comparing the quantitative analyses with the oral histories may generate new dialogues in new settings to recast and reshape concepts of community leadership.

When I reflected on this work, it became clear how the community research panel seven years ago anchored the work, stimulated the construction of the tree metaphor, and stimulated the creative efforts of Jill Williams, Dave Henry, and Mary Murray to create statistical analyses that embody the ideas, spirit, and philosophy of the DCP.

If we are even partially successful, we may be able to provide empirical testimony for Ella Baker's, Verna Worsham's, and Linda Bond's observations that there is indeed a variety of talent and points of view within the DCP community, and that as DCP participants have noted, the DCP organization attempts to create a place for each person.

The tree metaphor and the analogy of community leadership as being like preparing soup point to the possible pragmatic benefit of metaphors. Metaphors can establish a common ground between community participants and researchers and stimulate the expression of other unspoken metaphors in a way that means, percentages, and significant F ratios might not. Metaphors are very attractive when doing community research, as they are in other areas of psychology, because their use simultaneously demystifies the nature of inquiry and recognizes the natural explanatory models in use within the community (Gentner & Grudin, 1985; Gentner & Jeziorski, 1993; Gibbs & Hall, 1987; Lakoff, 1993; Loewenberg, 1981; Pillemer, 1998; Ricoeur, 1979).

An essential facet of this work is building the research relationship so that there are occasions for the metaphors to be expressed. Our work with the DCP has been going on for only nine years. Here is a thought: The French anthropologist Marcel Griaule worked in the African community of Dogon in Mali beginning in 1931. After 16 years the most esteemed elder (Ogotemmeli) said that the community was now ready to tell him about their beliefs and customs (Griaule, 1965)! In an issue of *Science* the archaeologist Judith Field, who is working to unearth the remains of human ancestors in Australia, said, "One third of my time is spent maintaining relationships with the local . . . community. In the end you get the cooperation of the land council because they trust you" (Finkel, 1998, p. 1342). On another occasion, perhaps, there will be an opportunity to discuss the development of trust, an essential construct for doing community research.

Coda

Clifford Geertz has been quoted as saying, "In order to make up our minds we must know how we feel about things; and to know how we feel about things we need the public images of sentiment that only ritual, myth, and art can provide." I believe that in this work, the art has been and continues to be the process of collaboration, the ability of the DCP and UIC to work together to provide compelling ways to display and frame the art (Kelly, 1995). The rituals, our lunch and dinner meetings, emerge from the collaborative relationship that creates the social settings for dialogue and reflection about the work (Bell, 1997; Kelly, 1994; Sarason, 1982).

Invoking the concept of myth may seem unorthodox. Myths are traditionally expected to be fabricated falsehoods; psychologists are expected to search for the empirical truth. I suggest an alternative idea that we are all participants in creating myths about the very good times, as well as about those times that are difficult. In fact, we may spend our lives constructing and deconstructing our views of what has happened to us in our various contexts. Developing community leadership may be a process of constructing meaning about the obstacles addressed, the gains made, the social bonds created, and the legacies maintained.

Editor's Note

James G. Kelly won the Award for Distinguished Contribution to Psychology in the Public Interest in 1997. This award address was delivered at the 106th Annual Convention of the American Psychological Association, San Francisco, CA, August 1998. Articles based on award addresses are not peer reviewed, as they are the expression of the winners' reflections on the occasion of receiving an award.

Author's Note

I have benefitted from the stimulating reviews and editorial comments from the following persons. Their interest in this work has been most appreciated: Isaac Balbus, Gersh Berkson, Rabbi Herb Bronstein, Becki Campbell, Dan Cervone, Paul Dolinko, Dave Henry, Rob Jagers, Caroline Leopold, Philip A. Mann, Andre Martin, Dana Meritt, Alison Miller, Robin L. Miller, Lynne Mock, Thom Moore, Joe Stokes, Debra A. Strickland, Darius Tandon, Mamie Thomas, David Mark Todd, Sharon Wasco, Jill Williams, and Marc Alan Zimmerman.

Some of the current persons involved in this work are Lynne Mock, Darius Tandon, Debra Strickland, and Mamie Thomas. Some others who have made special contributions are L. Seán Azelton, Dave Henry, Cecile Lardon, Caroline Leopold, Andre Martin, Mary Murray, Sandra Scheinfeld, and, from the University of Illinois Urbana-Champaign, Jill Williams and Thom Moore. People from the Developing Communities Project (DCP) include Margaret Bagby, Ceola Cheatam, the late Anna Dickerson, Desta Houston, Cora Long, Cassandra Lowe, John Owens, Rev. Albert M. Shears, and members of the community research panel and the DCP action task force. The members of the community research panel (1990–1991) were Hameedoh Akbar, Linda Bond, Anna Dickerson, Alma Jones, Doris Jones, Eugene Rogers, Rev. Booker Vance, and Verna Worsham. The members of the current DCP action task force (1997–present) are Rev. William Fristoe, Bobbie Henry, Sandra Sanders-Herrin, Rev. Frank Milton, Deacon T. R. Neuman, Alberta Roberts, Mamie Thomas, George Turk, Richard Watson, and Deacon James Woodson. From the Illinois Department of Human Services are Alvera Stern, Barbara Cimaglio, Karen Furlong, and Kimberly Fornaro.

Notes

1. For representative and influential works by or about these scholars, please see Ayers & Ford, 1996; Barone, 1995; Berkowitz, 1987; Colby & Damon, 1992; Coles, 1997; Dittmer, 1994; Gergen, 1991; Goldman, 1996; Hatch & Wisniewski, 1995; Lieblich & Josselson, 1994; Linde, 1993; MacAdams, 1996; Parker, 1996; Payne, 1995; Reinharz, 1994; Sarason, 1984; Vaze, 1997; Wandersman & Florin, in press; and Zinsser, 1986.

2. During the last two years, reliability has been established for the coding schemes of the five tree constructs, and methods of analysis have been generated (Tandon, 1996, 1998; Tandon et al., 1998; Williams, 1997).

References

Ayers, W., & Ford, P. (1996). *City kids, city teachers: Reports from the front row.* New York: New Press.

Azelton, L. S. (1996, July). The tree metaphor: A concept for visually representing data. In J. G. Kelly (Chair), *Documenting community leadership.* Symposium conducted at the 60th Anniversary Convention of the Society for the Psychological Study of Social Issues, Ann Arbor, MI.

Bales, R. F., & Cohen, S. P. (1979). *Symlog: A system for the multiple-level observation of groups.* New York: Free Press.

Barone, T. (1995). Persuasive writings, vigilant readings, and reconstructed characters: The paradox of trust in educational storysharing. In J. Hatch & R., Wisniewski (Eds.), *Life history and narrative* (pp. 63–74). London: Falmer Press.

Bell, C. (1997). *Ritual: Perspectives and dimensions.* New York: Oxford University Press.

Berkowitz, B. (1987). *Local heroes: The rebirth of heroism in America.* Lexington, MA: Heath.

Brydon-Miller, M., & Tolman, D. L. (Eds.). (1997). Transforming psychology: Interpretive and participatory research methods [Special issue]. *Journal of Social Issues, 53,* 597–827.

Colby, A., & Damon, W. (1992). *Some do care:Contemporary lives of moral commitment.* New York: Macmillan.

Coles, R. (1997). *Doing documentary work.* New York: Oxford University Press.

Conway, J. K. (1998). *When memory speaks: Reflections on autobiography.* New York: Knopf.

Dittmer, J. (1994). *Local people.* Urbana: University of Illinois Press.

Finkel, E. (1998, May 29). Aboriginal groups warm to studies of early Australians. *Science, 280,* 1342–1343.

Gentner, D., & Grudin, J. (1985). The evolution of mental metaphors in psychology: A 90-year retrospective. *American Psychologist, 40,* 181–192.

Gentner, D., & Jeziorski, M. (1993). The shift from metaphor to analogy in Western science. In A. Ortony (Ed.), *Metaphor and thought* (pp. 448–480). New York: Cambridge University Press.

Gergen, K. J. (Ed.). (1991). *Refiguring self and psychology.* Aldershot, UK: Dartmouth.

Gibbs, R. W., & Hall, C. K. (1987). What does it mean to say that a metaphor has been understood? In R. E. Haskell (Ed.), *Cognition and symbolic structures: The psychology of metaphoric transformation* (pp. 31–48). Norwood, NJ: Ablex.

Glaser, B., & Strauss, A. (1967). *The discovery of grounded theory: Strategies for qualitative research.* Chicago: Aldine.

Glidewell, J. C., Kelly, J. G., Bagby, M., & Dickerson, A. (1998). Natural development of community leadership. In R. S. Tindale, L. Heath, J. Edwards, E. J. Posavac, F. B. Bryant, Y. Suarez-Balcazar, E. Henderson-King, & J. Myers (Eds.), *Social psy-*

chological applications to social issues: Theory and research on small groups (pp. 61–86). New York:Plenum.

Goldman, A. E. (1996). *Take my word: Autobiographical innovations of ethnic American working women.* Berkeley: University of California Press.

Grant, J. (1998). *Ella Baker: Freedom bound.* New York: Wiley.

Griaule, M. (1965). *Conversations with Ogotemmeli: An introduction to Dogon religious ideas.* London: Oxford University Press.

Hartford, J. (1962). I would not be here. New York: Ensign Music, BMI.

Hatch, J. A., & Wisniewski, R. (Eds.). (1995). *Life history and narrative.* London: Falmer.

Henry, D. (1999, August). Reversing the typical flow: Using quantitative methods to enhance qualitative inquiry. In James G. Kelly (Chair), *Mixing qualitative and quantitative methods to explore community leaderships.* Symposium conducted at the 107th Annual Convention of the American Psychological Association, Boston, MA.

Hollander, E. P. (1983). Leadership and power. In G. Lindzey & E. Aronson (Eds.), *Handbook of social psychology: Vol. 2. Special fields and applications* (3rd ed., pp. 485–537). Hillsdale, NJ: Erlbaum.

Katz, D., & Kahn, R. L. (1978). *The social psychology of organizations.* New York: Wiley.

Kelly, J. G. (1992, August). *Ecological inquiry and a collaborative enterprise: A commentary on "The Chicago Experience."* Paper presented at the 100th Annual Convention of the American Psychological Association, Washington, DC.

Kelly, J. G. (1994). Generating social settings for a public's health. In D. G. Satin, E. B. Lindemann, & J. Farrell (Eds.), *Insights and innovations in community mental health: Ten Erich Lindemann memorial lectures* (pp. 125–146). Northvale, NJ: Jason Aronson.

Kelly, J. G. (1995, May). *Legacy of consultee-centered consultation for collaborative research.* Paper presented at the International Seminar on Consultee-Centered Case Consultation, Stockholm, Sweden.

Lakoff, G. (1993). The contemporary theory of metaphor. In A. Ortony (Ed.), *Metaphor and thought* (pp. 202–251). New York: Cambridge University Press.

Lieblich, A., & Josselson, R. (Eds.). (1994). *Exploring identity and gender: The narrative study of lives* (Vol. 2). Thousand Oaks, CA: Sage.

Linde, C. (1993). *Life stories: The creation of coherence.* New York: Oxford University Press.

Loewenberg, I. (1981). Identifying metaphors. In M. Johnson (Ed.), *Philosophical perspectives on metaphors* (pp. 154–181). Minneapolis: University of Minnesota Press.

MacAdams, D. P. (1996). Personality, modernity, and the storied self: A contemporary framework for studying persons. *Psychological Inquiry, 7,* 295–321.

Mishler, E. G. (1979). Meaning in context: Is there any other kind? *Harvard Educational Review, 19,* 1–19.

Murray, M. (1999, August). Using cluster analysis to understand qualitative data regarding community leaders. In J. G. Kelly (Chair), *Mixing qualitative and quantitative methods to explore community leaderships.* Symposium conducted at the 107th Annual Convention of the American Psychological Association, Boston, MA.

Neisser, U., Boodoo, G., Bouchard, T. J., Jr., Boykin, A. W., Brody, N., Ceci, S. J., Halpern, D. F., Loehlin, J. C., Perloff, R., Sternberg, R. J., & Urbina, S. (1996). Intelligence: Knowns and unknowns. *American Psychologist, 51*, 77–101.

Obama, B. (1995). *Dreams from my father.* New York: Random House.

Parker, T. (1996). *Studs Terkel: A life in words.* New York: Holt.

Payne, C. M. (1995). *I've got the light of freedom: The organizing tradition and the Mississippi freedom struggle.* Berkeley: University of California Press.

Pillemer, D. B. (1998). *Momentous events, vivid memories: How unforgettable moments help us understand the meaning of our lives.* Cambridge, MA: Harvard University Press.

Reinharz, S. (1994). Feminist biography: The pains, the joys, the dilemmas. In A. Lieblich & R. Josselson (Eds.), *Exploring identity and gender: The narrative study of lives* (pp. 37–82). Thousand Oaks, CA: Sage.

Ricoeur, P. (1979). The metaphorical process as cognition, imagination, and feeling. In S. Sacks (Ed.), *On metaphor* (pp. 141–157). Chicago: University of Chicago Press.

Rival, L. (1998). *The social life of trees.* London: Berg.

Sarason, S. B. (1982). *Psychology and social action.* New York: Praeger.

Sarason, S. B. (1984). *The creation of settings and the future societies.* London: Jossey-Bass.

Scheinfeld, S. J. (1992, August). *Documenting the community research panel.* Paper presented at the 100th Annual Convention of the American Psychological Association, Washington, DC.

Shapin, S. (1994). *A social history of truth: Civility and science in seventeenth-century England.* Chicago: University of Chicago Press.

Strauss, A. L., & Corbin, J. (1994). *Basics of qualitative research: Grounded theory procedures and techniques* (2nd ed.). Newbury Park, CA: Sage.

Tandon, S. D. (1996, May). Visual presentation and explanation of developing activist trees. In J. G. Kelly (Chair), *Varieties of community leadership: A method to define community activism.* Symposium conducted at the 60th Anniversary Convention of the Society for the Psychological Study of Social Issues, Ann Arbor, MI.

Tandon, S. D. (1998, August). A visual representation of community leadership. In T. Moore (Chair), *African American community leaders and university collaborators: Processes and products.* Symposium conducted at the 106th Annual Convention of the American Psychological Association, San Francisco, CA.

Tandon, S. D., Azelton, L. S., Kelly, J. G., & Strickland, D. (1998). Constructing a tree for community leaders: Contexts and processes in collaborative inquiry. *American Journal of Community Psychology, 26*, 669–696.

Tyler, F., Pargament, K., & Gatz, M. (1983). The resource collaborator role: A model for interactions involving psychologists. *American Psychologist, 38*, 388–398.

Vaze, K. M. (Ed.). (1997). *Oral narrative research with Black women.* Thousand Oaks, CA: Sage.

Wandersman, A., & Florin, P. (in press). Citizen participation and community organizations. In J. Rappaport & E. Seidman (Eds.), *Handbook of community psychology.* New York: Plenum.

Williams, J. H. (1997, May). *Profiling community leaders: A visual representation of the nature of and reasons for community involvement.* Paper presented at the Sixth Annual Biennial Conference of the Society for Community Research and Action, Columbia, SC.

Yukl, G. (1998). *Leadership in organizations* (4th ed.). Englewood Cliffs, NJ: Prentice Hall.

Zinsser, W. (Ed.). (1986). *Extraordinary lives: The art and craft of American biography.* New York: American Heritage.

13

The Spirit of Community Psychology

Reflections

This is a revised version of the address in the honor of Seymour Sarason, given at the annual meeting of the American Psychological Association in 2001. Previous winners had been Ed Zigler, Emory Cowen, Murray Levine, Julian Rappaport, and later Rudy Moos. I felt that I was in good company. Ira Iscoe, my professor at the University of Texas, nominated me for the award and introduced me. I used the occasion of my recent retirement to say some things that younger members of the field may not be able to say publicly.

I wanted to focus on issues that are not often addressed. It was my belief that the field may have lost some of its spirit since its founding in 1965. My three ideas for increasing our spirit were to advocate for more attention to the history of the field, to take time to share stories about our work, and to create safe settings for speaking frankly and openly about important issues facing us as researchers or practitioners. All fields are vulnerable to becoming insular and thereby restricted by their specialization. Responding to these issues could help community psychologists overcome isolation or find the connections to ideas and work of others doing community psychology in other fields. I quoted a few words from Ella Baker, Walter Goldschmidt, and George Kennan that spoke volumes, as did the words of community psychologists Don Klein, Murray Levine, and Julian Rappaport. I took note of the eloquence of William James to back me up.

Historical topics have always been inspiring to me. I find solace in the insights and struggles of others as they developed their careers. Historical topics also helped express qualities of the larger environment that shed light on the problems of the day and how topics of research shift as the times change. Murray and Addie Levine called attention to these matters much earlier than I did. In our day-to-day work, however, we give little energy or attention to the signif-

icance of historical topics. Seymour Sarason has been an exception throughout his career. I also discovered that rummaging around the history of community psychology gave me inspiration and increased my investment in the field. History was a tonic.

To increase our emotional spirit about our work and collective commitment to our field, I advocated for more time given to telling each other stories about our work. The norm of reporting research results without some public statements about the craft of our work limited our ability to communicate to the next generation of community psychologists how prevention programs and community-based research is done. We report our findings of the outcomes of our work but not how we carried out the work. This was my effort to reconnect with the theme of the processes of our work "Tain't What You Do It's the Way You Do It" (chapter 7). Knowing the steps you take to achieve a research activity or a preventive intervention makes the findings more meaningful, even when the work is modest and incomplete. I challenged colleagues to focus more on our own community in an attempt to generate new ways to increase our settings, our celebrations, and our occasions to appreciate the uniqueness of our enterprise as well as treasure our work and each other. Such topics, however soft and outside the conventions of science, are the essence of generating creativity and commitment to the field. Although I did not refer to it in the talk, I had been impressed with the biological laboratories at Woods Hole, Massachusetts, for making science personal and validating creativity. This approach is essential to a field like community psychology. I hope that the words reprinted here will energize others to treasure the significance of each other and the field.

Community psychology as a field may have lost some of its original spirit; a spirit dominant at the founding of the field. Spirit is a difficult concept to discuss since it is a concept beyond usual discourse in psychology as a denotative, measurable and verifiable concept. Taking the lead from William James, Spirit, however elusive, is most essential to a sense of self. I offer three suggestions to enhance and to make our individual and collective spirit more vital: (1) Continuing education in the history of community psychology; (2) Creating time to share stories about our work; (3) Creating safe settings to enlarge our spirit. These ideas are offered as pragmatic suggestions to enable us to create more coherence between our personal and professional selves.

What is most remembered about the May 1965 Swampscott Conference is the excitement that was so pervasive among the 39 participants. Don Klein, one of the primary organizers of the conference, commented in 1995 in a videotape interview: "The details of that conference, for me, have faded into the background; (but) the excitement of that conference is like it was today. It was one of the really highly significant events in my life and I suspect in the lives of many of the people who were there" (Klein, 1995).

The conference was an occasion to acclaim that beyond conventional methods and, with a focus beyond the individual, there were valid activities and meaningful roles for a new kind of psychologist, the community psychologist. The conference report proclaimed that psychologists could and should work at the community level and would be concerned with topics of culture and class, and issues of positive health, as well as illness (Bennett, Anderson, Cooper, Hassol, Klein, & Rosenblum, 1966).

In the years following, the field continues to become respectable within the academy, though only in a small way recognized in the larger psychological association. Nevertheless, we are building a knowledge base that is at the same time uniquely a community psychology. This is a substantial achievement!

There is now knowledge available, for example, about how to design and evaluate community-based interventions and how to generate social support systems that enhance positive well-being; how to implement a wide variety of preventive mental health programs; how to evaluate self-help groups and how to carry out participatory action research (Rappaport & Seidman, 2000; Sandler, 2001). As Lonnie Snowden and others have commented, community psychologists also have served as resources and catalysts for psychologists in other fields to adopt a community perspective (Snowden, 1987). Some facets of clinical psychology today have a preventive cast, albeit with foci on the individual. Although a small field, community psychology is a viable field and continues to attract new entrants.

At this point in the field's development, it may be time to think some more about ways to create and sustain occasions for making the spirit of the work as important as the science and the practice of the work. In our efforts to become acceptable within psychology we may have lost our spirit and our sense of excitement that was present at the founding of the field in the United States in 1965 as expressed by Don Klein.

Psychology's Heritage in Putting Aside the Concept of Spirit

This is difficult because as a discipline, psychology has had only modest success in addressing and conversing about concepts like spirit, a concept that does not have an established empirical basis. The concept of spirit is likely to be perceived to be beyond science, viewed close to a religious concept, and thereby not appropriate for serious study. In addition, our work settings, particularly in universities, do not encourage conversations about the spirit guiding or inspiring our work. Laura Nader has said it well: "The university buries emotions, and faculty look for 'balanced' opinions" (Nader, 1997, p. 117). It has been my experience that there are few ongoing traditions in departments of psychology to genuinely celebrate the spirit of our work.

If I was going to consider concepts related to spirit I would think of passion, personal vision, ideology, empowerment, resilience, persistence, and Seymour Sarason's concept of transcendence (Hill, 2000; Sarason, 1994). Plus a sense of humor and spirituality. That's my starter list.

Spirit is no doubt a multifaceted, multidimensional concept that varies from person to person and ecology to ecology. Each of these terms would have different salience at different times for various people. I think that Egon Brunswik would appreciate this approach (Brunswik, 1952, 1955, 1956; Hammond, 1966). Back in the 1940s and 1950s he advocated that psychology should give as much attention to the properties of the organism's environment as it does to the organism itself.

There is a potential connection between spirit and spirituality that should be explored. Particularly, the relationships between faiths, beliefs, and the persistence in carrying out social change activities.

This was most emphatically demonstrated in the beginning of the civil rights movement in the 1930s and '40s and no doubt is salient for those who participate in other social movements.

In the 1999 summer issue of *The Community Psychologist*, papers organized by Randolph Potts reaffirmed the historical connections between religious beliefs and social change. Five essays and examples on the connections between religious practice, spirituality, and community psychology were presented. They each asserted that spirituality was a resource for social activism (Abdul-Adil, 1999; Balcazar, 1999; Molock & Douglas, 1999; Potts, 1999; Ramos, 1999; Rodriguez & Quellette, 1999).

Bret Kloos and Thom Moore have put together a special issue of the *Journal of Community Psychology* on the topics of spirituality, religion, and psychology (Kloos & Moore, 2000). In this work the participants reaffirm the significance of the connections between religion and community psychology. They also point to analyses of religious experience and the ties to a sense of community. Ken Pargament and Ken Maton also have presented a schema for the pathways in which religious settings contribute to a variety of ways to bolster self-esteem and reduce stress (Pargament & Maton, 2000). There is now a small group of community psychologists doing research on spiritual beliefs. But I am not advocating a directed research effort on the concept of spirit, however laudable and potentially informative that may be. I am going to suggest some direct actions that we can take to enhance our individual spirit by our collective activities.

This is a tall order! We have a history within the larger field of psychology, which implicitly, if not explicitly, discourages conversations and dialogues about concepts that we cannot put to rigorous test and measure.

The zeal of the early founders was to have psychology accepted as a science. Thank goodness, there are examples throughout the larger history of psychology, where individuals have persevered when the dominant paradigm would not sanction inquiry outside the preferred view. For example, it was difficult for people like Mary Whiton Calkins, in the 1890s, to elaborate the meaning of the Self Concept, a research topic that was outside the standards for acceptable research topics. She met pervasive resistance to her investment in this topic, as well as for being a woman desiring an academic career (Calkins, 1915, 1930; Furumoto, 1991; Milar, 2000; Minton, 2000). William James was one of her few advocates. William James was also one of the few, if only, early pioneers who spoke up and spoke out against the emerging behaviorist direction. In the *Principles of Psychology*, he boldly asserted: "The spiritual self is so supremely precious that, rather than lose it, a man ought to be willing to give up friends and good fame, and property, and life itself" (Coon, 2000; James, 1890, p. 315). I would like to advocate the same significance for the concept of spirit!

Psychology, like many professions, has had difficulty in reducing insularity and expanding tolerances for varied methods. The History of Psychology in Autobiography series, dating from 1930, does include examples of eminent psychologists going against the preferred views of science at a particular point in time (Boring, Langfeld, Werner, & Yerkes, 1952; Boring & Lindzey, 1967, 1973; Lindzey, 1980, 1989; Murchison, 1930, 1932, 1936). Seymour Sarason also comments on these issues in his own autobiography (Sarason, 1988).

Yet, if we take as our source of inspiration those psychologists who became eminent in spite of going against the canons of their time, are we not reifying a Darwinian principle that there was something so special and unique about these individuals that we could never equal their accomplishments? For the rest of us, who may wish to do nontraditional work, can we survive if we do not conform to contemporary norms? There may be a tendency to exclude ourselves as we revere the accomplishments of eminent people. If we adopt the point of view of the unrepeatable achievements of special people, I think that we restrict ourselves from focusing on our own cultures, our own norms, our own traditions, and our own basic values.

The power of the cultures of universities and the power of the leaders of professional associations induce conformity pressures. It is indeed very challenging to create "safe" settings where there is active support to follow one's own direction in contrast to going along with the current paradigm or being undone by orthodoxy. Reflect on how long it has taken for nonlaboratory research to be carried out or for qualitative studies to be accepted in community psychology (Miller & Banyard, 1998). Think how long it might take for oral histories to be considered as an alternative and valid method.

We community psychologists need to feel validated when we expend our energies to understand topics in communities outside of our university or practice settings. Our work is carried out largely where we are not indigenous members;

where we are often guests and are required to earn the privilege to become a partner. This takes large amounts of commitment and zeal. We need sources of inspiration to maintain and uplift our spirit. We need to begin to look at our own professional communities for how we can create supportive environments that can enable us to share our values and struggles and aspirations.

In reading and listening to those who have devoted their lives to social justice it is clear that they have created ways to charge themselves, to enlarge their vistas, to sustain their morale, and to bolster their values. For example, nine White women in telling their stories about their work in the Freedom Movement in the 1950s and 1960s speak movingly about their mentors, their peers, their families, and their ideologies, as sources of their spirit. They also speak to their plight. One of these nine women, Casey Hayden, quotes the poet Gary Snyder: "In the political and spiritual loneliness of American life in the fifties, you'd hitch a thousand miles to meet a friend" (Hayden, 2000, p. 342).

Charles Payne, the sociologist and historian, in describing the role of ordinary African American citizens organizing for justice in the South in the face of life-threatening assaults, before and after World War II, points to the spirit of those who were embraced and maintained by their families and their churches as they organized themselves (Payne, 1995). These stories offer hope about the power of the sense of community when we go about tasks that diverge and confront the status quo. Isaac Prillentensky and Geoffrey Nelson have challenged community psychologists to work harder to not just ameliorate harsh conditions but to challenge the status quo, which too often provides the underlying legitimacy of many social interventions. (Prillentensky & Nelson, 1997; Prillentensky & Austin, 2001). If we accept their challenge we will need a fortified spirit!

Community Psychologists: We Are Resources of Our Own Spirit

It is we ourselves that bear the responsibility for creating our own solutions to overcome our constraints; those qualities of our settings that limit us realizing our goals. These constraints can be social norms, which are restrictive of our self-expression; they can be judgments of others that indicate that they do not know our needs or aspirations. But we are in a bind. Because we are part of the elite society of well-educated professionals, we often look to other professionals. Listen to an observation of Howard Zinn quoted by Charles Payne: "The idea of saviors has been built into the entire culture, beyond politics. We have learned to look to stars, leaders, experts in every field, thus surrendering our own strength, demeaning our own ability, obliterating our own selves" (Payne, 1995, p. 440; Zinn, 1980, p. 570).

Ella Baker, one of my heroes, said it directly when arguing against a too easy deference to established authorities in the civil rights movement: "My basic sense of it has always been to get people to understand that in the long run they themselves are the only protection they have against violence or injustice. . . . People have to be made to understand they cannot look for salvation anywhere but to themselves" (Payne, 1989, p. 891).

We community psychologists are often enmeshed in doing work that is in places that have their own independent political life, with their own histories and rivalries and intrigues. The community psychologist accepts these stresses as we become familiar with those settings so that we can carry out useful work.

Getting to know the community and its ways of working, whether it is a school, a shelter for the homeless, or a community organization, requires much of our emotional and intellectual resources. These are challenges as we do our work in places where we do not have ascribed power, nor are we initially valued. We are just one of several participants. We earn our way to be accepted as a trusted partner or observer. Building trust takes much time and much energy and can limit our spirit. Such challenges can also be the reservoir for the next community research or action.

So the challenge is how do we do work that we value while not becoming drained of our spirit? How can we respond to the tough substantive issues and problems of communities and do research or address these problems while keeping our values and visions intact and be rejuvenated as well?

What so often occurs is that we are left to create, as solitary persons, those proactive pleasures that enhance our spirit. Our churches, our faiths, our aerobic exercises, the nutritional programs, our extra intake of antioxidants, our pets, our leisure pursuits, the hobbies, the recreational interludes, the creation of our social support systems, our families, where intimacy and celebration go hand in hand with authentic exchanges, is what we can do for ourselves on our own time. For me the arts do it, especially music. I have a T-shirt with a quote from Nietzsche, "Without music life would be a mistake."

But these are treasured ballasts that so often make up for what is missing in our work settings. Sadly, we in community psychology are still faced with the traditions of the larger field of psychology where we are taught to be self-directed and to achieve status and recognition for our work that is solely our own and reflects our own individual talents.

Stan Schneider, in commenting on the uniqueness of community psychology, said in a videotaped interview in June of last year:

Not only is there the problem of how this field (community psychology) sort of manages to exist in psychology with the traditional remnants that are still there and the traditional ties to clinical and medicine that are still there in some sense, but how an academician with the kind of things that an academic needs to do could also be a community psychologist—It seems to me almost a total contradiction in terms. You have to satisfy being an academic, an entire list of things to do to get ahead. . . . Academics have been, as a group, as remote from the real world as any group you can think of. Community psychologists, on the other hand, have a mission really in their life to be connected with the real world. To do both of those things at the same time is a hell of a difficult job. (Schneider, 2000)

As an added constraint, psychology still attends to the achievements of a historically male-dominated definition of how we create a career—of gigantic individual achievements carried out in very competitive environments. I believe if we continue to follow that tradition we reduce our opportunities to achieve and sustain what William James prides as "the precious spiritual self." I add, a precious self that has spirit and has been nourished as we are contributing participants in the collective enterprise of community psychology.

Working as an individual in a competitive environment reduces the opportunities for shared, reciprocal learnings. The consequences of this socialization are to limit our own personal experiences of what community means and signifies. We particularly need this precious spirit, as we combine those two missions that Stan captured for us *and* as we embark on new ways of defining community psychology as a science. My guess is that new ways of doing community psychology involves new ways of understanding the processes of community change, which will require of us more shared learnings and more occasions in which we are vulnerable to learn.

At the Chicago Conference in 1988 there was a phrase that was called up to anchor the meeting. The phrase was "adventuresome research" (Tolan, Keys, Chertok, & Jason, 1990, pp. xvi). This phrase expressed a point of view to do research that is beyond contemporary conventions. We certainly need an ample supply of spirit to do new and different types of research, practice, and interventions.

Nicholas Lemann, in a New Yorker profile on George Kennan quotes Kennan: "If you're going to change a civilization, it can be done only as the gardener does it, not as the engineer does it. That is, it's got to be done in harmony with the rules of nature and can't all be done overnight" (Lemann, 2000, p. 98).

Wow! This changes the entire epistemology for thinking about preventive interventions. Prevention programs are not just technological innovations. They are grounded, engaged, and patient efforts at understanding the processes by which the resources of communities become part of the design of the prevention program. Kennan's assertion also changes the time line for thinking about making a positive difference in communities. The time period is not just a semester, but for substantial effects, perhaps several decades or longer. The Kennan thesis does argue for an ecological epistemology! Amen!

While all professions have their stresses and their conventions for helping their members to avoid "burn out," community psychology has the unique challenge to create settings within our daily activities to make the spirit of our work as central as the science and practice of our work.

We need to be able to establish ways that are energizing while we do the work that is demanding and worrisome and at times disheartening.

Settings for Nurturing and Enhancing Our Spirit

There are a variety of ways to promote the élan of the field. Some of these ways have been already working since 1987 when the first SCRA biennial organized by Jean Ann Linney was held at the University of South Carolina. The most recent eighth biennial at Georgia State University was definitely a spirited event where Jim Emshoff, John Peterson, Sarah Cook, Gabriel Kuperminc, Fran Norris, Rod Watts, Cindy Elrod, Harold Braithwaite, and many others created a setting where research and reflection and the presentation of a broad range of programs were nestled within occasions that inspired us, including the comments of Jane Fonda and Andrew Young. There are also increasing occasions for informal conversations at the biennials and e-mail exchanges and list serves. SCRA promotes various constituencies to create settings for communication and debate.

In addition to these established mechanisms, here are three more suggestions for protecting and preserving, and conserving, if you will, the spirit of community psychology. Each is complementary and even synergistic. I suggest that they collectively add to a supportive social environment for doing community psychology.

Continuing Education in the History of Community Psychology

Historians have a rule of thumb that topics do not have historical value until after 20 years go by. Consequently as the historian James Patterson comments, "there is a relative lack of historical perspective available concerning the very recent past" (Patterson, 1998, p. 190).

Because we are in our 36th post-Swampscott year, it is certainly time to review our history, examine our roots, and demythologize our heritage.

For example, David Fryer of the University of Stirling in Scotland, has reminded community psychologists of the pioneering work of Marie Jahoda in Marienthal, Austria, on the psychological impacts of unemployment that was published in 1933! This work combined multiple methods and a very active action component (Fryer, 1992; Jahoda, Lazerfeld, & Zeisl, 1972; McKenna & Fryer, 2001). That was 32 years before we in the United States thought that we had created the field of community psychology. This kind of review of historical contributors can set limits on our chauvinism *and* inspire us to dig deeper into people, events, and epics of the past.

Those involved in social change require and demand a thorough grounding in history; history has the potential of energizing us and reawakening our consciousness as we reassert our goals.

This is especially apt for our field because our history is derived from explicit historical forces, outside of the field of psychology, such as the turbulence about racism in the 1950s, the community mental health movement in the 1960s, the second wave of the women's movement, and the Vietnam War among others. I believe that without a constant reference to history we run the risk of becoming another scientific field adrift from our roots, devoid of a well-articulated set of values, and limited by our more restricted professional concerns. Attention to historical topics helps us understand those who came before us and those who also struggled to maintain an integration between our psychological work and our sense of justice.

Seymour Sarason has continuously reminded us and challenged us about the impact of history on our contemporary life and present plights. Most persuasively he has documented for our field the impacts of the economic depression of the 1930s, World War II, the Boulder Conference, and the sixties (Sarason, 1976a; 1993; 1994). He also called to our attention the limitations of our close association with federal legislation as a primary and limiting source for solving social problems (Sarason, 1978).

His address at the Austin Conference in 1975, published in the *American Psychologist*, as "Community Psychology, Networks and Mr. Everyman" referred to Carl Becker's 1931 Presidential Address to the American Historical Association. Here's a quotation from Becker, which can legitimate our choice of self-education about our own history: "If the essence of history is the memory of things said and done, then it is obvious that every normal person, Mr. Everyman, knows some history" (Becker, 1935, p. 235; Sarason, 1976b, p. 327).

We do not need any more rationale to make the history of our field a salient resource to enliven our spirit.

Meg Bond and Ann Mulvey's history of women and feminist perspectives in community psychology attest to the essential need to seek out and acknowledge multiple histories. For there is no one history but histories of different people working in varied places in diverse time periods. Our challenge is to create occasions to hear and learn from the multiple voices within our field so that we can benefit from a broader understanding of the roles of persons and events for different circumstances (Bond & Mulvey, 2000).

I personally was part of two groups that researched the history of SCRA and the domains of the field (Meritt, Greene, Jopp, & Kelly, 1999; Wilson, Hayes, Greene, Kelly, & Iscoe, in press). In carrying out both of these activities my understanding of historical issues was enlarged and my commitment to the field was renewed. Doing this work was like a tonic for my spirit. It helped me reconnect to heritages that I thought I once knew and to appreciate those past influences I was not even aware were a part of my professional self.

I also had the good fortune of teaching a graduate course in the History of Community Psychology for incoming doctoral students at the University of Illinois at Chicago between 1994 and 1997, plus one abbreviated modular version in 2000. During those five semester course offerings my consciousness was raised and I believe so was the sense of history of the students. Anecdotal student reports indicated that discussions of such topics as World War II and the GI Bill, the research of sociologists and anthropologists in the 1940s and 1950s, the side effects of the civil rights movement, and so forth, clarified the fields' origins and in some cases increased students' respect and investment in their chosen field. Bianca Wilson, a student in the class in 1997 said: "As the telling of history is essentially an exercise in sharing spirit, this course provided me an opportunity to embrace the connections between my passions and my work" (B. D. M. Wilson, personal communication, July 19, 2001).

On November 8, 1996, four women faculty at the University of Illinois at Chicago participated in a videotaped discussion in the History of Community Psychology Class (Feminist Panel Video, 1996). They focused on the talk that Naomi Weisstein gave at a meeting of the American Studies Association at the University of California, Davis, on October 26, 1968. This talk was "Psychology Constructs the Female." As Becki Campbell, Alice Dan, Stephanie Riger, and Margaret Stroebel pointed out, this paper, which has classic status among feminist scholars, is relatively unknown among community psychologists. It was inspiring to see the give-and-take discussion among the panelists and the impact of the discussion on the students. It was a beautiful example of the role of history in empowering reaffirmations of students.

Walter Goldschmidt, the anthropologist, published a historical essay in the recent *American Anthropologist*, which is a cogent example for community psychologists. As he recounted his own career he pointed out historical influences on him and his colleagues and pointed to the interconnections with the fields of psychology, sociology, and anthropology. In this 18-page essay there are gems like:

> Everything is factorially more complex at the end of an enquiry than it was at the outset. The areas of the brain that carry the names of the pioneering anatomists Broca and Wernicke are about as accurate as sixteenth-century maps of Africa; the A, B, and O blood types that were hot new discoveries in my Austin days gave no clue to the rich mulligatawny stew that flows in our veins; and even the simple business of sleep turns out to have two forms-and still doesn't tell us, when our souls go flying about. . . . This complexity tells us that anybody who says he has a magic bullet to solve the riddle of human existence is either a fool or a charlatan and this is true of all anthropological schools. (Goldschmidt, 2001, p. 893)

There is a substantial role for the community psychologist practitioner and members of other professions to be resources in teaching the history of our field. They can enrich our understanding of the nitty-gritty of community research and practice and can help establish the connections between historical legislation, community power dynamics, and how these topics evolve and affect the acceptance and the implementation of community programs. Their participation also enlarges the collective spirit of community psychology.

Last semester when I taught a seminar on the History of Psychology at UC Davis I realized again the suffocating power of dominating paradigms in psychology and the courage required to confront them.

I continue to be impressed by the significance of historical contexts upon the evolution of ideas and the development of us.

Creating Time to Share Stories About Our Work

The second way I think we can build upon our own spirit involves creating time to share stories about our work. Much of graduate work is devoted to learning methods and evaluating research, appraising theory, and doing research. The days seem compressed with duties, chores, responsibilities, and deadlines. There is little time to sit back to reflect and share our experiences with each other. Most occasions for social interaction are formal and focused on meeting grant, research, or course-related deadlines. Many of these activities are self-imposed demands, as well as externally imposed deadlines.

Without collective occasions to celebrate and acknowledge our efforts, we miss the chance to create our own local history. The comment I have often heard from former students is that it is not the classes, but the relationships that count in aiding graduate students to commit to a career.

Why not take these observations seriously and build a culture in our training programs that in fact makes time and gives sanction for listening to each other rather than trying to impress each other. Here again the contributions of the community psychologist practitioner are essential.

We can benefit from the work of Lynne Bond, Mary Field Belenky, and Jacqueline S. Weinstock and their pioneering work with the Listening Partners Program. They supported "very isolated, poor, White rural mothers of young children to claim the powers of mind and voice . . . and help their families and friends to do the same" (Bond, Belenky, & Weinstock, 2000, p. 699).

This program created safe places for conversation. They created norms, which are essential for listening and growing. "Thus, within a feminist framework, facilitators emphasized inclusive, mutually respectful and reciprocal relationships among all group members" (Bond et al., 2000, p. 705). Anne Brodsky has independently pointed out the significance when working with those labeled "poor" that the work directly consider the significance of power and resources (Brodsky, 2001).

Julian Rappaport has aptly noted the significance of creating space for stories: "Much of the work of social change, organizational and community development in the direction of greater personal and collective empowerment, may be about understanding and creating settings where people participate in the discovery, creation and enhancement of their own community narratives and personal stories." (Rappaport, 1995, p. 726).

Elinor Ochs and Lisa Capps in presenting research on living narratives mention the work of Mary Main (Main, 1996; Ochs & Capps, 2001). Main has found that American children who engage in secure patterns of attachment with their parents have parents who readily narrate numerous, elaborate, coherent childhood experiences with their own parents. Children who engage in avoidance patterns of attachment with their parents generally have parents who insist that they are unable to recall their own childhood experiences. To extrapolate: If the older community psychologists can tell their stories in the company of younger members of SCRA then we can add to the attachments and commitments of future generations to our field! Ochs and Capps offer one explanation. "While narrative does not yield absolute truth, it can transport narrators and audiences to more authentic feelings, beliefs, and actions and ultimately to a more authentic sense of life" (Ochs & Capps, 1996, p. 23). How about that?

Len Jason is a role model for this. He periodically offers on the SCRA list serve his observations and his encounters with national organizations or government agencies. He takes the risk to express his concerns and invites our comments. His openness to do this helps to create a climate for being vulnerable rather then being right and being courageous rather then being doctrinaire.

In creating individual oral histories with six community leaders on the south side of Chicago in the spring of 1999, I discovered that, although the six leaders had worked together for 10 years, they did not know some of the more detailed personal histories of each other in their prior community work or their individual struggles against racism. These struggles were revealed in the videotaped oral histories.

When they saw the videos of each other's personal stories their bonds increased. They had renewed appreciation for each other and their group and what they had done and what they were still doing. Viewing each of their stories increased their spirit and their pride and their resolve. I bet this also could happen in Community Psychology Training Programs. We could increase our professional connections as we tell our stories about our work.

The teaching of history and telling stories can come together. When I was teaching the history course, mentioned above, I had the good fortune to invite exemplary community psychologists who were active in the field, before the field was created, to be videotaped about their personal histories and their work. On October 25, 1996, Murray Levine talked about the powerful influence on him and his career when he worked with Seymour Sarason at the Yale Psycho-Educational Clinic in the 1960s. At one point, Murray paused and said:

"There was a building at 295 Crowne Street. I still remember it. In fact, to tell you how important it is in my life . . . I don't have my keys with me . . . I still carry the key to that building even though the building doesn't exist" (Levine, 1996).

What a testament not only to Seymour and the clinic staff, but also to the power of remembering critical events and preserving them in our key chains and in our hearts as an ever present memento of deep penetrating life enhancing events. We all need such experiences to inspire our spirit. As we increase our scholarly commitments to history coupled with creating settings to tell our ongoing stories we can engage knowledge of our past and enrich ourselves as we proceed with our futures.

Creating Safe Settings to Enlarge Our Spirit

Finally, we can actively work to create safe settings to enlarge our spirit. One of the major concepts in community psychology is the concept of setting. Seymour Sarason called the significance of this concept to our attention in celebrating the work of Roger Barker (Barker, 1963; Sarason, Levine, Goldenberg, Cherlin, & Bennett, 1966; Sarason, 1984). Recent discussions on the SCRA Lists serve have reemphasized the significance of this concept and the related ideas of place and sense of community. It is ironic that we do not practice what we preach. We do not do as much as we could to create safe places to express our feelings and our dreams and aspirations for our own work. I believe that our own settings can contribute to a public's health and enhance the interactions of persons from diverse backgrounds (Kelly, 1994; Kelly, Azelton, Burzette, & Mock, 1994).

One of the most meaningful safe settings I have experienced was in 1958. As a new PhD I was part of a small group of staff and postdoctoral students from different disciplines attending a seminar at the Massachusetts General Hospital on the topics of community mental health. Erich Lindemann led it. He was a psychoanalyst, psychiatrist, and psychologist who was Professor of Psychiatry at Harvard Medical School and Psychiatrist-in-Chief at the hospital (Satin, 1982). Even with all his degrees, and prestige, and status, it was abundantly clear that he valued our views and that he cared about creating a safe setting for dialogue. It was the most exhilarating scholarly experience I had up to that time. I still recall the excitement, the nonjudgmental tone, and the freedom that exuded from those occasions. I have benefited from that setting to this day. His talent for being unassuming and stimulating was outstanding. So, I do believe that it is possible to create safe educational settings because I was a part of one. I know what it feels like to be in a safe setting from that experience 43 years ago!

Cary Nelson, an English professor at the University of Illinois at Urbana, wrote a point of view piece in the Chronicle of Higher of Education this summer "10 Ways to Keep Graduate Students From Quitting" (Nelson, 2001, p. B20). One of his points focused on a hospitable departmental environment. Here he included such things as a departmental lounge. What community psychologists can do is much more to directly affect the quality of the social life of graduate education by creating social settings that are safe for intellectual exchanges and where humor is considered a treasure.

This is quite a challenge! It means that faculty are less directive and didactic and express less of the role of the all-powerful judgmental person. It means that the student takes risks in moving beyond a silent and passive role where by default the professor fills the space with directives and unilateral edicts, however charming and witty and playful. There is a need for more opportunities for faculty and students, the whole training community, to express enough about themselves to create a basis of shared understanding. Students can learn more about the pressures of tenure and grant submissions. Faculties learn more about the plights of students as they try to be themselves, especially when they are faced with financial debts and competing demands to excel in all areas of the curriculum, doing this while they try to figure out how to reconcile the competing paradigms of psychology and community psychology. More sharing may lead to more respect and then more trust and then more excitement about the collective enterprise of community psychology.

Deborah Tannen has observed that students "are taught that they must disprove others' arguments in order to be original, make a contribution, and demonstrate their intellectual ability" (Tannen, 1998, p. 269). If we agree to challenge Tannen's observation it means that the new safe settings for community psychology will now include historical treatment of topics. The social norms will be so arranged to deal with intellectual controversies where there is a minimum of self-aggrandizement and self-promotion and denigration of others. The spirit of community psychology is to listen, appraise, and generate ideas based on the ideas of all participants; where every participant is a potential resource.

These are the values of the Vermont Listening Project. Don Klein refers to this process as "social glue" (Klein & Morrow, 2001). Back in 1968, Don proposed that these processes contribute to our sense of significance, "the value placed on the person by key people in his/her environment" (Klein, 1968, p. 15).

If we embark on the creation of these three types of settings I believe we need to concentrate on knowledge that is ecological such as the work of Ed Trickett and Ken Maton as well as work that has been traditionally identified with organizational psychology (Maton, 2000; Maton, Hrabowski, & Grief, 1998; Trickett, 1984, 1996). Fortunately there are community psychologists such as Meg Bond, Cary Cherniss, Pennie Foster-Fishman, Don Klein, Chris Keys, Doug Perkins, Rick Price, Beth Shinn, and Steve Stelzner and colleagues, who have been working on linking community psychology and organizational psychology. We need more understanding about such topics as how people become leaders in groups, how group boundaries are spanned, and how cohesiveness is achieved in settings (Allen, Stelzner, & Wielkiewicz, 1998; Bond, 1999; Cherniss & Deegan, 2000; Foster-Fishman & Keys, 1997; Kelly, 2000; Keys & Frank, 1987; Klein, 1968; Shinn & Perkins, 2000; Price et al., 1998; Stelzner, Allen, & White, in press).

David Mosse, an organizational anthropologist, has commented that "The more participatory the analysis of communities and institutions is, the less it is likely to reveal about the social dynamics of the participants themselves" (Mosse, 2001, p. 179). This is a powerful and instructive observation about the unanticipated consequences of researcher–participant relationships in organizational settings.

I argue that we cannot be optimally sensitive and understanding as community psychologists *in* the community unless we can understand our *own* host communities. The lack of a congruent fit between how we live inside the academy and what we propose or advocate out there in communities lowers our personal spirit, and creates mixed messages to those with whom we work, *and* thereby pollute the spirit of community psychology.

There is a potential very significant side effect of working on our spirit. The cumulative impact may be to put the personal at the center of doing our work and in reporting on our work. Becki Campbell, in a forthcoming book, focuses on researching researchers' emotions when doing research on women who are victims of violence (Campbell, in press).

She quotes the philosopher Cheshire Calhoun who says simply and profoundly: "The pursuit of knowledge is always to some extent personal" (Calhoun, 1989, p. 200). The work of Becki offers us an honest way of carrying out our work where we have finally disabused ourselves of being the objective, value-free, dispassionate all-knowing scientist.

Amen, indeed!

Murray Levine also has pointed out that our focus on our methods may have alienated us by standing between the subject matter and ourselves as a person. He observed that it is a paradox that we must rely on method, but that these very methods may block our interest and enthusiasm especially when accompanied by a hypercritical stance (Levine, 1982). Attending to the wisdoms and efforts of Becki and Murray can increase our spirit.

The settings I remember, and the ones I draw upon, are the ones where there was an élan and all participants were learning. We were enriched by each other as we proceeded to acquire facts, test ideas, and analyze complex projects. By giving our energies to the setting we increase our learning and our commitment and our spirit.

Rachel Ramen has remarked that: "The places in which we are seen and heard are holy places. They remind us of our value as human beings. They give us the strength to go on. Eventually, they may even help us to transform our pain into wisdom" (Remen, 1996, p. 244).

Conclusion

Community psychology is a special field. That uniqueness was appreciated by the Swampscott participants. It is still a special field as noted by the informal remarks reported above by Don Klein, Stan Schneider, and Murray Levine.

I have offered three ideas and actions to preserve this special quality. By concentrating on our history and creating opportunities to tell our stories to each other we can contribute to the ongoing tradition to create settings that are protected—protected to engage intellectual ideas and controversies in ways that will inspire us to make organic connections between our work in the outside community and our work in our own professional communities. This process is an essential source of energy.

There may be a developmental sequence here. If we can focus more on our history, such steps may encourage us to be more comfortable and tell each other the "stories" about our work. If we can feel ok about the telling of our stories we can then establish safe places to directly focus on topics that really matter to us. Rachel Ramen said another thing: "When we do not live coherently with ourselves, something begins to erode in us. We may survive, but we will never be whole or fully alive" (Remen, 2000, p. 47).

What is at stake is what William James referred to as that "precious" source of self, which enables us and enlarges our vistas. Community psychology will be alive and well as we commit to preserving our individual and collective spirit.

Note

Address delivered as the 2001-year recipient of the Seymour Sarason Award, at the 109th annual convention of the American Psychological Association, San Francisco, CA, August 26, 2001. The following persons took time to give me a pat on the back, offer editorial suggestions, made substantive appraisals, or all of the above. Part of the pleasure in preparing the address was their seriousness as they gave me feedback on early drafts of the effort. I thank them indeed: Holly Angelique, Meg Bond, Cary Cherniss, Becki Campbell, Paul Dolinko, Erin Hayes, Len Jason, Chris Keys, Don Klein, Cecile Lardon, Murray Levine, Ken Miller, Robin Miller, Lynne Mock, Thom Moore, Dan Romer, Sharon Rosen, Susan Ryerson-Espino, Debby Salem, Lonnie Snowden, Steve Stelzner, Stanley Sue, Ed Trickett, Bianca Wilson, and Marc Alan Zimmerman.

References

Abdul-Adil, J. K. (1999). Inner-city Muslim action network: Islam as a resource in revitalizing urban communities. *Community Psychologist, 32*, 29–31.

Allen, K. E., Stelzner, S. P., & Wielkiewicz, R. M. (1998). The ecology of leadership: Adapting to the challenges of a changing world. *Journal of Leadership Studies, 5*(2), 62–82.

Balcazar, F. E. (1999). Lessons from liberation theology. *Community Psychologist, 32,* 19–24.

Barker, R. (1963). On the nature of the environment. *Journal of Social Issues, 19,* 17–38.

Becker, C. (1935). Every man his own historian. In *Essays on history and politics* (p. 235). New York: Crofts.

Bennett, C. C., Anderson, L. S., Cooper, S., Hassol, L., Klein, D. C., & Rosenblum, G. (1966). *Community psychology: A report of the Boston conference on the education of psychologists for community mental health.* Boston: Boston University.

Bond, M. A. (1999). Gender, race and class in organizational contexts. *American Journal of Community Psychology, 27,* 327–356.

Bond, L., Belenky, M. F., & Weinstock, J. S. (2000). The listening partners program: An initiative toward feminist community psychology in action. *American Journal of Community Psychology, 28,* 697–730.

Bond, M. A., & Mulvey, A. (2000). History of women and feminist perspectives in community psychology. *American Journal of Community Psychology, 28,* 599–630.

Boring, E. G., Langfeld, H. S., Werner, H., & Yerkes, R. M. (Eds.). (1952). *A history of psychology in autobiography* (Vol. 4). Worcester, MA: Clark University Press.

Boring, E. G., & Lindzey, G. (Eds.). (1967). *A history of psychology in autobiography* (Vol. 5). New York: Appleton Century-Crofts.

Boring, E. G., & Lindzey (Eds.). (1973). *A history of psychology in autobiography.* New York: Appleton Century-Crofts.

Brodsky, A. E. (2001). More than epistemology: Relationships in applied research with underserved communities. *Journal of Social Issues, 57,* 323–335.

Brunswik, E. (1952). *The conceptual framework of psychology.* Chicago: University of Chicago Press.

Brunswik, E. (1955). Representative design and probabilistic theory in a functional psychology. *Psychological Review, 62,* 193–217.

Brunswik, E. (1956). *Perception and the representative design of psychological experiments* (2nd Rev. ed.). Berkeley: University of California Press.

Calhoun, C. (1989). Subjectivity and emotion. *Philosophical Forum, 20,* 195–210.

Calkins, M. W. (1915). The self in scientific psychology. *American Journal of Psychology, 26,* 495–524.

Calkins, M. W. (1930). Mary Whiton Calkins. In C. Murchison (Ed.), *A history of psychology in autobiography* (pp. 31–62). Worcester, MA: Clark University Press.

Campbell, B. (2002). *Emotionally involved: The impact of researching rape.* New York: Routledge.

Cherniss, C., & Deegan, G. (2000). The creation of alternative settings. In J. Rappaport & E. Seidman (Eds.), *The handbook of community psychology* (pp. 359–378). New York: Kluwer.

Coon, D. (2000). Salvaging the self in a world without soul: William James's the principles of psychology. *History of Psychology, 3,* 83–103.

Feminist Panel Video. (1996, November 8). *Exemplars of community psychology* [video series]. James G. Kelly (Ed.). Chicago: University of Illinois at Chicago.

Foster-Fishman, P. G., & Keys, C. B. (1997). The person/environment dynamics of employee empowerment: An organizational culture analysis. *American Journal of Community Psychology, 25,* 345–370.

Fryer, D. (1992). Introduction to Marienthal and beyond. *Journal of Occupational and Organizational Psychology, 65,* 257–268.

Furumoto, L. (1991). From "paired associates" to a psychology of self: The intellectual odyssey of Mary Whiton Calkins. In G. A. Kimble, M. Werteimer, & C. White (Eds.), *Portraits of pioneers in psychology* (pp. 57–72). Washington, DC: American Psychological Association.

Goldschmidt, W. (2001). A perspective on anthropology. *American Anthropogist, 102,* 789–807.

Hammond, K. (Ed.). (1966). *The psychology of Egon Brunswik.* New York: Holt.

Hayden, C. (2000). Fields of blue. In *Deep in our hearts: Nine white women in the freedom movement* (pp. 335–375). Athens: University of Georgia Press.

Hill, J. L. (2000). A rationale for the integration of spirituality into community psychology [Special issue]. *Journal of Community Psychology, 28,* 139–149.

Jahoda, M., Lazersfeld, P. F., & Zeisl, H., (1972). *Marienthal: The sociography of an unemployed community.* London: Tavistock.

James, W. (1890). *The principles of psychology.* New York: Henry Holt.

Kelly, J. G. (1994). Generating social settings for a public's health. In D. G. Satin, E. B. Lindemann, & J. Farrell (Eds.), *Insights and innovations in community mental health* (pp. 125–146). Northvale, NJ: Jason Aronson.

Kelly, J. G., Azelton, L. S., Burzette, R., & Mock, L. (1994). Creating social settings for diversity: An ecological thesis. In E. J. Trickett, R. J. Watts, & D. Birman (Eds.), *Human diversity: Perspectives on people in context* (pp. 424–451). San Francisco: Jossey-Bass.

Kelly, J. G., Ryan, A. M., Altman, B. E., & Stelzner, S. P. (2000). Understanding and changing social systems. In J. Rappaport & E. Seidman (Eds.), *Handbook of community psychology* (pp. 133–159). New York: Kluwer.

Keys, C. B., & Frank, S. (Eds.). (1987). Organizational perspectives in community psychology [Special issue]. *American Journal of Community Psychology, 15.*

Klein, D. C. (1968). *Community dynamics and mental health.* New York: Wiley.

Klein, D. C. (1995, September 26). *Exemplars in community psychology* [video series]. J. G. Kelly (Ed.). Chicago: University of Illinois at Chicago.

Klein, D. C., & Morrow, K. (2001). *New vision, new reality.* Center City, MN: Hazelden.

Kloos, B., & Moore, T. (2000). Spirtuality, religion and community psychology [Special issue]. *Journal of Community Psychology, 28*(2).

Lemann, N. (2000. November 13). The provocateur. *New Yorker,* pp. 94–100.

Levine, M. (1982). Method or madness: On the alienation of the professional. *Journal of Community Psychology, 10,* 3–14.

Levine, M. (1996, October 25). *Exemplars in community psychology* (Video series). James G. Kelly (Ed.). Chicago: University of Illinois at Chicago.

Lindzey, G. (Ed.). (1980). *A history of psychology in autobiography* (Vol. 7). San Francisco: W. H. Freeman.

Lindzey, G. (Ed.). (1989). *A history of psychology in autobiography* (Vol. 8). Stanford, CA.: Stanford University Press.

Main, M. (1996). Introduction to the special section on attachment: Implications for psychoanalysis. In T. Shapiro, R. N. Emde, et al., (Eds.), *Research in psychoanalysis: Process, development, outcome* (pp. 209–244). Madison, CT: International Universities Press.

Maton, K. I. (2000). Making a difference: The social ecology of social transformation. *American Journal of Community Psychology, 28,* 25–57.

Maton, K. I., Hrabowski, F. A., III, & Greif, G. L. (1998). Preparing the way: A qualitative study of high-achieving African American males and the role of the family. *American Journal of Community Psychology, 26,* 639–668.

McKenna, S., & Fryer, D. (2001). The third European conference on community psychology: A Scottish perspective. *The Community Psychologist, 34,* 10–14.

Meritt, D. M., Greene, G. F., Jopp, D. A., & Kelly, J. G. (1999). A history of division 27 [Society for Community Research and Action]. In D. A. Dewsbury (Ed.), *Unification through division: Histories of the divisions of the American Psychological Association* (Vol. III: pp. 73–99). Washington, DC: American Psychological Association.

Milar, K. S. (2000). The first generation of women psychologists and the psychology of women. *American Psychologist, 55,* 616–619.

Miller, K. E., & Banyard, V. I. (Eds.). (1998). Qualitative research in community psychology [Special issue]. *American Journal of Community Psychology, 26.*

Minton, H. L. (2000). Psychology and gender at the turn of the century. *American Psychologist, 35,* 613–615.

Molock, S. D., & Douglas, K. B. (1999). Suicidality in the Black community: A collaborative response from a womanist theologian and a community psychologist. *Community Psychologist, 32,* 32–35.

Mosse, D. (2001). Social research in rural development projects. In D. N. Gellner & E. Hirsch (Eds.), *Inside organizations.* Oxford, England: Berg.

Murchison, C. (Ed.). (1930). *A history of psychology in autobiography* (Vol. 1). Worcester, MA: Clark University Press.

Murchison, C. (Ed.). (1932). *A history of psychology in autobiography* (Vol. 2). Worcester, MA: Clark University Press.

Murchison, C. (Ed.). (1936). *A history of psychology in autobiography* (Vol. 3). Worcester, MA: Clark University Press.

Nader, L. (1997). The phantom factor: Impact of the cold war on anthropology. In *The cold war & the university: Toward an intellectual history of the postwar years.* New York: New Press.

Nelson, C. (2001, June 29). 10 ways to keep graduate students from quitting. *Chronicle of Higher Education,* p. 1320.

Ochs, E., & Capps, L. (1996). Narrating the self. *Annual Review of Anthropology* (pp. 19–43). Palo Alto: Annual Reviews.

Ochs, E., & Capps, L. (2001). *Living narrative: Creating lives in everyday storytelling.* Cambridge: Harvard University Press.

Pargament, K., & Maton, K. (2000). Religion in American life: A community psychology perspective. In J. Rappaport & E. Seidman (Eds.), *Handbook of community psychology* (pp. 495–522). New York: Kluwer.

Patterson, J. T. (1998). Americans and the writing of twentieth-century United States history. In A. Molho & G. S. Wood (Eds.), *Imagined histories: American historians interpret the past* (pp. 185–205). Princeton, NJ: Princeton University Press.

Payne, C. (1989). Ella Baker and models of social change. *Signs, 14,* 885–899.

Payne, C. (1995). *I've got the light of freedom: The organizing tradition and the Mississippi freedom struggle.* Berkeley: University of California Press.

Potts, R. (1999). The spirit of community psychology: Spirituality, religion and community action. *Community Psychologist, 32,* 17–18.

Price, R. H., Friedland, D. S., Choi, J. N., & Caplan, R. D. (1998). Job loss and work transitions in a time of global economic change. In X. B. Arriga & S. Oskamp (Eds.), *Addressing community problems: Research and interventions* (pp. 195–222). Thousand Oaks, CA: Sage.

Prillentensky, I., & Austin, S. (2001). Critical psychology for critical action. *International Journal of Critical Psychology, 2,* 39–60.

Prillentensky, I., & Nelson, G. (1997). Community psychology: Reclaiming social justice. In I. Fox & I. Prillentensky (Eds.), *Critical psychology: An introduction* (pp. 166–184). London: Sage.

Ramos, C. M. (1999). Faith at work: Reflections on Catholic social teaching and community psychology. *Community Psychologist, 32,* 36–37.

Rappaport, J. (1995). Empowerment meets narrative: Listening to stories and creating settings. *American Journal of Community Psychology, 23,* 795–807.

Rappaport, J., & Seidman, E. (2000). *Handbook of community psychology.* New York: Kluwer.

Remen, R. (1996). *Kitchen table wisdom.* New York: Riverhead Books.

Remen, R. (2000). *My grandfather's blessings.* New York: Riverhead Books.

Rodriguez, E. M., & Quellette, S. C. (1999). The metropolitan community church of New York: A community of gay and lesbian Christians. *Community Psychologist, 32,* 24–29.

Sandler, I. (2001). Quality and ecology of adversity as common mechanisms of risk and resilence. *American Journal of Community Psychology, 29,* 19–61.

Sarason, S. B. (1976a). Community psychology and the anarchist insight. *American Journal of Community Psychology, 4,* 246–261.

Sarason, S. B. (1976b). Community psychology, networks and Mr. Everyman. *American Psychologist, 31,* 317–328.

Sarason, S. B. (1978). The nature of problem solving in social action. *American Psychologist, 33,* 370–380.

Sarason, S. B. (1984). *The creation of settings and the future societies.* San Francisco: Jossey-Bass.

Sarason, S. B. (1988). *The making of an American psychologist: An autobiography.* San Francisco: Jossey-Bass.

Sarason, S. B. (1993). American psychology and the needs for transcendence and community. *American Journal of Community Psychology, 21,* 185–203.

Sarason, S. B. (1994). *Psychoanalysis, general custer, and the verdicts of history: And other essays on psychology in the social scene.* San Francisco: Jossey-Bass.

Sarason, S. B., Levine, M., Goldenberg, I. I., Cherlin, D., & Bennett, E. (1966). *Psychology in community settings.* New York: Wiley.

Satin, D. G. (1982). Erich Lindemann: The humanist and the era of community mental health: *Proceedings of the American Philosophical Society, 126,* 327–346.

Schneider, S. F. (2000, June 30). *Exemplars in community psychology* [Video series]. J. G. Kelly (Ed.). Chicago: University of Illinois at Chicago.

Shinn, M., & Perkins, D. N. T. (2000). Contributions from organizational psychology. In J. Rapapport & E. Seidman (Eds.), *Handbook of community psychology* (pp. 615–642). New York: Kluwer.

Snowden, L. R. (1987). The peculiar successes of community psychology: Service delivery to ethnic minorities and the poor. *American Journal of Community Psychology, 15,* 575–586.

Stelzner, S. P., Allen, K. E., & White, R. M. (2002). *A developmental model of leadership.* Manuscript in preparation.

Tannen, D. (1998). *The argument culture: Moving from debate to dialogue.* New York: Random House.

Tolan, P., Keys, C., Chertok, F., & Jason, L. (1990). *Researching community psychology: Issues of theory and methods.* Washington, DC: American Psychological Association.

Trickett, E. J. (1984). Toward a distinctive community psychology: An ecological metaphor for the conduct of community research and the nature of training. *American Journal of Community Psychology, 12,* 261–279.

Trickett, E. J. (1996). A future for community psychology: The contexts of diversity and the diversity of contexts. *American Journal of Community Psychology, 24,* 203–234.

Weisstein, N. (1971). *Psychology constructs the female.* Boston: New England Press.

Wilson, B. D. M., Hayes, E., Greene, G. F., Kelly, J. G., & Iscoe, I. (in press). Contexts and domains of community psychology. In D. F. Freedheim (Ed.), *History of psychology (Vol. 1): Comprehensive handbook of psychology.* New York: Wiley.

Zinn, H. (1980). *People's history of the United States.* New York: Harper & Row.

PART II

FOUR CONTEMPORARY ESSAYS

More Thoughts

The story of my life and my thoughts about connections to my work hopefully has oriented you, the reader, to the previously published articles. The past journey is before you. Now what I present are more recent thoughts on ecological topics. These further reflections address four topics often considered central to the mental health professions and the behavioral sciences. In the following pages, the function of ecological theory is considered. Ecological theory explicates the discovery process that is intrinsic to being immersed in community programs for particular people in real places. Inquiry is another important focal point because it can apply multiple methods often in concert with members of other disciplines. Practice is also discussed as an ecological enterprise, implementing the steps. Finally, I suggest how professional and academic training can implement the principles promoted by the other essays. Throughout these contemporary essays, I refer to other publications beyond the 13 articles reprinted in this volume, as well as current work by others in other disciplines as well as in the field of community psychology. I hope that the cumulative contribution of these chapters both elaborates on the themes from the previous 13 chapters as well as suggests topics that are worthy of continued exploration.

14
Thinking Ecologically

Psychology has a history of reductionism. By forcing a limited range of methods, the researcher is constrained to minimize the complexity of topics. Biologist Steven Rose (1997) says it well: "Reductionism . . . freezes life at a moment in time. In attempting to capture its *being*, it loses its *becoming*, turning processes into reified objects. This is why reductionism always ends by impaling itself on a mythical dichotomy of materialist determinism and non-material free will" (Rose, 1997, p. 306). Ernst Mayr sums it up: "Reduction, by failing to consider the interaction of components, fails to fulfill what it promises" (Mayr, 2004, p. 80). Community psychology can potentially illustrate the dynamic interplay between the qualities of people and the attributes of smaller social settings and larger social environments. This requires research methods that attempt to illustrate environmental complexity.

The field of community psychology, while doing some of its work with more classical designs, can benefit from other notions of inquiry to help grasp this complexity. The ecological ideas expressed in the previous chapters have been presented as alternatives to reductionist procedures. One reason for having alternatives is that when the research is nested in the community and the researcher becomes educated about the community, hypotheses generated as a result of this educational process can be situated in the lived experiences of the community. Thinking psychologically and ecologically are interdependent approaches. The process of theory confirmation is adapted to informed insights from the community as well as current knowledge from the literature. An educated view of a particular place creates a dynamic interplay between prior knowledge and informed insights. The views of the place can be related to the concepts in the literature, and the concepts from the literature can be assessed based on their salience in this particular community.

Because communities are complex, the educational process is paramount *before* designing the research or preventive intervention. This is in contrast to prior traditions in psychology where the emphasis has been to derive hypotheses from a systematic theoretical position and then carry out research that will validate or invalidate the hypotheses. Other approaches, like oral histories and narrative analyses, are emerging but remain less visible. These nontraditional approaches are discussed in greater detail in the Autobiography, particularly the example of the work with African American community leaders. Although other points of view about inquiry are increasingly available, the reductionist approach is still very dominant.

Over the years, the theoretical concepts in the previous chapters have been presented more as heuristics—a set of ideas to guide research and practice—rather than full-blown propositions that if attended to, can be empirically tested. The ecological ideas are topics for further clarification and illustration in very specific locales. This point of view is a way to prevent psychological research from being defined only by the precepts of the psychologist. An explicit rationale ties psychological thinking to the surroundings and the places where the research takes place.

The virtues of ecological concepts are not that they are prescribed beforehand but are very much a function of a particular place in time. There is a theory of a specific school, for example, at a specific time with special traditions. Each setting will generate a "theory" derived from that place. Knowledge is particular, not universal. Marybeth Shinn and Siobhan M. Toohey (2003) reviewed substantial psychological literature, exploring connections between individuals and community contexts, concluding that "contexts also moderate other individual and family processes, suggesting that many psychological theories may not hold across the range of environments in which ordinary Americans live their lives" (p. 428).

Biological ecologists believe that it is "only by understanding the natural history of a species that general ecological theory can be tested in the wild" (Jiggins, 2004). One of dozens of recent examples is the research expeditions in studying the checkerspot butterfly in the San Francisco Bay area (Ehrlich & Hanski, 2004). Geographer and historian David N. Livingstone has argued that sites themselves are a source for the nature of scientific activities. He states that "different scientific traditions and practices, in different historical and geographical settings, deploy different understandings of evidence, demonstration, proof, objectivity, and so on" (Livingstone, 2003, p. 184). An ecology of scientific activities is directly congruent with thinking about the significance of particular knowledge rather than universal knowledge. The research of Roger Barker and the essays of Seymour Sarason have been intellectual catalysts for thinking about the power of place. Still, community prevention or research programs do not consistently account for settings or include them directly.

Chapter 9 focuses on the importance of social setting as a concept. Other chapters, such as chapters 2 and 7, also address the topic. Social settings provide the structure and support for social groups to cohere. By being in places, our identities are elaborated. Such ideas are not usually developed systematically in the research literature. I will give a few examples that have been meaningful to me.

Nat Hentoff, jazz critic and urban activist, mentions the power of one setting, the band bus, for the touring jazz musician of the 1930s. Phil Woods, a saxophonist, states how important the touring band bus was for younger musicians: "On the band bus, the young guys and the old guys would be together, and that's how us young guys learned. But there aren't any of those kinds of buses any more. There was a sharing thing, a family thing" (Hentoff, 2004, p. 88).

I read an article in the *New York Times* back in 1986 that I recall vividly. It was about the role of the ice house in San Antonio, Texas, and it carried a powerful message about the role of social settings. I referred to it in comments in honor of the retirement of Harold Raush from the University of Massachusetts at Amherst (Kelly, 1986). In the article, the journalist quotes Ron Zimmerman, a San Antonio filmmaker: "Anything that happens in human affairs happens in an ice house . . . they're the public living room of San Antonio. One man told us: 'A stop and go is just that. This is a stop and stay. You put down anchors here' " (Appelbome, 1986, p. A10). The function of the ice house is not only to give structure and meaning to the members but to create a tradition of a place, a predictable place, for the values and norms of the community to be realized.

In the *Sacramento Bee*, there was a more recent report on the "Porch Club" in the small village of Herald, California, several miles from Elk Grove (Wiener, 2004). The article described how the men of the club are a community resource in raising funds for the local school, digging fence posts, and doing other good deeds. Though the numbers vary, most days 15 men show up in front of the Herald Store to confab and have a good time while drinking coffee at 10 cents a cup.

Another inspiring example of commitment to a community is how the citizens of the south Bronx are documenting the history of their own community, Morrisania. The Bronx County Historical Society collaborates with Fordham University to compile a comprehensive record of the borough's black history. The residents are also conducting oral histories to help create a more nuanced history than a romanticized or monochromatic version. Before World War II this community was the residence of postal workers, nurses, social workers, and porters. Jazz musicians and their families, like Elmo Hope, Maxine Sullivan, Henry "Red" Allen, and others were residents. The most famous graduate of Morris High School is Colin Powell. Scholar Vincent Harding commented that Morrisania "was a healthy middle-class Black community. But it is easy to see nothing if you didn't see that" (as cited in Gonzales, 2004, p. C9).

These four examples illustrate the type of knowledge needed in conducting research or implementing a prevention program. How these settings evolve and bring meaning and solidarity not only to themselves but also to the larger community is a major topic for doing community research. This type of information is necessary to understand the various contexts that will host the intervention.

Such places can inform the outsider about the values, traditions, and lifestyles of that specific place and the larger community. Host communities and their participants are interdependent. My guess is that the band members on the bus and the regulars at the ice house and the Porch Club can serve as boundary spanners, as advocates, for good deeds and for educating the researchers about local knowledge before they begin their work. This type of history developed by the citizens in the Bronx is essential for doing community psychology not only in this Bronx community but in any community. The professional outsider gains many benefits from being aware of social and community functions. At some point, the implementation of the research or community-based program may depend on grasping these subtleties and complexities of places. Journalistic and anecdotal reports, as mentioned, are vital sources of information that are often not considered in the work of community psychology. Such knowledge is essential for understanding community life and community resources for that locale.

Ken Maton and colleagues have provided some empirical support for the power of social settings in buffering stress and empowering others. Reports from three churches and mutual help groups pointed to the impact that is illustrated in the journalistic reports. In particular, tangible help and opportunities for friendship were resources for buffering stress (Maton, 1989, 1993). Such settings also generated social support for the members and created a sense of community (Maton & Salem, 1995). Social settings become essential places to understand their power to orient, validate, and celebrate participants. An ecological perspective seeks out the informal community places for well-being and a sense of social solidarity.

The focus for ecological concepts is not just to verify them but also to stimulate thinking as well as discover new facets about the ways in which different persons and social settings are or are not connected. The ecological ideas are offered as a way to think anew about the connections between people and places. One of the basic concepts stimulated by research in biological ecology is the concept of niche. A niche, as an especially suitable habitat, is the primary source for energy and nutrients (Hardesty, 1977). Extending the thinking to personal and social systems, new questions can be formed: What are the contextual sources for personal resources and support? How well do the primary social structures generate needed personal and social resources? How are new personal and group resources developed? The concept of niche becomes a reference point for thinking about social systems as sources of energy and psychological nutrients. Maton and colleagues, for example, have presented ideas for examining how mutual help groups and church congregations as well as the settings stimulated by their beliefs can become resources for stimulating community support systems that are available more broadly in the community (Maton, 1993; Maton et al., in press; Pargament & Maton, 2000). Ed Trickett, Dave Todd, and I (1972), for instance, worked out a set of theoretical starting points that later were used to carry out empirical research in two Detroit high schools summarized briefly in chapter 2. What was significant about this approach is that we made guesses as to how high schools with different environmental qualities, such as the rate at which students entered and left the high school, would have different consequences for the social life and adaptation of the students. A partial validation of the propositions is mentioned in that chapter.

Another effort was to review community development in three Mexican villages as an ecological problem. Based on anthropological concepts and data assembled by scholars activating these three different programs, it was possible to see just how induced developmental programs affected different parts of the social systems of these three villages. It appeared that there were different adaptive requirements for the residents of the villages (Mills & Kelly, 1972). In this case, the ecological concepts were employed to evaluate the community development and economic efforts of other social scientists. In viewing community development from an ecological perspective, the Mexican villages varied in terms of acculturation, urbanization, and political accessibility. These variables in turn affected how development programs had different levels of effectiveness in assisting the villages. The nature of the interdependencies between the villages with their surroundings also affected the processes of development.

In another effort, theoretical ideas were presented to look at the interdependence of structure and process in social organizations. (Kelly et al., 2000). Again, the purpose was to illuminate how ecological thinking can help with the design of community-based research and preventive programs. The role of personal and social system resources plus the qualities of social settings and the boundaries of social systems are presented as structures (variables) to think about social systems. Most important, the qualities of these structures are linked to the social processes that such systems generate to carry out their activities. Social processes—like social norms for facilitating interpersonal reciprocity, networks, boundary expansions, and adaptations—are linked to social structures. These ideas are presented as heuristics to stimulate the reader on how to rethink not only concepts about persons and social settings but also, most important, how each of these eight qualities of social systems are intertwined. These ideas were proposed as criteria for evaluating a preventive intervention. A preventive intervention is considered effective when it stimulates efficient use of social structures, such as personal and social system resources, the access to the social settings available to the participants, and how permeable the boundaries of the host environment have become. These structures are also viewed as being interdependent with basic social processes, such as how reciprocal ties between members of the community have been strengthened, how the members have been able to establish functioning social networks for themselves and with others outside their community, how well the members have learned to span the boundaries of their major roles, and how individuals and the community at large have adapted to changing environmental forces. The integration of the interrelated concepts was offered as a pragmatic framework to begin and then evaluate the efficacy of community-based prevention efforts.

Barabasi has termed the persons who span boundaries and provide life generating information and relationships "connectors" (2003). These manifold interdependencies that link not only people but people within social systems become equivalent to maintaining hubs of food webs for ecosystems. There is an adaptive value in having interconnected networks. As Barabasi notes: "Most systems displaying a high degree of tolerance against failures share a common feature: their functionality is guaranteed by a highly interconnected complex network" (2003, p. 111).

As chapter 1 indicates, the purpose of presenting these ideas is to offer a point of view about designing preventive interventions. This is divergent from traditions in psychology where the role of theory is to suggest principles that apply to individuals outside of any context. Here, the purpose is to discover how persons and settings together might influence behavior in a special set of circumstances. The process of discovery and understanding of such questions are as important as verification alone. Although there was some partial verification of the notions about boys' adaptation to high schools presented in chapter 2, the discoveries about the intricacies of the social life of the high schools removed from truncated research findings are vastly more important.

One of the consequences of ecological thinking is the development of "street wisdom" about how the residents will respond to a new program. The local culture is a potential resource or potential constraint in accepting and implementing the new program. The beliefs, traditions, and wisdom of community residents are as salient as hypothetical deductions from a received view prior to dialogue with community representatives. This is so because an ecological reality has been considered. A commitment is fostered to understand the anxieties, aspirations, and potential contributions of the people who are considered the potential benefactors of the community program. It is plausible that persons in different communities develop their major orienting concepts for everyday life through their immersion in their natural surroundings. Cognitive scientists Douglas Medin and Scott Atran (2004) have reviewed evidence on how cultural and ecological inputs combine with innate propensities to determine cognition.

There is latent wisdom in ecological concepts because they derive from specific people in particular locales. The territory of living systems is the source of ideas. That there are consequences when good deeds are introduced to a community is not a new idea, but it is an idea that can stimulate new learning about the coupling of people and places. An ecological premise is that a preventive intervention, as an additive component to the community, affects the status quo for good or ill. Given this intrusion, overt as well as unexpressed views, opinions, and anxieties are expected about the value of the proposed potential help from different segments of the community. When something new is added, how people feel or behave about the new addition is emphasized. An induced innovation is likely to generate some anxieties and ripples throughout the setting or community, which are not always perceptible to the professional but may affect how different members of the community will support, oppose, deflect, or even subvert the proposed positive aspiration. Ecological ideas suggest that there is some wisdom in knowing how the community and the various constituents are likely to respond. Insufficient attention in the profession has been paid as to how to think about the processes of starting something new. There are, however, emerging efforts on how to view the new couplings between the person and the system (Livert & Hughes, 2002). Values change, norms may shift, roles maybe altered as a result of adding a new program in a community (Katz & Kahn, 1978).

One of the most inspiring examples of ecological work that influenced my own thinking was the report by anthropologist Ed Wellin that I mentioned in my autobiographical comments. I read his "Water Boiling in a Peruvian Town" (1955) when I was a student at the Harvard School of Public Health in 1959. It is a magnificent revelation of the subtleties in the responses of villagers to a local health advocate wanting the villagers to boil their water to reduce the incidence of cholera. For two years, Wellin was in the village observing and trying to grasp its social complexities. The report reveals that any positive innovation proposed from the outside by benign officials will flourish or fail depending on how the proponents understand the intricacies of the social life of the community. In this village, traditions existed for where and when water was boiled and by whom (women only). The long-held belief shared by persons of different social status positions is that people who were sick drank only boiled water; drinking cold water was a sign of good health. Who did respond and boil water was determined by such factors as where the person lived in the community and how long they had been a resident as well as their social status. Another insight was that some people decided to boil their own water without any prompting by the local native health worker. This work illustrates the realistic presence of competing demands that residents face when responding to a well-intentioned preventive effort.

When I asked professor Wellin some 40 years later about the impact of his work in the village of Los Molinos, his response was enlightening. The top-level administrators of the Ministry of Health and the local health workers were influenced by his work. The physicians, who were the local supervising Peruvian health authorities, thought that Wellin was gullible and too ready to believe what the villagers told him. These upper-class Peruvians distrusted what Wellin was told and what he reported. It was only those physicians who themselves were patients, often for tuberculosis, who gave credence to what Wellin was reporting (Wellin, 1998). Fascinating! One of the implications of Wellin's work is to emphasize that one major focus for thinking ecologically is to understand the socially established structures of meaning. This is what Robert Wilson refers to as "the trading zone in which psychology and anthropology exchange their goods" (Wilson, 2004, p. 21), which is a topic that anthropologist Clifford Geertz has emphasized throughout his career (1973).

A brief published note, which may have escaped notice, includes another example of inducing change and its effects. In this case, the focus was on introducing a new coffee pot into an organizational unit. Even though there was consent for the adoption, when the new system was introduced, previously established social relations were disrupted along with status-conferring tasks. The report concludes with the following insight: "The innovator must accept that the disturbance of the social structure, the confrontation of differing value hierarchies, the inertial resistance to doing something different, may be anticipated only in a very general way. The specific problems are revealed only after the attempt at innovation" (Anonymous, 1977, p. 241). These examples illustrate an apt principle.

If such complexity exists in a small village and a small organizational unit, there is likely to be more complexity in every rural town or city. Ecological concepts like interdependence, succession, cycling of resources, and adaptation provide the investigator, advocate, or proponent a point of view as to how one can think about and orient themselves by immersion in the local culture *before* introducing the research or prevention program in the community. The pragmatic benefit is not only to facilitate adoption of a proposed intervention but also to ensure that ample time is given for the local community to determine for themselves how to create the conditions for the proposed innovation to be adapted to their customs and traditions.

Some trends suggest that professionals can introduce new options like a new product, with savvy commercials and testimonials from celebrities and public officials. The ecological perspective is a resource, an antidote, to superficial and/or manipulative pressures. The use of ecological concepts affirms that there is need for a real interdependence between the wishes and aspirations of the community participants and the project staff. The premise is that a strong working relationship between professionals and citizens increases the odds of comprehensive adoption and offers a solid basis for local ownership of the proposed intervention.

15

Inquiry as Situated Methods With Processes for Mutual Discovery

The previous chapters have presented a point of view that is divergent from past traditions. The emphasis is on connecting inquiry to the culture and needs of the community based on the premise that knowledge is a two-way process because the community is an essential partner in the expedition. The traditional role of expert is replaced with the concept of being a collaborative resource. Discussions with community representatives create the context for what and how to study. This does not mean that there is no place for research generated by the community psychologist; rather, the process of planning and carrying out the research is in concert with community values, needs, traditions, and aspirations. Because the research enterprise is a potential resource for the community, it is essential to be inclusive during the research process.

Many previous investigators in the social and behavioral sciences have worked from an ecological perspective. Many would not share my premise; nevertheless, I have benefited from their contributions. I have been challenged and stimulated by reading and absorbing their work. Those include the following from psychology: Roger Barker, Urie Bronfrenbrenner, Egon Brunswik, James and Eleanor Gibson, Eleanor Maccoby, Rudy Moos, Ulric Nessor, Harold Raush; from social psychiatry: John Cassell, Alexander and Dorothea Leighton; from sociology: Glen Elder, Melvin Kohn, Leo Srole; and from anthropology: Gregory Bateson, Clifford Geertz, Walter Goldshmidt, Roy Rappaport, and of course Kurt Lewin. This is a partial roster of those who have inspired my own efforts. They provided the soil for the ideas about research presented in the following.

The key feature of ecological inquiry is the axiom that knowledge is place- and person-specific. More specific features are (1) how people are connected to their social environment, (2) the use of multiple methods for inquiry, and (3) the research relationship as the foundation for inquiry.

The major implication of this thesis is that there cannot be general laws that account for all people for every situation, only conclusions about specific persons in particular settings as mentioned previously. Although the insights gained from inquiry in one place can be the basis of more general hypotheses to be tried and adapted to another place, the primary goal of an ecological expedition is the discovery of specific places, people, and events in their particular and unique situations. These ideas run counter to historical traditions in psychology, where methods are more focused on posing research questions as general propositions to apply to all people. A brief discussion of each of these three ecological principles of research is presented next.

How People Are Connected to Their Social Environment

The increased attention to integrating information gained from individuals in their setting is one of the outcomes of an ecological perspective. The investigator is challenged not only to think in multilinear ways but also to conceive of time, people, place, and their interactions as the primary focus of inquiry. In their review of the literature about the association between socioeconomic status and health, Linda C. Gallo and Karen A. Matthews (2003) have pointed to the need for more research that focuses on the types of reciprocal associations between (environmental) resources and cognitive-emotional factors. They also advocate further study of "psychosocial risk factors in their naturally occurring configurations" (Gall & Matthews, 2003, p. 38).

Gary Evans's analysis of the environment of childhood poverty illuminates the multiple interacting events and conditions that precipitate poverty, which stem from such various conditions as low social support, fewer persons who read to children, polluted water and air, and so on. I read his concluding sentence with a shared conviction: "Psychologists need to come to grips with the ecological reality of poverty and desist relegating income and SES to unexplained confounding variables in their models of human behavior and well being" (Evans, 2004, p. 88).

This ecological view of research is captivating because it can express and illustrate the subtleties of how people interact in situations. This kind of knowledge is considered valuable because of the potential insights about the locales where community prevention programs will be situated. This information also can help clarify just how the interdependence between researcher and community can be illustrated. Will the interdependence be based on a congruent fit between the researcher and the resident who aspires for a social status like that obtained by professionals? Or will the interdependence between researcher and community be based on the demands of the community so that the professional becomes "educated" about their locale? Each of these contextual processes may be operating at once, thereby generating various simultaneous and contrasting role expectations and different arrangements for sharing power between the researcher and community representatives. These kinds of questions and sensitivities for both the community and the researcher test the ecological thesis. The process of coping with such topics is the proof in the pudding for these ideas.

The Use of Multiple Methods

The use of multiple methods is an exciting intellectual journey. In the high school study presented in chapter 2, the faculty and administrators in the two high schools over time began to see the connections between different levels of exploratory preferences and social settings. This awareness stemmed from knowledge gained through different methods: questionnaires, small group exercises, and experimental problem-solving groups.

While the investigations of individual expressions of exploratory behavior were ongoing, simultaneous efforts to document the social structures of the high schools occurred. Various approaches provided vital information. It was possible to appraise the student power structures of the schools and the settings that defined and elaborated the student power structure. For example, at one school cliques developed around schoolyard ledges where the youths congregated. At the other school, the major settings were with faculty in competitive games and sporting events. Following consultation with the faculty and students, a more veridical understanding of the socialization processes and connections to coping styles were revealed.

Different but equally compelling themes were revealed with the inquiry of African American community leaders conducted between 1990 and 2000, which is described in chapter 12. This project made it possible to assess the ecological perspective again in quite a different setting. This work demonstrated not only the conceptual but also the pragmatic benefits of another ecological expedition. The basis for defining what was important to study came from a series of 19 meetings with community representatives (Glidewell et al., 1998). Personal vision was the key component to this African American community, which became the focus during interviews with 80 community leaders and encouraged more in-depth explorations (Mock, 1994, 1999).

The context for expressing community leadership was the sponsoring organization Developing Communities Project, which promoted the development of citizens to encourage and motivate local leadership. As a result of the continuous conversations with community leaders, the research staff realized the importance of the concepts of hope and optimism in their daily lives as well as the pivotal role of spirituality that was a source for their commitment to the community. When it came time to analyze interview data with these community leaders, a metaphor was chosen that corresponded to the values of evolution, development, and strength.

At Christmas in 1984, my youngest daughter, Kathryn, presented me with a watercolor she composed. It was a tree with a poem by Herman Hesse:

> Trees are the most penetrating preachers
> The world rustles in their highest boughs,
> Their roots rest in infinity; but they do not lose themselves there
> They struggle with all the force of their lives for one thing only
> To build their own form to fulfill their own
> Laws, to represent themselves

The watercolor was on my wall, so it was always present. The poem spoke to the concepts underlying the purposes of the Developing Communities Project to train and develop persons who were strong and unyielding to outside forces. The tree metaphor fit. The metaphor of leadership as a tree was chosen to frame the analyses, present the information, *and* communicate it. Representing the diverse styles of community leadership became a congruent way to document that there was no hierarchy to leadership. The variety of different people playing different roles reflected the philosophy and the realities of community leadership as defined in this community at this time (Tandon et al., 1998).

The use of multiple methods was highlighted when oral histories were conducted with a small group of six of the leaders. What was learned was that the oral history information complemented the more quantitative data. For example, in compelling ways the stories reflected the power of religion and spirituality as well as placed an emphasis on the role of the church. These same themes obtained via the quantitative information were now made real.

In both these inquiries reported in chapters 2 and 12, the use of multiple methods elaborated the meaning and significance of the major concepts (exploration and community leadership) and enhanced the meaning of the findings for the participants. The research staff also expanded and refined our understanding of the research topics.

These various approaches provided an opportunity for us to develop a portrait of the socialization processes and connections to coping styles in two high schools as well as the dynamics of community leadership in one particular community. These experiences also convinced me that ecological approaches to inquiry were stimulating, challenging, inspiring, and, most important, workable. At a more conceptual level, Bent Flyvbjerg has pointed out the significance of case studies such as the oral histories mentioned: "It is worth repeating the insight that a discipline without a large number of thoroughly executed case studies is a discipline without systematic production of exemplars, and that a discipline without exemplars is an ineffective one" (2001, p. 87).

Among some ecological researchers in biology, the term *consilience* is used to describe the integration of knowledge via various methods. As Mark Taper and Subhash R. Lele have pointed out, this resurgence of interest while important emphasizes the need to develop technical methods for combining evidence. This is a challenge for the next ecological expeditions in community psychology as well (Taper & Lele, 2004, p. 533).

The Research Relationship

The theme weaving through the previous chapter is that research is indeed a relationship. Ecological inquiry is not just simply the scientist asking for the participant's approval but instead working out the bases and purposes of inquiry with those who will be informants. This topic has been recently articulated by Elizabeth Hawkins, Lillian Cummins, and Alan Marlatt (2004) in discussing substance abuse prevention among American Indian and Alaskan youth:

> One method of assuring that programs are appropriate for their target population is extensive collaboration with and involvement of community members. Often this means going beyond the boundaries of traditional academic research and grant funding. It requires making a significant commitment of time and resources toward developing the trust and respect of community members and learning from them the best methods of designing and implementing a local program. (p. 314).

The relationship between researcher and informant lays the groundwork for defining just what a prevention program will look like and what kinds of rules of engagement exist for the community and professional participants. Jacob Kretzmann and John McKnight have emphasized the relationship as the important phase of community development as

> the sense of efficacy [is] based on interdependence, [unfortunately] the idea that people can count on their neighbors and neighborhood resources for support and strength has weakened. For community builders who are focused on assets, rebuilding these local relationships offers the most promising route toward successful community development. (1993, p. 11)

This type of inquiry has the potential of making the proposed program more authentic and thus more connected to the community.

The consequence is that the research will have contributed to the dissolution of the dichotomy between expert and subject. This topic is the focus of *A Guide to Conducting Prevention Research in the Community* (1988), which can be consulted as an additional resource. My first major effort to evaluate ecological principles in research was the six-year project studying adaptations of high school youth reported in chapter 2 and discussed in this chapter. As was mentioned, a concerted effort was made to work collaboratively with the two schools. Frequent meetings were scheduled with the central office staffs of the districts in addition to regular meetings with the school principals. Most important, a faculty member was involved as a field coordinator in each school. These contributors authored chapters in the book summarized in chapter 2.

This very positive experience convinced me that it was possible to view and implement research as close as possible to being interdependent. This experience was codified into a formal set of principles by Ed Trickett, Trudy Vincent, and me (1985). The working relationship that was established between the university group and the high school communities and later the African American community residents made it possible to report findings that enlarged understandings of the topics of high school adaptation as well as community leadership by both the university teams and members of the two different communities. In both cases, interdependence informed the discovery process and created a generative mood for future explorations. There was goodwill.

The research relationship is not predictable. There are surprises and demands on time, talents, and goodwill. The more the researcher fosters the relationship and believes in reciprocal connections with the community, the outcome will include more refined methods, benefits for the organization, and knowledge for all participants. The experience of documenting community leadership is a powerful story that has been partially told in reports by some of the key participants (Kelly et al., 2004). It is not often recognized that university administrative and program support are essential for faculty to engage in collaborative research with community organizations. The Maternal and Child Community Health Sciences Consortium and the Great Cities Program at the University of Illinois at Chicago (UIC) were essential in enabling faculty from different departments to engage in collaborative research with local community organizations. This is illustrated in the reports of 12 UIC faculty who describe the processes and outcomes of their work with a variety of community groups (Sullivan & Kelly, 2001). Ed Trickett and Susan Ryerson-Espino have also presented a detailed analysis of the multiple facets of doing collaborative research. With ecological expeditions, as they illustrate, there are many nuances of the research relationship. These nuances reflect local conditions of time, place, traditions, and the nature of the various contexts for the collaborative work (Trickett & Ryerson-Espino, 2004).

Examples of Recent Ecological Inquiries

Currently there are new voices emerging, a new generation of community psychologists who have a renewed commitment to ecologic analyses in the field of community psychology. In the past, investigators such as Gary Fisher and Irma Strantz (1972) referenced my ideas to study drug use some 30 years ago. They employed multiple methods (questionnaires and interviews) to examine the components of social class and frequency of marijuana use.

More recently, Kenneth Miller and Lisa M. Rasco (2004) have used an ecological framework for understanding and responding to the mental health needs of refugees. Departing from the person-centered illness model that has guided most research and intervention with refugees, Miller and Rasco emphasize the problematic fit between the demands of the settings in which refugees find themselves and the range of coping resources to which they have access. This shift in frameworks suggested the need for rethinking the current emphasis placed on clinic-based mental health services and underscores the value of community-based interventions that build on existing strengths and enhance refugees' capacity to cope effectively with the new settings. Echoing the ecological model's emphasis on local context, Miller and Rasco also suggest that refugee interventions are most likely to succeed when they are culturally grounded, whereby researchers are informed by an understanding of how particular communities experience and express psychological well-being and distress.

Cecile Lardon and colleagues (2004) at the Center for Alaska Native Health research at the University of Alaska, Fairbanks are working with the villagers of six Yup'ik and one Cup'ik community on the west coast of Alaska. Their project focuses on the cultural-behavioral components contributing to obesity, diabetes, and heart disease among the people of the Yukon-Kuskokwin Delta. Illustrating the collaborative commitment of the team, they worked with community representatives from two of the villages and with Yup'ik health care professionals to better understand local Yup'ik concepts of wellness. A Yup'ik advisory council provided further clarification and refinement of these concepts, helping transform them into a measure of wellness to be used in the participating communities. This is an especially important step in conducting cross-cultural research, even in mostly English-speaking communities. The Yup'ik and Cup'ik conceptualization of health included eating native foods, getting fresh air, being outside, staying physically active, respecting one's elders, maintaining spirituality, and coping with cultural change over time. Although some of these broader concepts may sound familiar to mainland audiences, the more specific cultural expressions of each concept were carefully documented in collaboration with members of the Yup'ik culture. The fact that the members of the communities generated these topics suggests that they provide a firm basis for assessment and for further health promotion efforts in those communities. The research instruments developed will be further grounded in the host community's traditions, including sensitivity to the significance of generational differences in how these basic cultural values are experienced.

The research team had to prove its commitment to the participating communities by making several trips to each village and participating in community events such as potlatches, dances, and basketball games and providing part-time paid positions for community members as coresearchers. Travel in this area is often difficult and frequently delayed by weather conditions as the villages can only be reached by small aircraft or, in the summer, by boat. By taking on an ecological expedition, the person has to be prepared to overcome personal and environmental challenges, in this case geographical ones.

The synergistic process of focusing on persons and settings, recognizing their dynamic interactions with multiple methods, and viewing the research as a relationship are illustrated by the recent examples. They suggest that an ecological approach to inquiry is both possible and fruitful.

16

Practicing Ecology

Ideas for Community-Based Preventive Programs

The mental health professions in the United States have a long and venerable history of trying to improve the mental health of individual citizens. The tendency accompanying this tradition is to view the community as a larger number of individuals. The notion of ecological practice is to adapt concepts of individuals and transpose them to a larger unit of analysis, and eventually to the immediate and extended social settings of the individual. Transferring the helping tradition of the mental health professions to the level of the community is a relatively new enterprise.

The thesis of the ecological perspective is that a different vocabulary is needed. The unit of analysis shifts to groups, organizations, and larger communities. When framing the topics of help at a different level, the concepts discussed in the earlier chapters come into play. The ecological ideas have been stimulated by the concepts of public health, which has had a long history of defining professional help at the community level (Rosen, 1993; Starr, 1983). There has been some success with the prevention of infectious disease through public health measures at the community level, particularly in the 1920s and 1930s. After World War II, more interest developed in applying prevention programs to chronic diseases such as cancer, heart disease, and mental illness.

The concepts of prevention began to be stated as salient for mental health, à la public health, in the 1950s. The first step was to consider mental health professionals going to the community and providing services before a problem of a specific individual was observed. This new rationale was to do something beneficial before the fact, not after the fact. This was quite novel for the mental health professions in the period immediately before and after World War II. At that time, the services were available *after* the person, family members, friends, or public officials recognized the appearance of personal difficulties. Resources were typically private practicing specialists or, in some cases, community-based clinics.

Public health nurses represent one significant historical reference point for these community services because they have been doing community-based prevention work for decades with their tradition of home visiting. This was a well-established tradition in locating people in need and getting services to them. (There is often a long incubating period for novel ideas to be rediscovered.) Two of the foremost thinkers about translating concepts from the individual to the community were psychiatrists Erich Lindemann and Gerald Caplan (Kelly, 1984, 1992a). While at the Harvard School of Public Health and Massachusetts General Hospital from 1948 through the 1960s, they created concepts for working with the people in a position to spot incipient difficulties and consult with them about their clients. The idea was that if community resources could be supported and trained to understand and manage mental health difficulties, more opportunities would exist to provide early assistance without the stigma of seeing a mental health professional. Teachers, clergy, nurses, and police officers could become community resources and, in turn, educate their colleagues about how to address problems within their community or social organization.

These pioneering preventive concepts largely focused on the consultant–consultee relationship. Little discussion occurred about the qualities of organizations or communities that could facilitate or impede the consultation process. Only anecdotal reports existed by consultants who could not fully understand the social systems in which they were working. I was stimulated by these issues and wanted to expand a way to think about how consultants could consider the qualities of the settings in which they were working to identify and understand both the constraints and the resources present in the community organizations where the consultation was taking place. The intent was to provide a conceptual framework so that mental health consultants could be more informed when working in different social systems.

Doing ecological practice is a pragmatic activity. A spirit of improvisation develops as the work unfolds. A premium is placed on the consultant being able to expand concepts of help that include such activities as advocacy and community development, which are normally outside the methods of psychology. Such methods are very apt for schools, parents, and students, especially in poor communities. Over the years, I discovered and rediscovered that not all elementary schools had the same histories and qualities, creating a situation where a consultant in one school could not expect the same issues to be expressed in another school. Different solutions were required when working in varied places. Over the years, I have found the following ideas fruitful for the mental health professional, as an outsider, learning how to be helpful in different community institutions. Here are four insights about the processes of doing preventive work as an ecological practice.

1. Settings as Well as People Are Resources

The mental health consultant working from an ecological perspective begins with finding out the natural resources of the organization or group. The premise is that every place has people who are the resources for others, though they may lack titles or formal mental health roles. Secretaries, maintenance personnel, security guards, and assistants of various kinds are examples. School bus drivers and mail personnel are other examples. Persons in these roles are potential facilitators to make new programs work. They can do this in spite of union contracts and other organizational constraints. The goal is to move the work away from one elite mental health professional, the consultant, serving another elite person, the principal or schoolteacher. The entire school staff becomes a potential source of help for individual or groups of students in an ecological enterprise. The total environment becomes a resource for drawing on their combined solutions and help.

The ecological perspective is one conceptual resource for clarifying how all the participants of social systems and their shared culture can become resources for the proposed new mental health program. By illuminating how people are interdependent within their groups, it is possible to take the next step and point to how the role of the social system at large can be the basis for the improvement of service. Service, then, has been redefined. To do this, working knowledge is needed about the place as well as all the people in the community.

The focus becomes understanding the interdependence of participants and appreciating the traditions that foster and support interdependence in a particular place. Recognizing the cultural norms that facilitate or inhibit persons being connected to a social group augments the diagnostic process of the professional outsider who is trying to be a resource to the total system, such as an elementary school. Over and over again, it became clear that the principal, teachers, secretaries, and custodians in an elementary school, for example, could realize that they were interdependent with each other. A real beginning was made to link the consultation process to the culture of that specific school (Kelly & Hess, 1987).

2. Defining Community Programs as a Process of Creating Diverse Solutions

Going against traditional approaches by developing a diverse array of solutions presents many challenges. It is for the consultant to decide that not every organization or community will require and should have the same clinical program or solution to address a problem. Some community issues can benefit from the services of a consultant focusing on changes in communication patterns among adults. In other places, it may be literacy training for parents, job development in the community, or understanding lifestyles. Different social groups may emerge as the salient focus. Examining the negative consequences of social class differences or community values may be the most systemic solution rather than thinking primarily of clinical services for individuals or groups who are the casualties of the system itself.

This fundamental ecological premise is that *not* every problem needs a traditional, individual "psychological" solution. This new situation requires the professional to move beyond the revered techniques identified with their past training. This is particularly so when the problem and the setting are unfamiliar to the helping resource. Anglo professional resources will need to be open to education in nonwhite communities. Although this seems obvious, the processes for planning the workable solutions in a community that varies from the heritage of the consultant must be adapted to the constraints and resources of that specific community. The trained professional needs to be open to becoming educated by the community because the problems are often outside or beyond the methods sanctioned by formal training. By collaborating with persons from other disciplines, the consultant is modeling how to relate to and create a variety of resources that are appropriate for this problem at this time in this place.

After the educational process proceeds, the professional must remain informed about the utility and wisdom of the multifaceted nature of designing community-based programs. This translates into the ecological practitioner working in a multidisciplinary team or cooperative group. A recent presentation by Emilie Phillips Smith and colleagues (2004) points to the contributions of cooperative groups working with different elements of a preventive program. They developed an adolescent diversion program that focused on the individual, family, community, and juvenile justice contexts. They found that "attending to the youth in the ecological context of their family and community is a more powerful approach to decreasing juvenile delinquency than either ignoring the act (diversion without services) or punishing the act via the juvenile justice system" (Smith et al., 2004, p. 44). This ecological point of view can be a resource in itself for community residents to see that long-term solutions avoid blaming the victim (Ryan, 1971). The solution comes instead from concerted efforts from a coalition of citizens and professional resources. Susan Scherffius Jakes (2004) has developed a scale to assess social programs' descriptions with the goal of determining whether the program is ecological. Her results produced three considerations: community control of the program, focus on systemic change, and the extent to which the social program is multidimensional. This effort pushes thinking to specify in some detail what is meant by an ecological program. Jakes reemphasizes a point made by Ed Seidman in 1988: If an intervention does not seek to actually change the setting or person interaction, it is not ecological.

The following example illustrates how ecological thinking generates two complementary yet different services for subregions of a community. Philip A. Mann (1987) provides an illustration of developing diverse approaches in two contrasting neighborhoods in northern Iowa. Both neighborhood communities wanted to reduce child abuse. In the central city of this larger community, the ecologically focused consultation program was to facilitate coordination of the existing social agencies concerned with child abuse. The goal was to reduce repetition of services and strengthen the combined effects of services. Another ecologically developed but different program in the rural neighborhood of this same larger community emphasized a community development perspective where the approach to the problem of child abuse was community education and enlightenment of the citizens about the topic.

In one large geographical community with central city and rural neighborhoods, complementary yet different solutions were created that were based on the assessment of the natural resources in the two neighborhoods. When the community values the uniqueness of their human, economic, and political resources, models for services are needed that reflect this uniqueness. The solutions derive from the community, not the methods of the professional. Not every problem requires identical programmatic solutions. In doing community work, an ecological perspective means that not all problems are addressed with the same techniques and methods. Although this may seem obvious, one of the challenges in training professionals is to provide sufficient opportunities to engage with citizens to tailor the help so that it "feels right" for all concerned. Sensitivity, patience, and a commitment to work collaboratively are required.

3. Longitudinal View

The training of professionals tends to concentrate on techniques that are bounded in time. Discrete packages and programs are usually expected and preferred. The larger societal and professional values support the creation of time-limited efforts to solve a problem. Larger cultural values endorse what are often referred to as "quick fixes."

Moving from working with individuals in a professional way to collaborating at the community level is an entirely different enterprise. The community problem is nested in a combination of constraints, few of which are solvable by discrete solutions in a short time. In addressing systemic problems, more time is needed to understand and elaborate the various connections and unravel the intricacies of history, economics, community values, and traditions. Not only does it take time to assess the local community, but it also takes time to build relationships between the professional and various segments of the community. Understanding the various segments is clearly a pressing topic. Not all persons in a community will wish to work with some other members. Understanding the bases for these differences becomes essential to create a realistic and workable sense of the layers of the social structures that exist within a geographical area. The criteria for similarities in viewpoints or the bases for discord may include the length and location of residence, race, age, religious beliefs, leisure time activities, and the nature of the family unit. There might be other factors that bind people together, such as ethnic heritage, level of schooling, number of children, occupation, and so on. The task of the ecological practitioner is to learn the categories that unite or separate residents from sharing common purposes about solving a problem or enhancing the quality of life in their locale. This is where the commitment to the discovery of community takes place. It is also vital to reduce any unintended arrogance that encourages status differences between the professional and citizens. If the community has a history of being "the laboratory" for prior professionals, then the task for the ecologically sensitive professional is to overcome resistances and anxieties about the professional's motives and goals. Is the professional more interested in his or her career than the community's issues?

Ecological practice is not for everyone. The ecologically oriented worker is prepared to be present for the long haul. To enable the process to go forward for the long term, there are at least two requirements. One is that the ecological worker helps create a local community leadership structure that gives the work not only authenticity but also a grounded quality. Such structures could be an advisory committee or a group named by the community. Their function is to be an informed oversight group who watches the planning of new services and learns about themselves as well as their changing needs. Such a structure gives the work some insurance that if the professional unexpectedly needs to move away from this activity, the disruption will be minimal. The second requirement is for the workers to create supportive groups for themselves and community participants, which can help reduce the strains and frustrations that surface. Such a group could include local foundation leaders and persons who have previously gone through the process of designing and implementing community-based prevention services. Such a group can serve as a meaningful motivator and validate what has been proposed and hopefully accomplished. In both of these instances this can be achieved by encouraging others to contribute natural and varied resources. The practicing ecologist models ecological thinking for the community.

4. Unintended Consequences

One of the important but unrecognized principles in doing community work is the notion that every intervention generates unexpected consequences. In everyday conversation, there is reference to negative side effects of work strain on the family, the positive side effects of the birth of a new child on the life of grandparents and relatives, and sometimes positive and negative side effects on the parents. Also notable are the positive and negative side effects of occupational promotions and certainly the pernicious side effects of economic decline affecting an increase in gang violence. Although unintended consequences are the products of interventions, this anecdotal knowledge is rarely documented.

These experiences are not always factored into the rationale and purposes of prevention programs. The ecological perspective moves this concept of unintended consequences to a primary position. The concept does focus explicitly on the fact that there *will be* unanticipated consequences of imposed and even desired changes. An ecological evaluation looks for these effects and encourages citizens to be alert to possible positive and negative changes that occur in their lives as a result of being a codesigner of a prevention program. In appraising Head Start some years ago, Edward Fiske noted that these programs changed parents' relationship to schools, quoting one participant as stating: "Parents are no longer afraid to go to school and ask the teacher why their child doesn't have homework" (Fiske, 1975; Kelly, 1977). This is indeed a positive unanticipated consequence of concentrated attention to the social development of preschool children. Their parents become informed parents and advocates for community-wide efforts of early childhood education. Negative unintended consequences also occur when persons are released from hospitals without local community or health care. This negative side effect has tragically not been attended to during the past four decades when the "dumping phenomenon" has been the norm for transferring disabled persons back into neighborhoods. The concept of unintended consequences brings home the value framework of an ecological perspective: to be self-conscious and responsible for understanding the potential good as well as limitations from organized community helping programs.

There is another caveat. Tom Haydon (2004) in researching and writing about gang culture made the following observation: "The problem is the chasm that grows between an academic idea and its implementation in reality" (p. 352). The ideas expressed in these four topics are intended to reduce that chasm.

17

Education and Training for an Ecological Perspective

Graduate education in clinical or community psychology is often restricted to requiring doctoral students to learn only the precepts of their major discipline. In doing so, the unintended consequence is that education becomes insular and restrictive, losing useful knowledge about contextual topics necessary when practicing ecological research. This insularity may have another unwitting consequence of not encouraging students to search out the ideas, methods, and knowledge from other disciplines. These side effects of restricted training contrast with the precepts of an ecological orientation. These precepts ask the student not only to think anew and go outside their own profession but also to work with doctoral students from other disciplines.

Thinking ecologically is not an easy activity. Ludwig von Bertalanffy, one of the founders of general systems theory, referred to it as "uncommon sense" (Davidson, 1983). In understanding how to acquire this uncommon sense, opportunities must exist to examine the implicit premises of both U.S. culture and the psychology profession. Then, after some sensitivity to our own cultural and professional heritages, the education to acquire uncommon sense can begin.

I say this because for the most part, we are raised as citizens of the United States to focus explicitly on the individual rather than a larger group. If we choose psychology as a career, the individual is dominant. Both our culture and profession emphasize an individualistic view. Being too absorbed in American culture can make us believe that we as individuals account for our destiny without the presence of support and validation from legions of former, current, and future others. The concept of interdependence is not part of our philosophical heritage. Some religious organizations do embrace the notion of interdependence, but it is not absorbed as a general notion of everyday life. Two anthropologists have made a similar observation: "People in Western Societies tend to hold the view that humans are separate from the environment, above it in some way" (Sutton & Anderson, 2004, p. 1).

Paradoxically, those from different heritages and circumstances can often appreciate the value of community. Shinobu Kitayama and Hazel Rose Markus (1999), in studying the personality coherence of the Japanese self, provide insights about, for example, the differences between the Japanese values for toughness and warm-heartedness and the European-American values for independence. New immigrants, as persons from groups who have experienced racism or other forms of discrimination, may understand the value and place of community. In other words, those at the margins understand it best. Those who struggle to overcome obstacles and to create economic opportunities often end up developing a set of community resources to further combat oppression. Those of us who have experienced little discrimination and have lived relatively sheltered lives may find it more difficult to think ecologically because we have experienced our lives as primarily being our own doing. This may be a potential side effect of being in higher status, unless other opportunities are created to embrace other cultures or classes. It may be that acquiring a moral or ethical imperative bolsters thinking ecologically.

One of the potential positive, unanticipated consequences of learning to think ecologically in an interdisciplinary group is that as a result the American orientation to think analytically by separating the "I" from the "it" is grasped. There can be more of a tendency to view oneself as a group of interdependent selves. The "one" self will be moderated. Peter Senge and colleagues discuss these processes in more detail (Senge et al., 2004).

The paradox is that we cannot achieve individual goals without being part of a larger group and acquiring a sense of the power of others. Playwright Tony Kushner noted that the production of his play *Angels in America* was dependent on the contributions, advice, support, and commitment of many. In his view, he, even as the playwright, was just one contributor (Weber, 1993). Accomplishments solely by an individual are largely a fiction. Yet prizes are given for individual achievements. We revere the qualities of individuals alone. This custom can create myths that the individual makes the most difference.

Thus the instructor taking on the challenge to teach the significance of ecological points of view has several responsibilities: to stimulate motivation to reduce nonecological thoughts as well as to reduce the premise that learning and achievement is primarily an individual effort. In contrast to traditional pedagogical methods, interdependent learning is assessed and valued. The goal is to reduce student stress about traditional achievement, because it is not essential to be competitive. Empirical evidence shows that cooperative learning is a valid way to achieve goals (Johnson & Johnson, 1992). By focusing directly on the benefits of interdependent learning, the instructor can then clarify the principles of interdependent learning.

Graduate education is not always helpful in going beyond an individualistic value. There is a competition for grades, letters of recommendation, teaching awards, and postgraduate positions. Most times, the behavioral sciences and the mental health professions reward individual achievement rather than collaborative work. So the instructor of ecological concepts is obligated to put American culture and psychology in perspective before embarking on ecological education. I will elaborate on some of the points previously suggested in chapter 5.

The Title for a Course: Social Adaptation

The title of the course I have taught is Social Adaptation. This title reflects the purpose of the class, which is not only how the class adapts to the community but also how the students adapt to each other. The students also learn how to adapt to a teaching structure that is more than didactic, because it requires actively learning how to create and implement a community-based program. In addition to the basic ecological concept of interdependence, the class participants experience how they themselves adapt to multiple communities, which includes their own community of students as well as the groups in the community with whom they are working. This process is analogous to learning how to be a resource for each of the other class members.

Supports for the Instructor

The instructor works to reduce high expectations about the individual accomplishments of the different tasks generated by the students. It is really helpful if the instructor has one or more advanced doctoral students as teaching assistants, which is illustrated with greater detail in chapter 5. In addition, it may be useful for the instructor to create an informal support group where he or she can discuss the substantive issues and the process issues that are generic to learning how to be a resource to a community. Another major support would be other learning settings where the student is exposed to such concepts as systems theory and cultural norms or such methods as qualitative inquiry, oral history documentation, and the evolution of communities. Obviously, an educational locale that encourages interdisciplinary education can be a major intellectual resource. Jacob Tebes and colleagues (2002) have proposed various methods to create "effective practice networks" or "prevention study groups" to enhance communication and discussions of common experiences. These include an array of Web-based technologies.

Learning in Groups

If the students have some prior experiences where they have absorbed the values and benefits of being interdependent with others, they have experienced firsthand the potential utility of ecological thinking. Previous experiences in cooperative learning can be excellent preparation for understanding the diversity of cultures of persons different from themselves in a new group (Johnson & Johnson, 1992; Kelly et al., 1994; Stelzner, 1996). In retrospect, the ease with which doctoral students at the University of Michigan in the 1960s quickly engaged with interdependent learning in their work groups mentioned in "Community as Teacher" may have been due to their prior and then current involvement in feminist, civil rights, and/or environmental protection activities. Without the students having some deep and meaningful past experiences with interdependent learning, the instructor will need to create simulations or proxy group experiences *before* moving on to the ecological axioms and concepts. These can be simulated learning situations where the tasks are to establish social bonds as cocontributors to accomplishing shared goals. Education as an ecological enterprise is not just didactic education. Working in groups is a potential resource for seeing how it is easier and more profound to learn firsthand that the combined energies and talents of others can add to the quality of achieving an objective. Learning about the power of group norms may provide the doctoral student with an additional perspective that when work team members feel connected to each other some chance exists to increase the élan and the originality of ideas (Zander, 1985). This is surely important when working in the community as the combined energy, experiences, and points of view of participants enable the adaptation of a community-based preventive program. This cohesiveness makes it possible for more options to be generated by the participants with the result that the proposed community solution or program is unique to their own group at a particular time.

Learning in an Interdisciplinary Environment

Ecological education at the graduate level is an interdisciplinary activity, which can be a challenge as well. At some universities, doctoral students are traditionally discouraged from going outside their own departments. When this attitude of departmental insularity is explicit, students have fewer opportunities to shape their values about working in groups and with other disciplines.

Group experience is excellent preparation to work in interdisciplinary teams. Working in a group with members of other disciplines can give the student more confidence to go on and establish a working connection with members of a different "tribe" when their graduate education is completed. The value for interdisciplinary education is an asset in enabling students to dissipate stereotypes about other disciplines. Professional ethnocentrism is tempered. Each student begins to see the complimentary nature of information and knowledge. Ultimately, students who enter the field of community psychology will need to work with several disciplines, so this gap between academic training and professional development must be bridged. Research knowledge is beginning to accumulate so that the elements and processes of doing interdisciplinary work will have more clarity (Stokols et al., 2003). Ken Maton and colleagues are creating a set of guidelines for the Society for Community Research and Action to facilitate community psychologists' contributions to interdisciplinary research and practices (Maton et al., in preparation). Geographers and urban historians can illuminate the culture of the community, which is the seed for a new program. Anthropologists can illuminate the microstructures of places. Sociologists can alert us to the salience of community power structures. Working with members of other disciplines reduces the anxiety that one needs to be all knowing.

Ecological Learning Beyond a Semester

In addition to working in groups with students from other disciplines, a basic structure is needed. The Social Adaptation course is yearlong. It takes time for the groups to cohere and then for the groups to select a topic and a community. This is not a semester-long enterprise. In a single semester, there is only an illusion of learning, as the lack of time undermines any meaningful understanding of community work. An additional reason for the yearlong course is that this length of time makes it easier for students to understand the processes of innovation and to educate the team members about each other as well as the community with which they will be working.

This provides an opportunity for the team to learn how to be interdependent with each other and the community. This learning demands some tolerance of ambiguity and patience to encourage the community members to have an opportunity to trust the aspirations and motivations of the university team. These processes can further enhance the learning of the combined university and community group as they see what the rudiments are for an outsider designing a preventive intervention in a community. The collective value for the class is to resist quick solutions and to create ways for the community to be the primary host for deciding on the efficacy of the work.

The Jury Concept

This all comes together near the end of the year when a jury of citizens, selected as a representative group, evaluates the work carried out by each of the various teams. The presentations to the jury can be powerful events for the students as they witness the eloquence and wisdom of community residents. Students have told me that they take these jury sessions seriously and hold on to the resulting insights for a long time. Students not only earn community respect and see that their work has been worthwhile but also contribute a legacy to the community.

With current recording equipment, these jury events can be easily documented as a testimony for the students and the community participants. Part of the planning for the jury is to set in motion roles, structures, and means for the community groups to carry on. A significant part of the jury event is for the students to see what has to happen to sustain the momentum after they end their formal involvement. This provides an opportunity for the class to understand some of the ethics of an ecologically designed and implemented intervention. This is referred to as succession, the natural processes by which the evolution of the work progresses from the various stages. The significance of this concept was presented in chapter 1, which illustrates how the community takes over and carries on the work that it began with the students. The jury event is a success when the succession process has been discussed, organized, and planned. This gives both students and citizens closure for the work. It is instructive that one yearlong class with doctoral students from different disciplines working in groups can learn some of the basic concepts and principles of ecological thinking while contributing a workable plan to address a community problem.

Class projects that made a sizable contribution to the community, as judged by the juries themselves, have included creation of a rural health clinic, extension of a public transportation system to better serve African Americans, a proposal of a retirement program for university salaried employees, the establishment of a crime prevention program for elderly citizens, and a community-based program to improve the self-esteem of high school students. A description of this last project has been published (Gonzales, 1987). In each of these projects, the described format was implemented to enable the educational processes of the group to work toward an ecological approach (Kelly, 1992b).

Despite all of these benefits, one class is not enough. Hopefully the class is embedded in a culture that supports the values for these activities. But if not, the class can be a powerful and informative setting in which students take from the experience sufficient competences, hope, and patience, balanced with zeal, that enables them to be optimistic and informed resources for a future community.

A Summing Up

Some Facets of Interdependence

The concept of interdependence is the cornerstone of the ecological perspective. In biology, it represents the fundamental notion of life, particularly the exchange of nutrients and energy in an ecosystem. Roy Rappaport rightly maintains that "the ecosystem concept itself is a vital element in the construction, maintenance and reconstruction of the webs of life upon which, by whatever name we call them, we are absolutely dependent" (1990, p. 69). This axiom defines ecological biology and serves as an ecological perspective for community psychology.

As I mentioned in the previous essays, thinking ecologically in psychology has been at the margins of preferred thinking. With the exception of a few notable researchers—such as those mentioned previously, like Roger Barker, Urie Bronfenbrenner, Rudy Moos, Harold Raush, and Ed Trickett—psychology has only recently become a potential host for ecological thinking. The concept of interdependence has been employed in other fields and disciplines, however. For example, environmentalist James G. Speth has provided connections between economic indicators and sustainable environmental resources. He has demonstrated how continued growth, without controls, depletes supplies of fresh water and the quality of the atmosphere (Speth, 2004). Thomas Hughes, historian of science, has argued that technology and culture are interdependent (2004). The concept of interdependence has currency for many academic disciplines. Fortunately in community psychology, thinking ecologically and the concept of interdependence have currency. I have mentioned some examples in the various chapters and essays. For me, the concept of interdependence has been noteworthy because it has represented a personal and intellectual journey that has made my work come alive.

In the autobiography included in this book, the reader may see the ways in which my work and life have become interconnected. My intuitive sense of the vitality and salience of the concept of interdependence has personal roots. Fortunately, at a very early time I was aware of my feelings of being connected with other people and other places. Friends, teachers, and sometimes employers gave me energy and validation. I learned that in spite of less than organized family or neighborhood structures, life could be lived with some sense of not being alone. I was fortunate to have established a grounded sense of interdependence.

Interdependence is as much an emotional concept as an intellectual concept. This idea links the experiences we share with various people and places. In this sense, the concept provides a worldview of how to think about events, people, and places. By creating and stimulating the notion that there is no imperative to be isolated and fragmented, we are encouraged to create our places, especially our ties to people and places. This is so even in dire circumstances. This is all done in the spirit of Ella Baker's belief that it is "us" in our connected worlds that make the difference. Interdependence can support the design of community-based preventive interventions to the extent that the professional sees that the primary mission of inquiry is to be a resource for the members of the community. The hope is that members of the community can become interdependent as a result of the ecological research or practice.

Those periodic visits to downtown department stores in Cincinnati when I was younger and places like Crosley Field, the baseball stadium in Cincinnati, and the various jazz venues mentioned in the autobiographical statement gave meaning to me because I was a participant in these formative places of ritual and celebration. Friends and family reinforced the meaning of connections to these places. These places and cultural events oriented me. In both my brain and my gut I was feeling the benefits of what I later found to be the experience of interdependence. I was living an integrative life.

There is little doubt that I was attracted to the field of community mental health and later community psychology because I believed that mental health and well-being were nested and sustained by the interconnections with others in specific places. Early on, the implicit concept of interdependence was addressed in research about social support, which discussed individuals apart from the community context. Place was not considered. Later on, the significance of place was introduced to understand the sense of community mentioned earlier. Church groups, self-help groups, and political groups gave meaning to the concept and created opportunities to examine mutual relationships involved in building traditions. A sense of place was a salient host to appreciate ecological thinking. I discovered in my own life how having a sense of community was essential for personal growth as well as my own well-being and perhaps that of others. I was then ready to build on the community idea. My work has been an attempt to provide examples and illustrations of the various facets of ecological interdependence. I believed that I could not consider myself a *community* psychologist without thinking about and understanding how the connections between people and places were developed, nurtured, and evolved.

The following sections discuss seven themes that are inspirational to me and illustrate the preeminence of the concept of interdependence.

Interdependence Is a Resource for How to Think About People and Places

Every profession has a preferred paradigm for thinking about the world. Disciplines may reinforce these paradigms through a tradition of concepts, methods, and training. An unstated set of assumptions or epistemology about how to understand people is pervasive. To me, these traditions in psychology of viewing people outside their contexts not only were confining but also limited an understanding of behavior.

More important, without appreciation of contexts, the information about individuals was incomplete and possibly not representative of the complexities of the informants as they lived their lives in their own places. The concept of interdependence was a breakthrough. The construction of places for solidarity seemed essential as a social structure to support mutual understanding and personal well-being. The concept of interdependence stimulated new questions and insights about people and places. What were the social resources that people needed for their adaptation? What resources, less visible but present, were already available in the setting? What resources outside of their setting could be linked together to expand and diversify local resources? What were the implications of adding new resources to the setting? What social processes were needed to create new resources? These were the questions that interested me. These questions motivated me to construct hypotheses about how places succeeded or failed at meeting the psychological needs of their members. I then began what has turned out to be a lifelong expedition to think, study, try out, and evaluate various ways of thinking about such topics. I have not finished, nor do I think ecological expeditions will be ever finally completed. The expeditions will only evolve.

Instead, what is occurring is an elaboration of concepts; knowledge is accumulating. It is a unique knowledge where propositions and insights illuminate the qualities of people in a community at a particular time. The following assertion by Clifford Geertz gives some credence to this idea: "The road to the general, to the revelatory simplicities of science, lies through a concern with the particular, the circumstantial, the concrete" (1973, p. 53). Contexts change as new factors and events contribute to a new set of adaptive requirements for people and situations. Places change over time, so our methods must adapt and respond to each context. Stimulated by the concept of interdependence, the task is to understand how these environmental changes impact the participants and then how the participants create new criteria for being interdependent.

This does not mean that knowledge generated by other means is not considered. Basic facts are still essential as long as we grasp the requirements of the research setting and are explicit about how that knowledge was obtained. Our tendency to oblige authority, for example, is accepted and appraised in terms of the demand characteristics of the situation, which Urie Bronfenbrenner has suggested (1979). All methods are available, and diverse research styles can be employed in an ecological expedition.

This may be a good place to mention that the ecological perspective is not presented as a received view of correctness. Instead, thinking ecologically, by being open to multiple experiences and ideas, has some chance of not being stagnant. The organic process of discovering, revising, monitoring, and updating connections to external events allows for ideas to be reformulated for how people and places evolve. Thinking ecologically puts aside the need to think in fixed and irrefutable terms because there are no constants. There are only informed insights as a result of the knowledge gained from the exchanges between people and places.

Another important axiom in ecological analysis includes the places where data are collected and the methods used. The climate, for example, of an elementary school classroom, playground, or a graduate seminar is subject to a series of multilayered circumstantial, organizational, and community issues and events. Thinking ecologically expands our opportunities to consider varied interpretations depending on the locale. We can focus on the various facets of how people are and are not connected to one another. The agenda becomes understanding the dynamic energies and factors that promote connections, not just focusing on the qualities of persons or situations alone. We then have a new way of looking, observing, reflecting, and constructing meaning for ourselves and for the places in which we are situated.

Interdependence as a Resource for Linking Inquiry and Practice

Psychology traditionally separates inquiry and treatment. For the field of community psychology, this is particularly troublesome. For in thinking separately about inquiry and preventive interventions in the community, both the researcher and the practitioner reduce opportunities to link the two activities thereby losing potential benefits. Linking these two sources of information increases the chance that the choice of research topics or preventive interventions will bear directly on the selected problem in the community. As Rebecca Campbell and colleagues have illustrated, sexual assault can be tied to inquiry so that the community sees the benefit of a holistic view. The inquiry is also carried out with the shared consciousness with victims of violence about how the inquiry might be planned and realized (Campbell, 2002; Campbell et al., 2004).

There are potential unintended consequences. The polarities between researcher and interventionist are reduced while a shared view of the resources is increased among community members. The community participants can then see two different types of professional resources working together with the community. The community representatives can begin to see that there is some potential benefit to inquiry because they see for themselves the dialogue between the researcher and the practitioner. Two professional cultures now can realize their interdependence, which makes their actually being interdependent more likely. This is all very important because interdependence can serve as a reference point for the next generation of students to see on a personal level how community resources are really considered and employed to solve a problem. This is brought home when the researchers work together from different disciplines. There is a synergistic benefit of the presence of varied resources. The *process* of interdependent discovery, analysis, and learning replace the *concepts* of ecology.

A current social policy issue illustrates how the concept of interdependence can clarify competing interests. William H. Adams and other British colleagues are analyzing ways that conservation programs can contribute to the reduction of poverty (Adams et al., 2004). For a long time, conservation efforts were planned and begun without understanding that they eliminated jobs. Currently, a concerted effort is emerging to view conservation and the reduction of poverty as interdependent. Proposals for meeting both goals simultaneously can be carried out to "allow human society to meet its potential and share the fruits of economic growth while sustaining a biosphere that not only sustains full ecological functions but retains its living diversity" (Adams et al., 2004, p. 1148).

Rationale for the Use of Multiple Methods

I have been influenced by the notion that knowledge gained from only one method is limited. When multiple methods are employed in concert, there is potential for more comprehensive understanding of a topic. My own realization of this is related to two major research studies, first the high school study mentioned in chapter 2 and the community leadership study mentioned in chapter 12. Multiple methods not only provided a richer, more differentiated picture of high school youth or community leaders but also revealed qualities about the high school communities and the local community where the leaders were being developed. Multiple methods energize the process of discovery.

In the most recent example, I had a very positive experience in documenting community leadership. An interview was conducted as part of a collaborative process with residents of the community described in chapter 12. The interview material was analyzed in terms of themes for the 80 community leaders. The quantitative data revealed part of the thematic structure that was shared by the leaders. Then oral histories were documented via videotapes with six of the community leaders mentioned earlier. What was revealed were facets of information not revealed by the quantitative analyses. These rich recollections of personal histories complemented the more structured interview. The oral histories, for example, expressed the leaders' life struggles with racism. This topic was not revealed in the structured interviews because the interview questions, even though codesigned with community participants, were not focused on this essential topic. Viewing these videotaped stories with other leaders had a very positive impact because they could all share in their similar if not common experiences. The retelling of the oral history information created more interest by the leaders to examine the potential benefits of taking another look at the quantitative data. The combination of the methods was indeed synergistic.

The challenge is to disabuse ourselves of thinking that one method will approximate most of the meanings and significance of important topics. This is especially so in the field of community psychology where the complexity of the subject matter is such that a variety of methods are needed to grasp the various facets of a topic. These can also include methods generated in geography, economics, sociology, anthropology, public health, and history to indicate some of the most closely related fields. The ecological enterprise is an interdisciplinary enterprise that mirrors the multiple dimensions of the communities in which we work.

Interdependence Is a Resource for Visualizing and Creating Linked Settings

Behind the concept of interdependence is the fundamental notion that life is dependent on exchanges within multiple systems. The concept of coalitions rests on this premise. Linked systems are antidotes to tendencies toward competition, control, and the consequences of being in corporations and organizations where the norms are often self-preservation at the expense and others' quality of life. The documentary film *The Corporation* by Mark Achbar and Jennifer Abbott (2004) demonstrates this with incisiveness.

When parents are connected to schools and schools are connected to each other as well as to such community resources as human services and businesses, greater possibilities exist for redefining current plights. Linked systems can prevent isolation, a feeling of solitary angst, by suggesting that many persons may sense and share the same plights and aspirations. Self-help and community organizing draw out people from different segments of a community to convene as a larger resource for everyone. Being resourceful is not incidental to who you are or what position you have in society but results from an evolving notion that all members of linked systems are potential resources for each other.

Guidelines are essential to develop these linked systems. Discussions about doing collaborative-based research or community development often focus on guidelines for developing successful collaborations (Wolf, 2003). Creating and maintaining linked systems is both an art and a scientific activity. Hopefully in the coming decades, there will be more examples of how linked systems are nurtured and developed. One of the major challenges in creating linked systems is that they not become impediments themselves or inhibit community revitalization. Understanding how to adapt the linked systems to changing external opportunities and constraints is likely to be a major focus. Case examples and stories from the participants will be very important in developing principles for the care and support of linked systems.

Interdependence as a Reservoir Against Ideas and Concepts Becoming Obsolete

The community psychologist works in different settings and examines various topics of choice. I discovered that working from an ecological perspective helped me reject notions that could potentially be quaint. For example, the meaning of exploratory behavior was different not only for different boys but also for boys in different schools. With the core concept of interdependence, I prevented myself from accepting the notion that a psychological topic, such as exploratory behavior, has the same meaning in every context.

In working in the African American community, our definition of leadership was not the same as leadership required or measured in more corporate places. I found out that community organizing required involving persons independent of their personality. The value was to see everyone as a potential leader and to create new roles for him or her as the situation demanded. Some leaders would contribute by phoning or visiting others to invite them to become involved in the current activity; others would work on local arrangements or transport participants to events. These occasions provided opportunities for community leaders to emerge, as did the extracurricular activities in the high schools for students. From these two research experiences, I was able to revise and adapt my notions of coping behavior and leadership because the research team was being interdependent with the participants.

In analyzing results from an ecological perspective, I was able to update and enlarge my thinking. I was the beneficiary of learning as well as a contributor with the participants. The learning was not just the exchange of data between the investigator, research team, and recipients but in the very process of carrying out the research. Learning was derived from my emotional experiences as well as my intellectual experiences.

My perspective was updated as a consequence of being connected in multiple ways to the contributors, historically called subjects. There was no hierarchical relationship between collaborators and myself as researcher. The socialization process to train the next generation of scholars and practitioners in community psychology necessitates social norms to reduce elitism. One option is to build from the ideas presented in chapter 5 and the contemporary essay on education included in this book.

Interdependence as Sources of Empowerment for the Community Psychologist and Citizen Alike

Viewing research activities as a relationship is becoming more plausible. Judy Primavera and Anne E. Brodsky have advocated this idea by editing the publication of several recent research examples (2004). Via stories of their personal experiences, each contributor reveals that doing research is a relationship. Up until recently, the boundaries between researcher and subject were impermeable. When defined as a personal relationship, the research can be active and dynamic, creating opportunities for mutual insights. Knowledge creation is dialogic and egalitarian.

This does not mean research is always fun or free of discord. However, when the connections are made between dedicated citizens and open-minded researchers, they both can become more empowered to define the research as an activity that is central to their newly developed mutual interests. The research relationship can be a reservoir for long-term personal development. Not all participants, either citizens or researchers, will believe this to be so. Still, the very process of exchanges and discussions will enlighten both parties as to the ways in which power is defined. This is particularly so when both parties discuss, accept, or reject findings.

Even failures or incomplete processes of the research relationship are grounds for understanding the ecologies of conflict. Conflict can be thought of not just as a result of personality differences but set in the themes of the day and as a response to surprising or uncontrollable constraints. There may be pervasive external forces that impact the good intentions of community development. Understanding these externally generated plights can be new resources to create strategies for redefining a future situation. Understanding such plights can motivate the creation of new environmental conditions to reframe apparent dead ends facing the citizens and researchers.

Interdependence as a Resource for Learning About Oneself

Interdependence is an orientation to building relationships. As you view yourself as one potential resource in a social situation, you can perceive others as cultivated resources for a future known or unknown shared goal. People are no longer just benefactors or obligations—they are partners in research.

Introducing the concept of interdependence creates the opportunity to think about working toward common goals independent of gender, ethnicity, sexual orientation, or lifestyle. This is more than an implicit notion of interdependence rather it is an explicit foundation for working with others. This awareness is especially apt for doing community psychology because the ecological thinker has a more open view of the potential talents of the community needed to embrace a problem.

As I began to think ecologically about my work, these ideas contributed to my continued awareness that they were so basic they could be used as a framework to move beyond cultural values for individual achievement. They had (and still have) relevance for myself. They were protections against being too insular, judgmental, self-serving, or controlling of my professional work. Though I was not always explicitly aware of it, ecological thinking over time became part of my personal as well as professional identity.

This was energizing because my personal views were related to my professional aspirations. I was developing an epistemology that was edifying for both my chosen career and myself. I felt whole. Ecological thinking could bring solace and revitalize my energies by helping me remain committed to the tasks related to being part of a larger group. These ideas may seem idealistic or indefinable, but I believe they are anchors for keeping oneself in concert with one's work. There is integration and less a sense of being fragmented.

Daniel J. Siegel in reviewing the connections between the brain and day-to-day personal relationships affirms that "when interpersonal communication is 'fully engaged'—when the joining of minds is in full force—there is an overwhelming sense of immediacy, clarity and authenticity" (1999, p. 337). These are qualities that are intrinsic in the work of community psychology, energized by the concept of interdependence.

There is a feeling of wholeness that hopefully is a resource for building relationships with colleagues and community participants. I have found more harmony than turmoil as well as more energy than debilitating brooding, allowing me to participate in difficult and challenging assignments. As a result, I have been able to more effectively contribute to the cycling of resources and adapt to changing conditions. In completing this book, I have been able to see this work as a part of succession where others continue and revise ideas while contributing to new ecological expeditions.

Afterword

Reflections on the Journey

EDISON J. TRICKETT

You cannot talk about the field of community psychology without paying serious attention to the ideas and research of Jim Kelly

—Seymour Sarason

Reading through this collection of essays evoked many recollections of how Jim Kelly walked the ecological walk throughout his unusual and distinguished career. *Becoming Ecological* is a beautiful compilation of essays written over a 40-year span that portray the personal, challenging, evocative, revolutionary, pithy, erudite, and seamless efforts of one person to create a worldview for a new profession. The essays outline the many ways in which Kelly has sought to integrate social values, commitment to place, and a rich and multilayered conception of our context and ourselves into an energizing vision for the field of community psychology. They outline the evolving contours of a field of dreams whose realization is constantly under way not only in community psychology but also across the behavioral and social sciences concerned with community intervention and community betterment. Although community psychology has as a field been known for its periodic identity crises, Kelly never seemed to share those crises because he was on a mission, a calling, to create a rich identity for the field. His career has been an antidote not only for arrogance but also for much more; it has been one person's effort to reshape how we think about our profession and our relations with each other.

The hallmarks of Kelly's persistent urgings are found throughout: the importance of process; of respectful, dedicated, and unwavering commitment to community and the diversity therein; the centrality of relationships and collaboration across status lines in creating goodwill and energy for community understanding and change; and the value of remembering, learning from, and indeed revering the past and those on whose shoulders we now stand. Then there is the evolution of a dynamic ecological perspective, the conceptual glue that connected the interdependencies so dear to Jim's thinking: the interdependencies between the personal and professional, between the professional role and the context, interdependencies within the context itself, and between the often separated tasks of community research and intervention. As Kelly was becoming ecological, he was integrating all these potentially binary categories into a coherent, though complex whole, seamlessly weaving together a masterful worldview to help guide the creation of a new field. As he put it in his introductory comments to chapter 6: "I was advocating a broader role for doing community work than was the norm at the time. The conventional view was that community work was just another place to conduct professionally defined research or practice. Community psychology could be much more."

What were some of the components of this broad view? One can do no better than to quote Kelly himself.

On community research and methods shaped by context: "I found that the search for independent and dependent variables was not salient for living systems. Living systems do not stand still for the observer." "Methods by themselves do not produce tangible impact unless there is a directed effort to understand the relationships between the community psychologist, the method of choice, and the setting in which the work is done."

On the professional lifestyle and its vicissitudes: "The recommended way to prevent professional extinction is participation in the local community: the preferred antidote for arrogance is an ecological view of man [sic]." "The community asks the worker to have a defined and viable skill. The professional often substitutes jargon for performance, mistakes his social position for meaningful involvement, and fantasies his theoretical constructs as wisdom." "Too often professionals have a frail vanity about making sure that they get the credit for what they do. This need for explicit recognition for work too often means that professionals seek out the easy and short range problems that satisfies a neat and finite result. . . . I am proposing that a new flag be carried, namely, the flag for community service." And, quoting Ibsen, "One should never wear one's best trousers to go out and battle for freedom and truth."

With respect to the evolutionary ecological aspect of the change process, he quotes George Kennan: "If you're going to change a civilization, it can be done only as the gardener does it, not as the engineer does it. That is, it's got to be done in harmony with the rules of nature and can't all be done overnight" (in Lemann, 2000, p. 98).

Kelly's response? "Wow! This changes the entire epistemology of thinking. Prevention programs are not just technological innovations. They are grounded, engaged, and patient efforts at understanding the processes by which the resources of communities become part of the design of the prevention program" (2002, p. 50).

In the sound bite mentality of the day: "What the ecological perspective boils down to is assessing a natural setting and then redesigning the context surrounding a social problem so that a specific community problem is altered as the host environment is changed."

The elaborations of all these seemingly simple but indeed revolutionary theses are found in the preceding chapters. Reading them reminded me that one of the most interesting tensions in Kelly's career has been his uncanny ability to draw out the implications of what might be seen as the commonsensical, the retrospectively obvious, and form from them an elegant ecological conception integrating research, training, collaboration, and community development. Of course the possibility for authentic relationships between professional and citizen is compromised when one member assumes (indeed insists on) the elitist role; of course you need some competency of relevance to the community of concern if you expect to be credible and useful there; of course you need to know how people in a community frame and make sense of their situation if you hope to contribute to their well-being; of course multiple methods are valuable, indeed necessary, in understanding ecological complexity; of course people don't think of themselves as composites of variables but as whole people with agency going about their business.

But these seemingly straightforward ideas were and perhaps are still not part of the working worldview of many psychologists, even community psychologists. Jim's articulate insistence, his simple yet compelling truth, was that we look at and engage in the world around us as a source of ideas for the development of our field. We have been privileged to share the many ways in which he has become ecological, and this book beautifully outlines the ecological roadmap he has fashioned over the course of a distinguished career.

But how revolutionary the implications of the obvious are have not always been fully appreciated either within the field of community psychology or outside. As these chapters make clear, Kelly's is not an add-on approach to how most of us were trained and, in varying degrees, continue to train subsequent generations of students. You can't simply add a few paragraphs on context, or conduct a couple of focus groups, or add an additional outcome variable, or say you are collaborating with citizens and come close to understanding the depth and breadth of Kelly's perspective. As Sarason is wont to say: "The implications of the obvious are not always themselves obvious." To take on the perspective outlined in these pages is to engage in a thoughtful and critical self-reflection of the history of our discipline, question our increasing reliance on external funding to do community good, and reevaluate the tension between the professional demands of our field and the university cultures many of us inhabit. It means keeping constant vigilance, in all our activities, about how the devil is in the details of the rhetoric we use, the roles we adopt, and the kinds of relationships we develop with citizens in whose communities we work. Kelly puts it well in "Antidotes for Arrogance," asserting that an ecological perspective can allow us to be "professional *and* revolutionary without rhetoric and without arms." This is surely the aspiration for Kelly's own career.

The preceding chapters also show that Jim's ability to put into words images of what community psychology and community psychologists can be and must have to fulfill the aspirations underlying the creation of the field. Over 25 years ago, Dave Todd and I had the privilege of introducing Jim as recipient of Division 27's award for Distinguished Contribution to Research and Theory in Community Psychology. At that time we wrote, "As readers of Jim's work, we have come to see Jim as a person who knows how to find the phrase, the language which expresses precisely what he wants to say—there is a flow, a clarity of intent, and precision of meaning which strengthens and makes more vivid the impact of his ideas." Rereading the chapters in this volume only strengthened that earlier conclusion. How much more apt can the tension in community work between reflection and action be described than requiring a "metabolic balance of patience and zeal?" How better to capture the difference between using the community as a research site and caring about its development than through the distinction between professionals who "play with, but rarely play out, the crosscurrents of community events"? And how important it is for the community psychologist, in attending to community dynamics, to differentiate the peripheral from the core: "if he misjudges gossamer for grit, he is dead before he starts."

But it gets even better! The spirit of Jim's ecological journey captured by the preceding chapters hint at but do not fully dignify, the ways that his ecological journey applied not only to his publications but to his colleagues in the field. The chapters do not elaborate on his untiring efforts to serve as a common bond connecting aspiring young community psychologists to each other, such as Dave Todd and me many years ago; they do not mention his efforts to create settings for collegiality, such as the group outings to baseball parks when the annual meetings of the American Psychological Association coincided with home games. Nor do they clarify how he developed the community of community psychologists by creating settings and events in the history of the field, beginning with his active involvement in the Swampscott conference (read the report of that conference and listen for his influence with this book in mind) and the subsequent creation of Division 27 of the American Psychological Association in the late 1960s. Throughout his career he created settings and events to celebrate community psychology; events such as a symposia celebrating the 20th anniversary of the Swampscott conference and the development of a video celebrating the history of ideas and individuals on which community psychology was built.

Kelly lived out, in his relations with colleagues, all of his ideas on how community psychology could become ecological. For Jim, it was not only critical to understand and appreciate the community in which one worked: it was equally important to understand and appreciate the community of community psychology colleagues. Over the years, Jim has demonstrated a thoughtful and caring commitment to his colleagues and the organizational structures of community psychology. He has known what light touches the Division of Community Psychology (now the Society for Community Research and Action) needed to get beyond the morass du jour. He has appreciated how boundary spanning could be leveraged into social resources and connections to create a sense of community and retain the spirit of an emerging field. He has understood the opportunities for interdependence and mutual development that could be made of collaborative writing and the creation of community-supporting events. This book provides the reader with many aspects of Kelly the scholar, the thinker, and the journey to becoming ecological. The icing on the cake is that he has always been the real deal across the settings, time, roles, and relationships so central to his worldview.

Bibliography

Achbar, M., & Abbott, J. (Directors). (2004). *The corporation* [Documentary film]. United States: Big Picture Media.

Adams, A. H., Aveling, R., Brockington, D., Dickson B., Elliot, J., Hutton, J., et al. (2004). Biodiversity, conservation, and the eradication of poverty. *Science, 306,* 1146–1149.

Anonymous. (1977). The tale of the coffee pot: Lessons learned from a systems innovation. *American Journal of Community Psychology, 5,* 237–241.

Applebome, P. (1986, August 26). In world capital of the icehouse a way of life hangs on. *New York Times,* p. A10.

Barabasi, A. L. (2003). *Linked.* Cambridge, MA: Plume.

Blee, Kathleen. (2003). Studying the enemy. In B. Glassner & R. Hertz (Eds.), *Our studies, ourselves: Sociologists' lives and work* (pp. 13–23). Oxford: Oxford University Press.

Bronfenbrenner, U. (1979). *The ecology of human development: Experiments by nature and design.* Cambridge, MA: Harvard University Press.

Campbell, R. (2002). *Emotionally involved: The impact of researching rape.* New York: Routledge.

Campbell, R., Sefl, T., Wasco, S., & Ahrens, C. (2004). Doing community research without a community: Creating safe space for rape survivors. *American Journal of Community Psychology, 33,* 253–262.

Davidson, M. (1983). *Uncommon sense: The life and thought of Ludwig Von Bertalanffy (1901–1972).* Los Angeles: J. P. Tarcher.

Edwards, D., & Kelly, J. G. (1980). Coping and adaptation: A longitudinal study. *American Journal of Community Psychology, 8,* 203–216.

Ehrlich, P. R., & Hanski, I. (2004). (Eds.). *On the wings of checkerspots: A model system for population biology.* New York: Oxford University Press.

Evans, G. W. (2004). The environment of childhood poverty. *American Psychologist, 50,* 77–92.

Fisher, G., & Strantz, I. (1972). An ecosystems approach to the study of dangerous Drug use and abuse with Special reference to the marijuana issue. *American Journal of Public Health, 62,* 1407–1421.

Fiske, B. (1975). Head Start: After ten years, planning experiments. *New York Times,* June 8, p. 40.

Flyvbjerg, B. (2001). *Making social science matter.* Cambridge: Cambridge University Press.

Gallo, L. C., & Matthews, K. A. (2003). Understanding the association between socioeconomic status and physical health: Do negative emotions play a role? *Psychological Bulletin, 129,* 10–51.

Geertz, C. (1973). *The interpretation of cultures.* New York: Basic Books.

Glassner, B., & Hertz R. (Eds.). (2003). *Our studies, ourselves: sociologists' lives and work.* Oxford: Oxford University Press.

Glidewell, J. C. (Ed.). (1971). *Issues in community psychology and preventive mental health.* New York: Behaviorial Publications.

Glidewell, J. C., Kelly, J. G., Bagby, M., & Dickerson, A. (1998). Natural development of community leadership. In R. S. Tinsdale, L. Heath, J. Edwards, E. J. Posavac, F. B. Bryant, Y. Suarez-Balcazar (Eds.), *Theory and research in small groups* (pp. 61–86). New York: Plenum.

Gonzales, D. (2004). Lost and found: An era in the bronx. *New York Times,* October 22, p. C9.

Gonzales, L. (1987). A community service for a rural high school. In J. G. Kelly & R. E. Hess (Eds.), *The ecology of prevention: Illustrating mental health consultation* (pp. 37–71). New York: Haworth Press.

Hardesty, D. L. (1977). *Ecological anthropology.* New York: Wiley.

Hawkins, E. H., Cummins, L. H. & Marlatt, G. A. (2004). Preventing substance abuse in American Indians and Alaska native youth: Promising strategies for healthier communities. *Psychological Bulletin, 130,* 304–323.

Haydon, T. (2004). *Street wars: Gangs and the future of violence.* New York: New Press.

Hentoff, N. (2004). *American music is.* Cambridge, MA: Da Capo Press.

Hughes, T. P. (2004). *Human-built world: How to think about technology and culture.* Chicago: University of Chicago Press.

Jakes, S. S. (2004). Understanding ecological programming: Evaluating program structure through a comprehensive assessment tool. In S. S. Jakes & C. C. Brookins (Eds.), Understanding ecological programming: Merging theory, research and practice. *Journal of Prevention & Intervention in the Community, 27*(2), 13–28.

Jiggins, C. D. (2004). A checkered history. *Science, 305,* 1913.

Johnson, D. W., & Johnson, R. T. (1992). Positive interdependence: Key to effective cooperation. In R. Hertz-Lazorwitz & N. Miller (Eds.), *Interaction in cooperative groups: The theoretical anatomy of group learning* (pp. 174–199). Cambridge: Cambridge University Press.

Katz, D., & Kahn, R. L. (1978). *Social psychology of organizations.* New York: Wiley.

Kelly, G. A. (1955). *The psychology of personal constructs.* New York: Norton.

Kelly, J. G. (1966). Ecological constraints on mental health services. *American Psychologist, 21,* 535–539.

Kelly, J. G. (1970). Antidotes for arrogance: Training for community psychology. *American Psychologist, 25,* 254–531.

Kelly, J. G. (1971a). Qualities for the community psychologist. *American Psychologist, 26,* 897–903.

Kelly, J. G. (1971b). The quest for valid preventive interventions. In J. C. Glidewell

(Ed.), *Issues in community psychology and preventive mental health.* New York: Behavioral Publications.

Kelly, J. G. (1977). The search for ideas and deeds that work. In G. Albee & J. M. Joffe (Eds.), *Primary prevention of psychopathology* (Vol. 1, pp. 7–17). Hanover, NH: University Press of New England.

Kelly, J. G. (Ed.). (1979a). *Adolescent boys in high school: A psychological study of coping and adaptation.* Hillsdale, NJ: Lawrence Erlbaum.

Kelly, J. G. (1979b). Tain't what you do, it's the way that you do it. *American Journal of Community Psychology, 7,* 239–261.

Kelly, J. G. (Ed.) (1984). A tribute to Erich Lindemann. *American Journal of Community Psychology, 12,* 511–536.

Kelly, J. G. (1986, November 14). Makin' occasions. Opening address in honor of Harold Raush at the symposium Process, Context and Perspective in Psychology and Psychology Training, Mt. Holyoke College, South Hadley, MA.

Kelly, J. G. (1987a). An ecological paradigm: Defining mental health consultation as a preventive service. In J. G. Kelly & R. E. Hess (Eds.), *The ecology of prevention: Illustrating mental health consultation* (pp. 1–35). New York: Haworth Press.

Kelly, J. G. (1987b). Seven criteria when conducting community-based prevention research: A research agenda and commentary. In *Preventing mental disorders: A research perspective* (DHHS Publication no. ADM 87–1493, pp. 57–72). Washington, DC: U.S. Government Printing Office.

Kelly, J. G. (1992a). Gerald Caplan's paradigm: Bridging psychotherapy and public health practice. In W. P. Erchul (Ed.), *Consultation in community, school, and organizational practice: Gerald Caplan's contributions to professional psychology* (pp. 75–85). Washington, DC: Hemisphere.

Kelly, J. G. (1992b). On teaching the practice of prevention: Integrating the concept of interdependence. In M. Kessler, S. E. Goldston, & J. M. Joffe (Eds.), *The present and future of prevention: In honor of George W. Albee* (pp. 251–264). Newbury Park, CA: Sage.

Kelly, J. G. (2000). Wellness as an ecological enterprise. In D. Cicchetti, J. Rapapport, J. Sandler, & R. J. Weissberg (Eds.), *The promotion of wellness in children and adolescence* (pp. 101–132). Washington, DC: CWLA Press.

Kelly, J. G. (2002). The spirit of community psychology. *American Journal of Community Psychology, 30,* 43–63.

Kelly, J. G., Azelton, S. E., Burzette, R. G.m & Mock, L. O. (1994). Creating social settings for diversity: An ecological thesis. In E. J. Trickett, R. J. Wattsm, & D. Birman (Eds.), *Human diversity: Perspectives on people in context* (pp. 424–451). San Francisco: Jossey Bass.

Kelly, J. G., Azelton, L. S., Lardon, C., Mock, L. O., Tandon, S. D., & Thomas, M. (2004). On community leadership: Stories about collaboration in action research. *American Journal of Community Psychology, 33,* 205–216.

Kelly, J. G., Dassoff, N., Levin, I., Schreckengost, J., Stelzner, S. P., & Altman, B. E. (1988). *A guide to conducting prevention research in the community: First steps.* New York: Haworth Press.

Kelly, J. G., Dimento, J., & Gottlieb, B. H. (1972). The community as teacher. In D. M. Flournoy (Ed.), *The new teachers.* San Francisco: Jossey-Bass.

Kelly, J. G., & Hess, R. E. (Eds.). (1987). *The ecology of prevention: Illustrating mental health consultation.* New York: Haworth Press.

Kelly, J. G., Kingry-Westergaard, C. (1990). A contextualist epistemology for ecological research. In P. H. Tolan, C. Keys, F. Chertok, & L. Jason (Eds.), *The clinical psychology handbook* (2nd ed.) (pp. 762–779). Elmsford, NY: Pergamon Press.

Kelly, J. G., Ryan, A. M., Altman, B. L., & Stelzner, S. P. (2000). Understanding and changing social systems: An ecological view. In J. Rappaport & E. Seidman (Eds.), *The handbook of community psychology* (pp. 133–159). New York: Kluwer/Plenum.

Kitayama, S., & Markus, H. R. (1999). Yin and yang of the Japanese self: The cultural psychology of personality coherence. In D. Cervone & Y. Shoda (Eds.), *The coherence of personality* (pp. 242–302). New York: Guilford Press.

Kretzmann, J. P., & McNight, J. I. (1993). *Building Communities from the inside out: A path toward finding and mobilizing a community's assets from the inside out.* Evanston, IL: Institute for Policy Research.

Lardon, C. (2004). Understanding what health and wellness means to Yu'ik people: Working with Alaska native communities to conduct research and promote health. *Proceedings from the first nations nutrition and health conference.* Vancouver, British Columbia.

Lindemann, E. B. (1987). *Erich Lindemann: A biographical sketch.* Wellesley, MA: Elizabeth B. Lindemann.

Livert, D., & Hughes, D. L. (2002). The ecological paradigm: Persons in settings. In T. A. Revenson, A. R. D'Augelli, S. French, D. L. Hughes, D. Livert, E. Seidman, (Eds.), *A quarter century of community psychology* (pp. 51–77). New York: Kluwer.

Livingstone, D. N. (2003). *Putting science in its place: Geographies of scientific knowledge.* Chicago: University of Chicago Press.

Mann, P. A. (1987). Prevention of child abuse: Two contrasting support systems. In J. G. Kelly & R. E. Hess (Eds.), *The ecology of prevention: Illustrating mental health consultation* (pp. 73–112). New York: Haworth Press.

Maton, K. I. (1989). Community settings as buffers of life stress? Highly supportive churches, mutual help groups and senior centers. *American Journal of Community Psychology, 17,* 203–231.

Maton, K. I. (1993). Moving beyond the individual level of analysis in mutual help group research: An ecological paradigm. *Journal of Applied Behavioral Science, 29,* 272–286.

Maton, K. I., Dodgen, D. W., Sto. Domingo, M. R. & Larson, D. (In press). Religion as a meaning system: Policy implications for the new millenium. *Journal of Social Issues.*

Maton, K. I., Perkins, D., Saegert, S. (in press). Community-based interdisciplinary research: promise, processes and contexts. Special Issue, *American Journal of Community Psychology.*

Maton, K. I., & Salem, D. (1995). Organizational characteristics of empowering community settings: A multiple case study approach. *American Journal of Community Psychology, 23,* 631–655.

Mayr, E. (2004). *What makes biology unique?* New York: Cambridge University Press.

Medin, D. L., & Atran, S. (2004). The native mind: Biological categorization and reasoning in development across cultures. *Psychological Bulletin, 111*, 960–983.

Miller, K. E., & Rasco, L. M. (Eds.). (2004). *The mental health of refugees.* Mahwah, NJ: Lawrence Erlbaum.

Mills, R. C., & Kelly, J. G. (1972). Cultural adaptation and analogies: Analysis of three Mexican villages. In S. Golann & C. Eisdorfer (Eds.), *Handbook of community mental health* (pp. 157–210). Englewood Cliffs, NJ: Prentice Hall.

Mock, L. O. (1994). Validation of an instrument to assess the personal visions of African-American community leaders. Unpublished Master's Thesis, University of Illinois at Chicago, 1994.

Mock, L. O. (1999). The personal vision of African-American community leaders. Unpublished Doctoral Dissertation, University of Illinois at Chicago, 1999.

Pargament, K., & Maton, K. I. (2000). Religion in American life: A community psychology perspective. In J. Rappaport & E. Seidman (Eds.), *Handbook of community psychology* (pp. 495–522). New York: Kluwer/Plenum.

Primavera, J., & Brodsky, A. (Eds.). (2004). Special issue on the process of community research and action. *American Journal of Community Psychology, 33*(1–2), 177–277.

Rappaport, R. (1990). Two ecosystems, population and people. In E. Moran (Ed.), *The ecosystem approach in anthropology* (pp. 41–74). Ann Arbor: University of Michigan Press.

Rappaport, J., & Seidman, E. (Eds.). (2000). *The handbook of community psychology.* New York: Kluwer/Plenum.

Rose, S. (1997). *Lifelines: Life beyond the gene.* New York: Oxford University Press.

Rosen, G. (1993). *A history of public health* (expanded version). Baltimore, MD: Johns Hopkins Press.

Ryan, W. (1971). *Blaming the victim.* New York: Vintage Books.

Seidman, E. (1988). Back to the future, community psychology: Unfolding a theory of social intervention. *American Journal of Community Psychology, 25*, 197–206.

Senge, P., Scharmer, C. O., Jaworski, J., & Flowers, B. S. (2004). *Presence.* Cambridge, MA: Society for Organizational Learning.

Shinn, M., & Toohey, S. M. (2003). Community contexts of human welfare. *Annual review of psychology* (Vol. 54) (pp. 427–459). Palo Alto, CA: Annual Reviews.

Siegel, D. J. (1999). *The developing mind: How relationships and the brain interact to shape who we are.* New York: Guilford Press.

Smith, E. P., Wolf, A. M., Cantillon, D. M., Thomas, O., & Davidson, W. S. (2004) The adolescent diversion project: Twenty-five years of research on an ecological model of intervention. In S. S. Jakes & C. C. Brookins (Eds.), Understanding ecological programming: Merging theory, research, and practice. *Journal of Prevention & Intervention in the Community, 27*, 29–47.

Speth, J. G. (2004). *Red sky at morning: Crisis of the global environment.* New Haven, CT: Yale University Press.

Starr, P. (1983). *The social transformation of American medicine.* New York: Basic Books.

Stelzner, S. P. (1996). The jigsaw exercise: A learning tool for the community psychology course. *Community Psychologist, 29*(4), 26–29.

Stokols, D., Fuqur, J., Gress, J., Harvey, R., Phillips, K., Baezconde-Garbanati, L. (2003). Evaluating transdisciplinary science. *Nicotine and Tobacco Research,* 5(S1), 521–539.

Sullivan, M., & Kelly, J. G. (Eds.). (2001). *Collaborative research: University and community partnership.* Washington, DC: American Public Health Association.

Sutton, M. Q., & Andersen, E. N. (2004). *Introduction to cultural ecology.* Walnut Creek, CA: Altamira Press.

Tandon, S. D., Azelton, L. S., Kelly, J. G., & Strickland, D. A. (1998). Constructing a tree for community leaders: Contexts and processes in collaborative inquiry. *American Journal of Community Psychology, 26,* 669–696.

Taper, M. L. & Lele, S. R. (2004). The nature of scientific evidence: A forward-looking synthesis. In M. L. Taper & S. R. Lele (Eds.), *The nature of scientific evidence.* Chicago: University of Chicago Press.

Tebes, J. K., Kaufman, J. S., and Chinman, M. J. (2002). Teaching about prevention to mental health professionals. In L. A. Jason & D. Glenwick (Eds.) *Innovative strategies for promoting health and mental health across the life span* (pp. 37–60). New York: Springer.

Trickett, E. J., Kelly, J. G., & Todd, D. M. (1972). The social environment of the high school: Guidelines for individual change and organizational redevelopment. In S. Golann & C. Eisdorfer (Eds.), *Handbook of community mental health* (pp. 331–406). Englewood Cliffs, NJ: Prentice Hall.

Trickett, E. J., Kelly, J. G. & Vincent, T. (1985). The spirit of ecological inquiry in community psychology. In E. C. Susskind & D. C. Klein (Eds.), *Community research* (pp. 283–333). New York: Praeger.

Trickett, E. J., & Ryerson-Espino, S. (2004). Collaboration and social inquiry: Multiple meanings of a construct and its role in creating useful and valid knowledge. *American Journal of Community Psychology, 34,* 1–69.

Weber, B. (1993, April 25). Angels' angels. *New York Times Magazine, 28.*

Wellin, E. (1955). Water boiling in a Peruvian town. In B. D. Paul (Ed.), *Health, culture, and community* (pp. 71–106). New York: Russell Sage.

Wellin, E. (1998). Videotaped interview. Chicago: University of Illinois at Chicago Library.

Wiener, J. (2004, August 1). Porch club in session. *Sacramento Bee,* pp. B1&3.

Wilson, R. A. (2004). *Boundaries of the mind: The individual in the fragile sciences.* Cambridge: Cambridge University Press.

Wolf, T. (2003). A practical approach to evaluation of collaboration. In T. E. Blacker (Ed.), *Evaluating community collaborations* (pp. 57–112). New York: Springer.

Zander, A. (1985). *The purposes of groups and organizations.* San Francisco: Jossey-Bass.

Index

Developing Communities Project (DCP)
  African American leaders, 18
  community leadership, 208–209,
    210, 212, 261–262
developmental processes
  resiliency, 140–141
  tolerance of ambiguity, 141
differentiating settings, socialization
    structure, 35
Dimento, Joe, 92–93
direct, indirect, and side effects,
    interventions, 146–147
disciplinary boundaries, working
    across, 61–62
disciplinary connections, wellness,
    189–193
Dittmer, John, 211
diverse settings, expressing
    competences in, 126–128
diversity
  experiences and roles, 9–11
  tolerance, 106–107
  wellness, 198–200
dumping phenomenon, disabled into
    neighborhoods, 273

eco identity, community psychologist
    quality, 105–106
ecological analogy
  cycling of resources, 29–30
  ecosystem principle, 27–29
  environment and adaptation styles, 30
  evolution of natural communities,
    30–31
  functions with social unit are
    interdependent, 27–29
  guidelines for defining process,
    122–123
  studying and changing social
    environments, 26–27
  succession principle, 30–31
ecological approach
  collaborative style, 176–177
  contextualism, 171
  implications of contextualist,
    ecological epistemology, 177–178
  interdependence of facets, 177–178
  robustness, 173
  social construction of ecological
    knowledge, 176

social processes, 177
  theoretical propositions, 175
ecological concepts, preventive
    interventions, 25–26
ecological development, community,
    102–103
ecological expedition, community
    leadership, 212
ecological inquiry. *See also* inquiry
  connection of people to social
    environment, 260–261
  people of Yukon–Kuskokwin Delta,
    265–266
  place- and person-specific knowledge,
    259
  recent examples, 264–266
  refugees, 265
  research relationship, 263–264
  use of multiple methods, 261–263
ecological perspective
  community as teacher, 93
  local setting as focus for work,
    101–102, 103
  place, 8–9
  value of limited heritage, 6–7
ecological research, contextualist
    epistemology for, 174–177
ecological thinking
  boiling water in Peru, 189–190,
    257–258
  community development, 255
  concept of niche, 254
  concepts, 258
  interdependence, 280
  interdisciplinary enterprise, 17
  latent wisdom, 256–257
  personal and social system resources,
    255, 255–256
  Porch Club, 253, 254
  social setting, 252–254
  street wisdom, 256
  studying checkerspot butterfly, 252
  virtues, 252
ecology, relationship of organisms with
    environment, 27
ecology of competence, tentative
    conclusions, 51–52
The Ecology of Prevention, community-
    based research, 15–16
ecosystem, field biology, 27–29

high school study (*continued*)
   help-giving process, 50
   individual differences in boys, 49–50
   research on adolescent development,
      54–55
   settings for socialization, 48–49
   social exploration, 53–54
   socialization of students, 46–50
   social norms, 47–48
   vanity, 46
historical topics, inspiring, 226–227
Hobbs, Nicholas, 25
Holiday, Billie, jazz, 12
Hollander, Ed, 211, 215
Holtzman, Professor Wayne,
   coincidence, 19
homogenizing settings, socialization
   structure, 35
Hope, Elmo, 253
Houston VA hospital, community
   mental health, 19
Howe, Louisa, academic influence, 12
Hughes, Thomas, 280
Human Relations Service of Wellesley,
   Erich Lindemann, 153
Hunt, J. M., 25
Hyde Park, Cincinnati, social class, 7

Ibsen, Henrik, 71
ideas, power of, from other places,
   16–18
identity
   athletic competence, 53
   department stores, 8
independence, European-American
   values, 275
indirect and side effects, interventions,
   146–147
infectious disease, preventive programs,
   267
inquiry. *See also* ecological inquiry;
   situated inquiry
   interdependence linking, and
      practice, 283–284
integrative tasks
   interdependence of variables, 36
   theory and practice, 37–38
   utility of multiple methods, 37
interdependence
   biology, 280

conservation programs, 284
ecological thinking, 280
ecosystem principle, 27–29
emotional and intellectual concept,
   281
empowerment source, 287
facets of ecological approach,
   177–178
heritage and cultures, 274–275
learning about oneself, 287–288
rationale for multiple method use,
   284–285
researcher and community, 260–
   261
reservoir against ideas and concepts
   becoming obsolete, 286–287
resource for linking inquiry and
   practice, 283–284
resource for visualizing and creating
   linked settings, 285–286
resource thinking about people and
   places, 282–283
interdependence of variables, iterative
   task, 36
interdisciplinary interaction, student
   involvement, 61–62
interdisciplinary research
   learning to think ecologically, 275
   National Institutes of Health (NIH),
      192
   University of Illinois at Chicago,
      191–192
interdisciplinary teaching
   learning environment, 277–278
   University of Michigan, 92
interrelationships, community
   psychology, 11
intervention process
   committing time and energy,
      128–130
   creating resources for selves,
      123–126
   expressing competences in diverse
      settings, 126–128
interventions. *See also* contrasting
   interventions
   academic references, 15
   biological ecology, 58–59
   direct, indirect, and side effects of,
      146–147

Moran, Lou, 12
Morris High School, Colin Powell, 253
Mosse, David, 241
Mowbray, Carol, 43
multiple research methods
    adolescent development, 54–55
    data collection, 37
    ecological inquiry, 261–263
    rationale for use of, 284–285
Munoz, Ricardo, power of coincidence,
    21
Murray, Mary, 219, 221
museums, inspiration, 17–18
mutual accommodation, ethics of
    interventions, 148

National Institutes of Health (NIH),
    interdisciplinary research, 192
National Institutes of Mental Health
    (NIMH)
    academic influence, 12
    Jerry W. Carter, Jr., 25
natural communities, evolution, 30–31
Nessor, Ulric, 259
Neuman, Deacon, 221
Newman, Barbara
    cultures of high schools, 43–44, 49
    individual differences in boys, 49–50,
    53–54
Newman, Philip, 43–44, 49
niche, concept, 254
non-equivalent control group design, 80
novelists, inspiration, 17
noxious events and places, reducing
    impact, 13–16
null hypothesis significance testing,
    limitations, 198–199

observations, adolescent development
    study, 54
occupational behavior, role
    expectations, 10
Ohio, Cincinnati. *See* Cincinnati, Ohio
Ohio State University, 116
    academic influence, 12
    community as teacher, 92
    history of Social Adaptation class,
    94–95
    power of coincidence, 20
Oliver, Sy, 113

opera, introduction, 17
organizational change
    environmental restructuring, 78–83
    mental health programs, 82–83
organizational forms, creating, for
    preventive research, 149–150
Orwell, George, 17
Owens, John, 214, 221
Ozu, Yasujiro, 18

parenting, between communities, 186
patched up design, community
    development, 85, 87
patience, metabolic balance between,
    and zeal, 100–101, 109–110
patriotic, World War II, 4
patterns of behavior, wellness, 200
Payne, Charles, spirit, 211, 231
people
    interdependence, 282–283
    mental health consultation, 269
Pepinsky, Harold, academic influence,
    12
Percy, Walker, 18
personal integrity, community
    psychologist and events, 65
personal resources, ecological thinking,
    255–256
person-environment fit, situated
    inquiry, 185–186
person-environment interactions, Jack
    Glidewell, 117
persons at margin, revitalizing
    communities, 199–200
Peru, boiling water in village, 189–190,
    257–258
places
    creation of new settings, 162–163
    interdependence, 282–283
    power of, 7–9, 281
    power of ideas from other, 16–18
    reducing impact of noxious, 13–16
planning, exploratory behavior, 34
pluralistic methods, wellness, 189–193
poets, inspiration, 17
Pogues, identity, 8
population exchange
    effects of rate of, on social settings,
    34–35
    high school environments, 32

Porch Club
    local knowledge, 254
    raising funds, 253
postdoctoral fellowship, community
        mental health, 19–20
poverty, ecological reality, 260
poverty reduction, interdependence,
        284
Powell, Colin, Morris High School, 253
power
    coincidence, 18–21
    ideas from other places, 16–18
    place, 7–9
    social support, 11–13
practice. *See also* theory and practice
    interdependence linking inquiry and,
        283–284
precious self, William James, 233, 242
prevention research
    assessing social settings and persons
        simultaneously, 141–143
    creating new organizational forms
        for, 149–150
    direct, indirect, and side effects of
        interventions, 146–147
    finding a voice, 140
    learning to see, 139–140
    listening, 139
    mental health field, 139
    participant evaluation, 145
    promoting mental health vs.
        preventing mental illness, 139
    reciprocal effects between persons
        and social settings, 143–144
    relationship between social support
        and self–direction and health,
        138–139
    social settings appraising ethics of
        interventions, 147–148
    social settings for participant
        contribution and benefit, 144–145
    variable selection, 140–141
Prevention Research Branch, creation,
        137
preventive interventions
    approaches to community change,
        74
    community as evolutionary process,
        83–89
    ecological concepts, 25–26

mental health consultation, 74–77
motivating community resources, 73
organizational change as
        environmental restructuring,
        78–83
preventive programs
    consultation process, 268
    defining community programs,
        269–271
    ecological practice, 268
    educational process, 270
    longitudinal view, 271–272
    mental health, 267–268
    people and settings, 269
    process of creating diverse solutions,
        269–271
    public health, 267–268
    resources, 269
    unintended consequences, 272–273
Price, Rick, 117
Primavera, Judy, 287
process. *See also* intervention process
    elaboration, 120–121
    guidelines for defining, 121–123
    importance of work, and content,
        119–121, 289–290
    leadership, 211
    muddling through Social Adaptation
        class, 97
    term, 120
professional heritage, values, 274–275
professional interests, external factors,
        4
professional limbo, Social Adaptation
        class, 97
professionals
    engagement process, 157–158
    informal settings of community,
        158–160
    term, 155
    training by time-bound techniques,
        271–272
Project on Human Development in
        Chicago Neighborhoods, 196
Protestants
    Catholics vs., 6
    Jews and, 9–10
psychologists
    arrogance and disdain of radicals, 58
    redefinition of job, 58

reluctance to chart course of action, 59

psychology
  acceptance as science, 230
  contextualism in, 172–173
  needs of community and, 57–58
  putting aside concept of spirit, 228–231

public applause, community psychologist not seeking, 110–111

public health. *See also* preventive programs
  ecological perspective, 267–268
  home visiting, 268

qualities for community psychologist
  clearly identified competence, 104–105
  commitment to risk taking, 108–109
  creating an eco identity, 105–106
  developing communities without seeking credit, 110–111
  effectively coping with varied resources, 107–108
  metabolic balance of patience and zeal, 100–101, 109–110
  tolerance for diversity, 106–107

quasi experimental design, time and spatial effects, 75, 77

questionnaire, adolescent development study, 54

quick fixes, 271

radiating process
  consultation as preventive intervention, 83
  mental health consultation, 74–77

Ramen, Rachel, 241–242

Rappaport, Julian, *vii–ix*, 183, 226, 238

Rappaport, Roy, 17, 259, 280

Rasco, Lisa M., 265

Raush, Harold, 117, 259, 280
  academic influence, 12
  behavior of aggressive and normal boys, 8
  retirement honor, 253

reciprocal effects, between persons and social settings, 143–144

reciprocity, structure and function, 28

recognition, community psychologist not seeking, 110–111

reductionism, community psychology, 251

refugees, ecological inquiry of, 265

Reiff, Robert, 57, 70

Reinhardt, Django, jazz, 12

Reinharz, Shlamit, 211

relationship connectors, persons spanning boundaries, 256

relationships, interdependence, 287–288

religion, connection to community psychology, 229

religious status, Protestants and Jews, 9–10

research relationship, ecological inquiry, 263–264

resilience
  learning about resilient communities, 195–198
  studying developmental processes, 140–141

resistant setting
  committing time and energy, 128–130
  creating resources, 124–126
  diverse settings, 127–128
  social setting type, 122

resources
  coping effectively with varied, 107–108
  cycling, 29–30
  interdependence linking inquiry and practice, 283–284
  mental health consultation, 269
  people and places for interdependence, 282–283
  settings linking and exchanging, 165–166

responsive setting
  committing time and energy, 128–130
  creating resources, 124–126
  diverse settings, 127–128
  social setting type, 122

risk taking, commitment of community psychologist, 108–109

robustness, ecological approach, 173

community as teacher, 92
good resource, 17
group experiences, 276–277
high school study, 43
history of Social Adaptation class, 94–95
power of coincidence, 20
social status, 6–7
University of Oregon, 116
Lila Acheson Wallace School of Community Service and Public Affairs, 100
power of coincidence, 21
University of Osnabrück, Germany, 113, 116
University of Stirling in Scotland, community psychology, 234
University of Texas, 116
academic influence, 12
coincidence, 19
U.S. Public Health Service, power of coincidence, 20

validation, new social settings, 164–165
varied resources, coping effectively with, 107–108
Vaughn, Sarah, jazz, 12
Vaze, Kim Marie, 211
Vermont Listening Project, social glue, 240
Vincent, Trudy, 264
visibility, community psychologist not seeking, 110–111
von Bertalanffy, Ludwig, uncommon sense, 274

Walnut Hills High School
coincidence, 19
community resources, 11
Wandersman, Abe, 211
war, disciplining whole community, 71
water, boiling in Peru, 189–190, 257–258
Wayne Memorial High School
adolescent development study, 54–55
competences, 46
ecology of competences, 51
fluid high school, 44

help-giving process, 50
patterns of socialization, 52
socialization, 50
socialization setting, 48–49
social norms, 47–48
Weigl, Bob, 43
Weissberg, Roger P., 183
Wellin, Ed
forces establishing wellness, 183
Peru and boiling water, 189–190, 257–258
wellness
analysis of risk and protective factors, 184
analysis of variety and diversity, 198–200
contextual thinking; agenda for situated inquiry, 185–189
disciplinary connections and pluralistic methods, 189–193
Emory Cowen, 183, 200
learning about resilient and competent communities, 195–198
listening with others, 193–195
scholar, 184–185
wellness scholar, multiple causal systems, 190
Welty, Eudora
concept of listening, 141
lectures at Harvard University Graduated Program, 139
One Writer's Beginnings, 137–138
West Oakley
isolation, 14
power of place, 7
social class, 7
Wievel, Wim, Great Cities Program, 192
Williams, Jill, community leadership, 218–219, 221
Wilson, Robert, 258
wisdom
latent, in ecological concepts, 256–257
street, 256
Wittgenstein, Ludwig, power of ideas, 16
women, history in community psychology, 235